FLORIDA'S
CRIMINAL JUSTICE SYSTEM

CAROLINA ACADEMIC PRESS
State-Specific Criminal Justice Series

Arkansas's Criminal Justice System
Edward Powers and Janet K. Wilson

California's Criminal Justice System
Second Edition
Christine L. Gardiner and Pamela Fiber-Ostrow, eds.

Florida's Criminal Justice System
Second Edition
William G. Doerner

Georgia's Criminal Justice System
Deborah Mitchell Robinson

Illinois's Criminal Justice System
Jill Joline Myers and Todd Lough, eds.

Missouri's Criminal Justice System
Frances P. Reddington, ed.

North Carolina's Criminal Justice System
Second Edition
Paul E. Knepper and Mark Jones

Ohio's Criminal Justice System
Joshua B. Hill, Nancy E. Marion, Kevin M. Cashen,
R. James Orr, III, and Kendra J. Kec

Pennsylvania's Criminal Justice System
Mary P. Brewster and Harry R. Dammer, eds.

West Virginia's Criminal Justice System
Kimberly A. DeTardo-Bora, Dhruba J. Bora, and Samuel L. Dameron

Florida's Criminal Justice System

Second Edition

William G. Doerner

COLLEGE OF CRIMINOLOGY & CRIMINAL JUSTICE
FLORIDA STATE UNIVERSITY

CAROLINA ACADEMIC PRESS
Durham, North Carolina

Library of Congress Cataloging-in-Publication Data

Doerner, William G., 1949-
  Florida's criminal justice system / William G. Doerner. -- Second edition.
      pages cm -- (State-Specific Criminal Justice Series.)
  Includes bibliographical references and index.
  ISBN 978-1-61163-680-2 (alk. paper)
  1. Criminal justice, Administration of--Florida. I. Title.

HV9955.F6D64 2015
364.9759--dc23

                          2015005322

Carolina Academic Press
700 Kent Street
Durham, NC 27701
Telephone (919) 489-7486
Fax (919) 493-5668
www.cap-press.com

Printed in the United States of America

To my best friend, my wonderful wife Judy.

CONTENTS

List of Figures   xiii

List of Tables   xvii

Series Note   xix

Chapter 1 · Florida's Criminal Justice System   3
   Introduction   3
   Civic Responsibility   4
      Persistent Problems with High School Education   5
      Persistent Problems with College Education   6
   Criminology and Criminal Justice Students   9
   Criminology and Criminal Justice Mission Statements   10
   An Overview of *Florida's Criminal Justice System*   11
   Summary   12
   References   12

Chapter 2 · The Florida Constitution   15
   Learning Objectives   15
   Introduction   15
   Branches of Government   16
      The Legislative Branch   16
      The Executive Branch   17
      The Judicial Branch   17
      Summary   17
   Declaration of Rights   17
   Amending the Florida Constitution   18
   Summary   19
   Key Terms   20
   Selected Internet Sites   20
   Review Questions   20
   References   21

Chapter 3 · Florida Crime   23
   Learning Objectives   23
   Introduction   24

The Florida *Uniform Crime Reports* Program   25
  A Word of Caution   26
The Crime Clock   27
The Crime Rate   28
  Another Word of Caution   29
Crime Trends   30
  A Further Word of Caution   30
Crime in Florida Cities   34
  Even More Words of Caution   34
Summary   35
Key Terms   36
Selected Internet Sites   37
Review Questions   37
References   38

Chapter 4 · Florida Criminal Law   41
Learning Objectives   41
Introduction   42
Homicide   42
  Lawful Homicide   43
  Unlawful Homicide   43
Simple Assault   46
Simple Battery   46
Aggravated Assault   47
Aggravated Battery   48
Sexual Battery   49
Robbery   50
Larceny-Theft   51
Burglary   52
Summary   53
Key Terms   53
Selected Internet Sites   54
Review Questions   54
References   55

Chapter 5 · Florida Law Enforcement   57
Learning Objectives   57
Introduction   58
Becoming a Florida Law Enforcement Officer   58
  Minimum Standards   58
  Police Academy Training   59
  The Police Officer Certification Examination   62
The Law Enforcement Officer Selection Process   62
The Structure of the Florida Law Enforcement System   65
  State Law Enforcement Agencies   65
    Florida Department of Law Enforcement   66
    Florida Highway Patrol   68
  Local Law Enforcement Agencies   68
    County Sheriff Offices   69

Municipal Police Departments   71
Special Jurisdiction Agencies   73
Job Prospects   75
Accreditation   76
The National Effort   76
The Florida Effort   77
Summary   77
Key Terms   78
Selected Internet Sites   78
Review Questions   79
References   80

Chapter 6 · Florida Courts   85
Learning Objectives   85
Introduction   86
Florida Court Structure   87
Florida Supreme Court   87
District Courts of Appeal   90
Circuit Courts   92
County Courts   92
Court Administration   93
Florida Board of Bar Examiners   93
Florida Bar Association   95
Florida Office of the State Courts Administrator   95
Florida Court Operations   95
Court Personnel   99
State Attorney   100
Public Defender   100
Clerk of the Court   104
Attorney General   104
Post-Arrest and Pretrial Activities   106
Booking   106
First Appearance   107
Filing Formal Charges   108
Arraignment   108
Investigation and Deposition   108
Pretrial Motions   109
Section Summary   109
Trial Activities   109
Type of Trial   109
Jury Selection   110
Opening Arguments   111
State's Presentation   111
Defense's Presentation   112
Closing Arguments   112
Jury Instructions   112
Jury Deliberations   112
Post-Trial Activities   114
Pre-Sentence Investigation   114

Sentencing Hearing   115
The Development of Florida's Sentencing Guidelines   120
A Closer Look at Florida's Sentencing Guidelines   121
Summary   122
Key Terms   122
Selected Internet Sites   124
Review Questions   124
References   127

Chapter 7 · Florida Corrections   133
Learning Objectives   133
Introduction   134
Becoming a Correctional Officer in Florida   134
Minimum Standards   134
Correctional Officer Academy Training   134
The Correctional Officer Certification Examination   137
The Structure of the Florida Correctional System   138
Prisons   139
Jails   141
Community Supervision   144
Accreditation   145
The National Effort   146
The Florida Effort   147
Private Prisons   147
Growth   147
Savings   148
Thwarted Expansion   148
Civil Rights Restoration   149
A Graying Inmate Population   151
The Expanding Group of Senior Inmates   151
Health Needs of Senior Inmates   153
Summary   154
Key Terms   154
Selected Internet Sites   154
Review Questions   155
References   156

Chapter 8 · The Florida Death Penalty   161
Learning Objectives   161
Introduction   162
Making the Death Penalty Constitutional Again   164
The Case of *Furman v. Georgia* (1972)   164
The Florida Reaction   165
The Case of *Gregg v. Georgia* (1976)   167
The Resumption of Executions   168
Problems with Electrocutions   168
Embracing Lethal Injections   170
Confronting New Problems with Lethal Injection   170
The Jennings Commission   170

Lightbourne v. McCollum (2007)   171
Baze v. Rees (2008)   172
Further Challenges in Florida   172
The Post-Conviction Process   173
Hidden Costs with the Post-Conviction Process   174
Problems with Legal Representation   178
Three Contemporary Developments   179
The Demise and Resurrection of Formal Legal Representation   179
Florida's Death Penalty Statute Ruled Unconstitutional   181
A Call to Abolish Florida's Death Penalty   182
Summary   182
Key Terms   183
Selected Internet Sites   184
Review Questions   184
References   185

Chapter 9 · Florida Juvenile Justice   191
Learning Objectives   191
Introduction   192
Is Delinquency a Concern in Florida?   192
Violent Arrest Rates   193
Property Arrest Rates   196
The Offense Mix   196
Summary   196
The Florida Juvenile Justice System   198
Referral   199
Intake   202
Detention Hearing   202
Delinquency Petition   202
Arraignment   203
Waiver   204
Adjudicatory Hearing   205
Disposition Hearing   206
The Florida Department of Juvenile Justice   207
Special Topics   208
Curfews   208
Teen Court   210
Waiver   211
Gangs   213
The Death Penalty   216
Thompson v. Oklahoma (1988)   216
Stanford v. Kentucky (1989)   216
Roper v. Simmons (2005)   217
The Impact on Florida   217
Summary   218
Key Terms   218
Selected Internet Sites   219
Review Questions   220
References   221

Chapter 10 · Florida Victims   227
    Learning Objectives   227
    Introduction   228
    Victim Rights Amendment   228
        Reforming the Federal Constitution   229
        Reforming the State Constitutions   230
    Victim Compensation   231
        The Shortcomings of Offender Restitution   231
        The Promise of Victim Compensation   232
        Provisions   233
        Operations   234
    Victim Rights Legislation   234
    Victim Impact Statements   237
    Summary   240
    Key Terms   240
    Selected Internet Sites   240
    Review Questions   241
    References   242

Index   245

LIST OF FIGURES

Figure 1.1 Key Findings Regarding Florida's Civic Health   5
Figure 1.2 Public High School Graduation Rates, by State, 2009–10   7

Figure 2.1 The Hierarchy of Law   16
Figure 2.2 Recent Proposed Amendments to the Florida Constitution
    and Voter Outcome   19

Figure 3.1 FBI Definitions for Serious Violent Offenses   26
Figure 3.2 FBI Definitions for Serious Property Offenses   27
Figure 3.3 Crime Clock Comparing the United States and Florida, 2013   28
Figure 3.4 United States (Broken Line) and Florida (Solid Line) Serious
    Violent Crime Rates 1990–2013   31
Figure 3.5 United States (Broken Line) and Florida (Solid Line) Serious
    Property Crime Rates, 1990–2013   32
Figure 3.6 How Reporting and Recording Practices Influence the Production
    of Official Crime Statistics   33
Figure 3.7 The FBI Official Warning about the Pitfalls of Ranking   36

Figure 4.1 Excerpts from Standard Jury Instructions in Castle Doctrine Cases   44
Figure 4.2 Seriousness Levels of Assaults and Batteries in Florida   47
Figure 4.3 The Florida 10-20-Life Law   48
Figure 4.4 Percent of the Population by Age, United States and Florida, 2009   50

Figure 5.1 The Law Enforcement Officer Selection Process   63
Figure 5.2 Entrance Requirements of Florida Sheriff Offices and Police
    Departments   64
Figure 5.3 Oath of Office for Florida Public Officials   64
Figure 5.4 Entrance Requirements for Florida Department of Law
    Enforcement Agents   67
Figure 5.5 Entrance Requirements for Florida Highway Patrol Troopers   69

Figure 6.1 Diagram of the Florida State Court System   88
Figure 6.2 The First Page from the Florida Judge Application Form   89
Figure 6.3 Map of the Florida District Courts of Appeals   92
Figure 6.4 Map of the Florida Circuit Courts   93
Figure 6.5 Lawyer's Oath of Admission to the Florida Bar   94

Figure 6.6 State Courts System Appropriations ($443 Billion) for Fiscal
Year 2013–14   96

Figure 6.7 Cases Filed in Florida Trial Courts and District Courts of
Appeals, Fiscal Year 2012–13   96

Figure 6.8 Cases Filed in Florida District Courts of Appeals, Fiscal Year
2012–13   97

Figure 6.9 Criminal Cases per 100,000 Adults, Courts of General
Jurisdiction, 2010   98

Figure 6.10 Criminal Cases per 100,000 Adults, Courts of Limited
Jurisdiction, 2010   99

Figure 6.11 The Public Defender's Credo   101

Figure 6.12 Florida Application Form for Determining Criminal
Indigent Status   102

Figure 6.13 An Example of a *Subpoena Duces Tecum*   105

Figure 6.14 Right to Pretrial Release from Detention, Florida Constitution   107

Figure 6.15 U.S. Supreme Court Upholds Florida's Use of a Six-Person
Jury in Criminal Trials   110

Figure 6.16 Oath Administered to Trial Jurors   111

Figure 6.17 Principles Underlying the Florida Sentencing Guidelines   115

Figure 6.18 The Florida Criminal Punishment Code Scoresheet for
Felony Offenses   116

Figure 6.19 Mitigating Circumstances that Permit Departure from
Sentencing Guidelines   119

Figure 6.20 Sanctions Imposed by Florida Felony Courts, Fiscal Year
2011–12   119

Figure 6.21 Prior Felony Record and Sanctions Imposed by Florida
Courts, Fiscal Year 2011–12   120

Figure 7.1 Entrance Requirements for Florida Correctional Officers   135

Figure 7.2 Examples of Correctional Officer Duties and Responsibilities   137

Figure 7.3 Florida Correctional Officer Code of Conduct   138

Figure 7.4 Jail Functions and Services   139

Figure 7.5 Examples of Probation and Parole Officer Duties and
Responsibilities   145

Figure 7.6 Benefits of Accreditation   146

Figure 7.7 The Florida Clemency Application   150

Figure 7.8 Florida Prison Population Composition by Age Groups,
1996–2013   152

Figure 8.1 Annual Executions in the United States, 1930–November 30, 2014   162

Figure 8.2 The Eighth Amendment to the United States Constitution   164

Figure 8.3 The Prohibition against Excessive Punishments in the
Florida Constitution   164

Figure 8.4 Examples of Aggravating Circumstances   167

Figure 8.5 Examples of Mitigating Circumstances   167

Figure 8.6 The Post-Conviction Process in Florida Death Penalty Cases   175

Figure 8.7 The Death Warrant Gov. Rick Scott Signed on October 10, 2011,
for Death Row Inmate Chadwick Banks   176

Figure 8.8 Letter from Representative Vasilinda to Governor Scott
    Requesting a Moratorium on the Death Penalty   183

Figure 9.1 United States (Broken Line) and Florida (Solid Line)
    Juvenile Serious Violent Crime Arrest Rates, 2000–2013   194
Figure 9.2 Florida Serious Violent Arrest Rates for Juveniles (Solid Line)
    and Adults (Broken Line), 2000–2013   195
Figure 9.3 United States (Broken Line) and Florida (Solid Line)
    Juvenile Serious Property Crime Arrest Rates, 2000–2013   197
Figure 9.4 Florida Serious Property Arrest Rates for Juveniles (Solid Line)
    and Adults (Broken Line), 2000–2013   198
Figure 9.5 Relative Composition of Selected Juvenile Arrests in Florida
    (Black) and the United States (Gray), 2013   199
Figure 9.6 Florida Juvenile Delinquency Case Flowchart   200
Figure 9.7 The Florida Civil Citation Process   201
Figure 9.8 Common Juvenile Diversion Programs in Florida   203
Figure 9.9 A Florida Affidavit Form Regarding a Petition to Expunge a
    Juvenile Arrest Record   204
Figure 9.10 Department of Juvenile Justice Operating Budget, FY 2014–2015   207
Figure 9.11 Legislative Intent Section of the Statute Permitting Local Juvenile
    Curfew Ordinances   210
Figure 9.12 The Florida Constitution Provision Allowing Juvenile Waiver
    to the Adult Court   211
Figure 9.13 How Florida Determines Whether Someone Is a Gang Member   214
Figure 9.14 The Florida Gang Reduction Pyramid Strategy   215
Figure 9.15 Annual Number of Juvenile Murder Arrests in Florida,
    2005–2013   218

Figure 10.1 The Florida Victim Rights Amendment   229
Figure 10.2 The Proposed Change to the U.S. Constitution
    Recommended by the President's Task Force on Victims of Crime (1982)   229
Figure 10.3 The Proposed 26th Amendment to the U.S. Constitution
    Protecting Victim Rights   230
Figure 10.4 Legislative Intent Section of the Florida Crimes Compensation Act:
    An Example of the Social Contract or Social Welfare Philosophy?   232
Figure 10.5 Florida Victim Compensation Application Form   235
Figure 10.6 Text of the Announcement Judges Must Read at Criminal
    Proceedings or Display in Their Courtroom   237
Figure 10.7 Victim Impact Statement Form Used in the Florida 10th
    Judicial Circuit   238

LIST OF TABLES

Table 3.1 The Top Ten States with the Highest Serious Violent Crime
    Rates, 2001–2013   24
Table 3.2 The Top Ten States with the Highest Serious Property Crime
    Rates, 2001–2013   24
Table 3.3 Serious Crime Rates for the United States and Florida, 2013   29
Table 3.4 2010 Serious Crime Rates for Florida's 20 Largest Cities, 2013   35

Table 5.1 Instructional Hours Devoted to Topics during Police Academy
    Training   60
Table 5.2 Agency Sworn Size, Race and Gender of Full-Time Sworn
    Personnel, Florida State Law Enforcement Agencies, 2013   66
Table 5.3 Agency Sworn Size, Race and Gender of Full-Time Sworn
    Personnel, Florida Sheriff Offices, 2013   70
Table 5.4 Annual Salary by Sworn Size, Florida Sheriff Offices, 2013   71
Table 5.5 Agency Sworn Size, Race and Gender of Full-Time Sworn
    Personnel, Florida Municipal Police Departments, 2013   72
Table 5.6 Annual Salary by Sworn Size, Florida Municipal Police
    Departments, 2013   73
Table 5.7 Sworn Size, Race, Gender, and Entry-Level Salary, Florida College
    and University Law Enforcement Agencies, 2012   74

Table 7.1 Instructional Hours Devoted to Topics during the Florida
    Correctional Officer Academy Training   136
Table 7.2 Number of Prisoners and Imprisonment Rates, by State,
    as of December 31, 2013   140
Table 7.3 Sworn Size, Race, and Gender of Full-Time Sworn Personnel,
    Florida Correctional Facilities, 2012   141
Table 7.4 Entry-Level Salary, State and Private Correctional Facilities, 2013   142
Table 7.5 Number of County Correctional Facilities and Full-Time Sworn
    Correctional Officers, 2013   142
Table 7.6 Sworn Size, Race, and Gender of Full-Time Correctional Officers,
    Florida Sheriff Offices, 2012   143
Table 7.7 Sworn Size and Average Entry-Level Salary of Correctional Officers,
    Florida Sheriff Offices, 2013   143
Table 7.8 50 Largest Local Jails in the United States by Average Daily Inmate
    Population, 2010   144

Table 8.1 Death Row Population and Post-*Gregg* Executions by State as of December 31, 2013   163

Table 9.1 FDJJ Service Categories and Number of Clients, Fiscal Year 2012–13   207

Series Note

Carolina Academic Press' state-specific criminal justice series fills a gap in the field of criminal justice education. One drawback with many current introduction to criminal justice texts is that they pertain to the essentially non-existent "American" criminal justice system and ignore the local landscape. Each state has its unique legislature, executive branch, law enforcement system, court and appellate review system, state supreme court, correctional system, and juvenile justice apparatus. Since many criminal justice students embark upon careers in their home states, they are better served by being exposed to their own states' criminal justice systems. Texts in this series are designed to be used as primary texts or as supplements to more general introductory criminal justice texts.

FLORIDA'S
CRIMINAL JUSTICE SYSTEM

CHAPTER 1

FLORIDA'S CRIMINAL JUSTICE SYSTEM

Introduction

Welcome to the second edition of *Florida's Criminal Justice System*. This text is a member of the expanding innovative state-specific criminal justice series that Carolina Academic Press is sponsoring. Given the uniqueness of this approach, an explanation about the overarching theme behind this line of books would be helpful.

Understanding the criminal justice system and probing how it operates is a fundamental course in the criminology and criminal justice (CCJ) curriculum of most colleges and universities. A survey course is intended to provide novices with a basic understanding of concepts and a broad overview of the field before they move into more advanced topical classes (Williams, 2004). Such an introductory course is one of the basic requirements an undergraduate program must have in place in order to receive approval from the Academy of Criminal Justice Sciences (ACJS, 2014). As former ACJS President Ronald Hunter (2008) astutely reminds us, the field of criminal justice has developed into such a complex enterprise that newcomers now need very careful guidance before they move into the more detailed nuances of how the system works.

Most introductory criminal justice courses break down the criminal justice system into its various components (e.g., crime, police, courts, corrections, and the juvenile system). They then embark upon a closer, more intense inspection of the various facets within each segment. The thinking is that once all the pieces of this giant jigsaw puzzle are reassembled, the student walks away with a firm grasp of how the system operates. Such a strategy, while very simplistic, enables learners to become familiar with basic features in preparation for the more detailed focus that characterizes the specialized upper-level courses.

One drawback to the usual orientation these courses provide, as well as the textbooks instructors adopt for classroom use, is that the materials are very generic. The progression of topics is exactly the same, the coverage is fairly typical, the features are relatively standardized, and not much distinguishes one book from the rest of the pack (Withrow, Weible, & Bonnett, 2004). Another common trait is that most books pertain to the really non-existent "American" criminal justice system and completely ignore the local landscape. While many rules and regulations devised by the various branches of the federal government are applicable to the uniform application of justice in this country, the reality is that every single state runs its own independent criminal justice system. The separation of powers between the federal and state governments is a deliberate effort to remain responsive to local needs. As a result, each state has its own legislature, its own executive branch, its own court and appellate review systems, its own supreme court, its own law enforcement system, its own correctional system, its own juvenile justice apparatus, and so forth. So the idea of a monolithic "American" criminal justice system is not a particularly accurate portrayal of how justice is organized and dispensed within every single state of the Union.

Another consideration that frames *Florida's Criminal Justice System* is that many high school graduates go on to attend public and private colleges in the Sunshine State. A few years later after they have completed their collegiate studies, it is time to decide upon a career and to conduct a job search. Some candidates may have an eye on landing a federal position that probably will take them many miles away from home. However, many CCJ graduates launch their criminal justice careers in the surrounding communities or nearby areas. Yet these college-degreed job-hunters are moving into brand-new positions without having a firm understanding of what they are about to do or how things actually work in the Florida criminal justice system. They have been schooled in some mythical, non-existent criminal justice system.

Given these concerns, *Florida's Criminal Justice System* represents a very deliberate attempt to plug that gap. The premise behind the state-specific criminal justice series that Carolina Academic Press publishes is that CCJ students are better served if they are exposed to their own particular state's criminal justice system rather than to some non-existent entity. While the states face many similar problems, the remedies they choose are far from uniform and, sometimes, invite quite different results. What all this boils down to is that there is a very real need for an introductory text that showcases the Florida version of the criminal justice system. This book is designed to do just that. Further support for this orientation comes from a consideration of civic responsibility and how the current educational system leaves our young citizens unprepared for the roles they will assume one day.

Civic Responsibility

The National Conference on Citizenship (NCoC) is a nonprofit organization charged with promoting civic education and citizenship in the United States. As part of its mandate, the NCoC has joined forces with the Lou Frey Institute of Politics and Government at the University of Central Florida and the Bob Graham Center for Public Service at the University of Florida. The goal of this partnership is to enhance adult participation in civic activities and to promote civic education in K–12 schools.

Whenever a person enters a medical facility for treatment, one of the first things attending personnel do is take the patient's temperature, pulse, and blood pressure. This baseline is the initial step in the journey to chart an appropriate course of action. This is the exact same path the Florida stakeholders took. Their collaboration resulted in a project that focused on identifying key civic indicators and taking Florida's temperature, pulse, and blood pressure, so to speak.

The results of that initial assessment were not very flattering. As Figure 1.1 illustrates, the State of Florida did not fare very well in comparison with the rest of the country. The Sunshine State landed almost at the very bottom of the scale, ranking a distant 46th in 2008 and 45th in 2009. That diagnosis led the project team to conclude that "Florida's civic health is among the worst in the nation" (Dobson, Fine, & Henderson, 2009, p. 9.)

How bad is it to be "among the worst in the nation"? Here is a prime example. The Hillsborough County Supervisor of Elections listed 1,422 registered voters with addresses

Figure 1.1 Key Findings Regarding Florida's Civic Health

Florida has a weak civic culture. It is, in fact, one of the worst in the nation. For 2008, Florida ranked:

- 34th in average voter turnout;
- 49th in the percentage of its citizens who volunteered;
- 48th in the percentage of its citizens who attended a public meeting; and
- 37th in the percentage of its citizens who worked with others to address a community issue.

Florida's overall Civic Health Index for 2008 put the state at 46th in the nation.

Source: L. Douglas Dobson, Terri Susan Fine, and Ann L. Henderson (2009). *Florida Civic Health Index 2009: Communities and the State's Civic Destiny*, p. 2. Washington, DC: National Conference on Citizenship. Retrieved on October 20, 2011 from http://ncoc.net/2kc29.

on the University of South Florida campus. Despite this sizeable bloc of potential voters, only seven people showed up at the polls to cast a ballot in a recent local election (Shenkman & Heffner, 2011).

The most recent report regarding Florida's civic health focused on its "Millennial Generation," the cohort of young adults who fall in the 18–29 age bracket. Again, the results are quite dire. While less than half the Millennials had registered to vote, only a mere 21% cast a ballot in the gubernatorial race. These youth also ranked 48th in the country when it came to participation in civic, community, school, sports, or religious groups. They were also in the bottom ten states for volunteering, showing up at public meetings, and becoming involved neighborhood problems. In short, "Florida Millennials have the depressing distinction of being the most disengaged group in one of the most civically disengaged states in the nation" (Knuckey & Collie, 2012, p. 5).

So what would an appropriate cure or line of defense entail? One response is to turn to educational circles in the hope of instilling more appropriate values in students. Other suggestions are to encourage greater college enrollments and combat the Florida high school dropout rate (Knuckey & Collie, 2012, p. 16). As the following materials illustrate, these spheres have their own fair share of problems to overcome before they can become an integral part of a workable solution.

Persistent Problems with High School Education

The National Assessment Governing Board, a federal agency, periodically assesses how well American K–12 students perform on various standardized subject matter tests. The 2010 civics exam covered three general areas. The first section tapped knowledge about the political system, the Constitution, democracy, and citizen rights. The second portion of the instrument emphasized skills one would need to analyze and form opinions about various public interest issues. The final aspect dealt with citizen actions and responsibilities.

After administering a test of 153 questions to 9,900 twelfth-grade students around the country, it was determined that just 28% graded out as being proficient. All told, 64% had at least a minimal understanding of civic matters (National Center for Education Statistics, 2011a, p. 35). A similar report covering U.S. history produced even more dismal results. Only 12% of the 12,000 students who took the test achieved proficiency. The proportion of students exhibiting a basic or higher performance came in at 45% (National Center for Education Statistics, 2011b, p. 37).

Another recent national survey canvassed 1,200 American seventeen-year-olds. Utilizing a slightly different format, the report converted actual test scores to the more familiar letter-grade format. In terms of the history test, students earned an overall score of 73% for a "C" average. The misconceptions adolescents had about basic historical facts are appalling. Here are just a few observations from that report (Hess, 2008, p. 19):

- "Nearly a quarter of 17-year-olds did not know that George Washington commanded the American army in the Revolutionary War."
- "Forty percent could not identify the proper half-century in which the First World War took place."
- "One-fourth thought Christopher Columbus had landed in the New World after 1750."
- "More than a quarter did not know that it is the Declaration of Independence that declares that all men 'are endowed by their Creator with certain unalienable Rights.'"

Clearly, the American educational system has withered and become compromised. It is not in a position to provide much immediate assistance to the promoters of civic education. In other words, young Americans are growing up without an appropriate awareness of what it means to live in a democratic society.

Another way to track student progress through the education system is to look at high school graduation rates. This indicator counts the number of students entering ninth-grade and then determining how many of these students graduated four years later. Figure 1.2 maps high school state graduation rates for the entire country. A glance at Figure 1.2 shows that Florida is a cellar-dweller with a rank of 44th in the nation. The Sunshine State has one of the more dismal high school graduation rates in the country. Three out of every ten freshmen will become a high-school drop-out (National Center for Education Statistics, 2013, Table 124).

Bear in mind that the test results just mentioned came from students attending high school. They did not include high school drop-outs. More than likely, this disenfranchised group would have dragged those standardized scores down even further. Even more disturbing is that one out of every five applicants who held a Florida high school diploma and attempted to join the U.S. Army were turned away because of failing scores on the entrance examination (Christeson, Bishop-Josef, Taggart, & Beakey, 2013, p. 1). Thus, one could conclude that the actual level of knowledge about civics and American history among the general populace is even lower than what these results suggest. Unfortunately, this level of ignorance also extends to knowledge about the criminal justice system.

Persistent Problems with College Education

This educational malaise spills over into the lecture halls at many post-secondary institutions. A sizeable number of students who graduate from high school and move on to a college campus are simply not ready to undertake this academic challenge. For instance, 36% of all college freshmen signed up for at least one remedial course in 2007–08 (National Center for Education Statistics, 2013, Table 270). In other words, these

Figure 1.2 Public High School Graduation Rates, by State, 2009–10

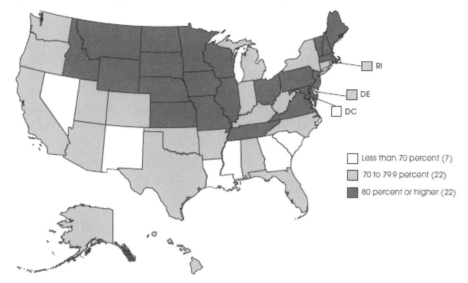

Source: Kena, Grace, et al. (2014). *The Condition of Education 2014*, p. 140. Washington, DC: U.S. Department of Education, National Center for Education Statistics. Retrieved on October 3, 2014 from http://nces.ed.gov/pubs2014/2014083.pdf.

students needed to take a preparation course in order to be able to occupy a seat in one of their first college courses. Furthermore, only 59% of the freshmen who enrolled in a four-year college program in 2006 ended up walking across the commencement stage over the next six years to receive a bachelor's diploma (Kena et al., 2014, p. 194).

Some commentators have hailed the release of the title *Academically Adrift* as the "most significant book on higher education written in recent years" (Vedder, 2011). The authors, Arum and Roksa, tracked 2,322 college students who enrolled in 24 institutions in the Fall 2005 semester until the completion of their sophomore year at the end of the Spring 2007 semester. Participants took the College Learning Assessment (CLA) exam three times during this period. This instrument presents students with tasks, such as writing a memorandum that explains an existing problem and suggests remedies, as a way of demonstrating their ability "to analyze and evaluate information, solve problems, and communicate effectively" (Council for Aid to Education, 2014).

The results amount to a chilling indictment of the limited amount of learning that actually takes place in the higher education environment. Astonishingly, 45% of the students show no change in their critical thinking, complex reasoning, and writing skills after being in college for two years (Arum & Roksa, 2011, p. 36). The researchers attribute this lack of learning to several factors. First, most colleges fail to challenge or engage students in the learning process. Many college students never see, talk, nor have contact with their professors outside the classroom. Second, the average student spends about 12 hours a week studying, with 37% saying they poured over their books for less than five hours per week (Arum & Roksa, 2011, p. 69). Instead, college students squander an inordinate amount of time socializing, going to bars, attending parties, watching television, playing on the computer, or participating in other recreational outlets. Third, students gravitate en masse to the less-than-demanding courses. They typically avoid classes where professors expect them to read forty pages a week or write a term paper.

A sequel that extends the time frame from the sophomore year through the end of the senior year of college does not contain findings that are any more encouraging (Arum, Roksa, & Cho, 2011). After four years of college, 36% of the seniors do not exhibit any gains above and beyond their freshmen CLA tests. Most students log less than nine hours a week studying alone. A little more than a third say they spend less than five hours every week preparing for their classes. Half the students take courses in which instructors do not require a term paper. In fact, the average college senior submits just one term paper per year throughout his or her college stay.

In a separate development, Senack (2014) surveyed 2,039 students representing 150 colleges and campuses across the United States. Perplexed by the rising cost of textbooks, two out of three college students reported they decided not to buy a required book in a course because they deemed the price too expensive. Boycotting the purchase of course materials would seem to be a disingenuous strategy to advocate in a post-secondary learning environment.

Tracking a segment of the *Academically Adrift* baccalaureate recipients for an additional two years after they left their campuses paints an even more disconcerting picture of these young adults (Arum & Roksa, 2014). Excluding subjects who were attending graduate school or pursuing professional studies leaves a batch of degree-holders poised to enter the work force. Despite being the proud owners of a four-year college diploma, over half of this group was unemployed, working only on a part-time basis, or earning less than $30,000 a year (Arum & Roksa, 2014, pp. 56–57). Given these bleak labor market conditions, a sizable chunk had decided to return home and live with their parents who, in turn, were absorbing a portion of their college-educated offspring's living costs. Obviously, the college credential does not signal the acquisition of critical skills so that the transformation to productive adulthood is well underway.

A more detailed analysis examined the "state of the state" and cited several crucial concerns with the Florida university system. According to Dewey and Denslow (2014), one effect of the latest recession is that Florida now ranks dead last among the states in terms of state appropriations for college education. In other words, Florida university budgets are starving for cash. Recurring budget cuts have forced college administrators to rely more heavily upon large classes to accommodate a growing number of students. As Dewey and Denslow (2014, p. 77) explain:

> Most students spend a large share of their time in very large classes in which they often fail to relate to teachers, to other students, or to course content. Such courses seldom assign term papers and tests are largely multiple-choice. Even with exceptional teachers, it is hard for such courses to motivate students to study.

Super-sized classes detract from the quality of the college educational experience. Grade inflation, spurred in part by this inferior learning atmosphere, means that the quality of a Florida public college diploma is of dubious value to both recipients and prospective employers. While a simple remedy does exist, it requires more funding. As the authors explain (2014, p. 78):

> A straightforward way to increase student effort would be to have smaller classes, with more carefully graded written assignments, more oral reports, and more essay tests. With little state funding and low tuition, however, smaller classes are just not affordable.

This calloused reluctance to invest in a quality educational environment should make taxpayers recoil with disdain. In addition, prospective employers would be abhorred if they knew there were deliberate decisions to not groom students for success and to not cultivate the critical skills needed in the 21st-century work force. But before we look more closely at the mission statements of some CCJ programs in Florida colleges and universities, it might be revealing to take a detour and gather a quick peak at CCJ students.

Criminology and Criminal Justice Students

One approach to curricular development is to find out what students plan to do after graduation and then design courses that match those needs. A consistent refrain that emerges from the literature is that CCJ students are very much future-oriented. That is, the vast majority intend to pursue a career within the criminal justice system, most likely in the law enforcement sector (Bumgarner, 2002; Courtright & Mackey, 2004; Dantzker, 2005; Krimmel & Tartaro, 1999; Tontodonato, 2006). Having made that decision, these students are looking for courses that are relevant to their aspirations and will help advance their careers. Seasoned law enforcement officers feel that a college background gives them an advantage and boosts their careers (Carlan, 2007; Payne, Blackwell, & Collins, 2010; Hilal, Densley, & Zhao, 2013).

What makes these grounded courses so critical is that all too often students have developed a distorted view of what takes place in the criminal justice world. One can trace these misperceptions to glamorous, but incorrect, portrayals in the media and Hollywood movies (Courtright & Mackey, 2004; Mackey & Courtright, 2012). Interestingly enough, these same students also import unrealistic expectations about the academic arena when they go to college.

Many freshmen who intend to major in CCJ arrive on campus ill-prepared and bring a host of unrealistic expectations. Martin and Hanrahan (2004) report that incoming CCJ students at their campus seriously underestimate the amount of time they need to set aside for class preparation. Almost a quarter of the arriving freshmen come to college with the intention to spend less than ten hours a week studying. Seventy percent of these new CCJ students figure they can get by with devoting no more than 20 hours a week to studying even though they have enrolled for 15 semester hours of credit (Martin & Hanrahan, 2004, p. 294). Those numbers amount to less than the standard 40-hour work week in the labor force.

Even more amazing is that a sizeable number of these CCJ freshmen fail to attend class on a regular basis. These students skip at least one class, if not more, every other week. Instead, they reserve the bulk of their time for participation in social activities. Needless to say, such a time allocation will not result in much collegiate, let alone occupational, success.

Given this documentation, it is no small wonder why police administrators do not view a college degree as an essential ingredient when hiring new officers. According to the *2013 Criminal Justice Agency Profile* sponsored by the Florida Department of Law Enforcement (2014), a college degree is not a vital requirement for most sworn criminal justice positions. Of the 258 Florida municipal police departments, only two (Coral Springs and Hillsboro Beach) require incoming sworn personnel to have a four-year college degree. Twenty-six other agencies look for candidates who have a two-year degree.

A similar picture emerges when attention turns to county sheriff offices. None of these agencies require new employees to have a Bachelor's degree and four others (Gilchrist, Hillsborough, Jacksonville, and Leon) expect candidates to have earned an Associate's degree before they apply for employment. None of the 85 state, county, private, or sheriff offices that operate a jail require new hires to have any college education.

Obviously, there is a need to cultivate more realistic expectations among CCJ students and to develop meaningful classes. Quite often, courses do not prepare CCJ students adequately for future employment opportunities. In addition, prospective employers are not swayed by bald claims that a college degree translates into a better prepared employee. In short, there is a large disconnect here. Dantzker (2005, p. 7) summarizes this situation very aptly:

> In the meantime … criminal justice programs need to be more aware of their students' goals and taper programs to fit that need, regardless of whether it's the direction in which the faculty would prefer to go. The reality is, it's not for them; it's for the students.

Criminology and Criminal Justice Mission Statements

Most formal organizations have constructed what is known as a mission statement. A *mission statement* explains what that group's top priorities are. Most colleges and universities have established mission statements that reflect their goals and objectives. For instance, the opening sentence of the Florida State University Mission sets the tone by noting that the institution "is a comprehensive, national, graduate research university that puts research into action for the benefit of our students and society" (Florida State University, 2005).

Quite a few departments and programs within colleges and universities have framed their own particular mission statements. In instances where a unit may not have put a formal mission statement into writing, there may be a program overview in the catalog or on the departmental web site that summarizes organizational expectations. These declarations can range from a single sentence to a paragraph or to multiple pages.

What does a mission statement look like? The following samples come from criminal justice programs located at several Florida public institutions. They include:

- To provide quality graduate and undergraduate education within a liberal arts context and is designed to prepare students for careers in criminal justice or other fields that become attractive to students (Florida Atlantic University, 2014).

- To prepare students with the skill sets that are in demand by employing, criminal justice agencies. The Department provides an intellectually challenging and supportive environment which allows for the students to develop and demonstrate competence in both theory and practice (Florida Gulf Coast University, 2014).

- To challenge students both intellectually and pragmatically to prepare them for a career in the criminal justice system, including policing, courts, corrections, juvenile justice, and private security, or for graduate school (University of West Florida, 2014).

- To provide students with an in-depth exposure to all facets of the criminal justice system including law enforcement, detention, the judiciary, corrections, and probation and parole . . . . to develop a sound educational basis either for graduate work or for professional training in one or more of the specialized areas comprising the modern urban criminal justice system (University of South Florida, 2014).

Two common themes stream throughout these statements. The first thread is the recognition that students should become familiar with how the criminal justice system works. The second emphasis is the acknowledgement that students are apprentices preparing for future careers.

As mentioned at the beginning of this chapter, *Florida's Criminal Justice System* is designed to help students achieve these twin goals. Examining each individual component of the criminal justice system presents readers with a panoramic view of the field. More importantly, an exclusive focus on state and local matters within Florida helps readers further their career development. It also heeds ACJS President Hunter's (2010) admonition that we need to become more aware of "real-world problems" and "expand beyond criminology/criminal justice parameters" to craft solutions that work.

An Overview of *Florida's Criminal Justice System*

This book delivers a similar treatment of the topics one would find in any standard introductory criminal justice text. The only difference is that it concentrates on topics that deal with what happens in the Sunshine State. For example, Chapter 2 examines the contents of the Florida Constitution. When Chapter 3 discusses how pervasive crime is, it explores crime in Florida. The fourth chapter deals with criminal law and uses *Florida Statutes* to demonstrate relevant points. Chapter 5 explains how Florida has structured its law enforcement system at the state and local levels. It also shows how potential law enforcement officers have to meet a series of state requirements in order to become certified. The next chapter describes how the Florida court system is organized and how criminal cases progress through the system. Chapter 7 offers details about the Florida corrections system and the adaptations that officials have made in the effort to punish and rehabilitate.

Chapter 8 marks the point at which the book turns to more topical chapters. The first member of that section deals with the Florida death penalty. It explains the key role that Florida played on the national scene after the United States Supreme Court banned capital punishment in 1972 and subsequently lifted the moratorium in 1976. That chapter then goes on to raise a number of issues that have trailed the execution process in Florida. Chapter 9 reviews the problem of juvenile delinquency and explores how the Sunshine State handles these cases. It also entertains some specific issues that Florida communities face when devising tactics to confront youthful crime. The final chapter examines the services that Florida provides to crime victims and visits the major developments this state has championed in victim rights.

Summary

This short synopsis should convince you that *Florida's Criminal Justice System* is a much needed enhancement to the typical introductory criminal justice course. By the time students work their way through this text, they will have gained a greater sensitivity to the problems associated with crime in the Sunshine State and the mechanisms put in place to deal with these issues. Readers should also become aware of some emerging issues and solutions. Hopefully, this spotlight on our own state will help create a cadre of knowledgeable Floridians who understand the inner workings of their own criminal justice system when they embark on their careers.

References

Academy of Criminal Justice Sciences (2014). *Certification Standards for College/University Criminal Justice/Criminology Baccalaureate Degree Programs.* Greenbelt, MD: Academy of Criminal Justice Sciences. Retrieved on October 3, 2014 from http://www.acjs.org/uploads/file/ACJSCertificationStandards-Baccalaureate.pdf.

Arum, Richard and Josipa Roksa (2011). *Academically Adrift: Limited Learning on College Campuses.* Chicago: University of Chicago Press.

Arum, Richard, Josipa Roksa, and Esther Cho (2011). *Improving Undergraduate Learning: Findings and Policy Recommendations from the SSRC-CLA Longitudinal Project.* New York: Social Science Research Council. Retrieved on May 14, 2014 from http://www.ssrc.org/workspace/images/crm/new_publication_3/%7Bd06178be-3823-e011-adef-001cc477ec84%7D.pdf.

Arum, Richard and Josipa Roksa (2014). *Aspiring Adults Adrift: Tentative Transitions of College Graduates.* Chicago: University of Chicago Press.

Bumgarner, Jeff (2002). An assessment of the perceptions of policing as a profession among two-year and four-year criminal justice and law enforcement students. *Journal of Criminal Justice Education, 13,* 313–334.

Carlan, Philip E. (2007). The criminal justice degree and policing: Conceptual development or occupational primer? *Policing: An International Journal of Police Strategies & Management, 30,* 608–619.

Christeson, William, Sandra Bishop-Josef, Amy Dawson Taggart, and Chris Beakey (2013). *A Commitment to Pre-Kindergarten Is a Commitment to National Security.* Washington, DC: Mission Readiness. Retrieved on October 3, 2014 from http://missionreadiness.s3.amazonaws.com/National_prek_report.pdf.

Council for Aid to Education (2014). *Performance Assessment: CLA+ Overview.* New York: Council for Aid to Education. Retrieved on October 3, 2014 from http://cae.org/participating-institutions/cla-overview/.

Courtright, Kevin E. and David A. Mackey (2004). Job desirability among criminal justice majors: Exploring relationships between personal characteristics and occupational attractiveness. *Journal of Criminal Justice Education, 15,* 311–326.

Dantzker, Mark (2005). Majoring in criminal justice: I want a job. *ACJS Today, 30* (4), 6–7.

Dewey, Jim and David Denslow (2014). *Tougher Choices: Shaping Florida's Future.* Tallahassee, FL: LeRoy Collins Institute. Retrieved on October 3, 2014 from http://collinsinstitute.fsu.edu/sites/collinsinstitute.fsu.edu/files/Tougher%20Choices%20FINAL%202-20-14.pdf.

Dobson, L. Douglas, Terri Susan Fine, and Ann L. Henderson (2009). *Florida Civic Health Index 2009: Communities and the State's Civic Destiny.* Washington, DC: National Conference on Citizenship. Retrieved on October 3, 2014 from http://www.ncoc.net/2kc29.

Florida Atlantic University (2014). *Introduction.* Boca Raton: School of Criminology & Criminal Justice. Retrieved on October 3, 2014 from http://www.fau.edu/dcj.

Florida Department of Law Enforcement (2014). *2013 Criminal Justice Agency Profile Survey Results.* Tallahassee: Florida Department of Law Enforcement. Retrieved on October 3, 2014 from http://www.fdle.state.fl.us/Content/CJST/Menu/Publications/test.aspx.

Florida Gulf Coast University (2014). *Mission.* Fort Myers: Division of justice Studies. Retrieved on October 3, 2014 from http://www.fgcu.edu/CAS/Departments/JS/index.html.

Florida State University (2005). *Florida State University Mission Statement.* Tallahassee: Florida State University. Retrieved on October 3, 2014 from http://facultyhandbook.fsu.edu/content/download/58091/674320/FSUmission2005.pdf.

Hess, Frederick M. (2008). *Still at Risk: What Students Don't Know, Even Now.* Washington, DC: American Enterprise Institute for Public Policy Research. Retrieved on October 3, 2014 from http://www.aei.org/files/2008/02/26/20080226_CommonCorereport.pdf.

Hilal, Susan, James Densley, and Ruohui Zhao (2013). Cops in college: Police officers' perceptions on formal education. *Journal of Criminal Justice Education, 24,* 461–477.

Hunter, Ronald G. (2008). Why we need certification standards in criminal justice education and what the impacts will be: A response to the concerns of JDs. *Journal of Criminal Justice Education, 19,* 193–204.

Hunter, Ronald G. (2011). Presidential address: The future of justice studies. *Justice Quarterly, 28,* 1–14.

Kena, Grace, Susan Aud, Frank Johnson, Xiaolei Wang, Jijun Zhang, Amy Rathbun, Sidney Wilkinson-Flicker, and Paul Kristapovich (2014). *The Condition of Education 2014.* Washington, DC: U.S. Department of Education, National Center for Education Statistics. Retrieved on October 3, 2014 from http://nces.ed.gov/pubs2014/2014083.pdf.

Knuckey, Jonathan and Tim Collie (2012). *2011 Florida Civic Health Index: The Next Generation.* Washington, DC: National Conference on Citizenship. Retrieved on October 3, 2014 from http://ncoc.net/FLCHI2011.

Krimmel, John T. and Christine Tartaro (1999). Career choices and characteristics of criminal justice undergraduates. *Journal of Criminal Justice Education, 10,* 277–289.

Mackey, David A. and Kevin E. Courtright (2012). Connecting academic criminal justice to the practitioner perspective: The efficacy of the professional interview. *Journal of Criminal Justice Education, 23,* 536–549.

Martin, Jamie S. and Kate Hanrahan (2005). Criminology freshmen: Preparation, expectations, and college performance. *Journal of Criminal Justice Education, 15,* 287–309.

National Center for Education Statistics (2011a). *The Nation's Report Card: Civics 2010.* Washington, DC: U.S. Department of Education. Retrieved on October 3, 2014 from http://nces.ed.gov/nationsreportcard/pdf/main2010/2011466.pdf.

National Center for Education Statistics (2011b). *The Nation's Report Card: U.S. History 2010*. Washington, DC: U.S. Department of Education. Retrieved on October 3, 2014 from http://nces.ed.gov/nationsreportcard/pdf/main2010/2011468.pdf.

National Center for Education Statistics (2013). Table 124: Averaged freshman graduation rates for public secondary schools, by state or jurisdiction: Selected years, 1990–91 through 2009–10. *Digest of Education Statistics: 2012*. Washington, DC: U.S. Department of Education. Retrieved on October 3, 2014 from http://nces.ed.gov/programs/digest/d12/tables/dt12_124.asp.

National Center for Education Statistics (2013). Table 270: Percentage of first-year undergraduate students who took remedial education courses, by selected student and institutions characteristics: 2003–04 and 2007–08. *Digest of Education Statistics: 2012*. Washington, DC: U.S. Department of Education. Retrieved on October 3, 2013 from http://nces.ed.gov/programs/digest/d12/tables/dt12_270.asp.

Payne, Brian, Brenda Sims Blackwell, and Sue Carter Collins (2010). Exploring the ties between career satisfaction and education: Trait versus situational approaches. *Journal of Criminal Justice Education*, *21*, 77–92.

Senack, Ethan (2014). *Fixing the Broken Textbook Market: How Students Respond to High Textbook Costs and Demand Alternatives*. Washington, DC: Center for Public Interest Research, Inc. Retrieved on October 3, 2014 from http://uspirg.org/sites/pirg/files/reports/NATIONAL%20Fixing%20Broken%20Textbooks%20Report1.pdf.

Shenkman, Rick and Alexander Heffner (2011). Fight civics ignorance. *St. Petersburg Times*, March 22. Retrieved on October 3, 2014 from http://www.tampabay.com/opinion/columns/fight-civics-ignorance/1158754.

Tontodonato, Pamela (2006). Goals, expectations, and satisfaction of criminal justice majors: Implications for faculty, students, and programs. *Journal of Criminal Justice Education*, *17*, 162–180.

University of South Florida (2014). *Undergraduate in Criminology*. Tampa: Department of Criminology. Retrieved on October 3, 2014 from http://criminology.cbcs.usf.edu/undergraduateCriminology/.

University of West Florida (2014). *Overview*. Pensacola: Department of Justice Studies. Retrieved on October 3, 2014 from http://uwf.edu/cops/departments/criminal-justice/about-us/overview/.

Vedder, Richard (2011). *Academically Adrift*: A must-read. *The Chronicle of Higher Education*, January 20. Retrieved on October 3, 2014 from http://chronicle.com/blogs/innovations/academically-adrift-a-must-read/28423.

Williams, Marian R. (2004). The role of prerequisites in a criminal justice curriculum. *Journal of Criminal Justice Education*, *15*, 19–31.

Withrow, Brian L., Kerry Weible, and Jennifer Bonnett (2004). Aren't they all the same? A comparative analysis of introductory criminal justice textbooks. *Journal of Criminal Justice Education*, *15*, 1–18.

CHAPTER 2

THE FLORIDA CONSTITUTION

Learning Objectives

After reading this chapter, you should be able to:

- Explain what the hierarchy of law means.
- Tell what the supremacy clause accomplishes.
- Differentiate the three branches of government and explain what their duties entail.
- List some of the items present in the Declaration of Rights within the Florida Constitution.
- Explain the various ways to amend the Florida Constitution.

Introduction

The very foundation for state government and the state criminal justice system is embedded within the Florida Constitution. While it is true that Floridians are subject to the provisions of the United States Constitution and the federal courts, there are a number of items that do not carry national prominence. By default, it is up to the states to decide the direction they wish to take in those instances. The *hierarchy of law*, displayed in Figure 2.1, provides a visual demonstration of this principle.

This hierarchy of law is based upon Article VI, Clause 2, of the United States Constitution. This article, also known as the *supremacy clause*, reads:

> This Constitution, and the Laws of the United States which shall be made in Pursuance thereof; and all Treaties made, or which shall be made, under the Authority of the United States, shall be the supreme Law of the Land; and the Judges in every State shall be bound thereby, any Thing in the Constitution or Laws of any State to the Contrary notwithstanding.

In other words, whenever a conflict or a difference of interpretation arises between two bodies, the higher authority prevails. For example, while the Florida Supreme Court is the highest judicial body under the state constitution, its holdings are subject to the federal court system and the decisions that are rendered there. We shall encounter plenty of examples of this process in work throughout this text. For instance, when we look at the oath of office that Florida public officials take, you will notice that office-holders swear to uphold both the federal and the state constitutions. Similarly, when we examine issues relevant to the juvenile justice process and to the death penalty, there will be instances in which the state courts bow to rulings issued by the United States Supreme Court.

15

Figure 2.1 The Hierarchy of Law

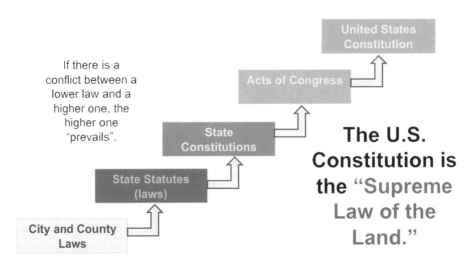

Source: Annette Boyd Pitts (2012). *Amending the Florida Constitution: The Role of the Courts*. Tallahassee: Florida Law Related Education Association, Inc., The Florida Bar. Retrieved on December 30, 2014 from https://www.floridabar.org/cmdocs/cm154.nsf/600714bc5772f53285257236004a107e/0c5af73dc 6a55aaf85257bf00055f84a/$FILE/Amending%20Florida%27s%20Constitution%20All%20Documents.pdf.

The Florida Constitution has a long history. Work began on assembling a state constitution in 1838 while Florida was still a U.S. territory. In 1845, Florida gained recognition as the 27th state. However, when the Civil War commenced, Florida seceded from the Union and joined the Confederate States of America. After the Civil War ended, Florida was placed under military rule until it could nullify the "Ordinance of Secession of 1861" and adopt a new state constitution, which the delegates did so in 1868.

The current state constitution came into being during 1968. This document has undergone several revisions since then, but the basic core has remained unchanged. What we shall do in this chapter is examine some of the relevant provisions in the state Constitution and discuss how these provisions have molded the way justice is dispensed in the Sunshine State.

Branches of Government

The Florida Constitution divides government into three distinct bodies: the legislative, executive, and judicial branches (Article II, Section 3). Each entity is independent of the other and no one branch is superior to the others.

The Legislative Branch

Article III explains the legislative branch and its powers. It defines the membership and organizes this body into the Senate and the House of Representatives. The contents also provide for an annual legislative session, enactment of laws, the process for overriding the Governor's veto of a bill, sets the term of office and qualifications for holding office, and drawing boundaries of legislative districts. The only specific directive that the Legislature is mandated to accomplish is the passage of an annual budget for running the state.

The Executive Branch

According to Article IV of the Florida Constitution, the executive branch consists of the governor, the lieutenant governor, and the cabinet (attorney general, chief financial officer, and commissioner of agriculture). In addition to spelling out candidate qualifications and election procedures, this portion of the state constitution also invests the power of clemency within the executive branch. *Clemency* refers to the restoration of civil rights after conviction, commutations of sentence lengths, and pardons. Further details about this process will appear in Chapter 7 of this book. The governor is also empowered to fill a host of vacancies at the state, county, and municipal levels. Chapter 6 will explain the role of the governor's office in handling judicial nominations and appointments to the bench.

The Judicial Branch

The judiciary is the topic of Article V of the Florida Constitution. It establishes the duties of the Florida Supreme Court, the District Courts of Appeal, circuit courts, and county courts. Later in Chapter 6, we will visit the qualifications judges, state attorneys, clerks of the circuit courts, and public defenders must satisfy, how the appointment process works, and how vacancies are filled.

Summary

The remaining Articles in the Florida Constitution address a host of topics. Some of these articles are tangentially related to the state criminal justice system. For instance, there are sections that deal with voter qualifications and election procedures, taxation, bonds, the structure and responsibilities of local governments, the public education system, and other sundry items. The more important features, which the next section handles, are individual rights.

Declaration of Rights

Article I of the Florida Constitution bears a strong resemblance to the federal Bill of Rights. Its basic principle is that "all political power is inherent in the people." Among the specific rights outlined there are:

- Religious freedom, including the separation of church and state;
- Freedom of speech and press;
- Right to assemble;
- Right to work and collective bargaining;
- Right to bear arms;

- Due process, protection against double-jeopardy, and privilege against self-incrimination;
- No bill of attainder and protection against *ex post facto* laws;
- Protection against imprisonment for debt;
- Search-and-seizure protections;
- *Habeas corpus*;
- Pretrial release in criminal cases;
- Grand jury indictment for a capital crime;
- Timely notice of charges, cross-examination of witnesses, subpoena power, speedy and public trial, and venue;
- Rights of victims in criminal proceedings;
- Protection against excessive punishments;
- Trial by jury;
- Right of privacy; and
- Access to public records and meetings.

As you can see, the Florida Constitution bears a very strong resemblance to the United States Constitution. This coordination is important because it makes the hierarchy of rule much easier to process and understand. While the Florida Constitution provides the foundation for the system of government in the Sunshine State, the document is not written in stone. As the next section explains, there are a variety of avenues for amending the Florida Constitution.

Amending the Florida Constitution

There are five different ways to amend the Florida Constitution. The first procedure lies with the state legislature. If 60% of the members serving in the House of Representatives and 60% of the Senate chamber agree to the language, then that proposal is put on the state ballot for Floridians to approve. If 60% of the voters are in favor of the change, then the proposal receives approval. If fewer than 60% of the voters do not approve the measure, it fails and the constitution is not modified or changed.

Another option comes from the realm of the Constitution Revision Commission (CRC). The Florida Constitution provides the CRC be empaneled every twenty years to review the contents of that document. The CRC recommendations go before Florida voters who then decide the fate of these suggestions. Again, the bar is set at 60% approval for the change to take effect.

A third path is a citizens' initiative. Interested parties must register their petition with the State Division of Elections and then canvass the state for voter signatures backing this plan. If a sufficient number of voters express interest in the matter, then the Secretary of State certifies the petition and presents it to the Florida Supreme Court for review. If the Florida Supreme Court validates the petition, then the question will appear on a statewide ballot for voter consideration. A 60% approval rating is needed before the state constitution is changed.

The fourth way to change the Florida Constitution is for 15% of Florida voters to sign a petition calling for a constitutional convention. The language that appears on the ballot is very simple. It asks, "Shall a constitutional convention be held?" If a simple majority of the voters approve the question, then the process begins to seat a constitutional convention. The items that pass the constitutional convention then appear on the next state-wide ballot for voter approval at the 60% level.

Finally, the last way to amend the Florida Constitution is via the Taxation and Budget Reform Commission (TBRC). The TBRC meets every twenty years to analyze whether the state budget process is in need of repair. This group examines the budget, revenue streams, and expenditures to determine whether the current structure is sufficient to satisfy demand. Should any gaps be identified, the TBRC can recommend ways to alleviate these conditions. The matter then goes on a state-wide ballot for voter approval. Once again, it takes a 60% voter approval for passage.

Efforts to amend the Florida Constitution in the 2014 and 2012 elections met with mixed success. As Figure 2.2 illustrates, quite a few of these initiatives fail to meet with voter approval.

Figure 2.2 Recent Proposed Amendments to the Florida Constitution and Voter Outcome

Year	Topic	Status
2014	Water and Land Conservation— Dedicating funds to acquire and restore Florida conservation and recreation lands	Passed
2014	Use of Marijuana for Certain Medical Conditions	Defeated
2014	Prospective Appointment of Certain Judicial Vacancies	Defeated
2014	State Courts	Defeated
2014	Religious Freedom	Defeated

Source: Adapted from Division of Elections (2014). *2014 Proposed Constitutional Amendments.* Tallahassee: Secretary of State. Retrieved on December 30, 2014 from http://elections.myflorida.com/constitutional-amendments/2014-proposed.shtml; Division of Elections (2012). *2012 Proposed Constitutional Amendments.* Tallahassee: Secretary of State. Retrieved on December 30, 2014 from http://elections.myflorida.com/constitutional-amendments/2012-proposed.shtml.

Summary

The Florida Constitution sets the environment in which the state's criminal justice system operates. Each of the three branches of government influence how justice is pursued in the Sunshine State. As the Preamble to the Constitution of the State of Florida explains:

> We, the people of the State of Florida, being grateful to Almighty God for our constitutional liberty, in order to secure its benefits, perfect our government, insure domestic tranquility, maintain public order, and guarantee equal civil and political rights to all, do ordain and establish this constitution.

The remainder of this book explains exactly how this mandate is discharged in the State of Florida.

Key Terms

clemency
hierarchy of law
supremacy clause

Selected Internet Sites

Florida Division of Elections, Secretary of State
    http://elections.myflorida.com/

Florida Law Related Education
    http://www.flrea.org

League of Women Voters of Florida
    http://www.thefloridavoter.org/

Review Questions

1. What does the "hierarchy of law" mean?

2. What is the importance of the "supremacy clause"?

3. What are the three branches of government?

4. What is the purpose of the legislative branch?

5. What is the role of the executive branch?

6. Who belongs to the executive branch?

7. What is the purpose of the judicial branch?

8. What is included in the "Declaration of Rights" portion of the Florida Constitution?

9. Explain the various ways in which the Florida Constitution can be amended.

References

Constitution of the State of Florida (2014). Tallahassee: State of Florida. Retrieved on December 30, 2014 from http://www.leg.state.fl.us/Statutes/index.cfm?Mode=Constitution&Submenu=3&Tab=statutes&CFID=44863504&CFTOKEN=99268941.

Division of Elections (2012). 2012 Proposed Constitutional Amendments. Tallahassee: Secretary of State. Retrieved on December 30, 2014 from http://elections.myflorida.com /constitutional-amendments/2012-proposed.shtml.

Division of Elections (2014). *2014 Proposed Constitutional Amendments*. Tallahassee: Secretary of State. Retrieved on December 30, 2014 from http://elections.myflorida. com/constitutional-amendments/2014-proposed.shtml.

Pitts, Annette Boyd (2012). *Amending the Florida Constitution: The Role of the Courts.* Tallahassee: Florida Law Related Education Association, Inc., The Florida Bar. Retrieved on December 30, 2014 from http://r.search.yahoo.com/_ylt=AwrBT8PYraJU078AtD-FXNyoA;_ylu=X3oDMTByNzA1YWV1BHNlYwNzcgRwb3MDOQRjb2xvA2JmMQR2d GlkAw—/RV=2/RE=1419976280/RO=10/RU=http%3a%2f%2fwww.flrea.org%2fcur-riculum%2fpowerpoint%2fAmendments.ppt/RK=0/RS=DHlldiorxZi4LyaolzuQ3 Gs1Iw4-.

CHAPTER 3

FLORIDA CRIME

Learning Objectives

After reading this chapter, you should be able to:

- Describe Florida's serious violent crime rate relative to the other states.
- Portray how Florida leads most of the other states in terms of serious property crime.
- List the four objectives of the Florida UCR Program.
- Explain where and how the Florida Department of Law Enforcement gets information for the *Uniform Crime Reports* Program.
- Provide the FBI definitions for murder, forcible rape, robbery, and aggravated assault.
- Do the same for burglary, larceny-theft, and motor vehicle theft.
- Tell how hierarchical reporting is used.
- Discuss the purpose behind the crime clock and how it works.
- Sketch out some findings based upon the national and Florida crime clocks.
- Criticize the use of the crime clock.
- Show how a crime rate is calculated.
- Compare U.S. and Florida crime rates.
- Offer a criticism of crime rate calculations based upon the appropriate population at risk.
- Speak to the benefits of a crime trend analysis.
- Compare and contrast the trends in national and Florida violent crime rates.
- Conduct a similar trend analysis for property crime rates.
- Probe how the "dark figure of crime" makes official crime reports less dependable.
- Explore how reporting and recording practices affect the production of crime statistics.
- Evaluate the FBI's warning on ranking crime statistics.
- Assess the Florida city rankings of crime.
- Demonstrate how external factors affect city crime rates.
- Specify how tourism can influence crime statistics.

Table 3.1 The Top Ten States with the Highest Serious Violent Crime Rates, 2001–2013

Rank	2001	2002	2003	2004	2005	2006	2007	2008	2009	2010	2011	2012	2013
1	*FL*	SC	SC	SC	SC	SC	SC	SC	NV	NV	TN	TN	AK
2	MD	*FL*	*FL*	*FL*	TN	TN	TN	NV	SC	AK	AK	NV	NM
3	NM	MD	MD	MD	*FL*	NV	NV	TN	TN	DE	SC	AK	NV
4	TN	NM	TN	TN	MD	*FL*	LA	DE	DE	TN	NM	NM	TN
5	SC	TN	NM	NM	NM	LA	*FL*	*FL*	AK	SC	NV	SC	LA
6	LA	LA	DE	LA	DE	AR	DE	LA	LA	NM	DE	DE	SC
7	ID	NV	LA	AR	AR	DE	NM	AK	NM	LA	LA	LA	DE
8	IL	IL	NV	NV	NV	MD	AL	NE	*FL*	MD	*FL*	*FL*	*FL*
9	CA	DE	AR	DE	LA	NM	MD	MD	MD	*FL*	MD	MD	*FL*
10	DE	CA	CA	CA	MI	MI	MI	OK	AR	AK	AR	OK	AR

Source: Compiled by author from annual FBI reports.

Introduction

Crime is a significant problem in Florida. As a matter of fact, Florida is one of the more violent states in the country. As Table 3.1 shows, the Florida violent crime rate typically lands the Sunshine State in the top five of the most violent states. In 2001, Florida had the dubious honor of leading the nation in serious violent crime statistics (murder, forcible rape, robbery, and aggravated assault). Florida slipped slightly in 2002 when South Carolina nudged out our state and overtook the number one spot. However, Florida has managed to land in the top-five bracket of states with the highest violent crime rate for eight of the past 13 years.

Florida has not been a slouch when the focus turns to property crime (burglary, larceny, and motor vehicle theft). At the turn of the millennium, Florida's serious property crime

Table 3.2 The Top Ten States with the Highest Serious Property Crime Rates, 2001–2013

Rank	2001	2002	2003	2004	2005	2006	2007	2008	2009	2010	2011	2012	2013
1	AZ	AZ	AZ	AZ	WA	AZ	AZ	AZ	TX	SC	SC	SC	WV
2	HI	HI	HI	WA	AZ	WA	SC	SC	*FL*	TX	AR	AR	NM
3	WA	WA	OR	HI	HI	SC	HI	*FL*	LA	WA	KA	WA	SC
4	*FL*	*FL*	WA	OR	OR	HI	TX	AL	AK	TN	GA	NM	AR
5	OR	TX	TX	SC	SC	TN	*FL*	NC	AL	LA	AL	LA	LA
6	LA	OR	SC	TX	TX	NC	TN	TN	TN	GA	TN	AZ	AZ
7	TX	SC	*FL*	LA	TN	NV	NC	GA	NM	AK	WA	AL	AK
8	NM	LA	TN	TN	NV	TX	LA	TX	NC	*FL*	AZ	GA	GA
9	NC	NM	LA	GA	GA	LA	WA	NM	WA	AZ	NM	OK	OK
10	TN	TN	OK	OK	NM	*FL*	AL	AK	GA	AL	NC	TN	TX

Source: Compiled by author from annual FBI reports.

rate was so pronounced that it secured a ranking as the fourth highest property crime-prone state. Florida did fall out of the top ten ranking during the middle of the decade, but then quickly resumed a relentless ascent back into the top cluster of crime-infested states. By 2010, Florida had regained its reputation as one of the top states in property crime, only to fall out of the top tier in 2011.

These numbers point to the need to study the Florida criminal justice system in greater depth. But before we embark on that journey, let us take a closer look at some other aspects of Florida crime statistics. By the time we finish this chapter, you should have a greater appreciation for the magnitude of the crime problem Floridians face.

The Florida *Uniform Crime Reports* Program

The Florida Legislature has tasked the Florida Department of Law Enforcement (FDLE) with the mammoth job of collecting and organizing crime data throughout the entire state. The need for centralized administrative oversight becomes evident when one takes into account the number of law enforcement agencies that operate in the state, the populations these agencies cover, and the geographical areas they encompass. The objectives of the Florida *Uniform Crime Reports* (UCR) Program are to:

- Gather summary crime data from all law enforcement agencies in the state;
- Maintain a statewide database regarding crime;
- Publish reports analyzing these data; and
- Collect other supplemental crime-related materials (FDLE, 2011, p. 4).

FDLE provides contributing agencies with instructions, definitions, forms, training, and periodic updates in order to ensure uniformity and completeness. Most agencies assign at least one clerk in the records section to serve as the agency liaison. This person reviews every single offense report submitted by agency members and classifies each event and its characteristics according to UCR standards. Sometimes, these standards differ from the specifications contained in *Florida Statutes*. For example, the Florida sexual battery law recognizes that both males and females can be victims of this offense. However, up until 2013 the UCR program restricted forcible rape incidents to certain types of intrusions and to just female victims. Starting with the 2013 UCR, the federal program expanded its collection to distinguish *legacy rape* (the older common law standard) from the newer rape categorization. This distinction is only one example of the classifications to which UCR clerks must be sensitive. The UCR definitions for some selected Part I violent offenses appear in Figure 3.1 and Figure 3.2 contains UCR descriptions for some selected Part I property offenses.

Agencies usually compile their UCR records on a monthly basis. After checking the information contained in these records, agencies then forward the reports to FDLE on a semi-annual basis. FDLE personnel scour the data for any irregularities, contact originating agencies and make any corrections that might be necessary, assemble the reports into statewide data files, analyze the information, and produce a variety of reports for local, state, and federal officials. As you can see, FDLE is the state hub for assembling Florida crime statistics.

Figure 3.1 FBI Definitions for Serious Violent Offenses

Murder and Nonnegligent Manslaughter

The willful (nonnegligent) killing of one human being by another. The UCR Program does not include the following situations in this offense classification: deaths caused by negligence, suicide, or accident; justifiable homicides [the killing of a felon by a peace officer in the line of duty or the killing of a felon, during the commission of a felony, by a private citizen]; and attempts to murder or assaults to murder, which are classified as aggravated assaults.

Forcible Rape (Legacy Definition)

The carnal knowledge of a female forcibly and against her will. Attempts or assaults to commit rape by force or threat of force are also included; however, statutory rape (without force) and other sex offenses are excluded.

Forcible Rape (Revised Definition)

Penetration, no matter how slight, of the vagina or anus with any body part or object, or oral penetration by a sex organ of another person, without the consent of the victim.

Robbery

The taking or attempting to take anything of value from the care, custody, or control of a person or persons by force or threat of force or violence and/or by putting the victim in fear.

Aggravated Assault

An unlawful attack by one person upon another for the purpose of inflicting severe or aggravated bodily injury. The UCR Program further specifies that this type of assault is usually accompanied by the use of a weapon or by other means likely to produce death or great bodily harm. Attempted aggravated assault that involves the display of, or threat to use, a gun, knife, or other weapon is included in this crime category because serious personal injury would likely result if the assault were completed.

Source: Federal Bureau of Investigation (2014). *Crime in the United States, 2013.* Washington, DC: U.S. Department of Justice. Retrieved on December 12, 2014 from http://www.fbi.gov/about-us/cjis/ucr/crime-in-the-u.s/2013/crime-in-the-u.s.-2013/cius-home.

A Word of Caution

The UCR program relies upon a classification strategy known as hierarchical reporting. *Hierarchical reporting* means that when one or more offenses occur during the course of a criminal event, the entire episode is classified according to the most serious crime (FDLE, 2013, pp. 8–10). Suppose that a robber enters a bank, presents a demand note to the teller, and points a gun at the employee. After taking the cash, the robber walks towards the exit, where a security person confronts the robber. The robber shoots and kills the security officer. The robber flees on foot, discovers an unattended car with keys left in the ignition, and uses the vehicle to flee the area. Although a number of crimes have taken place during this entire episode (bank robbery, aggravated assault for pointing a firearm at the teller, murder for killing the security person, and motor vehicle theft for stealing the get-away car), the only crime that would appear in the UCR tabulations is a murder. As you can see, the hierarchical reporting rule, while convenient for tallying purposes, can produce an undercount of how much crime actually takes place.

Figure 3.2 FBI Definitions for Serious Property Offenses

Burglary

The unlawful entry of a structure to commit a felony or theft. To classify an offense as a burglary, the use of force to gain entry need not have occurred. The UCR Program has three subclassifications for burglary: forcible entry, unlawful entry where no force is used, and attempted forcible entry.

Larceny-Theft

The unlawful taking, carrying, leading, or riding away of property from the possession or constructive possession of another. Examples are thefts of bicycles, motor vehicle parts and accessories, shoplifting, pocket-picking, or the stealing of any property or article that is not taken by force and violence or by fraud. Attempted larcenies are included. Embezzlement, confidence games, forgery, check fraud, etc., are excluded.

Motor Vehicle Theft

The theft or attempted theft of a motor vehicle. In the UCR Program, a motor vehicle is a self-propelled vehicle that runs on land surfaces and not on rails. Examples of motor vehicles include sport utility vehicles, automobiles, trucks, buses, motorcycles, motor scooters, all-terrain vehicles, and snowmobiles. Motor vehicle theft does not include farm equipment, bulldozers, airplanes, construction equipment, or water craft such as motorboats, sailboats, houseboats, or jet skis.

Source: Federal Bureau of Investigation (2014b). *Crime in the United States, 2013.* Washington, DC: U.S. Department of Justice. Retrieved on December 12, 2014 from http://www.fbi.gov/about-us/cjis/ucr/crime-in-the-u.s/2013/crime-in-the-u.s.-2013/cius-home.

The Crime Clock

One handy way to visualize how much crime takes place is to look at the annual crime clock devised by the FBI. The *crime clock* takes the number of crimes known to the police and calculates how often these offenses occur every twenty-four hours. Figure 3.3 portrays the crime clock for both the United States and the state of Florida.

Figure 3.3 reveals that a murder takes place every 37 minutes in the United States. A rape occurs every 7 minutes, while there is a robbery every 2 minutes and an aggravated assault materializes every 44 seconds. Property crimes are much more frequent. A burglary occurs every 16 seconds, a larceny-theft happens every 5 seconds, and a motor vehicle is stolen every 45 seconds of the day.

When one looks at how much crime takes place in Florida, the numbers are more reassuring. For example, a homicide surfaces every 9 hours in the Sunshine State compared to the national norm of every 37 minutes. A quick look at the other Part I offenses gives the impression that Floridians are much safer and crime-free than people who live in the rest of the country.

The astute reader would notice that arson, which historically was one of the four FBI's property index offenses, is not included in our treatment of Part I offenses. Most local police departments are ill-equipped to handle arson investigations. Instead, they rely upon nearby fire department investigators or representatives from the state fire marshal's office for expertise. While some arson investigators might be cross-trained and have arrest authority, fire departments are not participating agencies in the UCR Program. Instead, they contribute reports to the National Fire Incident Reporting System (NFIRS) sponsored

Figure 3.3 Crime Clock Comparing the United States and Florida, 2013

The
Crime Clock

	In the U.S.	In Florida
A **Murder** occurs every:	37 minutes	9 hours
A **Forcible Rape** occurs every:	7 minutes	78 minutes
A **Robbery** occurs every:	2 minutes	22 minutes
An **Aggravated Assault** occurs every:	44 seconds	9 minutes
A **Burglary** occurs every:	16 seconds	3 minutes
A **Larceny-Theft** occurs every:	5 seconds	1 minute
A **Motor Vehicle Theft** occurs every:	45 seconds	15 minutes

Source: Federal Bureau of Investigation (2014a). *Crime in the United States, 2013.* Washington, DC: U.S. Department of Justice. Retrieved December 12, 2014 from http://www.fbi.gov/about-us/cjis/ucr/crime-in-the-u.s/2013/crime-in-the-u.s.-2013/offenses-known-to-law-enforcement/crime-clock; Florida Department of Law Enforcement (2014). *Crime Clock 2013 Annual.* Tallahassee, FL: Florida Statistical Analysis Center. Retrieved October 4, 2014 from http://www.fdle.state.fl.us/Content/getdoc/4e1f64ee-b81f-4064-a46a-ea557c52cc5b/CRIME-CLOCK-2013.aspx.

by the U.S. Fire Administration. Further information about NFIRS is available at http://www.usfa.fema.gov/about/ for readers looking for more details.

While the crime clock is a convenient device, it has its own shortcomings. For one thing, FDLE and the FBI warn that crimes do not take place on such a regular basis. There are daily fluctuations and seasonal shifts, among other things. As we shall see in the next section, there is another way to standardize the crime picture a little more accurately.

The Crime Rate

One thing that the crime clock overlooks is the number of people in an area. The volume of crime might be a function of how many people reside in a location. One mech-

Table 3.3 Serious Crime Rates for the United States and Florida, 2013

Offense	United States Number of Offenses	United States Rate per 100,000	Florida Number of Offenses	Florida Rate per 100,000
Violent Crime				
Murder	14,196	4.5	972	5.0
Forcible Rape	79,770	34.4	6,760	34.6
Robbery	345,031	109.1	23,200	118.7
Aggravated Assault	724,149	229.1	61,054	312.3
Property Crime				
Burglary	1,928,464	610.0	138,916	710.5
Larceny-Theft	6,004,453	1,899.4	433,344	2,216.3
Motor Vehicle Theft	699,594	221.3	34,912	178.6
Total Violent	1,163,146	367.9	89,948	460.0
Total Property	8,632,512	2,730.7	607,172	3,105.3

Source: Federal Bureau of Investigation (2014). *Crime in the United States, 2013.* Washington, DC: U.S. Department of Justice. Retrieved on December 12, 2014 from http://www.fbi.gov/about-us/cjis/ucr/crime-in-the-u.s/2013/crime-in-the-u.s.-2013/tables/4tabledatadecoverviewpdf/table_4_crime_in_the_united_states_by_region_geographic_division_and_state_2012-2013.xls.

anism that criminal justice researchers use to sidestep this difficulty is to construct crime rates. A *crime rate* takes the number of offenses that have occurred, divides it by the number of residents, and multiplies that outcome by a constant, usually 100,000 people. That way, one can begin to conduct a better comparison across cities, counties, and other geographical divisions of varying sizes.

Table 3.3 displays the number of various offenses and the corresponding offense rates for both the United States and Florida. The 2013 population count for the entire nation was 316,128,839 persons; Florida's population registered 19,552,860 persons in 2013. The national murder rate was 4.5 (14,196 divided by 316,128,839 multiplied by 100,000), while Florida had a 5.0 murder rate (972 divided by 19,552,860 multiplied by 100,000). The other offense rates were calculated in a similar manner.

There are two interesting observations in the table. First, all the Florida violent crime rates exceed the national norms. Second, all the state's property crime rates also surpass the national averages. The conclusion generated from the crime clock comparisons is similar to what we saw in Table 3.1 and Table 3.2 a moment ago. Floridians do not live in a safer environment in comparison to other Americans.

Another Word of Caution

The way crime rates are constructed causes them not to be entirely accurate. As mentioned in the last section, the denominator reflects the number of residents in a particular location. If crime rates were completely accurate, then the base would represent the actual *population at risk*, the vulnerable units, in the calculations. For example, look at motor vehicle theft. That crime rate equals the number of stolen vehicles divided by the number of people living in an area. But, not everybody owns a motor vehicle. A more accurate representation would be the number of vehicles stolen divided by the number of registered vehicles in that area. When viewed in this context, some crime rates are calculated in a convenient, rather than completely accurate, manner.

Crime Trends

One shortcoming associated with viewing crime data from a single point in time is that they provide a static snapshot. Many people are concerned with the question of whether crime is rising or is on the decline. Such a question requires a *trend analysis*, a comparison of crime over time.

Figure 3.4 displays violent crime rates for both the United States and Florida from 1990 through 2013. A glance at the murder chart reveals that Florida tracks the national trend very closely. However, beginning in 2006, the Florida murder rate climbs above the national average. When attention turns to the other violent offenses, the Florida rates are higher than the national rates. In the early 1990s, the Florida rape rate surpassed the remainder of the country by a wide margin. That gap began closing somewhat after the turn of the century. Today, the Sunshine State forcible rape rate tracks the national norm. The Florida robbery and aggravated assault rates evidence a similar pattern. Whether these converging lines are the product of a concerted effort by the members of the criminal justice system will be discussed later.

The property crime rates, contained in Figure 3.5, paint a similar picture. During the 1990s, Florida had a much higher-than-average burglary, larceny-theft, and motor vehicle theft rates. However, as time goes by, the Florida property crime rates have started to resemble the national figures. Whether these patterns reflect policy enactments is an interesting question.

A Further Word of Caution

While the details derived from the UCR Program are informative, one must recognize that these crime statistics are somewhat incomplete and inaccurate. One troublesome aspect associated with official crime statistics is that they are based solely on "crimes known to the police." Another allied concern focuses on police recording practices.

Not all crimes come to the attention of the authorities. The true amount of crime consists of offenses that the police know about and offenses that the police do not know about. Incidents that the police are not aware of are called the *dark figure of crime*. As the dark figure of crime grows larger, official crime reports become less accurate and less dependable.

Estimates based upon the National Crime Victimization Survey (NCVS) provide some insights about *reporting practices* and the magnitude of the non-reporting problem. The NCVS, which does have its own quirks, advises that less than half of all violent victimization episodes and slightly more than one-third of all property crimes are reported to the police (Truman & Langton, 2011, p. 6). While reporting rates vary by type of crime, incident characteristics, and participant traits (Baumer & Lauritsen, 2010), victims express a variety of reasons for not making a disclosure. They may have told somebody other than the police about the event, considered it to be a private matter, thwarted the offender,

Figure 3.4 United States (Broken Line) and Florida (Solid Line) Serious Violent Crime Rates 1990–2013

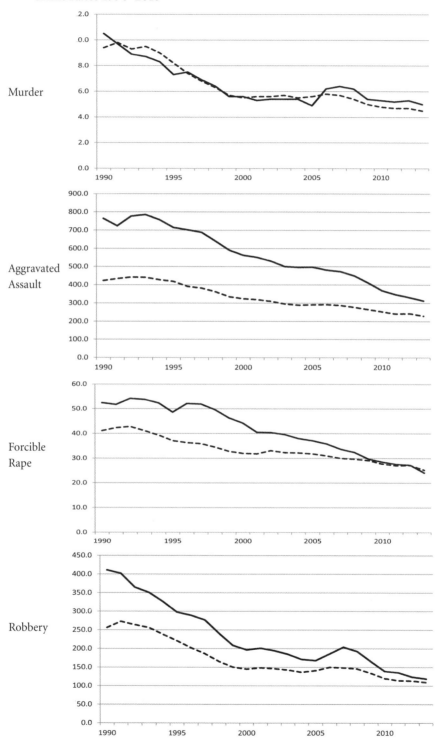

Source: Compiled by author from annual FBI UCR.

Figure 3.5 United States (Broken Line) and Florida (Solid Line) Serious Property Crime Rates, 1990–2013

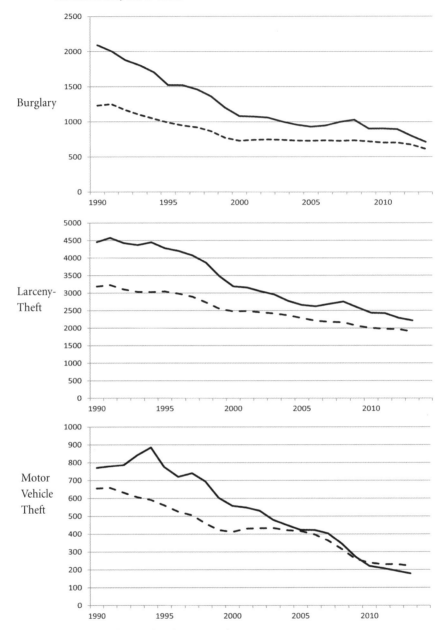

Source: Compiled by author from annual FBI UCR.

feared revenge from the suspect, or did not want to get involved with the police (Rand & Robinson, 2011, Table 102). Unfortunately, while the effects of the dark figure of crime are bothersome, it is not possible at this time to determine its exact impact upon official Florida crime statistics because victimization surveys are conducted at the national, not state, level.

The second intrusion on official crime statistics are *police recording practices*. Just because an incident comes to the attention of the police does not mean that the responding officer is obligated to generate a police report. A variety of legal and extralegal considerations may influence the officer's decision to write or not write a report (Boivin & Cordeau, 2011). Legal variables could encompass such things as whether a transgression has occurred, agency policy, offense seriousness, state law, sufficient probable cause, criminal history, and the like. Extralegal variables might include suspect demeanor, victim demeanor, whether a complainant is present, race, gender, social class and so forth. In any event, Figure 3.6 maps out this process. That sketch shows the many junctures and exit points involved in crime reporting and recording.

Back in the mid-1990s, the editors at *The Wall Street Journal* made a rather startling discovery. The Tallahassee crime rate was considerably higher than the New York City crime rate. The FBI UCR figures pegged the 1993 Tallahassee serious crime rate at 147 per 1,000 residents, compared with 82 for the Big Apple. In other words, despite the perception that New York City was not a safe haven, the crime rate in Tallahassee was 80% higher. Tallahassee residents were twice as likely to experience a burglary, had twice

Figure 3.6 How Reporting and Recording Practices Influence the Production of Official Crime Statistics

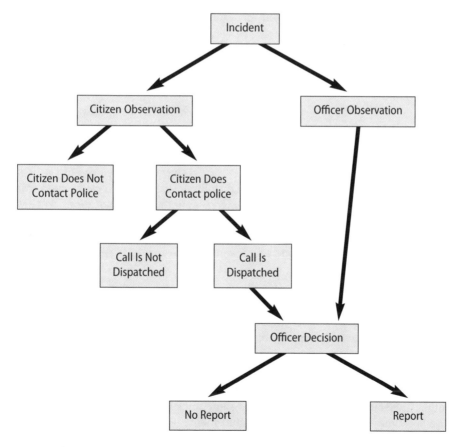

Source: Author.

the chances of having something stolen, were three times more at risk for forcible rape, and 60% more likely to become assault victims (Bennett, 1995). Intrigued by this oddity, newspaper reporters descended upon the Florida capitol to investigate further.

What the reporters found was interesting. While the New York Police Department was in the habit of not writing reports for minor offenses and discouraging citizen reporting, officers at the Tallahassee Police Department documented even the minutest crimes. Coupled with these intensive recording habits, the presence of three public colleges in Tallahassee (Florida State University, Florida A&M University, and Tallahassee Community College) translates into a sizeable youthful population who are not preoccupied with taking crime prevention measures. Thus, while the numbers painted one picture, the atmosphere was a lot more tolerant.

Crime in Florida Cities

Table 3.4 displays 2013 crime rates for the 20 largest cities in Florida. The total crime rate exhibits considerable variation. For example, Orlando leads the state with an overall serious crime rate of 7,510 per 100,000 persons. Port St. Lucie would appear to be the safest of these urban areas with a total crime rate of 1,646 per 100,000 persons. A closer look at the individual offenses shows some interesting patterns. Miami and Miami Gardens have exorbitant murder rates. Tallahassee, a college town, has a very elevated rape rate compared to other locales. Orlando, St. Petersburg, and Miami have hefty aggravated assault rates, with Gainesville and Tallahassee closely trailing behind. Orlando, Ft. Lauderdale, St. Petersburg, and Miami peak in terms of burglary, larceny, and motor vehicle theft rates.

Even More Words of Caution

Comparisons, just like what we have done thus far, have prompted the FBI to issue the warning that appears in Figure 3.7 and rightfully so. Variations in crime rates from one place to the next might exist because of differences in the various locations. We have already seen how the presence of a youthful population can affect forcible rape, aggravated assault, and burglary rates in college towns (Tallahassee and Gainesville). This recognition is what has prompted criminology and criminal justice researchers to study the correlates of crime.

Another focal concern, particularly for a state like Florida, harks back to our earlier discussion of how researchers calculate crime rates. If you recall, the crime rate is defined as the number of criminal episodes divided by the population, multiplied by a constant. Many urban areas predictably experience a daily influx of commuters who are traveling to their jobs in the mornings and then a decline of people as these workers make their way home at the end of the day. These temporary population swells increase the number of potential targets in an area that official head counts do not capture.

Another huge factor that gets overlooked sometimes is that Florida is a destination state. Being home to beaches, amusement and theme parks, attractions, recreational outlets, banking and financial institutions, businesses, travel, sports arenas, and other venues makes it difficult to create accurate population-at-risk estimates. For instance, tourism figures estimate there were almost 94 million out-of-state and international

Table 3.4 Serious Crime Rates for Florida's 20 Largest Cities, 2013

City	Population	Total	Murder	Forcible Rape	Robbery	Aggravated Assault	Burglary	Larceny	Motor Vehicle Theft
Jacksonville	876,075	4,649	11	56	169	395	849	2,978	191
Miami	419,777	6,164	22	23	528	610	951	3,578	456
Tampa	346,609	3,151	8	23	167	407	563	1,823	160
Orlando	250,415	7,510	7	50	229	639	1,392	4,786	407
St. Petersburg	249,704	6,231	6	62	254	631	1,098	3,730	450
Hialeah	229,766	3,188	6	18	101	213	332	2,211	308
Tallahassee	183,727	5,178	6	87	211	457	1,133	3,045	239
Ft. Lauderdale	170,065	6,530	8	43	412	393	1,561	3,780	333
Port St. Lucie	167,914	1,646	1	13	24	144	430	992	43
Cape Coral	161,069	2,218	2	4	25	91	499	1,507	90
Pembroke Pines	155,565	2,763	7	56	114	498	1,955	132	7
Hollywood	143,935	5,051	11	44	176	270	1,042	3,111	397
Miramar	126,619	2,875	3	29	128	216	845	1,471	183
Gainesville	124,391	4,656	5	50	125	469	597	3,216	196
Coral Springs	122,994	2,278	0	20	80	93	316	1,681	89
Clearwater	109,065	4,524	4	6	162	355	780	3,011	166
Miami Gardens	107,399	5,197	21	14	300	522	1,050	2,844	445
Palm Bay	104,693	2,301	3	20	41	367	494	1,267	110
Pompano Beach	103,189	5,764	7	62	265	460	1,182	3,469	319
West Palm Beach	103,038	5,400	15	28	273	365	994	3,351	375

Source: Compiled from Florida Department of Law Enforcement (2014b). *Crime in Florida, 2013.* Tallahassee, FL: Florida Department of Law Enforcement. Retrieved on December 13, 2014 from http://www.fdle.state.fl.us/Content/getdoc/2c79e16b-8846-4383-be92-c7c16e227813/CoMuOff2013annual.aspx.

visitors, coupled with slightly more than 20 million in-state travelers, during fiscal year 2013–14 (Visit Florida, 2010, p. 25). When we think about crime statistics in this manner, the elevated crime figures that Orlando displays are more understandable. The sheer number of targets and relative lack of guardians create ample opportunities for motivated offenders. When viewed in this context, the heightened figures for aggravated assault, burglary, larceny, and motor vehicle theft displayed in Orlando are more understandable.

Summary

The purpose of this chapter was to familiarize the reader with the crime situation in the state of Florida. A comparative analysis of official crime statistics reveals that crime is a substantial concern within the Sunshine State. Now that we recognize the breadth and depth of this social phenomenon, we are in a much better position to examine how various segments of the criminal justice system are designed to address this concern.

Figure 3.7 The FBI Official Warning about the Pitfalls of Ranking

Each year when *Crime in the United States* is published, many entities—news media, tourism agencies, and other groups with an interest in crime in our nation—use reported figures to compile rankings of cities and counties. These rankings, however, are merely a quick choice made by the data user; they provide no insight into the many variables that mold the crime in a particular town, city, county, state, region, or other jurisdiction. Consequently, these rankings lead to simplistic and/or incomplete analyses that often create misleading perceptions adversely affecting cities and counties, along with their residents.

Historically, the causes and origins of crime have been the subjects of investigation by many disciplines. Rankings ignore the uniqueness of each locale. Some factors that are known to affect the volume and type of crime occurring from place to place are:

- Population density and degree of urbanization.
- Variations in composition of the population, particularly youth concentration.
- Stability of the population with respect to residents' mobility, commuting patterns, and transient factors.
- Economic conditions, including median income, poverty level, and job availability.
- Modes of transportation and highway systems.
- Cultural factors and educational, recreational, and religious characteristics.
- Family conditions with respect to divorce and family cohesiveness.
- Climate.
- Effective strength of law enforcement agencies.
- Administrative and investigative emphases on law enforcement.
- Policies of other components of the criminal justice system (i.e., prosecutorial, judicial, correctional, and probational).
- Citizens' attitudes toward crime.
- Crime reporting practices of the citizenry.

Source: Federal Bureau of Investigation (2013). *Crime in the United States, 2012.* Retrieved on December 13, 2014 from http://www.fbi.gov/about-us/cjis/ucr/crime-in-the-u.s/2012/crime-in-the-u.s.-2012/resource-pages/caution-against-ranking/cautionagainstranking.

Key Terms

aggravated assault
burglary
crime clock
crime trend
dark figure of crime
hierarchical reporting
larceny-theft
motor vehicle theft
murder and nonnegligent manslaughter
National Crime Victimization Survey

police recording practices
population at risk
rape
reporting practices
robbery
Uniform Crime Reports

Selected Internet Sites

Federal Bureau of Investigation, Uniform Crime Reports
    http://www.fbi.gov/stats-services/crimestats

Florida Advisory Committee on Arson Prevention
    http://www.facap.org/

Florida Department of Law Enforcement, Uniform Crime Reports
    http://www.fdle.state.fl.us/Content/FSAC/Menu/UCR-Home.aspx

Florida Division of State Fire Marshall
    http://www.myfloridacfo.com/division/sfm/default.htm#.VI8LuHuYF6M

Florida Fire Investigators Association
    http://www.floridaarsonseminar.com/

Florida Statistical Analysis Center
    http://www.fdle.state.fl.us/content/FSAC/FSAC-Home.aspx

Review Questions

1. Where does Florida rank in violent crime compared to other states?

2. Where does Florida rank in property crime compared to other states?

3. What are the four goals of the Florida *Uniform Crime Reports* Program?

4. Which agency is in charge of administering the Florida *Uniform Crime Reports* Program?

5. What are the UCR definitions of murder, forcible rape, robbery, and aggravated assault?

6. What are the UCR definitions of burglary, larceny-theft, and motor vehicle theft?

7. What steps do local law enforcement agencies take when compiling UCR statistics from reports generated by patrol and investigative personnel?

8. What is "hierarchical reporting" and how does it affect crime statistics?

9. Explain what a "crime clock" is.

10. How does Florida's crime clock for violent crimes compare with the national version?

11. How does Florida's crime clock for property crimes compare with the national version?

12. What is a "crime rate" and what is its benefit?

13. Compare and contrast Florida crime rates with national figures.

14. Why is the "population at risk" an important concept?

15. What trends are there in Florida and national violent crime rates?

16. What trends are there in Florida and national property crime rates?

17. What is the "dark figure of crime" and why is it important?

18. Explain the FBI's concerns about crime rankings.

19. How do reporting practices and recording practices affect official crime statistics?

20. What are some reasons why people do not report victimization incidents?

21. What does a comparison of Tallahassee and New York City crime statistics reveal?

22. What insights does one gain when looking at crime rates of Florida cities?

23. How do commuter practices and tourism affect Florida crime figures?

References

Baumer, Eric P. and J. L. Lauritsen (2010). Reporting crime to the police, 1973–2005: A multivariate analysis of long-term trends in the National Crime Survey (NCS) and National Crime Victimization Survey (NCVS). *Criminology, 48*, 131–185.

Bennett, Amanda (1995). Apples & oranges: Is Tallahassee rally as plagued by crime as New York City? — Widely used statistics belie key variations in risks facing cities' residents — Murder vs. stolen mailboxes. *Wall Street Journal*, January 5, A1.

Boivin, Rémi and G. Cordeau (2011). Measuring the impact of police discretion on official crime statistics: A research note. *Police Quarterly, 14*, 186–203.

Federal Bureau of Investigation (2013). *Crime in the United States, 2012.* Retrieved on December 13, 2014 from http://www.fbi.gov/about-us/cjis/ucr/crime-in-the-u.s/2012/crime-in-the-u.s.-2012/resource-pages/caution-against-ranking/cautionagainstranking.

Federal Bureau of Investigation (2014). *Crime in the United States, 2013.* Washington, DC: U.S. Department of Justice. Retrieved on December 12, 2014 from http://www.fbi.gov/about-us/cjis/ucr/crime-in-the-u.s/2013/crime-in-the-u.s.-2013/cius-home.

Florida Department of Law Enforcement (2013). *Uniform Crime Reports Guide Manual.* Tallahassee, FL: Florida Department of Law Enforcement. Retrieved on December 13, 2014 from http://www.fdle.state.fl.us/Content/getdoc/7fad02e4-96bd-46d9-82fc-4a5c46f0be22/datahistory_ucrmanual-1-.aspx.

Florida Department of Law Enforcement (2014a). *Crime Clock 2013 Annual.* Tallahassee, FL: Florida Statistical Analysis Center. Retrieved October 4, 2014 from http://www.fdle.state.fl.us/Content/getdoc/4e1f64ee-b81f-4064-a46a-ea557c52cc5b/CRIME-CLOCK-2013.aspx.

Florida Department of Law Enforcement (2014b). *Crime in Florida, 2013.* Tallahassee, FL: Florida Department of Law Enforcement. Retrieved on December 13, 2014 from http://www.fdle.state.fl.us/Content/getdoc/2c79e16b-8846-4383-be92-c7c16e227813/CoMuOff2013annual.aspx.

Rand, Michael R. and Jayne E. Robinson (2011). *Criminal Victimization in the United States, 2008 Statistical Tables*. Washington, DC: U.S. Department of Justice. Retrieved on December 13, 2014 from http://bjs.ojp.usdoj.gov/content/pub/pdf/cvus0805.pdf.

Truman, Jennifer L. and Lynn Langton (2014). *Criminal Victimization, 2013*. Washington, DC: Bureau of Justice Statistics. Retrieved on December 13, 2014 from http://www.bjs.gov/content/pub/pdf/cv13.pdf.

Visit Florida (2010). *2013–14 Annual Report*. Tallahassee: Florida Tourism Industry Marketing Corporation. Retrieved on December 14, 2014 from http://www.visit florida.org/media/7939/yearinreview2014.pdf.

CHAPTER 4

FLORIDA CRIMINAL LAW

Learning Objectives

After reading this chapter, you should be able to:

- Explain what a homicide is.
- Separate a lawful from an unlawful homicide.
- Give an example of a justifiable homicide.
- Know what the castle doctrine means.
- Talk about what an excusable homicide is.
- Relay what a first-degree murder is.
- Discuss manslaughter.
- Explore vehicular/vessel homicide.
- Provide details about assisting self-murder.
- Appreciate the charge of killing of an unborn child by injury to mother.
- Acknowledge the ramifications of an unnecessary killing to prevent an unlawful act.
- Distinguish an assault from a battery.
- Differentiate a simple from an aggravated assault.
- Separate a simple from an aggravated battery.
- Know the difference between a misdemeanor and a felony.
- Appreciate the importance of a mandatory sentencing law.
- Show how sexual battery is broader than rape.
- Determine what a robbery is.
- Understand the distinction between an armed and a strong-armed robbery.
- Become familiar with the phrases "robbery by sudden snatching," "carjacking," and "home-invasion robbery."
- Understand the provisions of the offense larceny-theft.
- Explain the difference between a misdemeanor and a felony larceny-theft.
- Demonstrate how some statutes provide extra protection for elderly victims.
- Outline what a burglary is.

Introduction

Crime is a significant problem in Florida. As we saw in the Chapter 2, the Sunshine State is one of the most violent places in the entire country. However, we had to make allowances several times for different definitions. More specifically, we now know that police departments have to reclassify some of their incident reports because Florida law and the *Uniform Crime Reports* use different definitions.

We are going to visit a handful of Florida laws to see how certain offenses are defined. In keeping with Chapter 2, we will confine our explanations of violent crimes to homicide, simple assault, simple battery, aggravated assault, aggravated battery, sexual battery, and robbery. When it comes to property crimes, we will explore larceny-theft and burglary. While there are many other offenses on the books, these selections will mirror the information we developed in Chapter 2 about how much crime there is in Florida.

Homicide

Florida, like many other states, categorizes homicides as being either lawful or unlawful (*Florida Statutes 2014*, §782). A *homicide* refers to the killing of one human being by another. A convenient way to characterize these deaths is to realize that "all murders are homicides, but not all homicides are murders" (Edelfonso & Coffey, 1981, p. 61).

Suppose that Edgar enjoys growing roses in his garden. Edgar's neighbor, Sam, has a dog that has developed a habit of relieving himself on Edgar's rose bushes. The inevitable result from this unwanted spraying is that Edgar's prized roses die within a very short time of each exposure. Edgar has brought this undesirable situation to Sam's attention on several occasions. However, these attempts have failed to curb the dog's behavior and Edgar's roses keep wilting and dying. One evening, Edgar sees the mutt in the middle of the flower bed. In exasperation, Edgar grabs his handgun, approaches the animal, and mortally wounds the dog. Has a homicide taken place?

The answer is a resounding negative. The dog is an animal, not a person. Suppose, though, that upon hearing the gun blast, Sam runs out in the front yard and sees the motionless body of his pooch lying on the ground in a pool of blood. Sam yells some very unflattering phrases at Edgar. Edgar, who is incensed by all these events, points the gun at Sam and discharges the weapon. Sam falls to the ground and succumbs to his wounds. A homicide has definitely taken place here.

Let us alter the circumstances slightly. Edgar sees the errant critter in the rose bed and tries to shoo the animal away. Instead, the dog turns in Edgar's direction and issues a menacing growl. Edgar is scared by the dog's reaction and starts to run away from the area. However, the dog gives chase, knocks Edgar to the ground, and attacks him. The ensuing bites are so severe that Edgar is rendered unconscious and bleeds to death. Has a homicide taken place? The answer here is no because the dog is not a human being.

Take this same scenario and change it even further. Sam sees Edgar approaching the dog and the owner orders the canine to sic Edgar. The result is that Edgar dies from the dog's attack. Has a homicide taken place? In this instance, the answer would be yes. Sam used the canine as a deadly weapon when he ordered the dog to attack Edgar.

Lawful Homicide

There are two types of *lawful homicides* in Florida. The first is a justifiable homicide and the second is an excusable homicide. Let us look at each in greater detail.

A *justifiable homicide* occurs when a person kills another party in self-defense (*Florida Statutes 2014*, §782.02). Imagine that several police officers respond to a bank robbery-in-progress. As the bandit exits the building, he notices some of the police officers. The robber opens fire upon the officers and the officers return the volley. The rounds strike the robber and he falls to the ground dead. A justifiable homicide has taken place in this instance.

The *castle doctrine* becomes applicable in situations where a resident resorts to deadly force against an intruder in his or her home. Generally speaking, the average person has a duty to retreat when he or she finds himself/herself in a violent confrontation (*Florida Statutes 2014*, §776). However, under the castle doctrine, one does not have an obligation to retreat against an intruder who is trying to or has gained entry into one's residence (Jansen & Nugent-Borakove, 2007). The victim, in this instance, is entitled to use defensive force. Figure 4.1 displays portions of the standard instructions that judges read to a jury before the jurors retire to deliberate.

An *excusable homicide* is when an accidental death takes place despite reasonable measures of caution being in place. Suppose that construction workers are laying bricks on the front facade of a building. The company has posted signs that advise passersby of the construction and tell pedestrians to detour to the opposite side of the street. Malcolm notices the advisory warnings, but nonetheless continues to walk on the sidewalk underneath the scaffolding. At about this time, a bricklayer on the fifth floor stumbles over a brick and sends it on a descent. The flying object strikes Malcolm in the head and he dies instantly. Has a homicide taken place?

Yes, a homicide has occurred. One human being is dead because of another human being's actions. However, the situation is not a criminal homicide. The bricklayer had no intention of harming Malcolm. Furthermore, the company had posted sufficient warning signs that Malcolm chose to disregard as his own peril. Whether any civil liability is involved here is an entirely different matter.

Unlawful Homicide

Florida includes a number of categories under the rubric of "unlawful homicide." These types include (1) murder, (2) felony-murder, (3) manslaughter, (4) vehicular/vessel homicide, (5) assisting self-murder, (6) killing of an unborn child by injury to the mother, and (7) an unnecessary killing to prevent an unlawful act. Let us begin by looking at the first category.

First-degree murder is the appropriate charge in Florida whenever somebody plans to kill the victim or if somebody dies during the course of any one of a number of felonies. Suppose that Margaret's employer has fired her from her job. Margaret is incensed and decides to confront her former boss and get her old position back. Margaret places a handgun in her purse and drives to the business site. Once there, she engages in a heated argument with her former supervisor. Finally, Margaret takes the gun out and, in desperation, points it at her old employer in the hope of getting her job back. When the former boss refuses to reinstate her, Margaret fires the weapon and the bullet kills the ex-employer. Obviously, a homicide has taken place. The event is characterized as first-

Figure 4.1 Excerpts from Standard Jury Instructions in Castle Doctrine Cases

In deciding whether defendant was justified in the use of deadly force, you must judge [him/her] by the circumstances by which [he/she] was surrounded at the time the force was used. The danger facing the defendant need not have been actual; however, to justify the use of deadly force, the appearance of danger must have been so real that a reasonably cautious and prudent person under the same circumstances would have believed that the danger could be avoided only through the use of that force. Based upon appearances, the defendant must have actually believed that the danger was real.

If the defendant [was not engaged in an unlawful activity and] was attacked in any place where [he/she] had a right to be, [he/she] had no duty to retreat and had the right to stand [his/her] ground and meet force with force, including deadly force, if [he/she] reasonably believed that it was necessary to do so to prevent death or great bodily harm to [himself/herself/another] or to prevent the commission of a forcible felony.

If the defendant [was not engaged in an unlawful activity and] was attacked in any place where [he/she] had a right to be, [he/she] had no duty to retreat and had the right to stand [his/her] ground and meet force with force, including deadly force, if [he/she] reasonably believed that it was necessary to do so to prevent death or great bodily harm to [himself/herself/another] or to prevent the commission of a forcible felony.

If the defendant was in a(n) [dwelling/residence/occupied vehicle] where [he/she] had a right to be, [he/she] is presumed to have had a reasonable fear of imminent death or great bodily harm to [himself/herself/another] if (victim) had [unlawfully and forcibly entered/removed or attempted to remove another person against that person's will from] that [dwelling/residence/occupied vehicle] and the defendant had reason to believe that had occurred. The defendant had no duty to retreat under such circumstances.

If in your consideration of the issue of self-defense you have a reasonable doubt on the question of whether the defendant was justified in the use of deadly force, you should find the defendant not guilty.

However, if from the evidence you are convinced that the defendant was not justified in the use of deadly force, you should find [him/her] guilty if all the elements of the charge have been proved.

Source: Florida Supreme Court (2014). *Standard Jury Instructions, Criminal Cases: Section 3.6 Defenses: 3.6(f) Justifiable Use of Deadly Force.* Tallahassee: Florida Supreme Court. Retrieved on October 17, 2014 from http://www.floridasupremecourt.org/jury_instructions/instructions.shtml#.

degree murder because of all the thought and planning that Margaret put into her actions.

Another example of first-degree murder involves a married man whose wife discovers he is having an affair. Sandra comes home early from work one day only to find Mickey, her husband, upstairs in bed with the next-door neighbor. Sandra, in a fit of rage, stomps downstairs, and goes to the gun cabinet. She unlocks the door, takes out a revolver, meticulously loads it with six rounds, closes the cabinet door, locks it, and marches back up to the bedroom. Once there, she orders Mickey to get down on his knees and beg for her forgiveness. Although Mickey does as Sandra commands, she does not feel that Mickey is contrite enough. Sandra fires two rounds into Mickey's chest and he slumps forward on the floor. Then, Sandra straddles his body and fires four more bullets into Mickey who succumbs to his injuries. Given the amount of time that has transpired and the number of separate acts that Sandra has completed, a charge of first-degree murder aptly describes the situation.

Manslaughter involves the death of another person along with culpable negligence or reckless behavior (Goldman, 2012). Consider the following example. Mike and Ike have been picnicking all day long with their friends. Beer has been plentiful and both fellows are inebriated. Ten members of the party create a $100 pool by putting in $10 each. They then bet Mike that he cannot shoot a beer can placed on Ike's head from a distance of 20 feet. Both Mike and Ike are up to the challenge and are looking forward to splitting the pot and earning $50 each. Mike is very confident that he will win this game of skill. He takes out his pistol and aims very carefully at the beer can balanced on Ike's head. As Mike squeezes the trigger, though, Ike lets loose with a huge hiccup and moves. The weapon goes off and the bullet strikes Ike in the middle of his forehead. Ike slumps to the ground and later dies. The irrational behavior that Mike engaged in was negligent. Playing with a loaded weapon while drinking and exposing another person to serious harm are not responsible actions.

Vehicular homicide or *vessel homicide* describes a situation where the driver is operating the car or boat in a reckless manner and that behavior results in the demise of another person. Suppose that Rocket and Zoom-Zoom are bragging about who has the faster automobile. They arrange to race each other in a remote section of town. Halfway thru the contest, Rocket is leading as he rounds a curve in the road. Much to his dismay, there is a young lady pushing a baby stroller directly in front of him. Rocket swerves and narrowly misses the mother and toddler, but Zoom-Zoom is unable to avoid them. He strikes the two pedestrians, killing them both. Zoom-Zoom now faces two charges of vehicular homicide.

Anybody who helps another person commit suicide would be guilty of *assisting self-murder*. This charge is understandable when one considers the number of elderly persons who spend their "Golden Years" in the Sunshine State and all the nursing home facilities in Florida. Even though one might consider such behavior as being compassionate, senior citizens gain some reassurance by having this statute on the books. Of course, the State of Florida has an economic interest in making sure that the elderly have peace of mind.

The *killing of an unborn child by injury to mother* is another special provision in the Florida homicide statute. Suppose that Jenny and George are arguing. They are expecting a child any day now. George, in a fit of rage, throws Jenny down a flight of stairs. Medics arrive and transport Jenny to the hospital. However, the trauma that George inflicted causes Jenny to go into labor and the baby is born dead from those injuries.

The Sunshine State also recognizes an *unnecessary killing to prevent an unlawful act* as a form of homicide. Pops has invested his entire savings into a little store. He hopes that this enterprise will be a source of continuous income for him and his wife in their twilight years. Amy, a teenager, comes into the store and shoplifts a carton of cigarettes. As she starts to leave the store, Pops pulls out a gun that he keeps under the cash register to protect the premises and yells for Amy to stand still. Amy, though, runs out of the store with the purloined merchandise. Pops tries to give chase, but the years have taken a toll and he is unable to keep pace with Amy. In order to keep her from getting away scot-free, Pops fires the gun one time in her direction. That bullet strikes Amy in the back and she dies from that wound. Two considerations would frame the incident. First, the offense described in this scenario amounts to a misdemeanor. Second, the offense is a property, not a violent, type of a crime. Since Amy is not jeopardizing anybody's life, the shooting is not commensurate with the situation.

Simple Assault

A *simple assault* consists of three parts. First, there must be a verbal threat or a physical gesture aimed at harming the victim. Second, the person making the threat must have the ability to carry out that action. Finally, the threat the suspect issues must place the victim in genuine fear for his or her well-being (*Florida Statutes 2014*, § 784.011).

Suppose that Ralph is eating lunch in a restaurant. Max, who is sitting two tables away from Ralph, keeps staring at Ralph. In fact, Ralph cannot help but notice that he is the subject of Max's unwanted and constant gazes. Ralph is starting to feel more and more uncomfortable. He glances back at Max several times and sees that Max is still peering at him. Has an assault taken place? No, a crime has not taken place at this point.

Continuing further, suppose that Ralph gets up from the table and walks over to where Max is sitting. Ralph asks Max to explain why Max is staring at him constantly. Max replies that he was not looking at Ralph. Instead, he was admiring the art work hanging on the wall behind Ralph's chair. Instead of accepting this explanation, Ralph balls up his fist, shakes it in Max's direction, and tells Max to stop looking at him or else Max will have to face the consequences. At this point, Ralph has committed the crime of simple assault.

Let us change some details. Assume that Ralph has been in a car accident and sustained two broken arms. Both arms are immobilized in casts. Ralph threatens Max that when the casts are removed in two months and after he completes three additional months of physical therapy, he is going to return to the restaurant and beat up Max for staring at him. Because Ralph does not possess the apparent ability to hurt Max at the moment, no crime has occurred because a reasonable person would not be placed in fear of imminent harm (Goldman, 2012, p. 35).

Continuing further with the story, Ralph has two broken arms and they are in casts. He is holding a set of car keys in one hand. Ralph advises Max that after he leaves the restaurant, he is going to use the keys to scratch Max's car. Do these actions amount to an assault? No, because the harm that Ralph said he is going to inflict involves property and not physical injury to another person.

Simple Battery

A simple battery is nothing more than a simple assault performed to perfection. A *simple battery* involves three things. First, the suspect must touch or strike the victim. Second, that touching or striking is contrary to what the victim wants. Third, the suspect must intend to hurt the victim (*Florida Statutes 2014*, § 784.03).

Suppose that Juan is standing at a street corner, waiting for the traffic light to change so he can walk across the street. Angelina is standing next to Juan. She is carrying on a conversation with another person. Angelina notices that the pedestrian walk sign has changed. However, because she is in such a deep exchange with her friend, Angelina does not look both ways before starting to cross the street. Juan, though, observes an approaching vehicle and notices that the driver is not slowing down for the red traffic light. Rather than begin crossing the street, Juan watches the operator continue to drive into the intersection, contrary to the traffic signal device. Seeing that Angelina has stepped off

Figure 4.2 Seriousness Levels of Assaults and Batteries in Florida

	Assault	Battery
Simple	Misdemeanor	Misdemeanor
Aggravated	Felony	Felony

Source: Author.

the curb and is about to walk into the direct path of the oncoming vehicle, Juan reaches out, grabs Angelina by the arm, and forcibly yanks her back onto the sidewalk. The errant vehicle continues to pass by, narrowly missing Angelina.

Did a battery take place here? Although Juan touched Angelina on purpose, he had no intention of harming her. Instead, he was looking out for her safety. As a result, no crime has taken place.

Let us alter the circumstances somewhat so that oncoming traffic is not hazardous. As Angelina begins crossing the street, Juan purposively sticks out his foot and trips her. Angelina falls to the pavement and scratches her knee. Obviously, this situation involves a simple battery.

Let us return to the earlier example involving Ralph and Max in the restaurant. Ralph has approached Max's table. Ralph clenches his fist, shakes it in Max's direction, and tells Max to stop looking at him. Max simply laughs at Ralph and calls him an unflattering name. Then, Max slides his chair back, stands up, and pushes Ralph, who stumbles back a step or two. Once again, a simple battery has taken place.

Notice how two things are absent from all these scenarios and that keeps the incidents within the realm of a "simple" offense. The first observation is that none of the participants have a weapon nor are they using any objects as weapons. A second thing to note is that none of the victims sustain very harmful injuries. As we shall see in a moment, once these conditions change, then the situation moves from a "simple" to an "aggravated" offense.

Aggravated Assault

The seriousness of the transgression changes considerably whenever a weapon is involved or when the victim sustains serious physical harm. Under these circumstances, the offenses cease to be "simple" crimes and become "aggravated" crimes. As Figure 4.2 illustrates, a simple assault and a simple battery are misdemeanor offenses. In contrast, aggravated assault and aggravated battery are felonies. Under Florida law, a *misdemeanor* is punishable by a maximum term of one year in the county jail. A *felony* carries a penalty of death or imprisonment in a state penitentiary for more than a year (*Florida Statutes 2014*, §775.08).

Mandatory sentencing laws are another important consideration. As Figure 4.3 explains, Florida imposes additional sentences whenever a firearm is involved. Under the Florida 10-20-Life law, possession of a firearm during the commission of a crime results in a minimum 10-year prison term. Discharging a firearm during the course of a crime increases the penalty to twenty years in prison. If someone is injured or killed by a firearm, the minimum mandatory sentence is 25 years to life imprisonment (*Florida Statutes 2014*, §775.087).

Figure 4.3 The Florida 10-20-Life Law

- Mandates a minimum 10-year prison term for certain felonies or attempted felonies in which the offender possesses a firearm or destructive device.

- Mandates a minimum 20-year prison term when the firearm is discharged.

- Mandates a minimum 25-years-to-life if someone is injured or killed.

- Mandates a minimum 3-year prison term for possession of a firearm by a felon.

- Mandates that the minimum prison term is to be serviced consecutively to any other term of imprisonment imposed.

Source: Florida Department of Corrections (2014). *10-20-Life.* Tallahassee: Florida Department of Corrections. Retrieved on October 18, 2014 from http://www.dc.state.fl.us/secretary/press/1999/1020life.html.

In addition to the three elements that make up a simple assault, it is a fourth criterion that transforms the situation into a felony offense. That is, a deadly weapon was used during the assault (Goldman, 2010, pp. 95–96; *Florida Statutes 2014*, §784.021). For example, suppose that Dudley and Baxter are having an argument during a card game at Dudley's house. Dudley leaves the room. When he returns, Dudley has a gun in his hand. Dudley then announces to Baxter that it is time for Baxter to leave and go home. Baxter wisely takes advantage of the opportunity and walks out of the house. An aggravated assault has taken place here.

The weapon being used does not have to be just a firearm or a knife. Other objects can also suffice. However, non-deadly weapons, such as a Taser or a chemical spray, might not satisfy the definition of a deadly weapon (Adams, 2007, p. 3). Suppose in the last example, Dudley returned with either a tire iron, a hammer, or a baseball bat in his hand. Since these tools can inflict serious bodily harm, that situation would also constitute an aggravated assault.

Aggravated Battery

If you remember our earlier discussion, one way to think about a simple battery is to call it a simple assault done to perfection. Similarly, an aggravated battery is an aggravated assault carried out to its fullest extent. Keeping this idea in mind, there are two key components that determine whether a situation is an aggravated battery. The first is whether the suspect has inflicted serious bodily harm, permanent disability, or permanent disfigurement. The second consideration is whether the suspect used a deadly weapon to carry out the battery (*Florida Statutes 2014*, §784.045). Only one, not both, of these conditions must be met.

Suppose that Mike and David are engaged in a verbal argument. Mike gets very agitated and punches David in the face, breaking David's nose. Since a broken nose constitutes serious bodily harm, the crime here is an aggravated battery even though Mike did not use a weapon.

Let us look at another example. Alice and Juanita are in a restaurant. Their conversation becomes more heated and the argument escalates. Alice picks up a water pitcher and uses it to slug Juanita on the side of the head. The impact causes a deep cut to Juanita's face that will require stitches. Stitches leave a scar after a wound heals. As a result, Alice committed an aggravated battery. Not only did Alice use a weapon (the water pitcher), she also she inflicted a permanent disfigurement upon Juanita (the wound).

Returning to the earlier example, Dudley and Baxter have been feuding. Dudley arms himself with a baseball bat. Dudley swings the bat at Baxter, striking Baxter in the arm. Other than a red mark and some soreness, Baxter has not sustained any other injury. Even though there are no serious injuries, the fact that Dudley used a tool or an implement as a weapon renders this situation an aggravated battery.

There are also some special circumstances of which we need to be aware. Sometimes, statutes are crafted to protect certain interests. In Florida, any battery upon a pregnant woman becomes an aggravated battery. The law does require that the suspect be aware of the pregnancy or should have understood that the victim was pregnant if her physical condition is that obvious (*Florida Statutes 2014*, §784.045, 2(b)).

A simple battery gets elevated to a felony battery in Florida if the victim is a law enforcement officer, a correctional officer, a health services provider, or a sports referee. In addition, there are more severe penalties when the victim is 65 years of age or older. It does not make any difference if the suspect did not know the victim's actual age (*Florida Statutes 2014*, §784.08).

A look at Figure 4.4 helps understand why age is such an important concern. When one compares the age distributions of Florida and the nation, it is apparent that the elderly form a large segment of our state population. Given their economic power, their tendency to go to the polls at election time, and the large bloc the elderly constitute, law makers may wish to court their favor. As a result, extending special protections to senior citizens is one way that legislators can remain sensitive to the needs of their constituents.

Sexual Battery

In days gone by, people commonly referred to any unwanted sexual intercourse as "forcible rape." However, there was a dire need to revamp the outdated rape statutes. Many states, including Florida, did so by constructing sexual battery statutes.

The previous rape provisions were unacceptable for several reasons. First, only males could be perpetrators and only females could be victims. Second, the only transgression was forced sexual intercourse. Other forms of sexual abuse were not included. Third, a wife could not accuse her husband of forcible rape if they were married and resided together. Finally, the best way for a woman to prove that she did not consent to the intrusion was to incur severe injuries as proof of her refusal to be a willing participant.

The current sexual battery statute introduced considerable change (*Florida Statutes 2014*, §794). Today, anybody can be an offender and anybody can be recognized as a victim without regard to gender. In addition, the sexual battery statute governs any unwanted sexual intrusion, not just forced sexual intercourse. The former marital exemption is removed so that the matrimonial bond is not necessarily relevant. Finally, the level of resistance formerly required from a victim has become reduced.

The revised Florida sexual battery contains a number of other reforms. While sexual battery is a felony, the penalties are increased whenever aggravating circumstances are

Figure 4.4 Percent of the Population by Age, United States and Florida, 2009

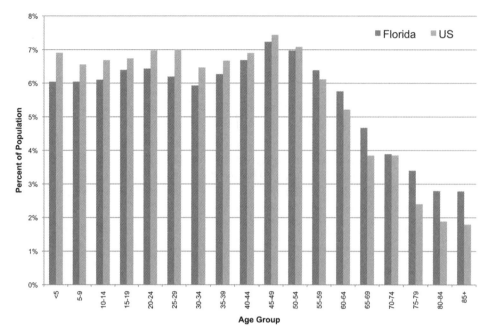

Source: Florida Department of Health (2014). *Florida Population Atlas.* Tallahassee: Division of Public Health Statistics & Performance Management. Retrieved on October 18, 2014 from http://www.florid-acharts.com/Charts/atlas/population/PopAtlas2012/Page_9_Percent_of_Population_by_Age_Group_US_Florida_2009.pdf.

present. The common law belief that young males are incapable of committing a sexual act before they reach a certain age has been rescinded. In addition, sexual battery victims are entitled to a number of protections from public embarrassment.

Robbery

Robbery is a violent offense in Florida. *Robbery* involves taking something, from a person, via the actual use or threat of force to the victim (*Florida Statutes 2014*, § 812.13). Using a weapon during the course of a robbery raises the situation to a more serious level.

Suppose that Steve goes into a bank and walks up to the teller. He points a gun at the teller and tells the bank employee to give him all the money in the till. The teller complies and Steve exits the bank. An *armed robbery* has occurred because (1) Steve took money, (2) from the teller, and (3) displayed a firearm to complete the act.

Let us change the circumstances slightly. Steven enters the bank and hands the teller a hold-up note that instructs the teller to hand over all the money in the drawer. Steve does not have a gun or any other kind of a weapon (there is no knife, no personal defensive spray, nor any other tool or mechanism) with him. Florida would classify this incident as a *strong-armed robbery*. In other words, a robbery took place, but without the use of a weapon.

Florida also recognizes other special kinds of robberies. Imagine that Sandra has been shopping at the mall. At the end of her excursion, Sandra exits the shopping center and walks out into the parking lot to get to her car. Sandra is carrying several packages in her hands and her purse is dangling from her shoulder. Vincent runs up behind Sandra, shoves her to the side, and pulls at her purse. Sandra tries to hang on to her purse, but the strap gives way and breaks. Vincent, who has a strong grip on the purse, feels it release and continues to run away with the purse. A *robbery by sudden snatching* has taken place in this instance. Vincent took the purse from Sandra's embrace and used force to do so (Adams, 2007, p. 11; *Florida Statutes 2014*, §812.131).

Carjacking presents another special set of circumstances. Suppose that Anthony is driving his car. Unfortunately, Anthony has forgotten to lock all the doors on his vehicle. As Anthony is sitting at a red signal light in a bad part of town, Bill walks up to the passenger side and flings open the door. Bill points a gun at Anthony and instructs Anthony to get out of the car. Anthony does so. Bill slides into the driver's seat and then speeds away. This vignette describes a special kind of a robbery known as a *carjacking* (*Florida Statutes 2014*, §812.133).

Another special type of a robbery is a *home-invasion robbery*. Matilda and Johnny are enjoying a quiet evening at home, watching television. There is a knock on the door. Johnny gets up, does not look through the peephole, and answers the door. After Johnny opens the door, two gunmen push Johnny back inside and demand cash. To avoid harm, Matilda runs into the bedroom, retrieves her purse, hands over some cash to the intruders, and the gunmen leave. A robbery, specifically, a home-invasion robbery, has taken place in this instance (*Florida Statutes 2014*, §812.135).

In summary, any time violence or the threat of violence is used to take money or property directly from a person, the crime is considered to be a robbery. As we shall see later, what distinguishes robbery from mere theft is that there is a direct confrontation with the victim. All robberies, no matter how large or little, are felonies under Florida law.

Larceny-Theft

The terms "larceny" and "theft" both refer to the exact same thing. *Larceny-theft* involves two elements. First, there is the taking, depriving, or using of some property. Second, that taking, depriving or using of property is done without the owner's permission, consent, or knowledge (*Florida Statutes 2014*, §812.014).

Imagine that it is summertime and Andy needs to mow his lawn. Andy goes to his garage and pulls out the lawn mower. Unfortunately, the darn thing will not start. Andy knows that all his neighbors have gone to work for the day. So, Andy walks down the street looking for any garage doors that might be open. He comes to Beth's house and notices that although the garage door is open, her car is not there. Andy knocks on the door, but Beth is not home. Andy spots a lawn mower that is not in use. He thinks to himself that if he takes the mower, uses and returns it, Beth will not be aware of the incident. Andy borrows Beth's lawn mower, wheels it over to his house, cuts his grass, and then returns the mower to its original location. Has a crime taken place? Yes. Andy appropriated the mower, albeit temporarily, without the owner's permission.

Suppose that Jessica is shopping and sees a pair of earrings that she likes. However, the jewelry costs more than what she can afford. Jessica looks around and does not see any sales personnel in the area. She takes the earrings, admires the pair for a moment, puts the items in her pocket, and then exits the store without paying for the merchandise. Obviously, a theft has taken place.

Florida uses a dividing line of $300 to distinguish a misdemeanor theft from a felony theft. Suppose the earrings in the last example had a $99.99 sales tag. That taking would be a misdemeanor offense. On the other hand, if the ear rings had sold for $525 a pair, then Jessica would have committed a felony offense.

As we saw earlier, legislators sometimes construct statutes to protect certain interests. Florida is no different when it comes to the larceny-theft statute. As we mentioned earlier, Florida prides itself on being a haven for those persons in their "golden years" and wishes to retain its prominence as a retirement destination. Almost one in every five Sunshine State inhabitants are 65 years of age or older (U.S. Census Bureau, 2014). In an effort to protect this constituency, the Florida Legislature has decreed that anybody who steals a person's last will and testimony or takes $1,000 worth of property from someone who is 65 years of age or older automatically commits a felony offense (*Florida Statutes 2014*, § 812.0145).

Florida also depends quite heavily upon tourism to support its economy. In fact, tourism is the most prominent component of Florida's economy today (Florida TaxWatch, 2014; Visit Florida, 2014). In order to safeguard this vested interest and keep the state's hallowed reputation as a vacation haven safe, stealing a fire extinguisher or using a fire extinguisher improperly is considered a felony offense. A similar protection extends to the theft of large amounts of citrus. Florida produces three-quarters of the nation's orange juice and is the world's second leading producer of the world's grapefruit supply (Florida Department of Citrus, 2014). Florida farmers also team up with California to produce the bulk of the tomato crop in the United States. Hence, legislators have a strong incentive to protect this powerful economic engine.

Florida also hikes the incident from a misdemeanor to a felony, despite the actual value, whenever the theft involves:

- a firearm;
- a motor vehicle;
- any commercial farm animal (horse, cow, or pig);
- an active construction site;
- a stop sign; or
- farm fertilizer.

Burglary

The crime of burglary involves two elements. The first condition is there must be an illegal trespass into a structure, dwelling, or conveyance. The second requirement is that the person who commits the trespass must also intend to commit another offense. That other offense, quite commonly, is a theft of some sorts (*Florida Statutes 2014*, § 810.02),

A very traditional way of viewing this offense is that it involves "breaking and entering." Suppose that Terry is looking for some quick cash. Late one evening, after a store has closed for normal business, she walks behind the building, breaks the window on a door, reaches inside, and opens the door. Terry then goes inside the business, locates the cash register, and takes the contents. Obviously, Terry has committed a burglary.

Burglary may also involve "breaking and exiting." Suppose that Terry is inside the store during normal business hours. An announcement over the intercom advises shoppers that the store is about to close and all customers should complete their purchases and leave the store. Instead of leaving the premises, Terry hides in a bathroom and waits until all the employees have left the store. Terry then goes to the cash register and rifles through the contents, taking all the cash. She then kicks open the door and exits the store. Once again, a burglary has occurred.

Suppose it is a very cold winter night. Gary, a homeless person, is in search of a warm place for the evening. He notices a church window that somebody failed to secure. Gary opens the window, climbs inside, spreads out his blanket on the floor, and goes to sleep. When morning dawns, Gary packs up his gear and exits the church without taking anything. In this instance, the only crime that has taken place is a trespass.

Summary

The purpose of this chapter was to make readers aware of some of the provisions contained in Florida criminal laws. Rather than just repeat the contents of the various Florida laws, examples were provided to help comprehend and appreciate some subtle distinctions. Now that we are more informed about these legal aspects, we will be in a better position to look at the other sectors of the Florida criminal justice system.

Key Terms

aggravated assault
aggravated battery
armed robbery
assisting self-murder
burglary
carjacking
castle doctrine
excusable homicide
felony
first-degree murder
home-invasion robbery
homicide
justifiable homicide
killing of an unborn child by injury to mother
larceny-theft
lawful homicide
mandatory sentencing law
manslaughter
misdemeanor
robbery
robbery by sudden snatching
sexual battery

simple assault
simple battery
strong-armed robbery
unlawful homicide
unnecessary killing to prevent an unlawful act
vehicular homicide
vessel homicide

Selected Internet Sites

Florida Coastal Law Review
    www.fcsl.edu/law-review

Florida Law Review
    http://www.floridalawreview.com

Florida State University Law Review
    http://www.law.fsu.edu/journals/lawreview

Florida Statutes
    http://www.leg.state.fl.us/Statutes/index.cfm?Mode=View%20Statutes&Submenu=
    1&Tab=statutes&CFID=72725658&CFTOKEN=42781737

Nova Law Review
    http://www.nsulaw.nova.edu/students/orgs/lawreview

Stetson Law Review
    http://www.law.stetson.edu/lawreview

University of Florida Journal of Law and Public Policy
    http://www.law.ufl.edu/student-affairs/additional-information/student-organization
    s/jlpp

University of Miami Law Review
    http://lawreview.law.miami.edu

Review Questions

1. What elements make up a homicide?

2. What is a lawful homicide?

3. List two types of lawful homicide.

4. Explain what a justifiable homicide is.

5. What is the "castle doctrine"?

6. What is an "excusable homicide"?

7. What is an "unlawful homicide"?

8. What is first-degree murder?

9. Explain what "manslaughter" is.

10. What do the terms "vehicular homicide" and "vessel homicide" mean?

11. To what does "assisting self-murder" refer?

12. Explain "killing of an unborn child by injury to mother."

13. What does "unnecessary killing to prevent an unlawful act" mean?

14. Distinguish an assault from a battery.

15. Differentiate a simple assault from an aggravated assault.

16. What is the difference between a simple battery and an aggravated battery?

17. What is the difference between a misdemeanor and a felony?

18. What is a mandatory sentencing law?

19. What is the importance of the terms "serious bodily," "permanent disability," and "permanent disfigurement" with respect to the crime of battery?

20. Why are their special provisions for situations involving elderly victims?

21. What is sexual battery and how does it differ from rape?

22. Define robbery.

23. What is the difference between an "armed robbery" and a "strong-armed robbery"?

24. What does the term "robbery by sudden snatching" mean?

25. What is a "carjacking"?

26. What is a "home-invasion robbery"?

27. What does "larceny-theft" mean?

28. What is the general difference between a misdemeanor and a felony theft?

29. Why are there special provisions in the Florida larceny-theft statute for elderly victims?

30. What are some of the special circumstances that make a situation a felony theft no matter what the value of the property?

31. Explain what burglary is.

References

Adams, William E., Jr. (2007). Criminal law: 2004–2007 review of Florida law. *Nova Law Review*, *32* (1), 1–20.

Edelfonso, Edward and Alan R. Coffey (1981). *Criminal Law: History, Philosophy, Enforcement*. New York: Harper and Row.

Florida Department of Citrus (2014). *Citrus Reference Book*. Bartow: Florida Department of Citrus. Retrieved on October 18, 2010 from https://fdocgrower.app.box.com/shared/dt42f2c7kk/1/76187836/19139928195/1.

Florida Department of Corrections (2014). *10-20-Life*. Tallahassee: Florida Department of Corrections. Retrieved on October 18, 2014 from http://www.dc.state.fl.us/secretary/press/1999/1020life.html.

Florida Department of Health (2014). *Florida Population Atlas*. Tallahassee: Division of Public Health Statistics & Performance Management. Retrieved on October 18, 2014

from http://www.floridacharts.com/Charts/atlas/population/PopAtlas2012/Page_9_
Percent_of_Population_by_Age_Group_US_Florida_2009.pdf.

Florida Supreme Court (2014). *Standard Jury Instructions, Criminal Cases: Section 3.6
Defenses: 3.6(f) Justifiable Use of Deadly Force.* Tallahassee: Florida Supreme Court.
Retrieved on October 17, 2014 from http://www.floridasupremecourt.org/jury_inst-
ructions/instructions.shtml#.

Florida Statutes 2014.

Florida TaxWatch (2014). *Unpacking the Benefits of Florida Tourism: Quantifying the Jobs
Created by Increased Florida Tourism.* Tallahassee: Florida Taxwatch. Retrieved on
October 18, 2014 from http://floridataxwatch.org/resources/pdf/UnpackingTourism
FINAL.pdf.

Goldman, Pearl (2010). Criminal law: 2007–2010 survey of Florida law. *Nova Law Review,*
35 (1), 95–136.

Goldman, Pearl (2012). Criminal law: 2010–2012 survey of Florida law. *Nova Law Review,*
37 (1), 1–67

Jansen, Steven and M. Elaine Nugent-Borakove (2007). *Expansions to the Castle Doctrine:
Implications for Policy and Practice.* Alexandria, VA: National District Attorneys Association. Retrieved on October 18, 2014 from http://www.ndaa.org/pdf/Castle
%20Doctrine.pdf.

U.S. Census Bureau (2014). Population 65 years and over in the United States: 2013
American Community Survey 1-year estimates. *American Factfinder.* Washington,
DC: U.S. Department of Commerce. Retrieved on October 18, 2014 from http://
factfinder2.census.gov/faces/tableservices/jsf/pages/productview.xhtml?pid=ACS_13_1YR_
S0103&prodType=table.

Visit Florida (2014). *2013–14 Annual Report.* Tallahassee: Florida Tourism Industry
Marketing Corporation. Retrieved on October 18, 2014 from http://visitflorida.org/
media/7939/yearinreview2014.pdf.

CHAPTER 5

FLORIDA LAW ENFORCEMENT

Learning Objectives

After reading this chapter, you should be able to:

- Explain what the phrase "minimum standards" for law enforcement officers means.
- List six minimum standards that one must satisfy to become a Florida law enforcement officer.
- Convey how minimum standards govern agency hiring practices.
- Understand what "certification" means.
- Compare and contrast the terms "weeding out" and "screening in."
- Outline the typical steps in the law enforcement officer selection process.
- Talk about how and why the police officer selection process resembles a funnel.
- Demonstrate what a *bona fide occupational qualification* (BFOQ) is.
- Explain what is included in the oath of office.
- Tell why jurisdiction is important.
- Pursue the relevancy of the terms "overrepresentation" and "underrepresentation" with respect to the characteristics of law enforcement officers.
- List some of the responsibilities with which FDLE is charged.
- Visit the entrance requirements for an FDLE agent position.
- Elaborate on the tasks that FHP discharges.
- Explore the entrance requirements for becoming a FHP trooper.
- Outline the responsibilities of the county sheriff.
- Develop a statistical portrait of county sheriff offices and city police departments.
- Apply the terms "overrepresentation" and "underrepresentation" to sheriff offices.
- Employ the terms "overrepresentation" and "underrepresentation" to city police departments.
- Explain how agency size affects the demographic composition of agencies.
- Explore the role of unionization with respect to sheriff offices.
- Summarize the Florida salary incentive program.
- Talk about what a special jurisdiction agency is.
- Paint a picture of what the job market looks like.

- Comment on how one might think about accreditation as minimum standards for law enforcement organizations.

- Distinguish national from state accreditation.

- List some benefits that are expected to materialize from accreditation.

- Relay some of the reluctance that has greeted the accreditation effort.

- Summarize the effect that accreditation has had on law enforcement organizations.

Introduction

Crime is a significant problem in Florida. As we saw earlier in Chapter 3, Florida is one of the most violent states in the entire country. That means there is plenty of grist for the Florida criminal justice system to process. More importantly, if law enforcement officers are the gatekeepers to the criminal justice system, then it makes sense to probe who they are, what they are, and how they get there.

This chapter pursues four themes in an effort to become more familiar with the law enforcement community. First, we will look at how people become law enforcement officers in the "Sunshine State." That means we will need to become familiar with the job requirements, as well as pre-service training. The second main feature of this chapter is to provide an overview of the selection process. We will examine the typical steps that agencies use in identifying who gets to wear a uniform. Our third goal is to understand the structure of the Florida law enforcement community. This objective entails looking at state agencies, county sheriff offices, city police departments, and special jurisdiction agencies. Finally, many efforts to upgrade the police have focused on enhancing the quality of law enforcement efforts. We will take a slightly different angle when we focus on the accreditation of law enforcement organizations. Once we have visited these four aspects, we should have gained a number of interesting insights into the Florida law enforcement community.

Becoming a Florida Law Enforcement Officer

The path to becoming a *sworn officer* (arrest power and authorization to carry a firearm) in Florida is pretty straight-forward. Candidates must fulfill a number of job requirements known as "minimum standards." Then, aspiring officers must attend a state-approved police academy and complete "basic recruit training." Once a student graduates from the police academy, then he or she must pass the state certification examination. Perhaps the best way to proceed at this point would be to examine each of these three facets (minimum standards, the academy training, and the certification examination) in greater detail.

Minimum Standards

Florida law requires that candidates for an appointment as a police officer or as a correctional officer must comply with a series of mandatory job requirements. These conditions, overseen by the Criminal Justice Standards and Training Commission (CJSTC), are known as *minimum standards*. In other words, these criteria are the basic expectations that all law enforcement officers must satisfy before CJSTC grants the person certification. *Certification* means that a person is licensed by the State of Florida to serve as a law enforcement officer.

Agencies are strictly forbidden from employing anybody who does not fit all the minimum requirements or who is denied certification. It is worth mentioning that these requirements are the absolute bare-bone job qualifications. Agencies are free to institute more stringent requirements (a college degree, for example) if they so desire. However, an agency cannot install more lenient ones or descend below any of the thresholds.

The Florida minimum standards that one must meet to gain certification as a law enforcement officer include the following:

- Be at least 19 years of age;
- Be a United States citizen;
- Hold a high school diploma or its equivalent;
- Have no felony convictions;
- Have no convictions for perjury or making a false statement;
- Hold an honorable discharge if one has served in the military;
- Submit to a fingerprint check;
- Pass a medical examination;
- Have a good moral character;
- Complete basic recruit training; and
- Pass the officer certification examination (*Florida Statutes 2014*, § 943.13).

Police Academy Training

There are more than three dozen police academies dispersed throughout the state that are recognized by CJSTC. Given this geographical distribution, CJSTC has established a list of qualifications for academy instructors, academy facilities, and the academy curriculum. More specifically, CJSTC has developed a series of modules that instructors must use when training recruits. This standardized curriculum represents a concerted effort to make sure that all Florida law enforcement officers meet certain basic expectations no matter where they are located in the state.

The Bureau of Justice Statistics, housed within the U.S. Department of Justice, recently initiated a periodic census of all 648 law enforcement training academies located throughout the country (Reaves, 2009). Florida requires its trainees to complete at least 770 hours of training compared to an average of 467 hours throughout the nation. Florida law enforcement academies spend much more time emphasizing report writing, patrol, investigations, and first aid. Table 5.1 displays the topics and instructional hours that take place at Florida law enforcement pre-service training academies. Recruits spend approximately one-third of their time at the academy acquiring weapons proficiency, learning defensive tactics, practicing first aid procedures, and participating in physical fitness training. In addition to classroom lessons, there are opportunities for role-playing exercises and scenario-based training modules.

Table 5.1 Instructional Hours Devoted to Topics during Police Academy Training

Training Topic	Hours of Training	
	n	%
Introduction to Law Enforcement	10	1
Training Program Overview		
Values and Ethics		
Sexual Harassment		
Structure of the Criminal Justice System		
Legal	62	8
Introduction to Law		
Legal Concepts		
Substantive Criminal Law		
Civil and Criminal Liability		
Civil Issues		
Juvenile Law		
Interactions in a Diverse Community	40	5
Communicating in Law Enforcement		
Communicating in a Diverse Society		
Communicating in a Crisis Situation		
Identifying High-Risk Groups		
Interviewing and Report Writing	56	7
Interviewing a Person		
Writing a Report		
Fundamentals of Patrol	35	5
Electronic Communications		
Crime Reduction and Prevention		
Officer Safety and Survival Skills		
Patrol Basics		
Responding to Calls		
Arrest Procedures		
Calls for Service	36	5
Community Services		
Responding to Disturbances		
Court Orders		
Resolving Vehicle Incidents		
Directing Traffic		
Responding to a Person in Crisis		
Criminal Investigations	50	6
Crimes Against Persons		
Crimes Against Society		
Crimes Against Property		
Economic Crimes		
Crime Scene to Courtroom	35	5
Processing the Crime Scene		
Follow-Up Investigations		
Court Procedures		
Critical Incidents	44	6
Incident Command System		
Critical Incident Overview		
Chemical and Hazardous Materials		
Biological Weapons of Mass Destruction		
Radiological and Nuclear Weapons of Mass Destruction		

Table 5.1 Instructional Hours Devoted to Topics during Police Academy Training,
continued.

Training Topic	Hours of Training	
	n	%
Traffic Stops	30	4
Traffic Law		
Conducting Professional Traffic Stops		
Unknown Risk Traffic Stops		
High-Risk Traffic Stops		
DUI Traffic Stops	24	3
Traffic Crash Investigations	32	4
Terms and Legal Considerations		
Traffic Crash Management		
Law Enforcement Vehicle Operations	48	6
Vehicle Inspection		
Proactive Driving Skills		
Principles of Driving		
Lights and Sirens		
First Aid for Criminal Justice Officers	40	5
Preparing to Respond to Emergencies		
Responding to Emergencies		
Trauma-Related Issues		
Medical Issues		
Criminal Justice Firearms	80	10
Firearms Safety		
Firearms Familiarization		
Fundamentals of Marksmanship		
Drawing and Holstering a Handgun		
Loading and Unloading		
Use of Cover		
Weapons Malfunctions		
Weapons Cleaning		
Survival Shooting		
Defensive Tactics Techniques	80	10
Dart-Firing Stun Gun	8	1
Physical Fitness Training	60	8
Total	770	99

Source: Author compilation from Florida Criminal Justice Standards and Training Commission (2014a). *Florida Basic Recruit Training Program: Florida Law Enforcement Academy, Volume 1;* (2014b) *Florida Basic Recruit Training Program: High Liability, Volume 2.* Tallahassee: Florida Department of Law Enforcement. Retrieved on October 8, 2014 from http://www.fdle.state.fl.us/Content/CJST/Menu/Publications/Curriculum-Home-Page.aspx.

The Police Officer Certification Examination

In an effort to ensure quality control, CJSTC mandates that training academy graduates must pass a competency examination known as the State Officer Certification Examination (SOCE) to gain certification or licensing as a law enforcement officer. This test is based upon the basic recruit training curriculum, is composed by experts in the field, and the questions are pre-tested to ensure validity and reliability. A total of 1,801 persons took the law enforcement SOCE during the first half of calendar year 2014 and 87% achieved a passing grade (Florida Criminal Justice Professionalism Program, 2014a, 2014b). These successful recruits are now considered to be "employable material."

The Law Enforcement Officer Selection Process

One can think of the police officer selection process as taking the shape of a funnel. The process starts out with a large number of applicants. Gradually, the pool gets smaller and smaller. Eventually, the list shrinks to what some people might regard as "the cream of the crop."

There are two contrasting approaches to the hiring process. The most common tack is to depend upon "weeding out" unacceptable applicants as opposed to "screening in" desirable candidates. *Weeding out* means that efforts concentrate on disqualifying candidates from further consideration. Applying minimum standards would be one example of this "thinning-the-herd" strategy. Unqualified applicants are discarded, while those persons who are not filtered out proceed to the next phase where they are subject to further scrutiny. What eventually emerges is a group of applicants for which no objections could be unearthed.

The opposite orientation, *screening in*, starts by identifying what traits or characteristics assure occupational success or good job performance. Applicants who match these qualities are ushered in while anybody who lacks these attributes is eliminated from further consideration. This procedure ensures that the survivors in the applicant pool have received a stamp of approval.

Figure 5.1 contains a sketch of the typical law enforcement officer selection process. There are two important general features to this figure. First, the applicant pool shrinks or diminishes throughout the entire process from start to finish. Second, a thrifty agency will rely upon less expensive methods at the start of employment consideration. The more costly junctures occur after the eligible pool of candidates decreases in size so as to save taxpayer dollars.

The first step is to submit a basic employment application. The items on the application are designed to see whether the job-seeker meets minimum standards. CJSTC will not allow agencies to hire anybody who does not comply with these minimum standards. Survivors in the pack continue to the written psychological stage. Paper-and-pencil tests cost very little to administer. In fact, office staff can score some inventories and quickly reject unsatisfactory applicants. More complete background checks will require contacting neighbors and past employers, conducting criminal and credit history checks, reviewing motor vehicle histories, and other investigative angles. At this point, the selection process starts to become more expensive for the agency. Polygraph testing and a face-to-face meeting with a psychologist are some of the more expensive tools used to ferret out questionable applicants.

Figure 5.1 The Law Enforcement Officer Selection Process

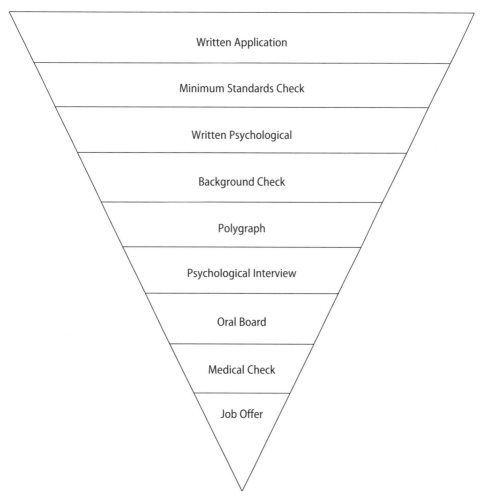

Written Application

Minimum Standards Check

Written Psychological

Background Check

Polygraph

Psychological Interview

Oral Board

Medical Check

Job Offer

Source: Author.

Candidates who survive the process to this point usually are invited to participate in an oral board interview. A panel of raters will sift through the applicant's files, ask a variety of questions, and grade the responses. While there are some concerns with this approach (Doerner, 1997; Doerner, 2001), it does remain as a time-honored practice.

Those individuals who are fortunate enough to have negotiated the process successfully up to this point undergo a medical check. Law enforcement can be a stressful and strenuous job. Conditions that can compromise a person's ability to deal with these occupational strains might be detected at this point. Of course, the "Americans with Disabilities Act" requires employers to make reasonable accommodations whenever feasible. However, there are some legitimate concerns that may form the basis for a valid bona fide occupational qualification. A *bona fide occupational qualification* (BFOQ) is a restriction that an employer deems necessary for employees to discharge job functions in a safe manner. For example, a candidate who is missing an index finger on one hand might be rejected from employment consideration as a law enforcement officer because he or she is not able to discharge a firearm with that hand.

Figure 5.2 Entrance Requirements of Florida Sheriff Offices and Police Departments

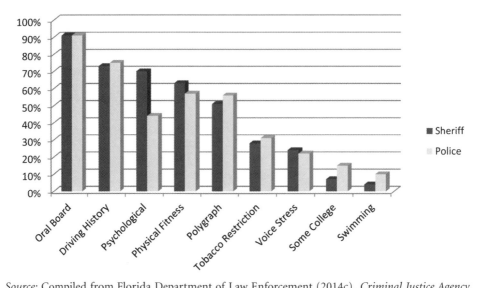

Source: Compiled from Florida Department of Law Enforcement (2014c). *Criminal Justice Agency Profile Report 2013.* Retrieved on October 15, 2014 from http://www.fdle.state.fl.us/Content/getdoc/ fe4a385f-32c8-445f-af50-b23e0216df70/2013-Sheriff-s-Office-Index-Page.aspx and also from http:// www.fdle.state.fl.us/Content/getdoc/b21c0049-41db-4ac1-bfe3-77bb5c026070/2013-Police-Department- Index-Page.aspx.

The common practices that Florida sheriff office and city police departments rely upon during the hiring process appear in Figure 5.2. The oral board and a review of the applicant's driving record are pretty standard. However, not as many police departments utilize psychological testing in comparison to sheriff offices. Both types of agencies exhibit a similar dependence on the remainder of the hiring tools.

Applicants who have traveled through all these steps are now in a position to receive a tentative job offer. After accepting the preliminary job offer and completing the police academy training, the person will take an oath of office (see Figure 5.3) at a swearing-in ceremony and will undergo any post-academy training the agency deems necessary.

Figure 5.3 Oath of Office for Florida Public Officials

I do solemnly swear (or affirm) that I will support, protect, and defend the Constitution and Government of the United States and of the State of Florida; that I am duly qualified to hold office under the Constitution of the state; and that I will well and faithfully perform the duties of (title of office) on which I am now about to enter. So help me God.

Source: Florida Constitution, Article II, §5 (b).

The Structure of the Florida Law Enforcement System

One can group Florida law enforcement agencies according to their geographical jurisdiction. *Jurisdiction* deals with the land boundaries in which an agency operates. For example, a municipal police officer normally does not have arrest authority outside the city limits. A sheriff deputy can provide law enforcement duties anywhere inside the county. Finally, state law enforcement officers can operate inside any city or county within the boundaries of Florida.

In order to illustrate how jurisdiction affects law enforcement activity, we will look closely at two state agencies: the Florida Department of Law Enforcement (FDLE) and the Florida Highway Patrol (FHP). After that, attention will turn to local authorities in terms of county sheriff offices and municipal police departments. Finally, the discussion will visit the role of special jurisdiction agencies.

State Law Enforcement Agencies

Florida, as Table 5.2 illustrates, has a number of agencies that contain sworn positions. The largest law enforcement employer is the Department of Highway Safety & Motor Vehicles which houses the FHP. The Fish and Wildlife Conservation Commission is the second leading employer, followed by FDLE. Because of their special importance, we will look more closely at FDLE and FHP in a moment.

According to the most recent census estimates, Florida is the third largest state in the Union with over 19.5 million residents. A look at the racial composition of Floridians reveals that 78% of the population is white, 17% is black or African American, and the remaining 5% falls into the "other" category. Women constitute 51% of the state's population (U.S. Census Bureau, 2014).

These benchmarks are important tools for understanding racial and gender distributions. For example, if whites compose 78% of the population, then one would expect that whites would constitute 78% of an agency's sworn members, all things being equal. If minority members have a 22% representation in the state population, then they should make up 22% of an agency's staff. Whenever an agency's characteristics exceed these benchmarks, there is an *overrepresentation* of the target group. Whenever an agency's characteristics fail to achieve these benchmarks, there is an *underrepresentation* of the target group.

A closer look at Table 5.2 reveals some imbalances within some state agencies. For example, white sworn personnel are overrepresented in Agriculture & Consumer Services; black and Hispanic law enforcement officials are underrepresented in that agency. Nonwhite persons are overrepresented in the Highway Patrol. When one looks at the total figures for all state law enforcement personnel, whites fall just short of parity representation in the sworn rank-and-file at 74% and nonwhites are slightly overrepresented at 26%.

Turning to gender, one would expect that if all things were equal, then 51% of the sworn members in an agency should be female. A glance at the last column of Table 5.2 shows that women are vastly underrepresented among state law enforcement personnel.

Table 5.2 Agency Sworn Size, Race and Gender of Full-Time Sworn Personnel, Florida State Law Enforcement Agencies, 2013

State Agency	Number of Full-Time Officers	% White	% Female
Agriculture & Consumer Services	226	90	8
Attorney General, Medicaid Fraud Control Unit	69	65	25
Business & Prof. Reg., Alcoholic Bevs. & Tobacco	97	68	32
Financial Services, Division of Insurance Fraud	131	70	15
Financial Services, Office of Fiscal Integrity	2	100	0
Fire Marshall, Fire Investigation	94	81	10
Fish & Wildlife Conservation Commission	742	89	8
Hwy. Safety & Motor Veh., Div. of Hwy. Patrol	1,749	63	12
Law Enforcement	404	81	17
Lottery, Division of Security	10	90	0
Marshal of the Supreme Court	12	67	25
State Attorney's Office (All Circuits Combined)	224	83	17
Total	3,760	74	12

Source: Compiled from Florida Department of Law Enforcement (2014c). *Criminal Justice Agency Profile Report 2013.* Retrieved on October 8, 2014 from http://www.fdle.state.fl.us/Content/CJST/Menu/Publications/test.aspx.

The question of why agencies experience an underrepresentation will be postponed until later in the chapter.

Florida Department of Law Enforcement

FDLE is the umbrella organization for a lot of members of the state's law enforcement community. Housed in the executive branch of state government, the FDLE Executive Director is appointed by the Governor, in conjunction with the Cabinet (which consists of the Attorney General, the Chief Financial Officer, and the Commissioner of Agriculture), and confirmed by a majority of the Senate (*Florida Statutes 2014*, § 20.201).

FDLE is charged with promoting public safety and security within the state. The agency maintains five programs (FDLE, 2014a). They include:

- Executive Direction and Business Support;
- Criminal Investigations and Forensic Science;
- Criminal Justice Information;
- Criminal Justice Professionalism; and
- Capitol Police.

Executive Direction is the section that provides administrative oversight of the entire FDLE operation. Some of those functions include planning, research, development, and management. The Business Support portion is responsible for the budget, human resources, finance, and accounting.

Criminal Investigations and Forensic Science contains three service areas. First is the state crime laboratory offices which offer crime scene analysis and evidence processing. Some key areas include toxicology, latent prints, DNA, firearms, document, and computer analyses. The second area involves Investigative Services. This arm conducts independent criminal investigations and coordinates criminal investigations that span multiple jurisdictions. Some typical areas would include major drug cases, ethics, fraud and economic crime, gang activity, domestic security, computers, and the procurement of criminal intelligence. The third component is mutual aid services which coordinates state and local responses during any emergency or mass disaster. A special emphasis is placed on coordinating homeland security plans.

Figure 5.4 Entrance Requirements for Florida Department of Law Enforcement Agents

Minimum Qualifications:

- Four years of sworn law enforcement experience; or
- A bachelor's or advanced degree from an accredited college or university with a major in criminology/criminal justice, accounting, finance, computer science or related fields.

Notes:

- Applicants must possess or, within 180 consecutive days after hire date, obtain Florida Criminal Justice standards.
- Based on the needs of the department, FDLE may pay for the applicant's Florida law enforcement certification course and examination.
- Preference will be given to applicants who possess a bachelor's degree or advanced degree.
- Preference will be given to applicants who are willing to relocate anywhere in the state.
- Preference will be given to applicants fluent in a foreign language.
- Preference will be given to applicants who are experienced sworn law enforcement investigators.
- Selected applicants will be required to sign an employment training reimbursement agreement.
- An applicant's probationary period will extend 12 months after completion of the FDLE Special Agent Training Academy.
- Applicants who do not currently possess certification as a Law Enforcement Officer in Florida will be hired at 5% below the base salary. Upon successful completion of the Florida Law Enforcement Basic Recruit Training Program and achieving a passing score on the State Officer Certification Examination, applicants will receive an increase to the base rate of pay.
- Internal applicants must have received at least an "achieves" on all work plan expectations during the last two rating periods. The applicant may not have received a "below" rating on any work expectation.

Source: Florida Department of Law Enforcement (2014b). *Special Agent Hiring Qualifications.* Tallahassee: Florida Department of Law Enforcement. Retrieved on October 8, 2014 from http://www.fdle.state.fl.us/Content/Employment-Information/Menu/Special-Agent-Hiring-Qualifications.aspx.

Criminal Justice Information is responsible for information storage systems. The Florida Crime Information Center (FCIC) is the computerized information system that patrol officers access when checking for such things as stolen vehicles, wanted persons, criminal histories, missing persons, and domestic violence injunctions. FCIC also provides local agencies with a link to the FBI National Crime Information Center (NCIC). NCIC coordinates similar databases from all the other states so that this information is immediately available to patrol officers in the field.

Criminal Justice Professionalism has responsibility for providing entry-level and in-service training. All the police academies in the state must adhere to a standardized set of rules and regulations. In addition, this program certifies new officers, provides training updates and advanced modules for officers throughout their careers, offers seminars for new police executives and leaders, oversees the state alcohol testing program for both equipment and operators, and administers the decertification process.

The Florida Capitol Police provides security protection for the governor, other high-ranking officials, and visiting dignitaries. This agency also provides law enforcement service to visitors and employees at the Capitol Complex in Tallahassee.

Figure 5.4 contains the entrance requirements for an FDLE agent. FDLE looks to hire applicants who have four years of prior law enforcement or a four-year college degree. The remaining list of desirable traits in the figure gives further indication as to the type of people FDLE wishes to employ.

Florida Highway Patrol

The Florida Highway Patrol, housed within the Department of Highway Safety and Motor Vehicles (DHSMV), is perhaps the most visible and widely-known state law enforcement agency. The mission of FHP is to promote safe driving, investigate traffic crashes, reduce the carnage associated with traffic violations on state highways, and make arrests for any criminal violations (*Florida Statutes 2014*, § 321). While campaigns to reduce traffic crashes, injuries, and fatalities are ongoing on a regular basis, FHP troopers are particularly visible during holidays and other peak periods. DHSMV is also responsible for administering driver's licenses, distributing Uniform Traffic Citations to all agencies within the state, and serving as the depository for the standardized traffic crash reports that all law enforcement officers utilize.

Figure 5.5 displays the entrance requirements for FHP. Notice how some of the expectations are more relaxed in comparison with FDLE. But, once again, prior law enforcement experience, in conjunction with some college exposure, is highly desired.

The DHSMV compiles an annual report that summarizes the activities in which FHP troopers engaged. During fiscal year 2012–13, FHP troopers issued over three-quarters of a million traffic citations to errant drivers, wrote warnings to another 320,000 motorists, and investigated more than 211,000 traffic crashes (Florida DHSMV, 2013a). To place these activities in perspective, local law enforcement officers throughout the state wrote over three million citations during the same period (Florida DHSMV, 2013b).

Local Law Enforcement Agencies

Local law enforcement agencies consist of both county sheriff offices and city police departments. There are some very distinctive differences between the two types of or-

Figure 5.5 Entrance Requirements for Florida Highway Patrol Troopers

- *Age:* 19 years or age or older.
- *Citizenship:* You must be a United States Citizen. Naturalized Citizens are welcome to apply. All naturalization documentation must accompany application.
- *Vision:* Applicants must have minimum correctable vision of 20/30, with normal color distinguishing capabilities and 140-degree field of vision. Any visual disability, which prevents the performance of essential functions of an applicant, for which no reasonable accommodation is possible, shall disqualify the applicant.
- *Weight Proportional to Height:* People of all heights are encouraged to apply. We do not have minimum or maximum height limits.
- *Education:* High school diploma or a general equivalency diploma is required.
- *Driver's License:* Applicants must possess a valid driver's license.
- *Relocation:* Applicants must be willing to serve anywhere in the state of Florida.
- <u>One</u> of the following:
  - o One year sworn or non-sworn law enforcement experience.
  - o Two years of active and continuous U.S. military service.
  - o Two years of public contact experience.
  - o Thirty semester-hours or 45 quarter-hours at an accredited college of university.

Employment preference is given to qualified applicants who have completed 60 semester-hours or 90 quarter-hours of college course work at an accredited college of university. Employment is given to qualified applicants who have two years of continuous U.S. military service with an honorable discharge.

Employment preference is given to Florida Certified Law Enforcement Officers with one year of sworn law enforcement experience.

Veterans' Preference is given to veterans and spouses of veterans as outlined in *Florida Statutes.*

Competitive Starting Salaries: $33,977.04 annually ($38,976.84 in Broward, Miami-Dade, Monroe, Palm Beach, Collier and Lee counties).

Source: Florida Highway Patrol (2014). *FHP Recruitment Information.* Tallahassee: Florida Department of Highway Safety and Motor Vehicles. Retrieved on October 8, 2014 from http://www.flhsmv.gov/fhp/Career/Requirements.htm.

ganizations. As a result, the following section describes county sheriff offices before turning to a similar presentation of city police departments.

County Sheriff Offices

The Florida Constitution (Article VIII, § 1(d)) establishes the local sheriff as the highest ranking constitutional officer in each of Florida's 67 counties. The state constitution further requires that an election be held every four years to determine who should occupy the top local law enforcement post. The duly elected sheriff is charged with four major responsibilities. They include:

- Providing law enforcement services throughout the entire county;
- Administering the county jail;
- Maintaining local courthouse security; and
- Delivering and serving court papers.

Table 5.3 provides a broad overview of the Florida sheriff offices. First, there are 67 sheriff offices which altogether employ 18,678 deputies. Second, because the sheriff offices provide coverage for the entire county, they tend to be relatively large organizations in terms of sworn size. Over half (54%) the sheriff offices carry at least 100 deputies on their rosters. Third, the eight largest sheriff offices account for over half the deputies who work in the Sunshine State.

The remaining portion of Table 5.3 presents the demographic characteristics of Florida sheriff deputies. If you remember our earlier discussion, the state population is 22% nonwhite, while females make up 51% of the state population. When looking at all the Florida SOs combined, nonwhite deputies account for 27% of the sworn membership. That is slightly more than what one would expect on the basis of chance so the relative composition amounts to an overrepresentation. Closer examination of the table reveals that much of this overrepresentation is due to agencies in the mega-category of a thousand or more sworn members. Compared to the overall population composition, the female presence at 14% constitutes a considerable underrepresentation. Women remain significantly underrepresented no matter what the agency size is. While a much more accurate assessment would use county population figures as a more pertinent comparative standard, the imbalance is not likely to fluctuate in a perceptible way.

One should frame these observations in a slightly different manner. If a law enforcement career spans 25 years, then it is reasonable that agency composition will lag behind these benchmarks somewhat. Also, the population-at-large may not be an entirely appropriate benchmark. As we saw earlier in this chapter, Florida has established a series of minimum standards for all sworn personnel (i.e., high school graduation, no felony convictions, and so forth). Even though the data are not readily available, it might be worthwhile to examine the available labor pool against those characteristics. In short, while these benchmarks might be convenient and readily available, they do not necessarily represent the final say in what an agency has accomplished over the years.

Table 5.3 Agency Sworn Size, Race and Gender of Full-Time Sworn Personnel, Florida Sheriff Offices, 2013

	Agencies			Sworn Personnel			
Sworn Size	n	%		n	%	% Nonwhite	% Female
1–9	2	4		18	—	0	25
10–24	12	15		171	1	7	6
25–49	10	16		375	2	14	10
50–99	5	11		509	3	9	11
100–249	19	24		2,854	15	10	11
250–499	11	18		4,214	23	13	12
500–999	2	3		1,134	6	11	14
1,000+	6	9		9,403	50	42	16
Total	67	100		18,678	100	27	14

Source: Compiled from Florida Department of Law Enforcement (2014d). *Criminal Justice Agency Profile Report 2013.* Tallahassee: Florida Department of Law Enforcement. Retrieved on October 11, 2014 from http://www.fdle.state.fl.us/Content/getdoc/fe4a385f-32c8-445f-af50-b23e0216df70/2013-Sheriff-s-Office-Index-Page.aspx.

Table 5.4 Annual Salary by Sworn Size, Florida Sheriff Offices, 2013

Sworn Size	Average	Entry-Level Salary Minimum	Maximum
1–9	$23,000	$20,000	$26,000
10–24	$30,459	$25,000	$36,756
25–49	$30,881	$28,000	$34,000
50–99	$32,883	$30,000	$36,167
100–249	$36,022	$29,120	$43,000
250–499	$36,735	$28,600	$42,645
500–999	$39,895	$38,506	$41,284
1,000+	$45,238	$38,148	$48,323
Total	$34,690	$26,000	$48,323

Source: Compiled from Florida Department of Law Enforcement (2014d). *Criminal Justice Agency Profile Report 2013.* Tallahassee: Florida Department of Law Enforcement. Retrieved on October 11, 2014 http://www.fdle.state.fl.us/Content/getdoc/fe4a385f-32c8-445f-af50-b23e0216df70/2013-Sheriff-s-Office-Index-Page.aspx.

Starting salaries for deputy sheriffs appear in Table 5.4, along with the minimum and maximum schedules, according to the size of the agency. The average deputy earns $34,690 upon being commissioned. That figure, of course, does not reflect geographical variation or other considerations. The figures in the table also indicate that entrance salaries tend to rise as agencies grow larger.

A number of factors affect the take-home earnings of a deputy sheriff. One of the more noticeable influences is whether deputies are represented by a union. A 2003 Florida Supreme Court decision extended the right to engage in collective bargaining to all deputy sheriffs. Deputies flocked to the bargaining table almost immediately. Today, deputies in 29 Florida sheriff offices are represented by a collective bargaining unit (FDLE, 2014b).

A quick look at this flurry of activity reveals that unionized deputies appear to have increased their take-home pay by a very noticeable margin (Doerner & Doerner, 2010). While further analyses probed the impact of other variables, it is safe to conclude that unionization ushered in higher earning powers for unionized deputies. Whether the benefits of engaging in collective bargaining spill over into other job-related areas (such as retirement options, cashing in unused vacation and sick time, shift differential premiums, and tuition reimbursement) remains to be determined.

Municipal Police Departments

Municipal police departments provide law enforcement services within a particular city. The Tallahassee Police Department, for example, works within that city's geographical boundaries. While the Leon County Sheriff's Office is responsible for law enforcement services outside the city limits, its members can also respond to calls for service inside the city.

The information contained in Table 5.5 provides a broad overview of Florida municipal police agencies and their personnel. First, there are 260 city police departments operating within the Sunshine State and those agencies employ 18,554 sworn officers. Second, almost half these agencies (46%) are staffed by less than two dozen officers and two-thirds of these departments have fewer than fifty sworn members. Much of the city policing efforts takes place in small towns. Third, the 13 largest municipal departments account

Table 5.5 Agency Sworn Size, Race and Gender of Full-Time Sworn Personnel, Florida
Municipal Police Departments, 2013

	Agencies		Sworn Personnel			
Sworn Size	n	%	n	%	% Nonwhite	% Female
1–9	44	17	247	1	17	7
10–24	75	29	1,181	6	18	10
25–49	53	20	1,918	10	25	12
50–99	36	14	2,541	14	29	13
100–249	39	15	6,144	33	28	15
250–499	8	3	2,488	13	15	12
500–999	3	1	1,933	10	16	14
1,000+	2	1	2,102	11	89	16
Total	260	100	18,554	98*	33	15

* Does not add up to 100% due to rounding error.

Source: Compiled from Florida Department of Law Enforcement (2014e). *Criminal Justice Agency Profile Report 2013.* Tallahassee: Florida Department of Law Enforcement. Retrieved on October 11, 2014 from http://www.fdle.state.fl.us/Content/getdoc/b21c0049-41db-4ac1-bfe3-77bb5c026070/2013-Police-Department-Index-Page.aspx.

for one-third of the local police officers who work in the Sunshine State. The bulk of Florida city police officers are concentrated in just a handful of agencies.

A look at the racial and gender backgrounds of municipal police officers is instructive. Using the state benchmarks (22% nonwhite population and 51% female) helps frame the presentation. Generally speaking, nonwhite officers are underrepresented in the smaller city police departments, have a more balanced presence in medium-sized agencies, and are below parity in the bigger agencies. The dominant presence in the 1,000+ category is due to large number of Hispanic officers in Miami. Females remain greatly underrepresented as a group. Once again, it would be much more accurate to examine a particular agency against the background of its local citizenry.

Annual beginning salaries, which appear in Table 5.6, are grouped by agency size. The average municipal police officer earns $38,021 annually. However, there are some wide variations in starting salaries, most of which reflect employment in upscale and more affluent communities. In general, though, salaries tend to climb as agency size increases. These average figures are also higher than the earnings we observed earlier for sheriff deputies. If you recall, city police officers have had collective bargaining rights since 1968, while the Florida Supreme Court extended this same benefit to sheriff deputies in 2003 (Doerner & Doerner, 2010).

One might also wonder whether the observed difference in starting salaries might stem from police departments having more stringent entrance requirements than sheriff offices. The average city police department pays its new employees $3,331 more than what the typical sheriff office does. If you recall from the discussion earlier in this chapter, agencies are free to enhance their expectations for new sworn personnel, but CJSTC will not allow them to dip below the established minimum standards. In actuality, there are some differences in entrance standards. About a quarter of Florida's municipal departments demand that recruits have earned at least a two-year college degree compared with 6% of the county agencies (FDLE, 2014c). In all fairness, while the number of individual

Table 5.6 Annual Salary by Sworn Size, Florida Municipal Police Departments, 2013

Sworn Size	Average	Entry-Level Salary Minimum	Maximum
1–9	$30,425	$20,800	$52,224
10–24	$35,880	$24,281	$56,638
25–49	$40,169	$28,436	$55,000
50–99	$24,272	$24,488	$52,241
100–249	$43,744	$32,968	$57,963
250–499	$41,239	$41,939	$51,558
500–999	$47,691	$43,616	$55,356
1,000+	$46,157	$45,929	$46,384
Total	$38,021	$25,000	$45,929

Source: Compiled from Florida Department of Law Enforcement (2014e). *Criminal Justice Agency Profile Report 2013.* Tallahassee: Florida Department of Law Enforcement. Retrieved on October 11, 2014 http://www.fdle.state.fl.us/Content/getdoc/b21c0049-41db-4ac1-bfe3-77bb5c026070/2013-Police-Department-Index-Page.aspx.

officers with exposure to college is increasing, the literature does not provide irrefutable evidence that a college education enhances on-the-job performance (Carlan, 2007; Hawley, 1998; Hilal, Densley, & Zhao, 2013; Roberg & Bonn, 2004; Rydberg & Terrill, 2010).

Part of the problem with establishing a minimum standard that would require all incoming personnel to have an associate's degree or bachelor's diploma is the undue burden that such a rule would impose upon smaller governments. For instance, some counties have significant holdings of national and state forest lands, parks, as well as recreational and agricultural areas, and state or local government buildings. These parcels do not generate any, or very little, tax revenues. Furthermore, the ongoing economic recession has ravaged local Florida government coffers (Doerner & Doerner, 2014). Paying for college-educated deputies or officers, especially when the expected benefits are not well-documented, is much more than what some locales can handle.

Government officials are aware of the economic difficulties that such a personnel prerequisite could create. As a result, the State of Florida has installed a *salary incentive program* in an effort to encourage officers to obtain a college education (*Florida Statutes 2014,* § 943.22). Utilizing trust fund dollars, as opposed to taxes, the state adds a supplement of $30 every month to the salaries of law enforcement officers who have earned an A.A. or an A.S. degree. Officers who have graduated from college receive a $50 monthly stipend in addition to their regular salaries.

Special Jurisdiction Agencies

A *special jurisdiction agency* refers to a law enforcement entity that provides service to a specific geographical location or is charged with special investigative authority. Some examples of special jurisdiction agencies would include college and university police departments, public housing authorities, some hospitals, mass transit police, port facilities and the like. For our purposes, we will concentrate on campus security.

Table 5.7 displays information regarding officer characteristics in Florida college and university law enforcement agencies. A glance at the table reveals that while some of these

Table 5.7 Sworn Size, Race, Gender, and Entry-Level Salary, Florida College and University Law Enforcement Agencies, 2012

College/University	Sworn Size	% Nonwhite	% Female	Entry-Level Salary
Edison State College	8	25	25	$32,000
Florida A & M U.	32	81	28	$34,176
Florida Atlantic U.	38	53	21	$38,868
Florida Gulf Coast U.	15	7	13	$37,000
Florida International U.	52	79	12	$41,232
Florida State U.	61	20	15	$37,917
New College	11	8	17	$35,000
Pensacola State C.	7	14	14	n/a
Santa Fe College	16	31	6	$27,505
Tallahassee Com. C.	12	33	17	$31,858
U. of Central Florida	59	25	12	$38,000
U. of Florida	80	22	19	$39,735
U. of North Florida	27	19	26	$31,444
U. of South Florida	52	19	12	$43,000
U. of West Florida	19	32	32	n/a

Source: Compiled from Florida Department of Law Enforcement (2014f). *Criminal Justice Agency Profile Report 2013.* Tallahassee: Florida Department of Law Enforcement. Retrieved on October 11, 2014 http://www.fdle.state.fl.us/Content/getdoc/2a0d8c02-9731-4b3a-9180-0adee2c3feb5/2012-CJAP-Schools-and-Ports-Index-Page.aspx.

agencies are small, others (University of Florida, Florida State University, and University of Central Florida) have a sizeable presence. There is also a wide variation in the representation of minority members. For example, Florida A&M University, an historically black institution, leads the pack at 81% minority presence. Women, while still under-represented, form an appreciable block at some institutions. As the final column indicates, starting salaries on some campuses can be competitive with local law enforcement agencies.

Some of what appears in Table 5.7 is the direct result of recommendations made by the Gubernatorial Task Force for University Campus Safety (2007). Following the rampage of a lone gunman on the Virginia Polytechnic Institute and State University campus which left 32 people killed and many others wounded, Florida Governor Crist issued an executive order convening a review team to examine "best practices" to ward off similar incidents on Florida college campuses. Of the many Task Force recommendations, three stand out because they address the need to attract and retain competent officers. The first proposal was to conduct a salary survey to ensure that campus police departments offered salaries that were comparable to other local agencies. The second recommendation was to hire seasoned officers with prior law enforcement experience. The third advisory was to develop a formula to arrive at a meaningful ratio of sworn personnel to the campus service population. Finally, the Task Force encouraged campus agencies to seek accreditation, a subject we will look at momentarily.

Job Prospects

The information compiled thus far enables us to take a crude look at job prospects in the state's public law enforcement sector. However, some assumptions need to be spelled out before we can undertake such an analysis. First, make the assumption that a law enforcement career spans 25 years. In other words, once every incumbent completes 25 years of service, he or she then automatically retires. Nobody leaves earlier and nobody departs later in this closed system. Second, assume that agencies replace these separated officers on a steady and regular basis. An agency that houses 100 officers will see four members leave each year and will bring four new replacements on board. Third, presume there are no lay-offs, hiring freezes, or other disruptions to the staffing situation.

Earlier Table 5.3 showed that Florida sheriff offices employed 18,678 deputies and, according to Table 5.5, there were another 18,554 sworn city officers in 2013. Together, these figures total 37,232 sworn local law enforcement officers working in the Sunshine State. With orderly departures over a 25-year period, each year would see the creation of 1,489 vacancies (37,232 law enforcement personnel divided by 25 years).

One can take a similar approach with the various state agencies. According to Table 5.2, there are 3,760 sworn personnel working in the various state agencies. FHP accounts for 1,749 sworn positions, Fish and Wildlife Conservation Commission (FWCC) houses 742 members, and the rest of the state agencies contain 1,269 law enforcement officers. Utilizing the same approach as the last paragraph outlined reveals that FHP and FWCC would be looking to hire 100 replacements each year. The remaining state agencies would have room for 51 newcomers annually.

As mentioned earlier, Figure 5.2 displays the requirements for landing an agent position with FDLE. FDLE, along with most state agencies, expects successful applicants will have a substantial amount of prior law enforcement experience in their backgrounds. Thus, state-level positions, with the exception of FHP and FWCC, would be beyond the reach of most college graduates.

The Florida Board of Governors is the body that oversees and guides the entire State University System. In other words, its policies and actions dictate the daily activities of the public universities. The Florida Board of Governors (2014) commissioned a study which tracked the Class of 2012 college graduates. That cohort consists of over 56,000 degree recipients. When the focus narrows to degree recipients in the area of "Security and Protective Services," 824 or less than half the graduates, had landed full-time jobs within Florida. These job-holders reported a median salary of $30,000 per year.

When viewed in this context, the public law enforcement sector in the Sunshine State is able to absorb the continuous influx of college graduates. However, college graduates are still vying with high-school graduates and community college degree-holders. Furthermore, the entry-level salaries these newcomers command are very much in line with the figures displayed in Tables 5.4 and 5.6 in this chapter. Obviously, the mere possession of a college sheepskin is not sufficient to impress law enforcement recruiters and human resources personnel. Applicants still need to demonstrate their worth.

Accreditation

Ever since the President's Commission (1967) issued a call for police officers to have college degrees, the major focal point for improving the police has riveted attention on the quality of individual officers. Accreditation takes the spotlight off these people and focuses on the organization or the agency itself. *Accreditation* means that an agency has undergone both internal and external reviews to make sure that its goals, objectives, and policies comply with the "best practices" in the field. One might think about accreditation as minimum standards for law enforcement organizations.

Two developments deserve some attention. They are the national accreditation movement throughout the United States and the accreditation efforts in Florida. Both topics are examined further.

The National Effort

The national campaign to upgrade police organizations began in the late 1970s. Representatives from the International Association of Chiefs of Police, the National Organization of Black Law Enforcement Executives, the National Sheriffs' Association, and the Police Executive Research Forum joined together to devise a series of standards that would assist law enforcement agencies to become more professionalized. These efforts concentrated on combatting crime more effectively, extending services more efficiently, enhancing co-operation with the other components of the criminal justice system, and boosting public support.

The Commission on Accreditation for Law Enforcement Agencies (CALEA) was formed to launch this endeavor and oversee operations. CALEA has established a series of mandatory standards and a set of voluntary standards for agency consideration. Agencies use these directives to evaluate their own practices. Once an agency completes a comprehensive self-study and updates its materials, a team of assessors visits and reviews these efforts. If everything is in tip-top shape, CALEA grants its seal of approval. Successful agencies must re-apply for accreditation every three years to make sure compliance is continuing and that administrators have addressed new developments that have materialized.

Since its inception over thirty years ago, CALEA has granted approval to 630 law enforcement agencies throughout the country. This number includes 15 sheriff offices, 25 municipal police departments, 2 state agencies, and 1 university police department from Florida (CALEA, 2014). Another perspective is that less than 3% of all local, state, and federal agencies have become accredited (Hougland & Mesloh, 2005). As one author team put it, "in other words, 97 percent of all U.S. agencies and 90 percent of all Florida municipal agencies have not seen a compelling need to pursue this opportunity" (Doerner & Doerner, 2009, p. 782).

The question of why national accreditation has not caught on looms large. For one thing, very little documentation and not much research exists about the effects that accreditation brings. A larger impediment is the cost that an agency incurs during this process. For example, the application fee ranges from $7,125 for agencies with fewer than 24 full-time sworn and non-sworn members to almost $19,000 for agencies that employ a thousand or more people. There are additional costs for office space and equipment, personnel salaries, assessor expenses, and other items. In short, national accreditation can be a very expensive undertaking.

The Florida Effort

A number of states, including Florida, have formed their own versions of the accreditation process. The Florida Sheriffs' Association and the Florida Police Chiefs' Association developed a state program that is administered by the Commission for Florida Law Enforcement Accreditation (CFA). The CFA followed the lead of CALEA and established a series of standards that agencies must meet to gain state accreditation. One attractive feature of this program is that it is tailored to more localized needs. In addition, CFA participation costs are considerably less. Those fees range from under $500 for smaller agencies to $3,900 with over 500 sworn members (CFA, 2014a). The latest count reveals that 7 state agencies, 32 county sheriff offices, 93 municipal police departments, 7 college or university police departments, and 2 special jurisdictions agencies have undergone the CFA process (2014b).

This last observation raises the question of which agencies pursue CFA recognition and why do they choose to participate. At the start, it appeared that the larger, more advanced, and more forward-thinking agencies were quick to pursue accreditation. However, a more detailed looked at the diffusion or spread of accreditation, along with an inspection of agency characteristics before and after accreditation, did not support this line of thinking. Doerner and Doerner (2009) found that accredited and non-accredited departments resembled each other quite closely. Furthermore, accreditation did not emerge as a catalyst for organizational change. Instead, the authors concluded that ambitious police executives pursued accreditation status so they could list this credential on their résumés and appear to be on the cutting-edge when applying for future positions.

An allied concern deals with the effects of accreditation. The CALEA webpage, as well as some state sites, extol the virtues derived from accreditation. However, a careful reading of these benefits reveals that just about all the supporting evidence is either anecdotal or testimonial. Very little independent third-party empirical research exists.

To counteract this vacuum, Doerner and Doerner (2012) examined whether accredited agencies exhibited higher clearance rates. Their thinking, based in part on some purported claims, was that refining organizational oversight, implementing state-of-the-art practices, and devising more efficient and effective services should result in better clearance rates. A *clearance rate* refers to solving a criminal case either through an arrest or the identification of a very likely suspect. Previous researchers have used clearance rates as a way of measuring investigative efficiency.

An examination was conducted of annual clearance rates for violent crimes (homicide, forcible rape, aggravated assault, and robbery) and property crimes (burglary, larceny-theft, and motor vehicle theft) from 1997 through 2006 that were reported to FDLE by 257 municipal police departments throughout the state. Contrary to what one might expect, CFA accreditation did not bolster clearance rates. In other words, both accredited and non-accredited city police departments produced similar clearance rates. Accreditation did not provide any crime-fighting advantages. Whether accreditation provides other advantages remains an open question.

Summary

Finishing this chapter means that we have accomplished four things. First, we now understand the various stages involved the law enforcement officer selection and hiring process. Second, we visited the preparation that goes into becoming a law enforcement officer in Florida. Third, invoking the concept of jurisdiction enabled us to see how the law enforcement community works at the state, county, municipal, and special jurisdiction levels. Fourth, while previous reform efforts focused on upgrading the quality of sworn members, there is the growing recognition that agencies themselves also need attention if we are to improve the administration of justice in our state.

Key Terms

accreditation
bona fide occupational qualification
certification
clearance rate
jurisdiction
minimum standards
overrepresentation
salary incentive program
screening in
special jurisdiction agency
sworn officer
underrepresentation
weeding out

Selected Internet Sites

Commission for Florida Law Enforcement Accreditation
    http://flaccreditation.org

Commission on Accreditation for Law Enforcement Agencies
    http://www.calea.org

Florida Criminal Justice Standards and Training Commission
    http://www.fdle.state.fl.us/Content/getdoc/91a75023-5a74-40ef-814d-8e7e5b622d
    4d/CJSTC-Home-Page.aspx

Florida Department of Law Enforcement
    http://www.fdle.state.fl.us/Content/home.aspx

Florida Deputy Sheriffs Association
    http://www.fldeputysheriffs.org

Florida Fraternal Order of Police
    http://www.floridastatefop.org/home.asp

Florida Highway Patrol
    http://www.flhsmv.gov/fhp

Florida Police Benevolent Association
    http://wwww.flpba.org

Florida Police Chiefs Association
   http://www.fpca.com

Florida Sheriffs Association
   http://www.flsheriffs.org

Office of the Attorney General of Florida
   http://myfloridalegal.com

Review Questions

1. Explain the term "sworn officer."

2. What are "minimum standards"?

3. List five specific minimum standards.

4. What does "certification" mean?

5. Comment about Florida's police academy training curriculum.

6. What is the "State Officer Certification Examination"?

7. Distinguish "weeding out" from "screening in" practices.

8. Diagram the law enforcement officer selection process.

9. What is a "bona fide occupational qualification"?

10. Why is "jurisdiction" an important concept?

11. Name at least three state law enforcement agencies.

12. Explain what the terms "underrepresentation" and "overrepresentation" mean.

13. Using Table 5.2 of your text, examine the demographic composition of sworn personnel in state law enforcement agencies.

14. What five programs does FDLE maintain?

15. What entrance requirements are expected of prospective FDLE agents?

16. What is the purpose or role of FHP?

17. What entrance requirements are expected of prospective FHP troopers?

18. List two findings regarding sworn size and number of personnel in Florida sheriff offices using Table 5.3 of your text.

19. What are the functions of the county sheriff?

20. Use Table 5.3 of your text to examine the demographic composition of sheriff deputies.

21. Conduct a comparison of entry-level salaries for sheriff deputies using Table 5.4 of your text.

22. Reach two findings regarding sworn size and number of personnel in Florida municipal police departments using Table 5.5 of your text.

23. Use Table 5.5 of your text to examine the demographic composition of city police officers.

24. Analyze the entry-level salaries for police officers using Table 5.6 of your text.

25. What problems would an agency encounter if it were to install a four-year college degree requirement for incoming personnel?

26. Explain the Florida salary incentive program.

27. Explain what a "special jurisdiction agency" is and give some examples.

28. What recommendations did the Gubernatorial Task Force for University Campus Safety make regarding campus police?

29. Explore the job prospects for people who are interested in a law enforcement career in the Sunshine State.

30. What is accreditation?

31. What are four aims of accreditation?

32. Has the Commission on Accreditation for Law Enforcement Agencies (CALEA) been successful in promoting accreditation throughout the United States? Why or why not?

33. What is the purpose behind the Commission for Florida Law Enforcement Accreditation (CFA)?

34. What obstacles did CALEA encounter and how does CFA avoid them?

35. Are accredited agencies different from non-accredited agencies?

36. What kind of evidence exists regarding the benefits of CALEA?

37. Why do some police executives pursue accreditation?

38. What is a clearance rate?

39. How might one expect accreditation to affect agency clearance rates? Does it?

References

Carlan, Philip E. (2007). The criminal justice degree and policing: Conceptual development or occupational primer? *Policing: An International Journal of Police Strategies & Management, 30* (4), 608-619.

Commission for Florida Law Enforcement Accreditation (2014a). *Program Requirements.* Orlando: Commission for Florida Law Enforcement Accreditation. Retrieved on October 15, 2014 from http://flaccreditation.org/programrequirements.htm.

Commission for Florida Law Enforcement Accreditation (2014b). *Accredited Agencies.* Orlando: Commission for Florida Law Enforcement Accreditation. Retrieved on October 15, 2014 from http://flaccreditation.org/accagencies.htm.

Commission on Accreditation for Law Enforcement Agencies (2014). *CALEA Client Database.* Gainesville, VA: Commission on Accreditation for Law Enforcement Agencies. Retrieved on October 15, 2014 from http://www.calea.org/content/calea-client-database.

Doerner, William G. (1997). The utility of the oral interview board in selecting police academy admissions. *Policing: An International Journal of Police Strategies & Management, 20* (4), 777–785.

Doerner, William G. (2001). Determinants of oral board scores for promotional candidates: serendipity amidst invalidity. *Police Forum, 11* (1), 1–5.

Doerner, William G. and William M. Doerner (2009). The diffusion of accreditation among Florida police agencies. *Policing: An International Journal of Police Strategies & Management, 32* (4), 781–798.

Doerner, William M. and William G. Doerner (2010). Collective bargaining and job benefits: The case of Florida deputy sheriffs. *Police Quarterly, 13* (4), 367–386.

Doerner, William M. and William G. Doerner (2012). Police accreditation and clearance rates. *Policing: An International Journal of Police Strategies & Management, 35* (1), 6–24.

Doerner, William M. and William G. Doerner (2014). Curtailing police academy sponsorships in Florida: A preliminary analysis of a budgetary adjustment to the economic downturn. Paper presented at the annual meeting of the Southern Criminal Justice Association, Clearwater Beach, FL.

Florida Board of Governors (2014). Graduate Follow-Up Study: Baccalaureate Class of 2012, First Year Outcomes. Tallahassee: State University of Florida. Retrieved on October 16, 2014 from http://www.flbog.edu/documents_meetings/0189_0826_6137_3.4.2%204.1%20Class_of_2012_Follow_Up_Study.pdf.

Florida Constitution.

Florida Criminal Justice Professionalism Program (2014a). State officer certification examination statistics second quarter, fy 2013–2014. *Quarterly Update, Spring 2014.* Tallahassee: Florida Department of Law Enforcement. Retrieved on October 10, 2014 from http://www.fdle.state.fl.us/Content/getdoc/bc16efd2-4c09-407a-8fad-a93832272357/Summer-2014-Quarterly-Update.aspx.

Florida Criminal Justice Professionalism Program (2014b). State officer certification examination statistics third quarter, fy 2013–2014. *Quarterly Update, Fall 2014.* Tallahassee: Florida Department of Law Enforcement. Retrieved on October 10, 2014 from http://www.fdle.state.fl.us/Content/getdoc/a9a4918f-f629-48be-a3bd-e477e2a56528/Fall-2014-Quarterly-Update.aspx.

Florida Criminal Justice Standards and Training Commission (2014a). *Florida Basic Recruit Training Program: Florida Law Enforcement Academy, Volume 1.* Tallahassee: Florida Department of Law Enforcement. Retrieved on October 8, 2014 from http://www.fdle.state.fl.us/Content/CJST/Menu/Publications/Curriculum-Home-Page.aspx.

Florida Criminal Justice Standards and Training Commission (2014b) *Florida Basic Recruit Training Program: High Liability, Volume 2.* Tallahassee: Florida Department of Law Enforcement. Retrieved on October 8, 2014 from http://www.fdle.state.fl.us/Content/CJST/Menu/Publications/Curriculum-Home-Page.aspx.

Florida Department of Highway Safety and Motor Vehicles (2013a). *Annual Performance Report: Fiscal Year 2012–2013.* Tallahassee: Florida Department of Highway Safety and Motor Vehicles. Retrieved on October 10, 2014 from http://www.flhsmv.gov/html/AgencyAnnualReport2013.pdf.

Florida Department of Highway Safety and Motor Vehicles (2013b). *Annual Uniform Traffic Citation Report 2013.* Tallahassee: Florida Department of Law Enforcement. Retrieved on October 10, 2014 from https://services.flhsmv.gov/SpecialtyPlates/UniformTrafficCitationReport.

Florida Department of Law Enforcement (2014a). *Statement of Agency Organization and Operation.* Tallahassee: Florida Department of Law Enforcement. Retrieved on October

10, 2014 from http://www.fdle.state.fl.us/Content/getdoc/3749abfa-3acc-4d9e-af97-f3016b86ccad/Quick-Facts.aspx.

Florida Department of Law Enforcement (2014b). *Special Agent Hiring Qualifications*. Tallahassee: Florida Department of Law Enforcement. Retrieved on October 8, 2014 from http://www.fdle.state.fl.us/Content/Employment-Information/Menu/Special-Agent-Hiring-Qualifications.aspx.

Florida Department of Law Enforcement (2014c). *Criminal Justice Agency Profile Report 2013*. Tallahassee: Florida Department of Law Enforcement. Retrieved on October 8, 2014 from http://www.fdle.state.fl.us/Content/CJST/Menu/Publications/test.aspx.

Florida Department of Law Enforcement (2014d). *Criminal Justice Agency Profile Report 2013*. Tallahassee: Florida Department of Law Enforcement. Retrieved on October 11, 2014 from http://www.fdle.state.fl.us/Content/getdoc/fe4a385f-32c8-445f-af50-b23e0216df70/2013-Sheriff-s-Office-Index-Page.aspx.

Florida Department of Law Enforcement (2014e). *Criminal Justice Agency Profile Report 2013*. Tallahassee: Florida Department of Law Enforcement. Retrieved on October 11, 2014 from http://www.fdle.state.fl.us/Content/getdoc/b21c0049-41db-4ac1-bfe3-77bb5c026070/2013-Police-Department-Index-Page.aspx.

Florida Department of Law Enforcement (2014f). *Criminal Justice Agency Profile Report 2013*. Tallahassee: Florida Department of Law Enforcement. Retrieved on October 11, 2014 from http://www.fdle.state.fl.us/Content/getdoc/2a0d8c02-9731-4b3a-9180-0adee2c3feb5/2012-CJAP-Schools-and-Ports-Index-Page.aspx.

Florida Highway Patrol (2014). *FHP Recruitment Information*. Tallahassee: Florida Department of Highway Safety and Motor Vehicles. Retrieved on October 8, 2014 from http://www.flhsmv.gov/fhp/Career/Requirements.htm.

Florida Statutes 2014.

Gubernatorial Task Force for University Campus Safety (2007). *Report on Findings and Recommendations*. Tallahassee: Office of the Governor. Retrieved on October 29, 2014 from http://cra20.humansci.msstate.edu/Florida%20Gubernatorial%20Task%20Force%20for%20University%20Campus%20Safety%20-%202007%20Final%20Report.pdf.

Hawley, Thomas J., III (1998). The collegiate shield: Was the movement purely academic? *Police Quarterly, 1* (3), 35–59.

Hilal, Susan, James Densley, and Ruohui Zhao (2013). Cops in college: Police officers' perceptions on formal education. *Journal of Criminal Justice Education, 24* (4), 461–477.

Hougland, Steven M. and Charles Mesloh (2005). Reliability of risk management data in measuring police performance: An initial empirical analysis. *Law Enforcement Executive Forum, 15* (1), 45–51.

President's Commission on Law Enforcement and Administration of Justice (1967). *The Challenge of Crime in a Free Society*. Washington, DC: U.S. Government Printing Office.

Reaves, Brian A. (2009). *State and Local Law Enforcement Training Academies, 2006*. Washington, DC: Bureau of Justice Statistics. Retrieved on October 15, 2014 from http://bjs.ojp.usdoj.gov/content/pub/pdf/slleta06.pdf.

Roberg, Roy and Scott Bonn (2004). Higher education and policing: Where are we now? *Policing: An International Journal of Police Strategies & Management, 27* (4), 469–486.

Rydberg, Jason and William Terrill (2010). The effect of higher education on police behavior. *Police Quarterly, 13* (1), 92–120.

U.S. Census Bureau (2014). *Florida QuickFacts from the U.S. Census Bureau.* Washington, DC: U.S. Census Bureau. Retrieved on October 10, 2014 from http://quickfacts.census.gov/qfd/states/12000.html.

CHAPTER 6

FLORIDA COURTS

Learning Objectives

After reading this chapter, you should be able to:

- Understand what the "Declaration of Rights" in the Florida Constitution means for the court system.
- Understand the mission statement of the Florida Supreme Court.
- Present the four levels of courts in Florida.
- Tell how Florida Supreme Court Justices are selected.
- Relay what a merit retention vote means.
- Appreciate the implications of Amendment #5 in the 2012 General Election.
- Give the three eligibility requirements that Supreme Court Justices must meet before taking office.
- Talk about the role of the Chief Justice of the Florida Supreme Court.
- List the different types of cases over which the Florida Supreme Court has jurisdiction.
- Speak about the functions of the District Courts of Appeal.
- Address what "judicial activism" means.
- Explore the implications that arise from Amendment #3 which appeared on the 2014 statewide ballot.
- Link circuit courts with the phrase "courts of general jurisdiction."
- Connect county courts with the phrase "courts of limited jurisdiction."
- Summarize the role of the Florida Board of Bar Examiners.
- Elaborate on the three criteria to become a lawyer in Florida.
- Describe what the term "suitable moral character" means for admission to the Florida Bar.
- Elaborate on the four major aims of the Florida Bar Association.
- Appreciate the role that the Office of the State Courts Administrator discharges.
- Understand how the judicial budget operates and where those monies go.
- Evaluate the caseload of Florida courts.
- Explore the role the state attorney plays in the Florida court system.
- List the requirements that one must satisfy in order to become a Florida state attorney.

- Amplify the issue decided by the federal Supreme Court in *Gideon v. Wainwright*.
- Present some of the standards used to determine whether a defendant qualifies for indigent status in Florida.
- Discuss efforts to recoup expenses from persons previously declared to be indigent.
- Talk about the conditions under which public defenders labor.
- Outline the responsibilities the clerk of the court discharges.
- Explain what a subpoena is.
- Identify some of the responsibilities of the Florida Attorney General.
- Appreciate the importance of Attorney General legal opinions.
- Expound upon what takes place during the booking phase.
- Account for what happens at first appearance.
- Explain what the filing of formal charges means.
- Elaborate on what occurs at arraignment.
- Amplify the activities that take place at a deposition.
- List some matters that pretrial motions explore.
- Differentiate between a bench trial and a trial by jury.
- Explore the jury selection process.
- Identify the goals involved in opening arguments.
- Summarize what takes place during jury instructions and jury deliberation.
- Appreciate the importance of sentencing guidelines.
- Present the principles that underlie Florida's sentencing guidelines.
- Evaluate whether Florida's sentencing guidelines have made progress towards satisfying the principles that underlie its construction.
- Understand why Florida turned to gain time as a way of dealing with prison overcrowding.
- Give a brief history of how Florida's sentencing guidelines came into existence.
- Evaluate whether Florida's Criminal Punishment Code has produced standardized and uniform sentencing practices throughout the state.

Introduction

The "Declaration of Rights" contained in the Florida Constitution (Article I, Section 21) gives a concise and very direct statement of how the Florida judicial system should carry on its daily business. That language reads, "The courts shall be open to every person for redress of any injury, and justice shall be administered without sale, denial or delay."

This cornerstone of justice is amplified in the mission statement prepared by the Supreme Court of the State of Florida. There the Court pronounces, "The mission of the judicial branch is to protect rights and liberties, uphold and interpret the law, and provide for the peaceful resolution of disputes" (Supreme Court of Florida, 2013). The Florida Supreme Court expands this foundation when it declares that "Justice in Florida will be accessible, fair, effective, responsive, and accountable" (Florida Office of the State Courts Administrator, 2014a).

Let us provide a backdrop to these pronouncements. Bear in mind that the boundaries of the State of Florida encompass almost 66,000 square miles (Bureau of Economic and Business Research, 2014). Florida is the third most populated state in the Union. It is currently home to more than 19 million persons who come from all races and all walks of life (U.S. Census Bureau, 2014). In addition, the state is subdivided into 67 counties which contain over 400 municipalities. When one considers how large and how diverse the State of Florida is, the mandate that the Florida state court system shoulders is a mammoth charge.

This chapter looks at how justice is delivered in the Florida courts. We will start by examining how the state court system is organized.

Florida Court Structure

The Florida court system is made up of two appellate-level courts and two trial-level courts. As Figure 6.1 portrays, the Florida Supreme Court and the five District Courts of Appeal form the appellate level. The twenty circuit court and 67 county courts are considered to be the basic trial courts. A closer examination of each court follows.

Florida Supreme Court

The Florida Supreme Court is the highest ranking judicial authority in the state. While seven Justices sit on the bench when it is full, at least five Justices are needed to form a quorum and at least four Justices must concur to form an opinion (*Florida Constitution*, Article V, Section 2). What would cause a Justice not to hear a case? It may be that the Justice had heard the case earlier and made a ruling at the lower court level prior to assuming a seat on the Florida Supreme Court. Another possibility is that the case is being handled by a law firm in which the Justice once held a proprietary interest. It may also be that a Justice has fallen ill and is not immediately available for service. As you can see, these circumstances might arise from time to time, but the Supreme Court's business must continue.

In years gone by, the Justices ran for office in an open, general election. However, having to muster a campaign and ask for monetary contributions while sitting on the bench led to some lapses in judgment and ethical matters. As a result, the selection process has taken many different forms over the years until evolving into the current practice (Rodriguez, 2005). Today, there is a Judicial Nominating Commission (JNC) in each circuit and in each county. The nine members of each JNC are appointed by the Governor. The local JNC fields applications from all interested parties whenever there is a post to be filled (see Figure 6.2). This Commission, operating as an arm of the Florida Bar Association, pares down the list of potential appointees to a minimum of three and a maximum of six names. The JNC then forwards the list to the Governor who makes the final choice of who should serve as a Supreme Court Justice (*Florida Constitution*, Article V, Section 11).

There have been some recent efforts to modify this scheme. After the Florida Supreme Court ruled that the language of several proposed constitutional amendments was confusing and, therefore, ineligible to appear on the 2012 ballot, the Legislature introduced legislation that would have modified the court's structure (No Author, 2011). House Bill 7111 called for dividing the Florida Supreme Court into two entities. The first would be a "Supreme Court of Civil Appeals" and the second would be a "Supreme Court of Criminal Appeals."

Figure 6.1 Diagram of the Florida State Court System

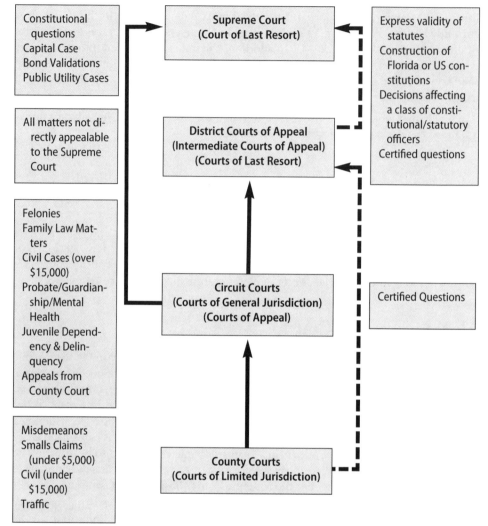

Source: Florida Office of the State Courts Administrator (2014b). *Diagram of the State Court System.* Tallahassee: Florida Supreme Court. Retrieved on October 22, 2014 from http://www.florida supremecourt.org/pub_info/CourtDiagram.pdf.

The plan also would have expanded the number of Justices from seven to ten positions, with the Governor appointing the three new Justices. While the measure passed the House, it stalled in the Senate and did not go further.

Supporters of House Bill 7111 quickly changed tactics. One popular reform mechanism is to bring state constitutional amendments directly before the voters. Such an initiative quickly materialized in this instance. The legislature placed this language on the November 2012 ballot which meant that Florida voters had the opportunity to decide on Amendment #5. Among other things, this proposal would have required Senate confirmation of any Supreme Court appointee advanced by the Governor before that person could sit on the state's high court bench. Voters defeated this proposal by a wide margin.

Figure 6.2 The First Page from the Florida Judge Application Form

APPLICATION FOR NOMINATION TO THE   COURT

(Please attach additional pages as needed to respond fully to questions.)

DATE: _____   Florida Bar No.: _____

GENERAL: Social Security No.: _____

1. Name _____   E-mail: _____

   Date Admitted to Practice in Florida: _____

   Date Admitted to Practice in other States: _____

2. State current employer and title, including professional position and any public or judicial office.

   _____

3. Business address: _____

   City _____ County _____ State _____ ZIP _____

   Telephone ( ) - _____ FAX ( ) - _____

4. Residential address: _____

   City _____ County _____ State _____ ZIP _____

   Since _____ Telephone ( ) - _____

5. Place of birth: _____

   Date of birth: _____ Age: _____

6a. Length of residence in State of Florida: _____

6b. Are you a registered voter? ☐ Yes ☐ No

   If so, in what county are you registered? _____

7. Marital status: _____

   If married: Spouse's name   _____

                 Date of marriage   _____

                 Spouse's occupation   _____

   If ever divorced give for each marriage name(s) of spouse(s), current address for each former spouse, date and place of divorce, court and case number for each divorce.

1

Rev. 100209-OGC

Source: Florida Bar (2014a). *Judicial Nominating Commission (JNC) Applications.* Tallahassee: The Florida Bar. Retrieved on October 22, 2014 from http://www.floridabar.org/TFB/TFBResources.nsf/Attachments/A3DFC294720BE5AE85257D270053B9B2/$FILE/REVISED%20JNC%20App%206-14.pdf?OpenElement.

As it stands right now, the initial appointment to the bench is followed by a merit retention vote after the Justice has been in office for at least a year. A *merit retention vote* is held during the general election. It involves all the registered voters in the state and the ballot carries a simple question. That is, "Shall Justice [insert name] be retained in office?" If the Justice receives a majority of the votes, he or she continues in that capacity for a six-year term. If the voters decline to retain a Justice in office, that action creates a vacancy which, once again, is vetted by the JNC which forwards an eligibility list to the Governor for final consideration (*Florida Constitution*, Article V, Section 10). This merit retention vote procedure is intended to spare judges from the onus of conducting a political campaign, reaching out for donations, and asserting political views when they are supposed to remain impartial (Hawkins, 2012). Florida judges face mandatory retirement once they reach their 70th birthday.

Candidates for the position of Florida Supreme Court Justice must meet certain eligibility requirements (*Florida Constitution*, Article V, Section 8). These standards include:

- Being a Florida resident;
- Being a registered voter in Florida; and
- Having practiced law in Florida for the past ten years.

The Supreme Court Justices select one member of the Court to serve a two-year term as Chief Justice. It is customary for the next most-senior Justice who has not served in that capacity to rotate into the position of Chief Justice (Anstead, Kogan, Hall, & Waters, 2005, p. 467). The Florida Supreme Court *Chief Justice* oversees all the courts in the state. He or she is in charge of the state court budget, appoints temporary judges when they are needed, and usually administers the oath when the Governor begins his or her term of office.

The Supreme Court, according to the Florida Constitution (Article V, Section 3), has jurisdiction over the following types of cases:

- Death penalty appeals;
- Advisory opinions to the Governor;
- Advisory opinions to the Attorney General regarding citizen petition initiatives to revise the state constitution;
- Reviews of local and state governmental bonds;
- Decisions regarding public utility matters reached by the Public Service Commission;
- Lower court rulings that deal with state statute or constitutional validity;
- Conflicting rulings among the district courts of appeal;
- Lower court rulings that have statewide implications;
- Applicability of federal decisions to the State of Florida; and
- Issuance of writs throughout the state.

District Courts of Appeal

As Figure 6.3 illustrates, there are five District Courts of Appeal (DCA) within the State of Florida. Each district court handles appeals from the lower courts in its geographical area. The 61 DCA judges must satisfy the same eligibility standards, appointment procedures, and merit retention requirements that apply to the state Supreme Court Justices.

There is some evidence that this judicial selection process permits the Governor to choose judges who are closely aligned with prevailing political viewpoints. There is an ongoing debate regarding *judicial activism*. Should judges act as champions of a cause and forge new territory with their rulings or should they show restraint and be content with merely offering an objective interpretation of the constitution and state laws? An analysis of judicial selections under Governor Bush concludes that "what now exists is closer to a system of gubernatorial appointments, in which a handpicked screening commission assists the governor, and but for errors in judgment, the commissioners will select nominees they believe share the administration's political, legal, ideological, and even religious views" (Salokar, Berggren, & DePalo, 2006, p. 139). Thus, Florida Governors are inclined to tilt matters by appointing judges who are sympathetic to their own views.

The issue of who has the authority to make judicial appointments and when culminated in Amendment #3 appearing on the November 2014 ballot. In the normal course of upcoming events, one Florida Supreme Court Justice is slated to retire in 2017 and the Governor will appoint a replacement at that time. Three more Florida Supreme Court Justices will have reached the mandatory retirement age by the end of 2018. They are scheduled to retire from the bench on January 8, 2019, the same day on which the incoming Governor will be sworn into office. These departures from the Florida high court carry two important implications. First, if replacements are not named in a timely manner, the Florida Supreme Court will not have a sufficient numbers of Justices to render decisions. If you recall, the Florida Constitution (Article V, Section 3) stipulates that five Justices constitute a quorum and all decisions require a majority of at least four Justices.

The second consideration is that the appointing Governor will have the power to stack the bench with justices who share his philosophy. Current Governor Rick Scott was re-elected to a second term in the November 2014 election. According to the Florida Constitution (Article IV, Section 5), Governor Scott will be term-limited and vacate office on January 8, 2019. The issue before the voters in the 2014 election was whether the exiting or the incoming Governor would fill the vacant judicial slots. The problem will be minimal if both Governors share the same political party affiliation. However, if the departing Governor and the incoming Governor come from opposite sides of the political spectrum, an inevitable squabble will arise over who has the power to fill the vacancies. If Florida voters had approved Amendment #3, then the outgoing Governor would make the appointment. However, Floridians rejected Amendment #3 in the 2014 election. In other words, the voters wish to see the incoming Governor assume the role of making judicial appointments. Obviously, those choices will shape the composition of the Florida Supreme Court and could alter its course for years to come.

In another related development, the Florida Bar (2014c) empaneled a special task force to examine the diversity of potential judicial appointees that emerged from the various JNCs and the Governor's subsequent selections. A certain amount of frustration became apparent. Governor Scott had rejected the slate of candidates that JNCs had forwarded on eighteen occasions. While that action is the Governor's prerogative, "no prior Governor of Florida has rejected a slate of JNC nominees presented by The Florida Bar" (Florida Bar, 2014c, p. 12). At the same time, one observer noted that of the 981 judges who presided in the state court system, only 16% were nonwhite and 34% were women (Taylor, 2014). Further inspection revealed a similarly disturbing trend. The JNCs themselves were largely devoid of minority members on the committees (Pettis, 2014). As a result, the Florida Bar formulated a series of recommendations aimed at seating a more representative judiciary.

Figure 6.3 Map of the Florida District Courts of Appeals

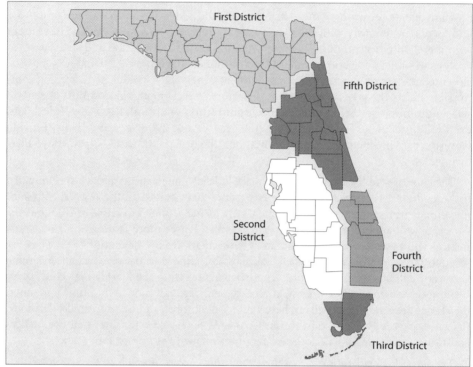

Source: Florida Office of the State Courts Administrator (2014c). *Florida Courts: District Courts of Appeal*. Tallahassee: Florida Supreme Court. Retrieved on October 22, 2014 from http://flcourts.org/ florida-courts/district-court-appeal.stml.

In terms of jurisdiction, each DCA reviews lower court decisions in its territory, decisions reached by state agencies, and a variety of writs. A party can appeal a DCA decision to the Florida Supreme Court and eventually to the United States Supreme, if necessary. However, there is no requirement that either the state or the federal supreme courts must review the case.

Circuit Courts

The circuit courts, *courts of general jurisdiction*, are where most criminal felony and civil trials typically originate. There are twenty judicial circuits in Florida with 599 judges appointed for six-year terms (Florida Office of the State Courts Administrator, 2014e). Each judge presides over his or her own courtroom. Some of the other cases that circuit courts have jurisdiction over include family law, juvenile cases, mental health, probate, guardianship, and civil lawsuits involving more than $15,000 in damages.

County Courts

County courts are sometimes considered to be *courts of limited jurisdiction*. They handle misdemeanor crimes, violations of municipal and county ordinances, small claims, land-

Figure 6.4 Map of the Florida Circuit Courts

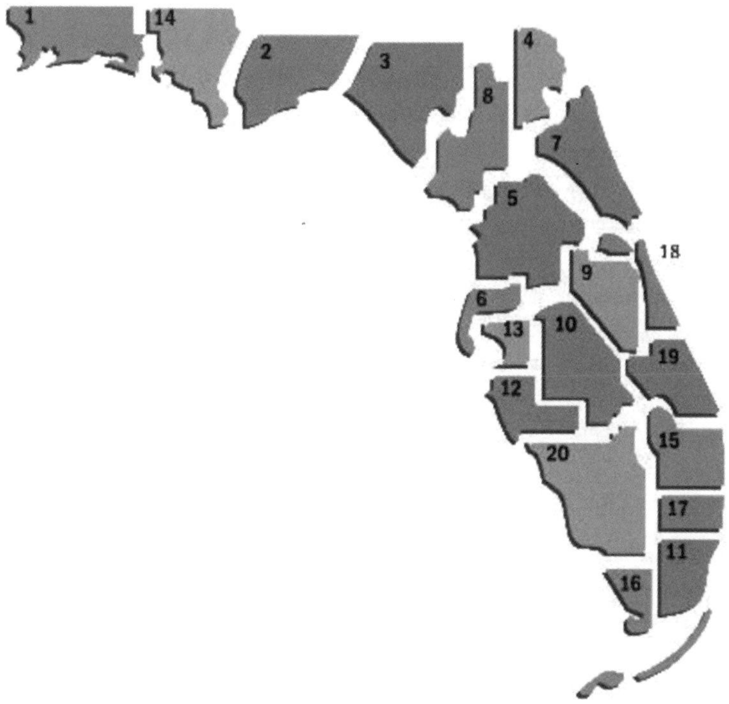

Source: Florida Office of the State Courts Administrator (2014d). *Florida Courts: Trial Courts–Circuit.*
Tallahassee: Florida Supreme Court. Retrieved on October 22, 2014 from http://flcourts.org/florida-courts/trial-courts-circuit.stml.

lord-tenant complaints, minor civil disputes, and traffic infractions. While the actual number of judges in each county depends upon the population size and caseload, there are a total of 322 county judges (Florida Office of the State Courts Administrator, 2014f).

Court Administration

There are three organizations within the Florida court system that play prominent roles in court administration. They are the Florida Board of Bar Examiners, the Florida Bar Association, and the Office of the State Courts Administrator. The Florida Board of Bar Examiners deals with admitting new lawyers to practice, the Florida Bar Association monitors attorney behavior, and the Office of the State Courts Administrator oversees judicial operations throughout the entire state. The following subsections will examine each of these groups more closely.

Florida Board of Bar Examiners

The Florida Board of Bar Examiners (FBBE) is an arm of the Florida Supreme Court. Its primary function is to ensure that all attorneys meet certain minimum standards to justify admission to the practice of law in Florida. Applicants must demonstrate competency in three general ways. They include:

- Graduate from a law school that is approved by the American Bar Association;
- Pass the Florida Bar Examination; and
- Demonstrate suitable moral character.

The Bar Exam is given twice a year and the latest administrations have a pass rate in the vicinity of 80% of the exam-takers (FBBE, 2014). The two-day test consists of both essay and multiple-choice questions that tap knowledge of Florida law, constitutional procedures, and court practices.

Suitable moral character means that the aspirant meets academic standards, has completed the appropriate academic preparation, has not been disbarred elsewhere, is not a convicted felon whose rights have not been restored, is financially responsibility, has not violated any professional obligations, is of sound mind, is not dependent on drugs or alcohol, and has not been disciplined by any other professional group (FBBE, 2011).

Once an aspirant satisfies these professional entrance criteria, then he or she is eligible to take the lawyer's oath and join the Florida Bar Association. Figure 6.5 reprints the Florida Lawyer's Oath. In addition to swearing to uphold the United States Constitution and the Florida Constitution, there is the recognition of ethical practices and appropriate conduct. Should a lawyer stray from this oath, that misbehavior falls under the purview of the Florida Bar Association.

Figure 6.5 Lawyer's Oath of Admission to the Florida Bar

I do solemnly swear:

I will support the Constitution of the United States and the Constitution of the State of Florida;

I will maintain the respect due to courts of justice and judicial officers;

I will not counsel or maintain any suit or proceedings which shall appear to me to be unjust, nor any defense except such as I believe to be honestly debatable under the law of the land;

I will employ for the purpose of maintaining the causes confided to me such means only as are consistent with truth and honor, and will never seek to mislead the judge or jury by any artifice or false statement of fact or law;

I will maintain the confidence and preserve inviolate the secrets of my clients, and will accept no compensation in connection with their business except from them or with their knowledge and approval;

I will abstain from all offensive personality and advance no fact prejudicial to the honor or reputation of a party or witness, unless required by the justice of the cause with which I am charged;

I will never reject, from any consideration personal to myself, the cause of the defenseless or oppressed or delay anyone's cause for lucre or malice.

So help me God.

Source: Florida Bar (2013a). *Oath of Admission to the Florida Bar.* Tallahassee: The Florida Bar. Retrieved on October 22, 2014 from http://www.floridabar.org/tfb/TFBProfess.nsf/basic+view/04E9EB581 538255A85256B2F006CCD7D?OpenDocument.

Florida Bar Association

Membership in the Florida Bar Association (FBA) is a requirement for all lawyers who practice law in Florida. Founded in 1889, the FBA today has over 90,000 members. The FBA has four major aims. They include public service, protecting rights, encouraging professionalism, and pursuing justice.

As the introduction to this chapter stated, the Florida Constitution envisions the ideal court system as one that is available to everybody. The Florida Supreme Court also echoes this same sentiment. Unfortunately, though, justice is out of the reach of many people. They simply cannot afford to hire an attorney and pay court fees. The FBA promotes access to justice by sponsoring a *pro bono* program. The phrase "pro bono" means for the public good. When translated into practice, it means that every Florida lawyer is expected to donate at least 20 hours of legal services or $350 a year to a legal aid organization (Florida Bar, 2013b). Lawyers can fulfill this duty by taking on cases at no charge to a deserving client, providing legal guidance to a charity, or in other ways.

A second FBA responsibility is to monitor and regulate the activities of its members. Clients can file a complaint if they feel they have received less than adequate legal representation from their attorney. The FBA investigates these matters, tries to resolve these concerns, and refer any unethical practices to the Florida Supreme Court. The Florida Supreme Court, in turn, handles attorney discipline and can, if need be, suspend or revoke a lawyer's license to practice.

The FBA requires members to update their education by completing 30 hours of professional education every three years. Another mechanism to maintain competency is the Board Certification Plan. This effort allows practicing lawyers to become immersed in specialty areas by taking courses, passing exams, and demonstrating proficiency in their practices. Publishing various trade journals, providing legal updates, and sponsoring conferences round out the FBA activities in this area.

Finally, regulating the practice of law is a dominant concern. The FBA oversees the FBBE and updates regulations for existing members. The FBA also engages in a number of outreach activities to school children and the general public.

Florida Office of the State Courts Administrator

The Office of the State Courts Administrator (SCA) is housed within the Florida Supreme Court. The SCA has oversight over all the court operations within the state. These functions range from research and planning to budgeting and staffing. This office prepares the annual state judiciary budget, makes legislative appearances, and serves as a liaison between the judiciary branch and other portions of state government. In one sense, then, the SCA is the hub of all judicial operations within the state.

Florida Court Operations

It might be worthwhile to look at the Florida court operations in a very broad context so as to place it within a proper context. The budget for the entire Florida judicial branch of government was $444 million for fiscal year 2012–13, down from $491 million allocated

**Figure 6.6 State Courts System Appropriations ($443 Billion) for
Fiscal Year 2013–14**

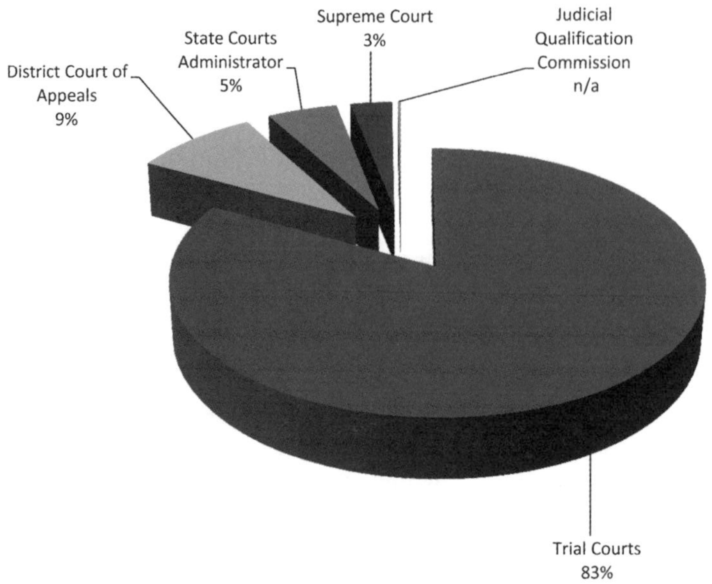

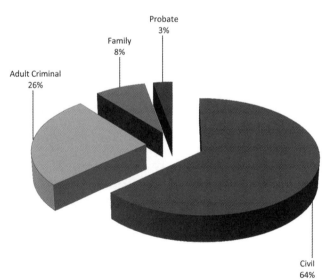

Source: Supreme Court of Florida (2013). *Florida State Courts: 2012–2013 Annual Report.* Tallahassee, FL: Florida Office of the State Courts Administrator. Retrieved on October 22, 2014 from http://www.flcourts.org/core/fileparse.php/248/urlt/annual_report1213.pdf.

**Figure 6.7 Cases Filed in Florida Trial Courts and District Courts of Appeals,
Fiscal Year 2012–13**

Source: Office of the State Courts Administrator (2011c). *The 2009–10 Florida State Courts Annual Report.* Tallahassee: Florida Supreme Court, p. 52. Retrieved on August 11, 2011 from http://www.flcourts.org/gen_public/pubs/bin/annual_report0910.pdf.

during the pre-recession 2007–08 fiscal year (Supreme Court of Florida, 2013). That current share represents 0.6% of the $70 billion budget for the entire state. As Figure 6.6 shows, the lion's share of these monies (83%) goes to the trial courts. If you recall from our earlier discussion, the trial courts include both the circuit courts and the county courts. The circuit courts are the courts of general jurisdiction. They handle felony cases, family law matters, civil disputes involving more than $15,000, probate, juvenile matters, and any appeals from the lower county courts. The county courts have much more limited jurisdiction. These courts process misdemeanors, small claims, small civil suits, and traffic cases.

Further inspection of Figure 6.6 reveals that the district courts of appeals receive a much smaller portion of the budget (9%). The DCAs handle matters that are referred from the lower trial courts. Finally, the Supreme Court garners 3% of the allocations. When all is said and done, approximately 95% of the judiciary funding is reserved for court operations.

The different mandates that the trial courts and courts of appeals become very evident in Figure 6.7 which describes the caseloads. Civil cases account for 64% of the proceedings and adult criminal cases occupy 26% of dockets in the Florida trial courts. While both criminal cases and post-conviction matters make up 61% of the agenda in the DCAs, 21% are post-conviction hearings (see Figure 6.8). Civil matters constitute 21% of the workload, while the remainder is devoted to administrative matters, juvenile concerns, family law, worker compensation, and probate.

A curious reader might wonder about what citizens get in return for these expenditures. A look at Figure 6.9 helps respond to this question. The National Center for State Courts

**Figure 6.8 Cases Filed in Florida District Courts of Appeals
Fiscal Year 2012–13**

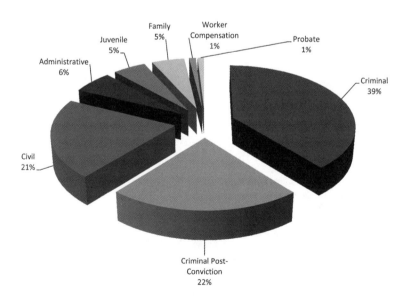

Source: Supreme Court of Florida (2013). *Florida State Courts: 2012–2013 Annual Report*, p. 64.Tallahassee, FL: Florida Office of the State Courts Administrator. Retrieved on October 22, 2014 from http://www.flcourts.org/core/fileparse.php/248/urlt/annual_report1213.pdf.

compiles information about judicial operations in various states. However, not all the states participate in this endeavor. The Florida circuit courts dealt with 1,817 criminal cases per 100,000 adults in 2010. When compared to the other reporting states, the Florida circuit courts carry a sizeable caseload.

Figure 6.10 contains a similar comparison of limited jurisdiction courts. With a caseload of 4,941 filings per 100,000 adults, the Florida courts have a medium-sized work schedule. When viewed in the context of case volume, it is understandable that the trial courts corral much of the judicial funding in the Sunshine State.

Despite the intensity of case processing, the judicial branch has faced the challenge of budget cuts. Recurring deficits in state revenues prompted the Florida Legislature to make across-the-board cuts. Judges and staff members took a 2% pay cut in 2009 (Florida Office

Figure 6.9 Criminal Cases per 100,000 Adults, Courts of General Jurisdiction, 2010

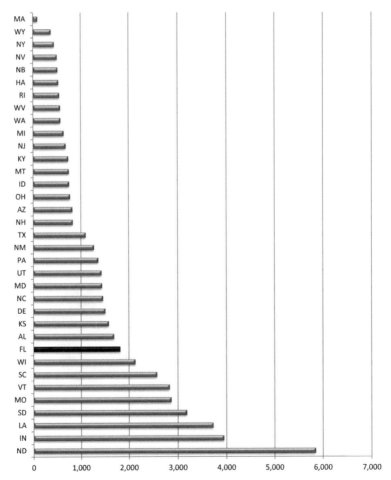

Source: LaFountain, Robert C., Shauna M. Strickland, Kathryn A., Holt, Brenda G. Otto, and Neal B. Kauder (2012). *Examining the Work of State Courts: An Analysis of 2010 State Court Caseloads*, p. 22. Williamsburg, VA: National Center for State Courts, p. 46. Retrieved on October 24, 2014 from http://www.courtstatistics.org/~/media/Microsites/Files/CSP/DATA%20PDF/CSP_DEC.ashx.

Figure 6.10 Criminal Cases per 100,000 Adults, Courts of Limited Jurisdiction, 2010

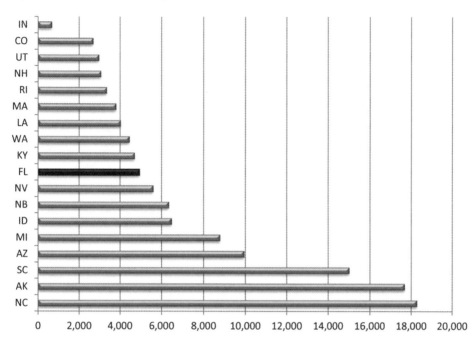

Source: LaFountain, Robert C., Shauna M. Strickland, Kathryn A., Holt, Brenda G. Otto, and Neal B. Kauder (2012). *Examining the Work of State Courts: An Analysis of 2010 State Court Caseloads*, p. 23. Williamsburg, VA: National Center for State Courts, p. 46. Retrieved on October 24, 2014 from http://www.courtstatistics.org/~/media/Microsites/Files/CSP/DATA%20PDF/CSP_DEC.ashx.

of the State Courts Administrator, 2010, p. 6). When the Legislature proposed an additional 10% cut for the 2010 budget on the heels of reductions during the previous three years, Chief Justice Quince balked at the idea. The Legislature was attempting to siphon monies from the "State Courts Revenue Trust Fund" and use these dollars for other purposes. In light of increased caseloads and the availability of fewer judges, the Chief Justice pled for a reprieve. While the judicial budget was spared, it is easy to envision that court budget needs will remain a sore spot in these troublesome economic times. As Chief Justice Polston recently explained:

> Funding remains a top concern for the judiciary. The branch of government does not have programs, it has people. In fact, 82 percent of our budget goes to pay salaries and benefits. So decisions made at the state level as to all state employees on pay and benefits have a dramatic effect on us (Supreme Court of Florida, 2013, p. 1).

Court Personnel

Court proceedings require a number of persons to do a variety of tasks in order to ensure smooth operations. Some of these roles include judges, bailiffs, stenographers, clerks, record custodians, judicial assistants, lawyers, jurors, witnesses, legal experts, and other parties. Without trying to diminish the importance of these court personnel, in the interest of space we will skip over their functions and focus on three more prominent roles. They include (1) the state attorney, (2) the public defender, and (3) the clerk of the court.

State Attorney

While prosecutors in some states are called "district attorneys," in Florida they are known as *state attorneys*. The Florida Constitution (Article V, Section 17) stipulates that each of the twenty judicial circuits shall be serviced by a state attorney. The state attorney or chief prosecutor is responsible for processing the cases of all persons arrested in that circuit and determining whether prosecution is warranted (*Florida Statutes 2014*, § 27).

Voters elect the state attorney to a four-year term of office. The Florida Constitution (Article V, Section 17) requires state attorneys to have been a member of the Florida Bar for at least five years and reside in the circuit they represent. State attorneys are allowed to hire assistant state attorneys to carry out actual prosecutorial duties in court. However, state attorneys are forbidden to practice law in a private capacity while they occupy office (*Florida Statutes 2014*, § 27.015) in order to avoid any pretense of a conflict of interest.

State Attorney Offices (SAO) employ assistant state attorneys to carry out actual prosecutorial duties on a day-to-day basis (*Florida Statutes 2014*, § 27.181). These lawyers appear before the circuit courts and county courts, representing the state's interests. Their caseloads involve felonies, misdemeanors, traffic violations, juvenile delinquency, and enforcement of local ordinances.

SAOs also require the services of special investigators. As we saw earlier in Table 5.2 when discussing law enforcement personnel, there were 224 SAO investigators working throughout Florida in 2013. In addition to possessing the full array of arrest powers, these individuals conduct criminal investigations, execute search and arrest warrants, and perform other related tasks (*Florida Statutes 2014*, § 27.255).

Public Defender

The counterpart of the state attorney is the public defender. The role of the *public defender* is to provide legal services to poor people who are facing criminal charges and the potential deprivation of liberty (see Figure 6.11). The public defender's office (PDO) came about as a result the United States Supreme Court decision *Gideon v. Wainwright* in 1963. Constitutional law was in its infancy in those days, but was evolving rapidly. Gideon was charged with burglary. Burglary, as we saw earlier in Chapter 4, is categorized as a felony in Florida. After he was arrested, Gideon asked the court to provide him with an attorney because he could not afford legal representation. It was the practice in those days that only defendants facing the death penalty were entitled to legal representation at no cost. Hence, the trial court denied Gideon's request for public counsel.

Because he had no money, Gideon had no choice except to proceed *pro se*. *Pro se* means that a person is representing himself or herself in court and lacks the advice or "guiding hand of counsel." Gideon's feeble attempts at self-representation ended very predictably in a finding of guilt, accompanied by a five-year prison sentence.

Gideon appealed his conviction and the United States Supreme Court granted *certiorari*. In other words, the Justices reviewed the case, determined that it involved a significant question, and agreed to hear Gideon's case. Given the magnitude of the case, the Court went so far as to appoint a lawyer to represent Gideon.

Figure 6.11 The Public Defender's Credo

I am a Public Defender.

I am the guardian of the presumption of innocence, due process and fair trial.

To me is entrusted the preservation of those sacred principles.

I will promulgate them with courtesy and respect but not with obsequiousness and not with fear.

For I am partisan; I am counsel for the defense.

Let none who oppose me forget that with every fiber of my being I will fight for my clients.

My clients are the indigent accused, they are the lonely, the friendless.

My voice will be raised in their defense.

I will resolve all doubt in their favor.

This will be my credo; this and the Golden Rule.

I will seek acclaim and approval only from my own conscience.

And upon my death, if there are a few lonely people who have benefited, my efforts will not have been in vain.

Source: Holt, Julianne M. (2014). *The Public Defender's Credo.* West Palm Beach, FL: Office of the Public Defender, 13th Judicial Circuit. Retrieved on October 24, 2014 from http://www.pd13.state.fl.us/Home.aspx.

The 6th Amendment to the United States Constitution, among other things, guarantees the right to an attorney in any criminal prosecution. Even though the Florida Constitution was silent on one's right to counsel, Gideon maintained that states had such an obligation under the due process clause of the 14th Amendment of the federal Constitution to provide for a fair trial. To make a long story short, the U.S. Supreme Court sided with Gideon. The Justices concluded that "any person hauled into court, who is too poor to hire a lawyer, cannot be assured of a fair trial unless counsel is provided for him" (p. 344). The Court remanded Gideon's case back to the trail court where, with the able assistance of counsel, he was acquitted of the burglary charge. As a result of *Gideon*, the public defender's office (PDO) came into being. Today, there is a PDO in each of Florida's judicial circuits, as well as throughout the United States.

As one might imagine, an outcry soon emerged from critics of the Court's ruling. They contended that the provision of legal counsel at taxpayer cost amounted to an exorbitant luxury. In response to this discontent, the states have tried numerous ways to restrict eligibility to meritorious cases. Florida has been one of those states. Figure 6.12 displays the application form that Florida uses today to determine whether an accused person qualifies for indigent status. *Indigent status* means that a person is too poor to afford to retain a lawyer. As you can see from the contents, there are specific inquiries into a person's income, assets, and liabilities and other obligations to help determine whether a public defender is warranted.

If after reviewing the indigent status application the Clerk of the Court (COC) determines the applicant is experiencing a substantial financial hardship, then the COC can declare the defendant eligible for public defender representation. That means the state will provide counsel at no cost or at a reduced cost. Should the defendant's financial circumstances change at a later date, it is always possible for a judge to enter an order for partial or full recovery of the PDO expenses. In the event that the court does appoint an attorney to represent the indigent defendant, then that attorney is charged with representing the best interests of his or her client.

Figure 6.12 Florida Application Form for Determining Criminal Indigent Status

IN THE CIRCUIT/COUNTY COURT OF THE SECOND JUDICIAL CIRCUIT
IN AND FOR LEON COUNTY, FLORIDA

STATE OF FLORIDA,

vs.   Case #: _____

_____
Defendant/Minor Child.

APPLICATION FOR CRIMINAL INDIGENT STATUS

_____I AM SEEKING THE APPOINTMENT OF THE PUBLIC DEFENDER

OR

_____I HAVE A PRIVATE ATTORNEY OR AM SELF-REPRESENTED AND SEEK DETERMINATION OF INDIGENT STATUS FOR COSTS.

Notice to Applicant: The provision of a public defender/court appointed lawyer and costs/due process services are not free. A judgment and lien may be imposed against all real or personal property you own to pay for legal and other services provided on your behalf or on behalf of the person for who you are making this application. There is a $50.00 fee for each application filed. If the application fee is not paid to the Clerk within 7 days, it will be added to any costs that may be assessed against you at the conclusion of this case. If you are a parent/legal guardian making this application on behalf of a minor or tax dependent adult, the information contained in this application must include your income and assets.

1. **I have _____dependents.** *(Do not include children not living at home and do not include a working spouse or yourself.)*

2. **I have a take home income of $_____** paid ( ) weekly ( ) every two weeks ( ) semi-monthly ( ) monthly ( ) yearly
*(Take home income equals salary, wages, bonuses, commissions, allowances, overtime, tips and similar payments, **minus** deductions required by law and other court-ordered support payments.)*

3. **I have other income** paid ( ) weekly ( ) every two weeks ( ) semi-monthly ( ) monthly ( ) yearly. *(Circle "Yes" and fill in the amount if you have this kind of income, otherwise circle "No")*

Social Security benefits......................Yes $ _____ No	Veterans' benefits ....Yes $ _____ No	
Unemployment compensation....................Yes $ _____ No	Child support or other regular support	
Union Funds...Yes $ _____ No	from family members/spouse ....Yes $ _____ No	
Workers Compensation............................Yes $ _____ No	Rental income ....Yes $ _____ No	
Retirement/pensions ....Yes $ _____ No	Dividends or interest.......................................Yes $ _____ No	
Trusts/gifts...Yes $ _____ No	Other kinds of income not on the list ....Yes $ _____ No	

4. **I have other assets:** *(Circle "yes" and fill in the value of the property, otherwise circle "No"; use the back to provide additional information)*

Cash..Yes $ _____ No	Savings ....Yes $ _____ No
Bank account(s) ....Yes $ _____ No	Stocks/bonds..Yes $ _____ No
Certificates of deposit or	*Equity in real estate (excluding homestead) ....Yes $ _____ No
money market accounts ....Yes $ _____ No	List the address of this property _____
*Equity in motor vehicles/boats/ ....Yes $ _____ No	* Equity means value minus loans. Also list any
other tangible property	expectancy in an interest in such property.
List the year/make/model & tag #_____	

5. **I have total liabilities and debts in the amount of $_____.**

6. **I receive:** *(Circle "Yes" or "No")*
   Temporary Assistance for Needy Families – Cash Assistance ....Yes   No
   Poverty-related Veterans' Benefits...Yes   No
   Supplemental Security Income (SSI) ....Yes   No

7. **I have been released on bail in the amount of $_____.   Cash ___ Surety ___   Posted by: Self ___ Family ___ Other _____**

A person who knowingly provides false information to the clerk or the court in seeking a determination of indigent status under FS 27.52 commits a misdemeanor of the first degree, punishable as provided in FS 775.082 or 775.083. **I attest that the information I have provided on this application is true and accurate to the best of my knowledge.**

Signed on _____ day of _____, 20____.

_____   Signature of Applicant for Indigent Status
                                                 Print Full Legal Name _____
Date of Birth   Driver License #   Phone Number: _____
                                                 _____
                                                 _____
                                                 Address, City, State, Zip Code

- -

CLERK DETERMINATION

_____ Based on the information in this Application and the statutorily required motor vehicle and property records review, I have determined the applicant to be ( ) Indigent and the Public Defender is appointed to this case until relieved by the Court; or ( ) Not Indigent.

_____ I certify that a review of motor vehicle and property records was performed and no vehicle or property records were found or those found match those listed in this application.

_____ I certify that a review of motor vehicle and property records was performed and records were found that are not listed in this application.

Date: _____.   Clerk of the Circuit Court by _____

This form was completed with the assistance of: _____
                                                        Clerk/Deputy Clerk/Other authorized person

APPLICANTS FOUND NOT TO BE INDIGENT MAY SEEK REVIEW BY A JUDGE BY ASKING FOR A HEARING TIME. Sign here if you want the judge to review the clerk's determination of not indigent. _____

Rev. 07/09/2010   Developed by the Florida CCOC

Source: Leon County Clerk of Courts (2010). *Application for Criminal Indigent Status.* Tallahassee, FL: Leon County Clerk of Courts. Retrieved on October 23, 2014 from http://www.clerk.leon.fl.us/sections/clerk_services/online_forms/criminal/criminal_indigent.pdf.

A recent high-profile case provides an example of how the authorities might recoup their costs. Casey Anthony, the mother of a two-year-old, was charged with the murder of her daughter. After spending three years in pretrial detention, an Orlando jury voted for an *acquittal*. In other words, the jurors found Anthony not guilty of homicide on July 5, 2011. Since the court had declared Anthony indigent, the state shouldered almost $1 million dollars in legal fees, court costs, and other expenses. Some observers speculate that Anthony is now in a position to profit from her experience. Granting movie rights, writing a book, giving interviews, appearing on television shows, participating in media stories, and other sundry activities could land Casey Anthony a windfall profit. Prosecutors in the case have argued that Anthony ought to be required to reimburse the state should an unexpected bounty materialize. Because Anthony filed for and was granted bankruptcy protection, this question is moot for the moment.

There are also some concerns about the quality of representation clients receive from the PDO. Funding cuts have stretched resources thinly and have forced some PDOs to operate on a shoe-string budget. One estimate is that Florida PDOs, given the volume of cases, are able to devote an average of two hours per client (Young, 2013). Despite having been in existence for more than forty years, the first census of PDOs was conducted in 2007 (Farole & Langton, 2010a; Langton & Farole, 2010). Those results paint a troubling picture across the nation. PDOs typically operate with extremely high caseloads, inadequate staffing, and limited resources. As Farole and Langton (2010b, p. 88) explain:

> If public defenders are available to work 1,800 hours per year, they can devote, on average, about 5 to 6 hours per case. This would include pre-trial activities and preparation, client contact, investigation, legal research, filing motions, time in court, and all other relevant activities. This calculation further relies on the unrealistic assumption that public defenders have no additional responsibilities, such as continuing legal education, staff meetings, and other administrative duties, all of which reduce the time they can devote to direct client representation.

On top of all the responsibilities and demands that assistant state attorneys (ASA) and assistant public defenders (APD) shoulder, salaries are simply inadequate to retain competent staff members. As a result, these offices have become short-term grooming grounds. The average entry-level salary ($42,000) that a Florida ASA/APD earns lags behind their counterparts throughout the nation. K–12 teachers in the Sunshine State have higher annual earnings even though their pay ranks 47th in the country (TaxWatch, 2014). This dismal situation translates into an inability to retain experienced and talented employees. With turnover rates hovering in the vicinity of 17–20%, staff departures have become a huge administrative nightmare.

Given this dire picture of the strain between workload demand and available resources, what happens to the quality of PDO representation? Williams (2002) raised this very question when she compared criminal case outcomes between PDOs and private attorneys in one north Florida county. The results indicated that the type of attorney had no impact on sentencing outcome and length of sentence. Thus, PDOs were on par in terms of job performance with private attorneys.

Despite Williams' (2002) reassuring finding, there are other indications that not all is well with the delivery of indigent defense services. Funding shortages are rampant, prompting deep budget cuts in several Florida counties (National Right to Counsel Committee, 2009, p. 60) and there are instances where PDOs are not able to service all their clients in a timely manner (National Right to Counsel Committee, 2009, p. 100). Obviously, reforms need to be introduced and the situation will continue to require ongoing monitoring. As one commentator (Mandel, 2009, p. 44) recently wrote:

Florida's public defender offices are at the mercy of government funding. Florida's public defender offices are so under-funded and under-staffed that it is virtually impossible to adequately and completely fulfill the scope of representation to indigent defendant as defined by law.

Clerk of the Court

The Florida Constitution (Article V, Section 16) establishes the clerk of the circuit court (CCC) in each of Florida's 67 counties. The actual duties of the CCC are spelled out in Chapter 28 of *Florida Statutes*.

The major duty of the CCC is to act as a depository for all the official records in the county. Theoretically, court rulings are not finalized until they are recorded with the CCC. Some of these instruments kept on file include:

- Deeds, leases, bills of sale, mortgage papers, liens, and tax warrants;
- Court judgments;
- Military discharge papers of residents;
- Tax liens;
- Bankruptcy petitions;
- Copies of death certificates;
- Marriage and divorce records; and
- Wills and probate records (*Florida Statutes 2014*, § 28).

The CCC also collects filing fees for both civil and criminal court cases, traffic citations, mortgage foreclosures, child support payments, and other matters. This office also handles the disbursement of monies into various trust funds, collecting fines and forfeitures, costs of documentary stamps, witness and juror fees, and other legal fees. One of the more important criminal justice tasks the CCC discharges is issuing jury summons and witness subpoena. A *subpoena* is an official court document that commands the recipient's presence at a legal proceeding so that he or can give testimony. A *subpoena duces tecum* also requires the subpoenaed person to bring any relevant papers, reports, and other pertinent documents to the hearing. Usually, civilian witnesses receive the first type of a subpoena and law enforcement personnel receive the *subpoena duces tecum*. Figure 6.13 contains a blank copy of the *subpoena duces tecum* form.

Attorney General

The premier legal officer in Florida is the state attorney general. The *attorney general* (AG), an elected official, defends the state in any litigation, acts as a statewide prosecutor, is involved in capital collateral or death penalty appeals, renders advice to governmental officials, handles cases in front of all the District Courts of Appeals and the Florida Supreme Court, protects civil rights, and assumes several other functions (*Florida Statutes 2014*, § 16.01). The AG has played a prominent role in such things as the BP Deepwater Horizon oil spill in the Gulf of Mexico, gang-related and organized crime activity, suppressing price-gouging during disaster conditions, prosecuting white-collar and racketeering offenses, convening the statewide grand jury, promoting sunshine laws in local government and public records requests, combating child pornography, and other things.

Figure 6.13 An Example of a *Subpoena Duces Tecum*

IN THE CIRCUIT/COUNTY COURT OF THE SECOND JUDICIAL CIRCUIT
IN AND FOR LEON COUNTY, FLORIDA

_____
              Plaintiff,   CASE NO. _____

vs.

_____
              Defendant.

SUBPOENA DUCES TECUM

STATE OF FLORIDA

TO:

        YOU ARE HEREBY COMMANDED to appear before the Honorable _____,
Judge of the Court, at the Leon County Courthouse, 301 S. Monroe Street, Tallahassee, FL
32301, on _____, 20___, at _____ .m., to testify in this action and to have
with you at that time and place the following:

        If you fail to appear, you may be in contempt of court.
        You are subpoenaed to appear by the following attorney and unless excused from this
subpoena by this attorney or the court, you shall respond to this subpoena as directed.
        DATED_____.

_____   BOB INZER
Attorney for _____   CLERK OF THE CIRCUIT COURT
_____
_____   By: _____
FL Bar #: _____   Deputy Clerk

**IF YOU ARE A PERSON WITH A DISABILITY WHO NEEDS ANY
ACCOMMODATION IN ORDER TO PARTICIPATE IN THIS
PROCEEDING, YOU ARE ENTITLED, AT NO COST TO YOU, TO THE
PROVISION OF CERTAIN ASSISTANCE. PLEASE CONTACT DANNY
DAVIS, OFFICE OF THE COURT ADMINISTRATOR, 301 S. MONROE
ST., ROOM 215, TALLAHASSEE, FL 32301, (850) 577-4444, AT LEAST 7
DAYS BEFORE YOUR SCHEDULED COURT APPEARANCE, OR
IMMEDIATELY UPON RECEIVING THIS NOTIFICATION IF THE
TIME BEFORE THE SCHEDULE APPEARANCE IS LESS THAN 7 DAYS.
IF YOU ARE HEARING OR VOICE IMPAIRED, CALL 711.**

Rev. 06/08/2010

Source: Leon County Clerk of the Courts (2010). *Online Forms: General Court Forms, Subpoena Duces
Tecum.* Tallahassee: Leon County Clerk of the Courts. Retrieved on October 23, 2014 from http://
www.clerk.leon.fl.us/sections/clerk_services/online_forms/general/subpoena_duces_tecum.pdf.

One of the more important functions the AG shoulders is to issue legal advice to governmental officials. Quite often, state laws have unintended gaps in their provisions. Whenever state and local officials encounter an absence of any legislative guidance or court rulings on the matter, they can ask the AG to render an opinion as to what course of action they should pursue. When the AG issues a legal opinion, that interpretation is considered to be "persuasive authority," but not necessarily a "binding order." Nevertheless, AG opinions are useful stop-gap measures. For instance, several years ago when "designer drugs" first became popular, they were not listed explicitly by name under the schedule of drugs within state laws. In a legal opinion, General Butterworth declared that since the underlying chemical compounds were of a similar nature to already outlawed substances, law enforcement officials could conduct investigations and make arrests for possession and use of the so-called "date-rape drug" rohypnol or "roofies" under existing statutes (Butterworth, 1996). The Legislature fixed this gap in the next session by amending the pertinent state statutes so that it complied with the AG legal opinion.

More recently, General Bondi invoked the powers of her office when she filed an emergency rule on January 26, 2011 declaring a 90-day temporary ban on the sale, possession, and use of mephedrone and methyloine, more commonly known as "bath salts" (Bondi, 2011). The Florida Legislature eventually approved House Bill 1039 which classified these substances as a Schedule I drug. Governor Scott signed the bill into law on May 31, 2011.

Post-Arrest and Pretrial Activities

As mentioned earlier, this guide to the Florida criminal justice system does not intend to replace the major textbook in your course. Instead, its goal is to supplement and augment the course text by highlighting practices that are pertinent to the State of Florida. The interested reader will find the *Florida Rules of Criminal Procedure* (FRCP), distributed by the Florida Bar (2014), to be an indispensable reference when dealing with the intricacies of the criminal justice procedures in the Sunshine State.

This section examines the post-arrest and pretrial activities. One thing that Florida is attempting to do is to standardize criminal justice operations so there is some uniformity in how justice is delivered. The FRCP represents a concerted effort in that direction. As a result, this section will look at what takes place during booking, what happens at first appearance, the filing of formal charges, arraignment, as well as pretrial investigation and motions. Later, we will turn to the activities associated with the trial phase.

Booking

Booking refers to the post-arrest situation where a law enforcement officer takes a suspect into physical custody, delivers that arrested person to the jail, and completes additional paperwork. Among other things, the arresting officer constructs a written *affidavit* (a sworn statement to the court) in which he or she provides the details behind the offense and the arrest. In that document, the officer must (1) establish proper *jurisdiction* (when and where the crime took place), (2) match the suspect's behavior with the elements of the offense, and (3) develop *probable cause* or an explanation as to why the officer thinks this is the person who committed the crime. Once these tasks are completed, the

Figure 6.14 Right to Pretrial Release from Detention, Florida Constitution

> Unless charged with a capital offense or an offense punishable by life imprisonment and the proof of guilt is evident or the presumption is great, every person charged with a crime or violation of municipal or county ordinance shall be entitled to pretrial release on reasonable conditions. If no conditions of release can reasonably protect the community from risk of physical harm to persons, assure the presence of the accused at trial, or assure the integrity of the judicial process, the accused may be detained.

Source: Florida Constitution, Article I, Section 14.

arresting officer turns over custody of the suspect to the correctional officers at the sheriff's office.

The booking officer at the jail checks the arresting officer's paper work to determine what crime with which the suspect is charged and then consults a standard bail/bond schedule. The *standard bail/bond schedule* contains a list of all criminal offenses and the corresponding bond amount for each offense. While there is no one standard bail/bond schedule for the entire state, usually the circuit court in an area has established such a guide. As you can imagine, maintaining somebody in custody can be expensive item for taxpayers to shoulder. If the suspect does not pose a threat to public safety and is not expected to flee the jurisdiction, then releasing him or her from jail will save taxpayer dollars.

Crimes are divided into bondable or nonbondable offenses. A *bondable offense* means that a person accused of this crime is eligible to post a bond and be released from jail pending trial (see Figure 6.14). A *nonbondable offense* refers to a crime for which the court has declined to set a release amount. Some nonbondable offenses would include homicide, any life felony, numerous violent felonies, domestic violence charges, and stalking. Persons charged with a nonbondable offense are not given the opportunity to make bail and must remain in jail until first appearance. The judge may consider bail options at that time.

If the arrested person is charged with a bondable offense, then he or she is eligible for release. Suppose that Frank is charged with simple battery, a first-degree misdemeanor, and the schedule lists a $500 bond. If Frank can make a $500 deposit, then he will be released from custody pending trial. This practice is considered to be a *cash bond*. If Frank does not have sufficient funds available, he can contact a bondsman. Should Frank pass that evaluation, then the bondsman will post a surety bond for Frank. A *surety bond* means that Frank will pay the bondsman a nonrefundable 10% deposit, in this case $50. The bondsman then posts bail on behalf of Frank and Frank will be released from jail pending trial.

First Appearance

Depriving a person of his or her freedom is a serious matter in a democratic society. As the *Florida Constitution* (Article I, Section 9) explains, "No person shall be deprived of life, liberty or property without due process of law." Furthermore, Section 14 states, "every person charged with a crime or violation of municipal or county ordinance shall be entitled to pretrial release on reasonable conditions."

An arrested person must be brought before a judge within 24 hours of his or her arrest (FRCP, 2014, Rule 3.130). The purpose of *first appearance* is to inform the defendant of the charges, provide the arrested person with a copy of the complaint, and inform the defendant of the right to counsel. If the person is unable to afford an attorney, the judge may appoint counsel to represent the defendant. If you recall, Figure 6.12 contains a copy of an application for indigent status.

The judge may also consider pretrial release at first appearance. The purpose of bail is to ensure that the defendant is neither a menace to society nor a *flight risk* (*Florida Statutes 2014*, § 903.046). In other words, bail is used to guarantee that the accused will appear for trial. The judge will consider the nature of the charge, the evidence, ties to the local community, previous criminal history, and any other relevant facts. The judge can also impose special conditions for pretrial release (surrender a passport, no out-of-state travel, no victim contact, etc.).

Filing Formal Charges

If the defendant remains in pretrial detention after first appearance, the state attorney has 21 days to investigate and decide whether formal charges are forthcoming. If the state attorney does not file an *information* or notice of charges, the defendant can ask the court to be released on his or own recognizance (ROR). The prosecution can counter with a request for a seven-day extension. However, if the state still has not filed charges at the end of thirty days, the court can order the release of the defendant from pretrial confinement on a "released on recognizance" (ROR) basis. *Released on recognizance* means the person is released from custody without having to put up any bail or bond money. If the state can convince the court otherwise, the defendant will remain in pretrial detention. However, there is a mandatory release on the 40th day if the state attorney has not filed charges by that time.

Arraignment

The *arraignment* is the court hearing at which the defendant is informed of the pending charges. After the charges are read, the court will ask the accused to enter a plea of either nolo contendere, guilty, or not guilty. If the defendant enters a "not guilty" plea, then the judge will schedule the case for trial. Should the defendant plead guilty or not contest the charges, the judge can move to a sentencing hearing and dispose of the case.

Investigation and Deposition

As part of its investigation and trial strategy development, the defense may decide that it wishes to speak with witnesses in order to gather more information. Some witnesses may agree to talk freely with the defense attorney in an informal setting; other witnesses may decline to do so. If that is the situation, then the defense attorney may decide to depose a witness. A *deposition* means that a witness is subpoenaed to produce testimony. Three parties, in addition to the subpoenaed witness, are usually present at a deposition. They are the defense attorney, the assistant state attorney to whom the case is assigned, and a court stenographer. Typically, a judge is not present. The court stenographer will swear in the witness and then record the session. The defense attorney is entitled to ask the witness questions and the witness must respond truthfully to the queries. At the end of the deposition, the witness can either sign a waiver that he or she does not wish to review the printed script of the recording or the witness can indicate that he or she wishes to read the deposition before signing it. If a witness does not dispute the contents of a deposition or corrections have been made, then he or she will be asked to sign the deposition. That signature indicates the contents of the transcript are accurate and true.

There are two advantages behind deposing witnesses. The first reason is to learn more about the circumstances surrounding the alleged crime and suspect. The second is to create a record that can be used, if necessary, to discredit a witness. Should a witness change his or her testimony during trial, the defense attorney can point to a discrepancy with what the witness stated during the deposition. Of course, should a witness disappear or die and not be able to attend the trial, the deposition might be an acceptable substitute for that testimony.

Pretrial Motions

There are a number of motions the defense attorney can file prior to the start of a trial. Some of these motions may argue the legitimacy of the charges on technical grounds, problems with unlawful searches and/or seizures, defective warrants, illegally obtained confessions, the defendant's mental competency, discovery, and other matters.

Speedy trial is one of those matters. *Speedy trial* means that the state must commence prosecution within 90 days of arrest for a misdemeanor and within 175 days for a felony case (FRCP, 2014, Rule 3.191). If the state attorney fails to meet those deadlines, then the court will terminate the case.

Section Summary

Once all these steps are completed, the case is ready to move into the trial phase. As we shall see in a moment, the trial phase involves a number of critical decisions. We shall examine some of the more prominent junctures.

Trial Activities

The trial phase is where a determination is made as to whether the defendant is guilty or not guilty of the charges. This section examines the activities that take place during this period. As a result, we will look at the two types of criminal trials, jurors, how the trial proceeds, and jury deliberations.

Type of Trial

The first decision the defense must make is whether to seek a bench trial or a jury trial. A *bench trial* means that the judge will hear the case and determine whether the defendant is guilty or not guilty of the charges. A *jury trial* occurs when the defendant asks for a group of peers, not the judge, to decide whether he or she is guilty or not guilty of the charges. The judge, of course, still presides over the trial.

The Florida Constitution (Article I, Section 22) guarantees citizens the right to a jury trial. It reads "The right of trial by jury shall be secure to all and remain inviolate. The

**Figure 6.15 U.S. Supreme Court Upholds Florida's Use of a Six-Person Jury in
Criminal Trials**

> The question in this case, then, is whether the constitutional guarantee of a trial by "jury"
> necessarily requires trial by exactly 12 persons, rather than some lesser number—in this case,
> six. We hold that the 12-man panel is not a necessary ingredient of "trial by jury," and that re-
> spondent's refusal to impanel more than the six members provided for by Florida law did not
> violate petitioner's Six Amendment rights as applied to the States through the Fourteenth.

Source: Williams v. Florida, 399 U.S. 86 (1978).

qualifications and the number of jurors, not fewer than six, shall be fixed by law." Although
the actual size of the jury may vary depending on the type of trial (see Figure 6.15), this
same sentiment about the availability of a trial by jury is embodied in the United States
Constitution. There, the 6th Amendment states "In all criminal prosecutions, the accused
shall enjoy the right to a speedy and public trial, by an impartial jury of the State and
district wherein the crime shall have been committed …."

Now that we understand the basis for a jury trial, the next consideration is how a jury
is empaneled. The jury selection process is explored next.

Jury Selection

In the past, potential jurors were identified through county voter registration lists.
This procedure, though, did not always ensure that jurors were representative of the
local population. As a result, Florida now relies upon a list of adult citizens who have
received either a driver's license or state-issued identification card or have volunteered
for jury duty to form the potential juror pool (*Florida Statutes 2014*, § 40.01-40.011).
However, convicted felons whose civil rights have not been restored, persons found
guilty of perjury or other forms of lying, anybody who is being prosecuted for a crime,
and mentally incompetent individuals are disqualified from juror service (Florida Office
of the State Courts Administrator, 1996, pp. 2–11). Other persons (i.e., law enforcement
officers, elderly persons, persons who have performed juror duty within the past year,
and pregnant women) are exempted automatically from jury duty. Judges can excuse
practicing attorneys, medical doctors, disabled persons, and anybody with an extreme
hardship from jury duty.

The document that commands a person to report to the courthouse for this civic duty
is called a *jury summons* and the group that arrives at the courthouse for jury duty is
called a *venire*. The process of *voir dire* ("speaking the truth") can begin once the venire
is assembled. Both the defense attorney and the state attorney are allowed to question
prospective jurors to see whether these persons can be fair and impartial deliberators. If
there is an indication of an interfering bias (i.e., a personal relationship, prejudice, a
preformed opinion), then either lawyer can ask the judge to dismiss the juror. This request
is called a *challenge by cause* and both sides have an unlimited number of such objections.

A second mechanism for removing a potential juror is called a *peremptory challenge*.
The objecting attorney does not have to explain his or her reasons to the judge in this
type of a challenge. He or she registers the objection with the court and the judge then
excuses the juror. There is not an endless supply of peremptory challenges. If the trial

Figure 6.16 Oath Administered to Trial Jurors

Do you solemnly swear (or affirm) that you will well and truly try the issues between the State of Florida and the defendant and render a true verdict according to the law and the evidence, so help you God?

Source: Florida Bar (2014b). Rule 3.360: Oath of Trial Jurors. *Florida Rules of Criminal Procedure.* Tallahassee: Florida Bar. Retrieved on October 23, 2014 from http://www.floridabar.org/TFB/TFB Resources.nsf/Attachments/BDFE1551AD291A3F85256B29004BF892/$FILE/Criminal.pdf?OpenElement.

involves a capital or life felony case, then each side is entitled to ten peremptory challenges. That number drops to six for all other felonies and three for misdemeanors (FRCP, 2014, Rule 3.350). However, the court at its discretion can allow additional peremptory challenges.

Once a jury is seated, the members are sworn into service. Figure 6.16 presents the oath that jurors take when they are sworn into duty at the start of a trial. Florida utilizes a jury of twelve persons in capital cases and six persons in all other criminal cases (*Florida Statutes 2014*, § 913.10).

Opening Arguments

Once the jury is seated, it is time to start the actual trial. One of the first things to occur is that either the state attorney or the defense attorney will ask the judge to invoke "The Rule." What "The Rule" means is that the judge will instruct all the witnesses in the case that they are not to discuss any details of the case with each other. The state attorney or the defense attorney are the only persons with whom a witness may confer outside the courtroom. The purpose behind this warning is to preserve each witness' individual testimony rather than a recollection shared by others.

Under our adversarial system of justice, the defendant is assumed to be innocent and the burden of proof falls upon the state. As a result, the state makes its opening arguments first. The *opening argument* is an opportunity for the state attorney to explain what type of a crime took place and why the defendant is accused of being the perpetrator. Once the state attorney finishes, the defense attorney presents a rebuttal. More than likely, the defense attorney will remind jurors that the standard of proof they are to apply is *proof beyond a reasonable doubt*. That is, by the time the trial ends, the state needs to have shown that there is no doubt the defendant is the one who committed the crime.

State's Presentation

The state attorney opens the prosecution by calling witnesses to the stand. After a witness is sworn in, the state attorney asks a series of questions designed to demonstrate certain facts. Usually, the first person to testify is the law enforcement officer who was the first to arrive at the scene. The *direct examination* will consist of the state attorney asking the witness to provide a narrative of the events and how he or she came to learn what took place. Once the state attorney is finished asking questions, the defense attorney has the opportunity to conduct a *cross-examination* of the witness. In other words, the defense attorney will ask further questions aimed at undermining some of the facts that the state has attempted to establish. Once the state has cross-examined all the witnesses it intends to call to the stand, the prosecution will rest and attention turns to the defense.

Defense's Presentation

Once the state has concluded its presentation, the defense may make a motion for *judgment of acquittal*. In other words, the defense attorney is asking the judge to rule on whether or not the state has proved its case against the defendant. The trial ends if the judge agrees that the state has not proven the defendant is guilty beyond a reasonable doubt. Should the judge deny this motion, the defense begins to call its witnesses to the stand for direct examination. The defense attorney may try to impeach the testimony of earlier witnesses or may introduce new evidence in an attempt to raise doubts about the state's case. Of course, the prosecutor will have the opportunity to cross-examine the defense witnesses. Once all the witnesses have testified in the case, the trial moves to closing arguments.

Closing Arguments

The *closing argument* phase of the trial allows the state to summarize the facts and the evidence in the case. Once the state attorney has completed his or her presentation, the defense has the opportunity to present a similar concluding argument. Once both sides have completed their arguments, the focus turns to the jury.

Jury Instructions

After both sides have rested, the judge takes over and explains to the jury what questions or issues they need to discuss. Both the state and the defense have had the opportunity to discuss the points they would like the judge to make and refrain from making to the jury. Florida has constructed a set of pre-printed instructions for judges to use (Florida Office of the State Courts Administrator, 2014g). Those *jury instructions* explain what the elements of the particular crime are, reiterate what level of proof applies, and provide explicit definitions for the various terms. The judge will read the instructions to the jury and provide jurors with a written copy of those same instructions. Once the judge has completed this task, the jury will leave the courtroom to deliberate in private.

Jury Deliberations

Only the jurors are allowed to be present during their discussion in the jury room. The first task is to select a *jury foreperson* who will chair the session and act as the moderator. The jury deliberations are not recorded and there is no time limit on how long a jury has to reach a *verdict* or a decision as to whether the defendant is guilty or not guilty.

Sometimes the judge will find it necessary to sequester a jury. *Sequestering* means that jurors are not allowed to return home until they reach a verdict. In addition, the jurors cannot communicate with anybody in the outside world. Newspapers that carry stories about the case will have that information excised before jurors can read them and any television programs jurors may view are monitored. Meals are brought in and, at night, jurors are taken to an undisclosed location where they remain under constant guard.

Whenever all the jurors cannot agree on a verdict, that outcome is called a *hung jury*. However, once the jurors have reached a final decision, they re-assemble back in the courtroom and deliver the verdict form to the clerk of the court. If the jury finds the defendant is not guilty, then he or she is released. On the other hand, should the jury believe the defendant is guilty, the case enters the post-trial phase.

The high-profile Casey Anthony case, discussed earlier in this chapter, had another interesting development. The trial jury returned a not guilty verdict, an unpopular finding to some observers. An outraged crowd gathered at the courthouse immediately after the verdict was read. Some protestors carried signs deriding the jurors. An area restaurant even posted a sign on its door stating "Pinellas County jurors NOT welcome!!!" In addition, one juror received numerous death threats. She ended up quitting her job and fleeing town. Other jurors found it necessary to contact the local sheriff's office because of threats they received to their safety. In an effort to balance the media's right to access juror identities against juror privacy and safety, Judge Perry decided not to release the names of the jurors immediately. After a three-month cooling-off period, Judge Perry did release the names of the jurors. In addition, he called for the Florida Legislature "to examine whether an exemption barring release of jurors' names, albeit limited to specific, rare cases, is needed in order to protect the safety and well-being of those citizens willing to serve" (*State of Florida v. Casey Marie Anthony*, 2011, pp. 11–12).

Judge Nelson took a similar stance in the George Zimmerman case. George Zimmerman, who was involved in a neighborhood watch program, was accused and later acquitted of killing seventeen-year-old Trayvon Martin. According to Zimmerman, Martin was acting suspiciously prior to the confrontation in which Martin attacked Zimmerman. Because Zimmerman shot Martin during a ferocious struggle, Zimmerman invoked protection under the Florida "Stand-Your-Ground" law. In other words, reliance upon deadly force was a reasonable alternative to the beating that Martin was administering to Zimmerman.

This high-profile case attracted considerable national attention and numerous demonstrations were held, both locally and throughout the country. Eventually, the case made its way to trial amidst intense media coverage. While seating the jury, several members expressed worries about their safety due to threats. After the jury returned a finding of not guilty, public outcry deploring the verdict mounted. As a result, the judge elected to delay the immediate release of the jurors' names. The identities of the jurors were made public eight months after the conclusion of the trial (Weiner & Stutzman, 2014).

The issue of whether judges have the authority to suppress the release of juror names has not been resolved. A legal opinion authored by Florida Attorney General Butterworth (1995) concluded that the identities of grand jury members were privileged and not subject to public disclosure. However, that decision did not address other types of juries. That issue surfaced in another AG legal opinion. There, General Crist (2005) opined that juror names were not protected information. As of this writing, the Florida Legislature has not taken up this issue.

Post-Trial Activities

Once a person is found guilty of the charges, he or she moves to the sentencing phase. There is a flurry of activity that takes place prior to the actual sentencing hearing. It is to these matters that we now turn.

Pre-Sentence Investigation

The pre-sentence investigation (PSI) takes place during the interim between *adjudication* (determination of guilt) and sentencing. Prior to 1983, Florida engaged in unstructured sentencing practices. The judge would refer the case to a probation officer to construct a PSI. A *PSI* involved assembling a complete social and historical background of the person facing sentencing. Information would involve social characteristics (education, childhood development, marital status, employment, etc.), legal history (past record, prior sentences, etc.), along with a forecast about the prospects for rehabilitation.

The judge would review the PSI and then develop a sentencing plan that was guided by legislatively imposed maximum penalties for the offense. A life felony carried a term of life imprisonment, a first-degree felony warranted a maximum sentence of thirty years, a second-degree felony was matched by fifteen years, and a third-degree felony was worth five years. In *unstructured sentencing*, the judge would sentence the defendant to a term that would fall anywhere between a minimum and a maximum number of years. However, the availability of parole, gain time, time off for good behavior, and other administrative schemes often meant there was no actual "truth in sentencing." In other words, inmates very rarely remained in prison for the entire amount of time to which they were sentenced. In fact, prior to 1989, the average sentence served by a Florida prisoner was one-third of what the sentencing judge had imposed (Florida Department of Corrections, 2010, p. 6). This brand of justice was ripe for inequities and differential practices. As a result, Florida moved to a plan that provided for *structured sentencing* by adopting sentencing guidelines.

Florida has been through several versions of sentencing guidelines and has struggled to articulate the philosophy that underlies this approach (see Figure 6.17). What happens today is that responsibility for completing the PSI has shifted. Now the assistant state attorney handling the prosecution of the case also prepares the sentencing scoresheet. The *sentencing scoresheet*, a copy of which appears in Figure 6.18, is an attempt to impose *sentencing guidelines* or standardize felony sentencing practices throughout the entire state. Points are assigned according to the seriousness of the criminal episode, the degree to which the victim was injured, the defendant's prior criminal history, any record of past legal status violations (escape, flight, failure to appear, etc.), and any use of a firearm. When these points are summed, the resulting score represents the number of months imprisonment the defendant must serve (Florida Department of Corrections and Florida Office of the State Courts Administrator, 2014).

The scoresheet calculations are not iron-clad. In other words, there is room for the judge to depart from the guideline. The judge can lower the sentence if any of the conditions presented in Figure 6.19 are present. However, the judge does not have the

Figure 6.17 Principles Underlying the Florida Sentencing Guidelines

- Sentencing should be neutral with respect to race, gender, and social and economic status.
- The primary purpose of sentencing is to punish the offender. Rehabilitation and other traditional considerations continue to be desired goals of the criminal justice system but must assume a subordinate role.
- The penalty imposed should be commensurate with the severity of the convicted offense and the circumstances surrounding the offense.
- The severity of the sanction should increase with the length and nature of the offender's criminal history.
- The sentence imposed by the sentencing judge should increase with the length and nature of the offender's criminal history.
- While the sentencing guidelines are designed to aid the judge in the sentencing decision and are not intended to usurp judicial discretion, departures from the presumptive sentences established in the guidelines shall be articulated in writing and made when circumstances or factors reasonably justify the aggravation or mitigation of the sentence.
- Because the capacities of state and local correctional facilities are finite, use of incarcerative sanctions should be limited to those persons convicted of more serious offenses or those who have longer criminal histories.

Source: Florida Bar (2014). Rule 3.701: Sentencing Guidelines. *Florida Rules of Criminal Procedure.* Tallahassee: Florida Bar. Retrieved on October 23, 2014 from http://www.floridabar.org/TFB/ TFBResources.nsf/Attachments/BDFE1551AD291A3F85256B29004BF892/$FILE/ Criminal.pdf?OpenElement.

authority to raise the sentence arbitrarily even though that heightened sentence still remains within the sentencing guideline range. For example, when one judge translated a scoresheet value of 73.95 months into 6.16 years and then rounded that figure to a seven-year sentence because rounding up was the judge's personal "sentencing philosophy," the Florida Supreme Court ruled that pronouncement (which translated into an actual harsher 84-month sentence) violated the defendant's right to due process (*Cromartie v. State of Florida*, 2011).

Sentencing Hearing

The *sentencing hearing* is the point at which the judge formally pronounces the punishment. If the sentence requires a period of incarceration, the defendant is remanded to the custody of the state.

Figure 6.20 displays the distribution of 72,003 sanctions imposed by Florida judges in felony cases for fiscal year 2011–12. Florida judges sentenced defendants to prison in 22% of the cases and to jail in 24% of the cases. Judges placed almost half the guilty parties on probation.

If you recall from Figure 6.17, one of the principles that legislators used to anchor the sentencing guidelines is that sentencing practices ought to reflect the offender's criminal history. What Figure 6.21 does is that it sketches sanctions against the number of prior

Figure 6.18 The Florida Criminal Punishment Code Scoresheet for Felony Offenses

Rule 3.992(a) Criminal Punishment Code Scoresheet

The Criminal Punishment Code Scoresheet Preparation Manual is available at: *http://www.dc.state.fl.us/pub/sen_cpcm/index.html*

1. DATE OF SENTENCE	2. PREPARER'S NAME	3. COUNTY	4. SENTENCING JUDGE	
5. NAME (LAST, FIRST, MI.I.)	6. DOB	8. RACE ☐B ☐W ☐OTHER	10. PRIMARY OFF. DATE	12. PLEA ☐
	7. DC #	9. GENDER ☐M ☐F	11. PRIMARY DOCKET #	TRIAL ☐

I. **PRIMARY OFFENSE:** If Qualifier, please check ___A ___S ___C ___R (A=Attempt, S=Solicitation, C=Conspiracy, R=Reclassification)

FELONY DEGREE F.S.# DESCRIPTION OFFENSE LEVEL **POINTS**

____/ ____/ ____/ ____/

(Level - Points: 1=4, 2=10, 3=16, 4=22, 5=28, 6=36, 7=56, 8=74, 9=92, 10=116)

Prior capital felony triples Primary Offense points ☐ **I.** ____

II. **ADDITIONAL OFFENSE(S):** Supplemental page attached ☐

DOCKET# FEL/MM DEGREE F.S.# OFFENSE LEVEL QUALIFY A S C R COUNTS POINTS TOTAL

____/ ____/ ____/ ____ ☐☐☐☐ ____ x ____ = ____
DESCRIPTION ____

____/ ____/ ____/ ____ ☐☐☐☐ ____ X ____ = ____
DESCRIPTION ____

____/ ____/ ____/ ____ ☐☐☐☐ ____ X ____ = ____
DESCRIPTION ____

____/ ____/ ____/ ____ ☐☐☐☐ ____ x ____ = ____
DESCRIPTION ____

(Level - Points: M=0.2, 1=0.7, 2=1.2, 3=2.4, 4=3.6, 5=5.4, 6=18, 7=28, 8=37, 9=46, 10=58)

Prior capital felony triples Additional Offense points ☐ Supplemental page points ____

II. ____

III. **VICTIM INJURY:**

		Number		Total			Number		Total
2nd Degree Murder	240 x	____	=	____	Slight	4 x	____	=	____
Death	120 x	____	=	____	Sex Penetration	80 x	____	=	____
Severe	40 x	____	=	____	Sex Contact	40 x	____	=	____
Moderate	18 x	____	=	____					

III. ____

IV. **PRIOR RECORD:** Supplemental page attached ☐

FEL/MM DEGREE	F.S.#	OFFENSE LEVEL	QUALIFY: A S C R	DESCRIPTION	NUMBER		POINTS		TOTAL
____	____/	____	☐☐☐☐	____	____	X	____	=	____
____	____/	____	☐☐☐☐	____	____	X	____	=	____
____	____/	____	☐☐☐☐	____	____	X	____	=	____
____	____/	____	☐☐☐☐	____	____	X	____	=	____
____	____/	____	☐☐☐☐	____	____	X	____	=	____
____	____/	____	☐☐☐☐	____	____	X	____	=	____
____	____/	____	☐☐☐☐	____	____	X	____	=	____
____	____/	____	☐☐☐☐	____	____	X	____	=	____
____	____/	____	☐☐☐☐	____	____	X	____	=	____

(Level = Points: M=0.2, 1=0.5, 2=0.8, 3=1.6, 4=2.4, 5=3.6, 6=9, 7=14, 8=19, 9=23, 10=29)

Supplemental page points ____

IV. ____

Page 1 Subtotal: ____

Effective Date: For offenses committed under the Criminal Punishment Code effective for offenses committee on or after October 1, 1998 and subsequent revisions.

24

Source: Florida Department of Corrections and Florida Office of the State Courts Administrator (2014). Appendix B: Scoresheet Form Rule 3.992: Criminal Punishment Code Scoresheet. *Florida Criminal Punishment Code: Scoresheet Preparation Manual.* Tallahassee: Florida Supreme Court. Retrieved on October 23, 2014 from http://www.dc.state.fl.us/pub/sen_cpcm/cpc_manual.pdf.

felonies a defendant has committed. The data indicate that probation is the most often preferred sentence when judges face a first-time defendant. Probation falls out of favor as one's criminal history increases. There is also a reluctance to rely upon community control and other methods.

Figure 6.18 The Florida Criminal Punishment Code Scoresheet for Felony Offenses, *continued*

NAME (LAST, FIRST, MI)	DOCKET #

Page 1 Subtotal: _____

V. Legal Status violation = 4 Points
☐ Escape ☐ Fleeing ☐ Failure to appear ☐ Supersedeas bond ☐ Incarceration ☐ Pretrial intervention or diversion program
☐ Court imposed or post prison release community supervision resulting in a conviction **V.** _____

VI. Community Sanction violation before the court for sentencing
☐ Probation ☐ Community Control ☐ Pretrial Intervention or diversion **VI.** _____

☐ 6 points for any violation other than new felony conviction x _____ each successive violation OR

☐ New felony conviction = 12 points x _____ each successive violation if new offense results in conviction before or at same time as sentence for violation of probation OR

☐ 12 points x _____ each successive violation for a violent felony offender of special concern when the violation is not based solely on failure to pay costs, fines, or restitution OR

☐ New felony conviction = 24 points x _____ each successive violation for a violent felony offender of special concern if new offense results in a conviction before or at the same time for violation of probation

VII. Firearm/Semi-Automatic or Machine Gun = 18 or 25 Points **VII.** _____

VIII. Prior Serious Felony - 30 Points **VIII.** _____

Subtotal Sentence Points _____

IX. Enhancements (only if the primary offense qualifies for enhancement)

Law Enf. Protect.	Drug Trafficker	Motor Vehicle Theft	Criminal Gang Offense	Domestic Violence in the Presence of Related Child (offenses committed on or after 3/12/07)
___ x 1.5 ___ x 2.0 ___ x 2.5	____ x 1.5	____ x 1.5	____ x 1.5	___ x 1.5

Enhanced Subtotal Sentence Points **IX.** _____

TOTAL SENTENCE POINTS _____

SENTENCE COMPUTATION

If total sentence points are less than or equal to 44, the lowest permissible sentence is any non-state prison sanction. If the total sentence points are 22 points or less, see Section 775.082(10), Florida Statutes, to determine if the court must sentence the offender to a non-state prison sanction.

If total sentence points are greater than 44:

_____ minus 28 = _____ x .75 = _____
total sentence points   lowest permissible prison sentence in months

The maximum sentence is up to the statutory maximum for the primary and any additional offenses as provided in s. 775.082, F.S., unless the lowest permissible sentence under the Code exceeds the statutory maximum. Such sentences may be imposed concurrently or consecutively. If total sentence points are greater than or equal to 363, a life sentence may be imposed.

_____
maximum sentence In years

TOTAL SENTENCE IMPOSED

	Years	Months	Days
☐ State Prison ☐ Life	_____	_____	_____
☐ County Jail ☐ Time Served	_____	_____	_____
☐ Community Control	_____	_____	_____
☐ Probation ☐ Modified	_____	_____	_____

Please check if sentenced as ☐ habitual offender, ☐habitual violent offender, ☐ violent career criminal, ☐ prison releasee reoffender,

or a ☐ mandatory minimum applies.

☐ Mitigated Departure ☐ Plea Bargain ☐Prison Diversion Program

Other Reason _____

JUDGE'S SIGNATURE	

Effective Date: For offenses committed under the Criminal Punishment Code effective for offenses committed on or after October 1, 1998, and subsequent revisions.

25

Source: Florida Department of Corrections and Florida Office of the State Courts Administrator (2014). Appendix B: Scoresheet Form Rule 3.992: Criminal Punishment Code Scoresheet. *Florida Criminal Punishment Code: Scoresheet Preparation Manual.* Tallahassee: Florida Supreme Court. Retrieved on October 23, 2014 from http://www.dc.state.fl.us/pub/sen_cpcm/cpc_manual.pdf.

There is a very predictable pattern when attention focuses on the imposition of prison sentences. Judges are more likely to issue an imprisonment order as recidivism increases. Jail terms also factor into the mix as a tool to hold convicted persons out of society.

Figure 6.18 The Florida Criminal Punishment Code Scoresheet for Felony Offenses, *continued*

RULE 3.992(b) Supplemental Criminal Punishment Code Scoresheet

NAME (LAST, FIRST, MI.I)	DOCKET #	DATE OF SENTENCE

II. ADDITIONAL OFFENSES(S):

DOCKET#	FEL/MM DEGREE	F.S#	OFFENSE LEVEL	QUALIFY A S C R	COUNTS	POINTS	TOTAL
___/	___/	___/	___	☐ ☐ ☐ ☐	___ x	___ =	___
DESCRIPTION
___/	___/	___/	___	☐ ☐ ☐ ☐	___ x	___ =	___
DESCRIPTION
___/	___/	___/	___	☐ ☐ ☐ ☐	___ x	___ =	___
DESCRIPTION
___/	___/	___/	___	☐ ☐ ☐ ☐	___ x	___ =	___
DESCRIPTION
___/	___/	___/	___	☐ ☐ ☐ ☐	___ x	___ =	___
DESCRIPTION

(Level - Points: M=0.2, 1=0.7, 2=1.2, 3=2.4, 4=3.6, 5=5.4, 6=18, 7=28, 8=37, 9=46, 10=58)

II. _____

IV. PRIOR RECORD

FEL/MM DEGREE	F.S.#	OFFENSE LEVEL	QUALIFY: A S C R	DESCRIPTION	NUMBER	POINTS	TOTAL
___	___	/___	☐ ☐ ☐ ☐	___	___ X	___ =	___
___	___	/___	☐ ☐ ☐ ☐	___	___ X	___ =	___
___	___	/___	☐ ☐ ☐ ☐	___	___ X	___ =	___
___	___	/___	☐ ☐ ☐ ☐	___	___ X	___ =	___
___	___	/___	☐ ☐ ☐ ☐	___	___ X	___ =	___
___	___	/___	☐ ☐ ☐ ☐	___	___ X	___ =	___

(Level = Points: M=0.2, 1=0.5, 2=0.8, 3=1.6, 4=2.4, 5=3.6, 6=9, 7=14, 8=19, 9=23, 10=29)

IV. _____

REASONS FOR DEPARTURE - MITIGATING CIRCUMSTANCES

(reasons may be checked here or written on the scoresheet)

☐ Legitimate, uncoerced plea bargain.
☐ The defendant was an accomplice to the offense and was a relatively minor participant in the criminal conduct.
☐ The capacity of the defendant to appreciate the criminal nature of the conduct or to conform that conduct to the requirements of law was substantially impaired.
☐ The defendant requires specialized treatment for a mental disorder that is unrelated to substance abuse or addiction, or for a physical disability, and the defendant is amenable to treatment.
☐ The need for payment of restitution to the victim outweighs the need for a prison sentence.
☐ The victim was an initiator, willing participant, aggressor, or provoker of the incident.
☐ The defendant acted under extreme duress or under the domination of another person.
☐ Before the identity of the defendant was determined, the victim was substantially compensated.
☐ The defendant cooperated with the State to resolve the current offense or any other offense.
☐ The offense was committed in an unsophisticated manner and was an isolated incident for which the defendant has shown remorse.
☐ At the time of the offense the defendant was too young to appreciate the consequences of the offense.
☐ The defendant is to be sentenced as a youthful offender.
☐ The defendant is amenable to the services of a postadjudicatory treatment-based drug court program and is otherwise qualified to participate in the program.
☐ The defendant was making a good faith effort to obtain or provide medical assistance for an individual experiencing a drug-related overdose.

Pursuant to 921.0026(3) the defendant's substance abuse or addiction does not justify a downward departure from the lowest permissible sentence, except for the provisions of s. 921.0026(2)(m).
Effective Date: For offenses committed under the Criminal Punishment Code effective for offenses committee on or after October 1, 1998 and subsequent revisions.

Source: Florida Department of Corrections and Florida Office of the State Courts Administrator (2014). Appendix B: Scoresheet Form Rule 3.992: Criminal Punishment Code Scoresheet. *Florida Criminal Punishment Code: Scoresheet Preparation Manual.* Tallahassee: Florida Supreme Court. Retrieved on October 23, 2014 from http://www.dc.state.fl.us/pub/sen_cpcm/cpc_manual.pdf.

**Figure 6.19 Mitigating Circumstances that Permit Departure from
Sentencing Guidelines**

- A legitimate plea bargain agreement exists;
- The defendant was an accomplice and relatively minor participant;
- The defendant's ability to understand the nature of the crime was substantially impaired;
- The defendant requires specialized treatment for a mental disorder;
- The need for restitution supersedes the need for confinement;
- The victim initiated or provoked the incident;
- The defendant acted under extreme duress;
- The defendant has provided reimbursement to the victim;
- The defendant cooperated with the state;
- The offense was an isolated incident and the defendant is remorseful;
- The defendant was too young to appreciate the consequences of the crime;
- The defendant is sentenced as a youthful offender; and
- The offense was nonviolent and the scoresheet total is minimal.

Source: Florida Statutes 2011, §921.0026(2).

Figure 6.20 Sanctions Imposed by Florida Felony Courts, Fiscal Year 2011–12

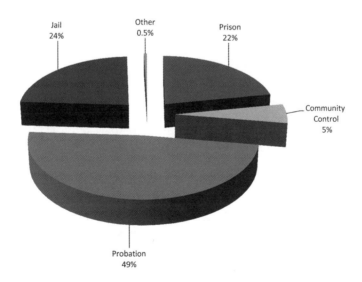

Source: Florida Department of Corrections (2013). Table 3: Sanction Imposed by Judicial Circuit and County. *Florida's Criminal Punishment Code: A Comparative Assessment September 2013.* Tallahassee: Florida Department of Corrections. Retrieved on October 23, 2014 from http://www.dc.state.fl.us/pub/sg_annual/1213/index.html.

Figure 6.21 Prior Felony Record and Sanctions Imposed by Florida Courts, Fiscal Year 2011–12

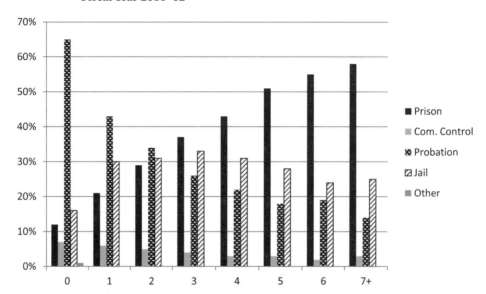

Source: Florida Department of Corrections (2013). Table 9: Prior Felony Record and Sanction Imposed. *Florida's Criminal Punishment Code: A Comparative Assessment September 2013.* Tallahassee: Florida Department of Corrections. Retrieved on October 23, 2014 from http://www.dc.state.fl.us/pub/sg_annual/1213/desclevels.html.

The Development of Florida's Sentencing Guidelines

Sentencing practices in Florida have changed dramatically over the past three decades. As we shall see in the next chapter, the Florida corrections system came under scrutiny from the federal government. Florida's prisons were so overcrowded that federal judges considered the living conditions to be "cruel and unusual punishment," a federal constitutional violation (*Costello v. Wainwright*, 1976).

Officials struggled mightily to maintain an acceptable inmate population count. Because of overcrowded conditions, the Florida Secretary of Corrections refused to accept any new prisoners on two different occasions. In addition, the Florida Department of Corrections had to resort to housing inmates in tents as another way of dealing with this congestion (Kaufman, 1999).

As Griset (1996, p. 129) explains, "prison population growth is a result of the number of prison admissions and the duration of each admittee's stay." Since prison administrators could not control the number of defendants sentenced to confinement, they had to make other adjustments to reduce the overall inmate population in order to remain under the federally imposed inmate cap. Florida simply had to find innovative ways to increase prison bed capacity or start building more correctional facilities, an expensive and lengthy venture. Early-release mechanisms, such as gain time and parole, became common tools to help manage the prison population crisis.

Gain time is time credited to inmates for good behavior. Credits are also given for participation in work programs and other rehabilitative activities (Griset, 1996; Griset, 1999; Kaufman, 1999). Generous gain time schemes, coupled with *parole* (early release from prison prior to completing the full sentence), meant that prisoners often serve minimal sentences. Prison officials can turn this early-release faucet on or off depending upon how intense the demand is for prison beds. Under this approach, "truth in sentencing" became a relic or a thing of the past.

Public outcry in the aftermath of several homicides committed by former inmates freed because of early-release provisions prompted the Florida Legislature to reevaluate sentencing practices. These conditions led to the imposition of state sentencing guidelines in 1983. This initial effort to promote uniform sentencing irked local prosecutors, sheriffs, and police leaders. The legislature had also passed several habitual offender laws, mandatory sentencing provisions, and harsher penalties (Bales & Dees, 1992; Harris, 2013). In addition, citizen backlash prompted the Florida Legislature to enact a law requiring prisoners to serve at least 85% of their imposed sentences (*Florida Statutes 2014*, § 944.275 (4)(b)(3)). All these developments produced a new sense of urgency for prison expansion.

Feeling hemmed in by these sentencing laws, Florida judges responded by making downward departures from the guidelines wherever possible. Judges felt these statutes were too harsh and unbending. As a result, judges *mitigated* or imposed less severe sentences than what the guidelines suggested. From the middle of 1994 to the end of 1996, 57% of the defendants whose scores warranted a prison term under the new sentencing guidelines were mitigated. Judges sentenced 41% to non-prison sentences and the other 15% received much shorter prison terms (Griset, 1999, p. 325).

Prosecutors railed against these deviations and critics wondered whether justice was being imposed arbitrarily. For example, the overall mitigation rate for Miami courts was 74%, compared to just 46% in Panama City (Griset, 1999, p. 325). Obviously, justice was not being administered uniformly throughout the state. Observations like these prompted the Florida Legislature to revamp the sentencing guidelines in an effort to curtail judicial discretion and to impose more stringent penalties. It was against this backdrop that the Criminal Punishment Code (CPC) went into effect in 1998. This chain of events led one observer to write:

> It is difficult to reconcile the proper use of this power with a punishment system that invites geographic disparity, racial discrimination, unconstitutional violations of *ex-post facto* protections, and unpredictable and unaccountable sentencing. Further research will seek to determine the existence and extent of geographic, class, racial, and gender disproportionality (Griset, 2002, p. 299).

A Closer Look at Florida's Sentencing Guidelines

Griset's (2002) cry for greater research was soon answered. An evaluation of Florida's sentencing guidelines requires a two-pronged approach. The first concern focuses on the "in/out" decision. In other words, was the defendant sentenced to a prison term as opposed to some form of community control? The second focal point is the length of the sentence. How long will the defendant remain behind bars?

Florida's odyssey to craft a more perfect sentencing structure provided Crow and Bales (2006) with an opportunity to compare and contrast 345,000 sentences under the 1983 guidelines with 353,000 sentences generated under the 1994 guidelines. The newer guidelines resulted in 56% fewer incarcerations. Although racial discrepancies existed, the gap between blacks and whites receiving prison sentences grew smaller with the 1994 guidelines. Furthermore, the odds of receiving a prison sentence vary according to geographical location. Turning to sentence length, Crow and Bales (2006) determined that prison terms are about 2½ years shorter under the current provisions. While black and white defendants received similar sentence lengths under the older rules, there is a four-month discrepancy (blacks receiving the longer terms) under the latest policy. Geographical differences also persisted.

These findings prompted further investigation. Crow (2008) updated the data so he could compare the 1994 guidelines with the 1998 CPC and also paid greater attention to any adjudication patterns generated by offense type and criminal history. The results showed that judges were more apt to incarcerate violent recidivists. Sentence differentials were more likely to arise in drug cases where the defendant was either Hispanic or black as opposed to white. Other studies of habitual-offender sentencing practices in Florida also uncover differential sentencing practices based upon race (Crawford, 2000; Crow & Johnson, 2008; Kovandzic, 2001; Kunselman, Johnson, & Rayboun, 2003). Whether or not these observations represent a "get-tough-on-crime" stance or stem from bias remains unknown. It would appear, though, that the CPC guidelines have not been entirely successful in eradicating biased sentencing.

Summary

As you have seen in this chapter, the Florida court system involves a myriad of actors. Each group has its own agenda. Yet, these factions come together to represent a coordinated effort to mete out justice. This apparatus is in place to dispense justice, equally and uniformly. Court cases move through the labyrinth in a very predictable way. Yet, there is still some discord and tension with the end stage. Obviously, Florida's odyssey to craft a sound sentencing scheme still has plenty of room to grow and improve. As Clemens and Stancil (2009, p. 58) explain:

> Our current approach to criminal sentencing is not only fiscally irresponsible—it is morally questionable.... Why should judges be so abhorred that the legislature can decide that judges shall no longer be trusted to make the important criminal sentencing decisions that they've been making for centuries? The best solution to Florida's increasing need for money to build and operate more prisons is to return parity to the judicial branch so that it can operate equally with the executive and legislative branches, particularly on the key issue of criminal sentencing.

Key Terms

acquittal
adjudication
affidavit

arraignment
attorney general
bench trial
bondable offense
booking
cash bond
challenge by cause
Chief Justice
closing argument
courts of general jurisdiction
courts of limited jurisdiction
cross-examination
deposition
direct examination
first appearance
flight risk
gain time
hung jury
indigent status
information
judgment of acquittal
judicial activism
jurisdiction
jury foreperson
jury instructions
jury summons
jury trial
merit retention vote
mitigate
nonbondable offense
opening argument
parole
peremptory challenge
pre-sentence investigation
pro bono
pro se
probable cause
proof beyond a reasonable doubt
public defender
released on recognizance (ROR)
sentencing guidelines
sentencing hearing
sentencing scoresheet
sequestering
speedy trial
standard bail/bond schedule
state attorney
structured sentencing
suitable moral character
subpoena

subpoena duces tecum
surety bond
the rule
unstructured sentencing
voir dire

Selected Internet Sites

Florida Association of Court Clerks and Comptrollers
http://www.flclerks.com

Florida Bar Association
http://www.floridabar.org/

Florida Bar of Examiners
http://www.floridabarexam.org/web/

Florida Clerks of Court Operations Corporation
http://www.flccoc.org/index.php

Florida Legal Services, Inc.
http://www.floridalegal.org

Florida Prosecuting Attorneys Association
http://www.myfpaa.org

Florida Public Defender Association
http://flpda.org

Florida State Courts Administrator
http://www.flcourts.org/administration-funding/

Florida Supreme Court
http://www.floridasupremecourt.org

Review Questions

1. What does Article I, Section 21 of the Florida Constitution mean?
2. Explain the mission statement of the Florida Supreme Court.
3. Which two courts are considered to be appellate courts in Florida?
4. Which two courts are considered to be trial courts in Florida?
5. How many Justices does the Florida Supreme Court have?
6. What is the function of the Chief Justice?
7. What role does the Judicial Nomination Commission play?
8. What is a merit retention vote with respect to Florida judges?
9. What qualifications do Florida Supreme Court Justices have to meet?
10. What kinds of cases come before the Florida Supreme Court?
11. What is judicial activism?

12. What are the issues associated with Amendment #3 on the statewide 2014 general election ballot?

13. What kinds of cases come before the District Courts of Appeal?

14. Address the issue of diversity among Florida judges.

15. What kinds of cases do the circuit courts handle?

16. What kinds of cases do the county courts handle?

17. What role does the Florida Board of Bar Examiners play?

18. What qualifications does one need to satisfy to practice law in Florida?

19. What does suitable moral character entail?

20. What does *pro bono* work mean?

21. What does the Florida Bar Association regulate?

22. What does the Office of the State Courts Administrator do?

23. On what does the bulk of the state court budget get spent?

24. What is the role of the state attorney?

25. What is the role of the public defender?

26. What are some of the things contained in the "Public Defender's Credo"?

27. Why is *Gideon v. Wainwright* (1963) so important?

28. What does *pro se* mean?

29. What is indigent status and how is it determined?

30. What is an acquittal?

31. What kind of staffing and budgetary conditions do public defenders face?

32. What functions does the clerk of the court discharge?

33. What is a *subpoena*?

34. What is a *subpoena duces tecum*?

35. What is the role of the Florida Attorney General?

36. What is an Attorney General Opinion?

37. What happens during booking?

38. Link the terms affidavit, probable cause, and jurisdiction?

39. What is a standard bail/bond schedule?

40. What is a bondable offense?

41. What is a nonbondable offense?

42. How does a cash bond differ from a surety bond?

43. What takes place at first appearance?

44. What is a flight risk?

45. What is the state attorney doing when he or she files an information?

46. What is the purpose of arraignment?

47. What happens at a deposition?

48. What does speedy trial mean?

49. Explain the difference between a bench trial and a jury trial.

50. How many people sit on a jury in Florida?

51. How does Florida locate people for potential jury service?

52. What eligibility restrictions are there for jury service?

53. What is a person expected to do when he or she receives a jury summons?

54. What is *voir dire*?

55. Explain the difference between a challenge by cause and a peremptory challenge?

56. What is the purpose of opening arguments in a trial? Which side goes first?

57. What is the difference between a direct examination and a cross-examination of a witness?

58. What is a judgment of acquittal?

59. What happens during closing arguments?

60. What are jury instructions?

61. What happens during jury deliberations?

62. What is a verdict?

63. What issues have surfaced regarding the public disclosure of juror identities?

64. What is a pre-sentence investigation?

65. What problems did Florida experience with unstructured sentencing?

66. How do sentencing guidelines address the problems with unstructured sentencing?

67. What principles underly the Florida sentencing guidelines?

68. What items are considered in the Florida Criminal Punishment Code Scoresheet?

69. What happens at the sentencing hearing?

70. What are mitigating circumstances and how do they affect sentencing?

71. What happened in *Costello v. Wainwright* (1976)?

72. What does the equation "prison population = admissions + duration" mean?

73. What is gain time?

74. What is parole?

75. How do gain time and early parole affect the size of the prison population?

76. What is the 85% requirement mean for Florida prisoners?

77. What is a downward departure or mitigation when it comes to sentencing?

78. What are researchers looking at when they study "in/out" sentencing decisions?

79. What are some of the findings that researchers reach when examining Florida's sentencing guidelines?

80. How do these research findings fit with the underlying principles outlined in Figure 6.17?

References

Anstead, Harry Lee, Gerald Kogan, Thomas D. Hall, and Robert Craig Waters (2005). The operation and jurisdiction of the Supreme Court of Florida. *Nova Law Review*, *29*, 431–570.

Bales, William D. and Linda G. Dees (1992). Mandatory minimum sentencing in Florida: Past trends and future implications. *Crime & Delinquency*, *38*, 309–329.

Bondi, Pam (2011). Protecting Floridians. *Weekly Briefing*, *9*(20), June 3. Tallahassee: Florida Office of the Attorney General. Retrieved on October 24, 2014 from http://myfloridalegal.com/__85256F35006DDEA1.nsf/0/FBB4C9898261212D852578A40066FA2A?Open&Highlight=0,june,3,2011.

Bureau of Economic and Business Research (2014). *Florida State Summary*. Gainesville: University of Florida. Retrieved on October 22, 2014 from http://www.bebr.ufl.edu/data/state/Florida.

Butterworth, Bob (1995). Disclosure of names and addresses of grand jury. *Florida Attorney General Advisory Legal Opinion*, September 8. Tallahassee: Attorney General. Retrieved on October 27, 2014 from http://www.myfloridalegal.com/ago.nsf/Opinions/E3CEBB447DA36161852562880076AF7D.

Butterworth, Bob (1996). *Hearing Set on Date Rape Drug Rescheduling Request*. Tallahassee: Attorney General News Release. Retrieved on August 9, 2011 from http://myfloridalegal.com/__852562220065EE67.nsf/0/4BBE9438B8E7876D85256324004FDDCC?Open&Highlight=0,rohypnol,schedule,i.

Clemens, Aaron M. and Hale R. Stancil (2009). Unhandcuffing justice: Proposals to return rationality to criminal sentencing. *Florida Bar Journal, February*, 54–58.

Costello v. Wainwright, 525 F.2d 1239 (1976).

Crawford, Charles (2000). Gender, race, and habitual offender sentencing in Florida. *Criminology*, *38*, 263–280.

Crist, Charlie (2005). AGO 2005-61: Records, disclosure of jurors' names. *Florida Attorney General Advisory Legal Opinion*, November 21. Tallahassee: Attorney General. Retrieved on October 27, 2014 from http://myfloridalegal.com/ago.nsf/Opinions/4A410DA4389543CC852570C000750D51.

Cromartie v. State of Florida, No. SC09-1868 (Fla. 2011).

Crow, Matthew S. (2008). The complexities of prior record, race, ethnicity, and policy: Interactive effects in sentencing. *Criminal Justice Review*, *33*, 502–523.

Crow, Matthew S. and William Bales (2006). Sentencing guidelines and focal concerns: The effect of sentencing policy as a practical constraint on sentencing decisions. *American Journal of Criminal Justice*, *30*, 285–304.

Crow, Matthew S. and Kathrine A. Johnson (2008). Race, ethnicity, and habitual-offender sentencing: A multilevel analysis of individual and contextual threat. *Criminal Justice Policy Review*, *19*, 63–83.

Farole, Jr., Donald J. and Lynn Langton (2010a). *Census of Public Defender Offices, 2007: County-Based and Local Public Defender Offices, 2007*. Washington, DC: Bureau of Justice Statistics. Retrieved on October 24, 2014 from http://bjs.ojp.usdoj.gov/index.cfm?ty=pbdetail&iid=2211.

Farole, Jr., Donald J. and Lynn Langton (2010b). A national assessment of public defender office caseloads. *Judicature*, 94, 87–90.

Florida Bar (2013a). *Oath of Admission to the Florida Bar*. Tallahassee: The Florida Bar. Retrieved on October 22, 2014 from http://www.floridabar.org/tfb/TFBProfess.nsf/basic+view/04E9EB581538255A85256B2F006CCD7D?OpenDocument.

Florida Bar (2013b). *Pro Bono Information*. Tallahassee: Florida Supreme Court. Retrieved on October 22, 2014 from http://www.floridabar.org/tfb/TFBConsum.nsf/840090c1 6eedaf0085256b61000928dc/8cf2326423a41d9d85256d5500704974?OpenDocument.

Florida Bar (2014a). *Judicial Nominating Commission (JNC) Applications*. Tallahassee: The Florida Bar. Retrieved on October 22, 2014 from http://www.floridabar.org/TFB/TFBResources.nsf/Attachments/A3DFC294720BE5AE85257D270053B9B2/$FILE/REVISED%20JNC%20App%206-14.pdf?OpenElement.

Florida Bar (2014b). *Florida Rules of Criminal Procedure*. Tallahassee: Florida Bar. Retrieved on October 23, 2014 from http://www.floridabar.org/TFB/TFBResources.nsf/Attachments/BDFE1551AD291A3F85256B29004BF892/$FILE/Criminal.pdf?OpenElement.

Florida Bar (2014c). *The Florida Bar President's Special Task Force to Study Enhancement of Diversity in the Judiciary and on the JNCs*. Tallahassee: Florida Bar. Retrieved on October 25, 2014 from http://www.floridabar.org/TFB/TFBResources.nsf/Attachments/8E7CB3755C3E15BC85257CE10049AFDD/$FILE/Report%20of%20The%20Florida%20Bar%20President%27s%20Special%20Task%20Force%20to%20Study%20Enhancement%20of%20Diversity%20in%20the%20Judiciary%20and%20on%20the%20JNC%27s.pdf?OpenElement.

Florida Board of Bar Examiners (2011*). Rules of the Supreme Court Related to Admissions to the Bar*. Tallahassee: Florida Supreme Court. Retrieved on October 22, 2014 from http://www.floridabarexam.org/web/website.nsf/rule.xsp.

Florida Board of Bar Examiners (2014). *July 2014 General Bar Examination Overall Method*. Tallahassee: Florida Supreme Court. Retrieved on October 22, 2014 from http://www.floridabarexam.org/__85257bfe0055eb2c.nsf/52286ae9ad5d845185257c07005c3fe1/6218b265c9a9302b85257d5e0051dff4.

Florida Constitution. Retrieved on October 24, 2014 from http://www.leg.state.fl.us/Statutes/index.cfm?Mode=Constitution&Submenu=3&Tab=statutes&CFID=33578 521&CFTOKEN=62723874.

Florida Department of Corrections (2010). *Florida's Criminal Punishment Code: A Comparative Assessment*. Tallahassee: Florida Department of Corrections. Retrieved on October 27, 2014 from http://www.dc.state.fl.us/pub/sg_annual/0910/sg_annual-2010.pdf.

Florida Department of Corrections (2013). *Florida's Criminal Punishment Code: A Comparative Assessment September 2013*. Tallahassee: Florida Department of Corrections. Retrieved on October 23, 2014 from http://www.dc.state.fl.us/pub/sg_annual/1213/index.html.

Florida Department of Corrections and Florida Office of the State Courts Administrator (2014). *Florida Criminal Punishment Code: Scoresheet Preparation Manual*. Tallahassee: Florida Supreme Court. Retrieved on October 23, 2014 from http://www.dc.state.fl.us/pub/sen_cpcm/cpc_manual.pdf.

Florida Office of the State Courts Administrator (1996). *Jury Managers' Manual*. Tallahassee: Florida Supreme Court. Retrieved on October 24, 2014 from http://www.flcourts.org/core/fileparse.php/259/urlt/manual.pdf.

Florida Office of the State Courts Administrator (2010). *Florida State Courts: 2008–2009 Annual Report*. Tallahassee: Florida Supreme Court. Retrieved on October 25, 2014 from http://www.flcourts.org/core/fileparse.php/248/urlt/annual_report0809.pdf.

Florida Office of the State Courts Administrator (2014a). *Florida Courts: Mission & Vision*. Tallahassee: Florida Supreme Court. Retrieved on October 22, 2014 from http://www.flcourts.org/florida-courts/mission-and-vision.stml.

Florida Office of the State Courts Administrator (2014b). *Diagram of the State Court System*. Tallahassee: Florida Supreme Court. Retrieved on October 22, 2014 http://www.floridasupremecourt.org/pub_info/CourtDiagram.pdf.

Florida Office of the State Courts Administrator (2014c). *Florida Courts: District Courts of Appeal*. Tallahassee: Florida Supreme Court. Retrieved on October 22, 2014 from http://flcourts.org/florida-courts/district-court-appeal.stml.

Florida Office of the State Courts Administrator (2014d). *Florida Courts: Trial Courts–Circuit*. Tallahassee: Florida Supreme Court. Retrieved on October 22, 2014 from http://flcourts.org/florida-courts/trial-courts-circuit.stml.

Florida Office of the State Courts Administrator (2014e). *Historic Statewide Judgeships: Fiscal Year 1972–73 to Fiscal Year 2014–15*. Tallahassee: Florida Supreme Court. Retrieved on October 22, 2014 from http://flcourts.org/publications-reports-stats/statistics/historic-statewide-judgeships.stml.

Florida Office of the State Courts Administrator (2014f). *Florida Courts: Trial Courts–County*. Tallahassee: Florida Supreme Court. Retrieved on October 22, 2014 from http://flcourts.org/florida-courts/trial-courts-county.stml.

Florida Office of the State Courts Administrator (2014g). *Florida Standard Jury Instructions*. Tallahassee: Florida Supreme Court. Retrieved on October 24, 2014 from http://www.floridasupremecourt.org/jury_instructions.shtml.

Florida Statutes 2014. Retrieved on October 24, 2011 from http://www.leg.state.fl.us/Statutes/index.cfm?Mode=View%20Statutes&Submenu=1&Tab=statutes&CFID=72725658&CFTOKEN=42781737.

Florida TaxWatch (2014). *When It Costs More to Pay Less: Starting Salaries for Assistant State Attorneys & Assistant Public Defenders in Florida among Lowest in Nation*. Tallahassee: Florida Taxwatch. Retrieved on October 25, 2014 from http://www.floridataxwatch.org/resources/pdf/ASAAPDFINAL.pdf.

Gideon v. Wainwright, 372 U.S. 335 (1963).

Griset, Pamela L. (1996). Determinate sentencing and administrative discretion over time served in prison: A case study of Florida. *Crime & Delinquency, 42*, 127–143.

Griset, Pamela L. (1999). Criminal sentencing in Florida: Determinate sentencing's hollow shell. *Crime & Delinquency, 45*, 316–333.

Griset, Pamela L. (2002). New sentencing laws follow old patterns: A Florida case study. *Journal of Criminal Justice, 30*, 287–301.

Harris, Maggie E. (2013). The cost of mandatory minimum sentences. *Florida Coastal Law Review, 14*, 419–450.

Hawkins, Scott G. (2012). Perspective on judicial merit retention in Florida. *Florida Law Review, 64*, 1421–1432.

Holt, Julianne M. (2014). *The Public Defender's Credo*. West Palm Beach, FL: Office of the Public Defender, 13th Judicial Circuit. Retrieved on October 24, 2014 from http://www.pd13.state.fl.us/Home.aspx.

Kaufman, Chet (1999). A folly of criminal justice policy-making: The rise and demise of early release in Florida, and its ex *post facto* implications. *Florida State University Law Review*, *26*, 361–449.

Kovandzic, Tomislav V. (2001). The impact of Florida's habitual offender law on crime. *Criminology*, *39*, 179–203.

Kunselman, Julie C., Kathrine A. Johnson, and Michael C. Rayboun (2003). Profiling sentence enhancement offenders: A case study of Florida's 10–20–lifers. *Criminal Justice Policy Review*, *14*, 229–248.

LaFountain, Robert C., Shauna M. Strickland, Kathryn A., Holt, Brenda G. Otto, and Neal B. Kauder (2012). *Examining the Work of State Courts: An Analysis of 2010 State Court Caseloads*, p. 22. Williamsburg, VA: National Center for State Courts, p. 46. Retrieved on October 24, 2014 from http://www.courtstatistics.org/~/media/Microsites/Files/CSP/DATA%20PDF/CSP_DEC.ashx.

Langton, Lynn and Donald Farole, Jr. (2010). *Census of Public Defender Offices, 2007: State Public Defender Programs, 2007*. Washington, DC: Bureau of Justice Statistics. Retrieved on October 24, 2014 from http://www.bjs.gov/content/pub/pdf/spdp07.pdf.

Leon County Clerk of the Courts (2010). *Online Forms: General Court Forms, Subpoena Duces Tecum*. Tallahassee: Leon County Clerk of the Courts. Retrieved on October 23, 2014 from http://www.clerk.leon.fl.us/sections/clerk_services/online_forms/general/subpoena_duces_tecum.pdf.

Leon County Clerk of Courts (2010). *Application for Criminal Indigent Status*. Tallahassee, FL: Leon County Clerk of Courts. Retrieved on October 23, 2014 from http://www.clerk.leon.fl.us/sections/clerk_services/online_forms/criminal/criminal_indigent.pdf.

Mandel, Roberta G. (2009). The appointment of counsel to indigent defendants is not enough: Budget cuts render the right to counsel virtually meaningless. *Florida Bar Journal*, April, 43–47.

National Right to Counsel Committee (2009). *Justice Denied: America's Continuing Neglect of Our Constitutional Right to Counsel*. Washington, DC: The Constitution Project. Retrieved on October 24, 2014 from http://www.constitutionproject.org/wp-content/uploads/2012/10/139.pdf.

No Author (2011). Editorial: Courts under attack. *Judicature*, *94*, 258–259.

Pettis, Eugene K. (2014). Diversity losing ground in the judicial system. *Florida Bar Journal*, *88* (3), 4.

Rodriguez, Raquel A. (2005). Judicial selection in Florida: An executive branch perspective. *Florida Bar Journal*, January, 16–19.

Salokar, Rebecca Mae, D. Jason Berggren, and Kathryn A. DePalo (2006). The new politics of judicial selection in Florida: Merit selection redefined. *Justice System Journal*, *27*, 123–142.

State of Florida v. Casey Marie Anthony (2011). Case No. 48-2008-CF-015606-AO. Orlando: Ninth Judicial Circuit. Retrieved on October 24, 2014 from http://media.trb.com/media/acrobat/2011-07/155178900-26150904.pdf.

State of Florida v. George Zimmerman (2012). Case No. 592012CF001083A. Seminole County: 18th Judicial Circuit.

Supreme Court of Florida (2013). *Florida State Courts: 2012–2013 Annual Report.* Tallahassee, FL: Florida Office of the State Courts Administrator. Retrieved on October 22, 2014 from http://www.flcourts.org/core/fileparse.php/248/urlt/annual_report 1213.pdf.

Taylor, Aaron N. (2014). The integrity of our judiciary depends on diversity. Pp. 1–2 in The Florida Bar (2014), *The Florida Bar President's Special Task Force to Study Enhancement of Diversity of the Judiciary and on the JNC's, Appendices to Task Force Report.* Tallahassee: Florida Bar. Retrieved on October 25, 2014 from http://www.florida-bar.org/TFB/TFBResources.nsf/Attachments/A4E41688279C883585257CE10 04A0B9E/$FILE/Appendices%20to%20Task%20Force%20Report.pdf?OpenElement.

U.S. Census Bureau (2014). *State & County QuickFacts.* Washington, DC: U.S. Census Bureau. Retrieved on October 22, 2014 from http://quickfacts.census.gov/qfd/states/ 12000.html.

Weiner, Jeff and Rene Stutzman (2014). Names of six jurors who acquitted George Zimmerman made public. *Orlando Sentinel,* April 3. Retrieved on October 26, 2014 from http://articles.orlandosentinel.com/2014-04-03/news/os-george-zimmerman-juror-names-20140403_1_george-zimmerman-trayvon-martin-circuit-judge-debra-nelson.

Williams, Marian R. (2002). A comparison of sentencing outcomes for defendants with public defenders versus retained counsel in a Florida circuit court. *Justice System Journal,* 23, 249–257.

Williams v. Florida, 399 U.S. 78 (1978).

Young, Gwynne A. (2013). *Gideon's* promise. *Florida Bar Journal,* 87 (3), 4, 6.

CHAPTER 7

FLORIDA CORRECTIONS

Learning Objectives

After reading this chapter, you should be able to:

- Explain what the phrase "minimum standards" means for Florida correctional officers.
- List the minimum standards that one must satisfy to become a Florida correctional officer.
- Understand what "certification" means.
- List some examples of correctional officer duties and responsibilities.
- Outline some of the provisions contained in the Florida correctional officer code of conduct.
- Explain the overall structure of the Florida correctional system.
- Separate the role of a prison from that of a jail.
- Elaborate on various categories of persons who are detained in jails.
- Distinguish probation from parole.
- Appreciate how the Florida correctional system compares with the remainder of the country in terms of the number of prisoners it holds and the imprisonment rate.
- Discuss the demographic characteristics of the correctional officers who staff the Florida prisons.
- Paint a picture of county jails and their sworn personnel.
- Assess how Florida jails rank in comparison to similar facilities throughout the country.
- Draw a picture that compares number of persons under correctional supervision with the number of college students in the state.
- Distinguish national from state accreditation.
- List some benefits that are expected to materialize from accreditation.
- Tell what privatization means.
- Analyze the growth in privatization.
- Visit the recent controversy surrounding privatization of Florida prisons.
- Link the loss of civil rights with convicted felons.
- Summarize how the Florida inmate population has become older.
- Appreciate how the expenses associated with medical care are expanding.

Introduction

Crime is a significant problem in Florida. As we saw earlier in Chapter 3, Florida has experienced some of the highest crime rates in the country. The apparatus that Florida has set up to deal with persons convicted of crimes is the topic of this chapter.

This chapter, like the earlier one on law enforcement, opens with an explanation of what it takes to become a correctional officer in Florida. It then details how the correctional system is organized before delving into a selected group of topics. The effort to promote professionalism is addressed within the context of both national and state accreditation standards. Privatization, currently a controversial item in the Sunshine State, is presented in an effort to clarify what is taking place today. Civil rights restoration, a post-release concern, receives attention. Finally, the chapter visits the issue of an aging inmate population and the special considerations this group requires.

Becoming a Correctional Officer in Florida

Florida correctional officers are considered to be sworn law enforcement officers and follow a similar path as do police officers to become certified (*Florida Statutes 2014*, § 943.13). Just like police officers, correctional officers must meet certain job requirements known as "minimum standards." Then, candidates must enroll in a state-approved correctional officer academy and undergo basic recruit training. Once a person successfully completes this pre-service training, then he or she is eligible to take the state certification examination. All correctional officers (persons employed by the State of Florida and those individuals employed by private corporations who have contracted services with the State of Florida) must complete these steps. Thus, correctional officers in private facilities have the same pre-service training as correctional officers in state-run facilities.

Minimum Standards

The Criminal Justice Standards and Training Commission (CJSTC), housed within the Florida Department of Law Enforcement (FDLE), oversees the employment of correctional officers. All public and private correctional officers must achieve certification prior to employment. *Certification* means that a person is licensed by the state to serve as a correctional officer. There are certain minimum standards that candidates must satisfy prior to becoming certified. Figure 7.1 explains what these *minimum standards* include.

Agencies are not allowed to hire anybody who does not comply with all these minimum standards. However, agencies can install more stringent requirements (e.g., raise the minimum educational requirement or increase the minimum age) if they deem it beneficial.

Correctional Officer Academy Training

The CJSTC licenses a number of correctional officer training academies throughout the state. Each academy must demonstrate that its instructors, facilities, and curriculum are in compliance with CJSTC expectations. The pre-service instruction is standardized

Figure 7.1 Entrance Requirements for Florida Correctional Officers

Minimum Qualifications:

- Be at least 19 years old;
- Be a citizen of the United States notwithstanding any laws of the State to the contrary;
- Be a high school graduate or its "equivalent" as the term may be determined by the Criminal Justice Standards and Training Commission;
- Not have been convicted of any felony or of a misdemeanor involving perjury or a false statement, nor have received a dishonorable discharge from any of the Armed Forces of the United States;
- Have his/her processed fingerprints on file with the employing agency;
- Have passed a medical examination by a licensed physician based on specifications established by the Commission;
- Have good moral character as determined by a background investigation under procedures established by the Commission;
- Have completed the basic recruit training course for Correctional Officers and be eligible for, or possess, a current employment certificate of compliance for Correctional Officers issued by the Criminal Justice Standards and training Commission; and
- Have a valid driver's license.

Salary Information:

- Trainee Officer: $28,007 annually;
- Certified Officer: $30,808–45,034 annually;
- Annual salary additive of approximately $1,200 when employed in Indian River, Martin, Okeechobee, or St. Lucie counties. Annual salary additive of approximately $2,500 when employed in Palm Beach, Broward, Dade or Monroe counties;
- Annual uniform and shoe allowance of $325; and
- Criminal Justice Incentive Pay up to $1,560 annually ($130 per month).

Source: Florida Department of Corrections (2014a). *Correctional Officer Careers: Minimum Qualifications.* Florida Department of Corrections: Tallahassee. Retrieved on October 28, 2014 from http://www.fldocjobs.com/paths/co/qualifications.html; Florida Department of Corrections (2014b). *Correctional Officer Careers: Salary Information.* Tallahassee: Florida Department of Corrections. Retrieved on October 28, 2014 from http://www.fldocjobs.com/paths/co/salary.html.

throughout the entire state. That means a correctional officer academy in northwest Florida teaches the same materials as a pre-service academy located in the southeast portion of the state. The purpose behind this standardization is to make sure that all entry-level correctional officers meet the same basic criteria.

Table 7.1 describes the pre-service training academy curriculum. The academy spans a 11-week period and includes 449 hours of instruction. Almost all the training is devoted to defensive tactics, weapons, and physical fitness. The remainder is spent in the classroom familiarizing recruits with legal aspects, communications, interpersonal skills, emergency procedures, basic functions in correctional operations, and first aid. A comparison of the academy curriculum with the duties and responsibilities of correctional officers, listed in Figure 7.2, illustrates how the pre-service training is aligned on-the-job activities.

Table 7.1 Instructional Hours Devoted to Topics during the Florida Correctional Officer Academy Training

Training Topic	Hours of Instruction		Training Topic	Hours of Instruction	
	n	%		*n*	%
Introduction to Corrections	32	8%	**First Aid**	40	10%
Training Program Overview					
Values and Ethics			**Defensive tactics**	80	19%
Professionalism					
Chain-of-Command			**Firearms**	80	19%
Criminal Justice System					
Constitutional Rights			**Wellness**	30	7%
Inmate Rights					
Legal Issues with Contraband					
Criminal Acts					
Use of Force					
Criminal and Civil Liability					
Communications	40	10%	**Facility and Equipment**	8	2%
Interpersonal Comm.			Equipment Management		
Telecommunications			Hazardous Materials		
Interviewing			Entering, Exiting Facilities		
Report Writing			Inspections		
			Security		
			Facility Safety Concerns		
			Sanitation and Health		
Officer Safety	16	4%	**Response to Emergencies**	16	4%
Safety and Security			Identifying Emergencies		
Identification			Determining a Response		
Manipulation and Deception			Types of Emergencies		
Contraband			Investigating Crimes		
Searches					
Supervising a Corrections Facility	40	10%	**Supervising Special Pops.**	20	5%
Observing/Monitoring Inmates			Diversity		
Supervising Referral Process			Security Threat Groups		
Inmate Discipline Process			Substance Abuse		
Inmate Count			Mentally Ill Inmates		
Inmate Dining			Juvenile & Youth Inmates		
Processing Mail			Elderly Inmates		
Visitation			Inmates and Gender		
Escorting Inmates			Inmates and Sexuality		
Transporting Inmates			Physically Disabled		
Work Squads			Inmates w Medical Needs		
Hospital			Inmates in Confinement		
			Death Row Inmates		
Intake and Release	18	4%			
Intake and Assessment					
Searching and Inventory					
Fingerprinting, Photos					
Classification and Housing					
Release					
			TOTAL	420	102%

Source: Author compilation from Florida Criminal Justice Standards and Training Commission (2014a), *Florida CMS Correctional Basic Recruit Training Program, ATMS #1190, Instructor Guide.* Tallahassee: Florida Department of Law Enforcement. Retrieved on October 28, 2014 from http://www.fdle.state.fl.us/Content/getdoc/e0f681e3-e361-4c21-a095-7c7ae787dd4e/2014_CO_IG.aspx.

Figure 7.2 Examples of Correctional Officer Duties and Responsibilities

- Supervise inmates in housing units and those segregated for administrative or punitive measures;
- Instruct inmates in housekeeping and sanitation;
- Supervise the issuance of clothing and other personal effects to inmates;
- Make periodic patrols of quarters and work areas and initiate counts of inmates at regular and irregular intervals;
- Maintain control and discipline including use of physical restraint and restraining devices;
- Prevent the introduction of contraband into the institution;
- Check inmate mail for possible contraband;
- Maintain a periodic patrol either inside or outside the institution to ensure the security and integrity of the institution;
- Monitor, supervise and screen inmate visitor traffic;
- Monitor periguard system;
- Observe traffic in and around the compound;
- Instruct inmates and maintain control in areas such as the inmate food service area, auditorium, etc.;
- Observe for signs of disorder or tension and report such observations to a higher authority;
- Counsel with inmates regarding institutional, domestic or emotional adjustment problems;
- Maintain a record of equipment, supplies and other items;
- Maintain and demonstrate proficiency in the use and care of firearms, restraint methods and equipment and emergency measures;
- Maintain knowledge of communication and other electronic equipment;
- Instruct inmates in the proper care and use of institutional equipment;
- Maintain master inmate location counts;
- Setup and receive inmate counts and be familiar with the entire operation of the Control Room;
- Initiate and participate in search of inmate recreation areas, work areas, and housing units to prevent the introduction of contraband items;
- Maintain proper security of inmates being transported;
- Ensure that all transportation permits are completed accurately and signed by the appropriate authority;
- Institute proper restraints as appropriate for inmate's custody classification; and
- Check transportation vehicles daily.

Source: Florida Department of Corrections (2014c). *Correctional Officers Careers: Examples of Duties and Responsibilities.* Tallahassee: Florida Department of Corrections. Retrieved on October 28, 2014 from http://www.fldocjobs.com/paths/co/duties.html.

The Correctional Officer Certification Examination

The CJSTC requires aspiring correctional officers pass a competency examination known as the State Officer Certification Examination (SOCE) after they complete the pre-service academy training. The exam is fashioned after the basic recruit training

Figure 7.3 Florida Correctional Officer Code of Conduct

I. I will never forget that I am a public official sworn to uphold the Constitutions of the United States and the State of Florida.

II. I am a professional committed to the public safety, the support and protection of my fellow officers, and co-workers, and the supervision and care of those in my charge. I am prepared to go in harm's way in fulfillment of these missions.

III. As a professional, I am skilled in the performance of my duties and governed by a code of ethics that demands integrity in word and deed, fidelity to the lawful orders of those appointed over me, and, above all, allegiance to my oath of office and the laws that govern our nation.

IV. I will seek neither personal favor nor advantage in the performance of my duties. I will treat all with whom I come in contact with civility and respect. I will lead by example and conduct myself in a disciplined manner at all times.

V. I am proud to selflessly serve my fellow citizens as a member of the Florida Department of Corrections.

Source: Florida Department of Corrections (2014d). *Code of Conduct.* Florida Department of Corrections: Tallahassee. Retrieved on October 28, 2014 from http://www.dc.state.fl.us/code.html.

curriculum. A total of 1,811 persons took the corrections SOCE during the first half of calendar year 2014 and 76% achieved a passing grade (Florida Criminal Justice Professionalism Program, 2014a, 2014b). These successful recruits are now considered to be "employable material."

Successful aspirants who travel through all these steps are now postured to receive a job offer as a correctional officer. Once they acquire a position, recruits will participate in any post-academy training the agency deems necessary. The Florida correctional officer code of conduct appears in Figure 7.3. It demonstrates the principles to which all correctional officers subscribe.

The Structure of the Florida Correctional System

The Florida correctional system maintains facilities at the state level. As Figure 7.4 illustrates, the FDOC operates 143 prison facilities within the state. These locations include major prisons, annexes, work camps, work release centers, road prisons, and forestry camps. *Prisons* are reserved for adults or persons sentenced as adults to more than one year imprisonment (FDOC, 2013).

Local jails contain a different set of inmates. As Figure 7.4 explains, *jails* are intended to handle defendants who are sentenced to confinement for a period of less than one year. Out of necessity, though, local jails often house several other categories of persons.

Probation and parole facilities are the third component in the Florida correctional system. As Herberman and Bonczar (2014, p. 2) explain, *probation* refers to "a court-ordered period of correctional supervision in the community, generally as an alternative to incarceration." *Parole*, on the other hand, "is a period of conditional supervised release in the community following a prison term." People sometimes refer to both probation and parole as *community supervision*.

Figure 7.4 Jail Functions and Services

Jails are correctional facilities that confine persons before or after adjudication and are usually operated by local law enforcement authorities. Jail sentences are usually for 1 year or less. Jails also:

- Receive individuals pending arraignment and hold those awaiting trial, conviction, or sentencing.
- Remit probation, parole, and bail-bond violators and absconders.
- Temporarily detain juveniles pending transfer to juvenile authorities.
- Hold mentally ill persons pending transfer to appropriate mental health facilities.
- Hold individuals for the military, for protective custody, for contempt, and for the courts as witnesses.
- Release inmates to the community upon completion of sentence.
- Transfer inmates to federal, state, or other authorities.
- House inmates for federal, state, or other authorities because of crowding of their facilities.
- Sometimes operate community-based programs as alternatives to incarceration.

Source: Bureau of Justice Statistics (2011). *Local Jail Inmates and Jail Facilities.* Washington, DC: U.S. Department of Justice. Retrieved on October 28, 2014 from http://www.bjs.gov/index.cfm?ty=tp&tid=12.

Prisons, jails, probation, and parole have their own set of priorities and operational procedures. As a result, the following materials present information regarding each of these three subsystems.

Prisons

One way to place Florida prisons into a more understandable context is to compare the Sunshine State with the remainder of the nation. As Table 7.2 demonstrates, the Florida prison system is the third largest operation in the United States. It houses 103,028 inmates. One way to place this number in perspective is to match it with the full-time equivalent undergraduate enrollment in Florida public universities during the summer 2013, fall 2013, and spring 2014 semesters. The Florida prison inmate count is about the same as the number of college students attending Florida State University, University of Florida, University of Central Florida, and University of South Florida (Florida Board of Governors, 2014).

One can also compare states in terms of the imprisonment rate. The *imprisonment rate* reflects the number of prisoners divided by the state population, multiplied by 100,000 persons. According to this calculation, Florida drops a few notches to eighth place among the states.

As mentioned earlier in Chapter 5, the racial composition of Florida residents is 78% white, 17% black or African American, and 5% other. Women account for 51% of the population (U.S. Census Bureau, 2014). These benchmarks help observers understand whether there is an overrepresentation or underrepresentation of select groups among sworn personnel.

Table 7.2 Number of Prisoners and Imprisonment Rates, by State, as of December 31, 2013

	Prisoners			Imprisonment Rate	
Rank	State	Number	Rank	State	Rate
1	Texas	168,280	1	Louisiana	847
2	California	135,981	2	Mississippi	692
3	Florida	103,028	3	Oklahoma	659
4	Georgia	54,004	4	Texas	602
5	New York	53,550	5	Arizona	586
6	Ohio	51,729	6	Arkansas	578
7	Pennsylvania	50,312	7	Georgia	533
8	Illinois	48,653	8	Florida	524
9	Michigan	43,759	9	Missouri	521
10	Arizona	41,104	10	Idaho	466

Source: Compiled by author from Heather C. West, William J. Sabol, and Sarah J. Greenman (2010). *Prisoners in 2009.* Washington, DC: Bureau of Justice Statistics, pp. 16, 24. Retrieved on November 17, 2011 from http://bjs.ojp.usdoj.gov/content/pub/pdf/p09.pdf.

Table 7.3 displays the number of correctional officers in the state and their demographic composition. The FDOC employed 15,601 sworn personnel in a full-time capacity. Looking at race, the correctional officer population comes close to tracking the state figures. A total of 67% of the correctional officers are white and 33% are black. In other words, whites are underrepresented among the rank and file while minority members are over-represented. While women are underrepresented relative to their presence in the Florida population, their numbers in the correctional surpasses their presence in the law enforcement sector. However, one does need to keep facility location in mind. Many correctional facilities are sited in outlying rural areas. Correctional facilities often become a dominant economic engine in these poorer, agricultural areas.

The entries in Table 7.3 also hint at another recent development, the rise of private prisons, which we will examine in greater detail later in this chapter. The State of Florida has signed contracts with Corrections Corporation of America, Management and Training Corporation, and The GEO Group to operate several private prison facilities in Florida. These locations employ almost 1,500 certified correctional officers. A quick glance at Table 7.3 might lead the reader to suspect the data contain some discrepancies. For example, 87% of the correctional officers who work in the Gadsden facility are black and 68% are female. Gadsden County is the only county in the state where people of African-American descent represent a majority of the local population (Gadsden County, 2014). In addition, the Gadsden Correctional Institute is a women's prison. Similarly, the residents of the City of South Bay are 63% African American and 25% Hispanic (U.S. Census Bureau, 2014).

Table 7.4 presents the entry-level salaries for correctional officers in both state and private prisons. Generally speaking, starting salaries are higher in public facilities than in private institutions. The annual pay for a state correctional officer is almost $31,000 while a correctional officer working for a private corporation most likely will earn around $29,000 a year.

Table 7.3 Sworn Size, Race, and Gender of Full-Time Sworn Personnel, Florida Correctional Facilities, 2012

Institution	Number of Full-Time Officers	% White	% Non-white	% Female
State Facilities:				
Dept. of Corrections	15,601	67	33	21
Dept. of Corrections Inspector General	69	81	19	29
FL State Hospital Correctional Staff	69	68	32	25
FL State Hospital Persons with Disabilities	30	37	63	27
North FL Evaluation & Treatment Center	38	47	53	16
Private Facilities:				
Bay Correctional Facility	159	70	30	36
Blackwater River Correctional Facility	245	80	20	24
Florida Civil Commitment Center	75	61	39	33
Gadsden Correctional Institution	184	13	87	68
GEO Care/S. FL Evaluation & Treatment Center	49	4	96	35
GEO Care Treasure Coast Forensic Treatment Ctr	54	43	57	17
Graceville Correctional Facility	180	65	35	42
Lake City Correctional Facility	142	58	42	28
Moore Haven Correctional Facility	142	46	54	34
South Bay Correctional Facility	240	10	90	45

Source: Compiled from Florida Department of Law Enforcement (2013). *Criminal Justice Agency Profile Report 2012.* Retrieved on October 29, 2014 from http://www.fdle.state.fl.us/Content/getdoc/8670ee78-1114-445c-ba74-cd0d03a14abe/2012-CJAP-Correctional-Agencies-Index-Page.aspx.

Jails

The usual arrangement is for the sheriff to assume responsibility for operating the county jail. However, some local governments have established their own separate jails or have hired private corporations to provide these services. As Table 7.5 reveals, 61 sheriff offices (SOs) run county jails and another 19 local jails are either separate county departments or private facilities. Together, these local facilities employ a total of 12,973 correctional officers on a full-time basis. As you can see, a number of these facilities are relatively small in size. About half the SOs and 22% of the private and county facilities are less than 50 sworn members.

Table 7.6 displays the number of correctional officers who work in the Florida SOs and their demographic composition. Looking at race, the correctional officer population consists of 58% white persons and 42% nonwhite. Women account for almost one-third of the correctional officer population. When one takes agency size into consideration, certain dynamics emerge. Larger agencies have the capacity to assemble a more racially diverse staff. Smaller agencies, on the other hand, are more likely to employ female correctional officers.

As Table 7.7 illustrates, the average entry-level salary of a correctional officer working in a Florida SO can be competitive with the wages earned in a state or private facility. On average, though, a beginning correctional officer will make $33,271 on an annual basis. As one might suspect, the starting salary will vary depending upon agency size and location.

Table 7.4 Entry-Level Salary, State and Private Correctional Facilities, 2013

Institution	Entry-Level Salary
State Facilities:	
Department of Corrections	$30,808
FL State Hospital Correctional Staff	$30,808
FL State Hospital Persons with Disabilities	$30,808
North Florida Evaluation & Treatment Center	$32,208
Private Facilities:	
Bay Correctional Facility	$29,120
Blackwater River Correctional Facility	n/a
Florida Civil Commitment Center	$29,099
Gadsden Correctional Institution	$27,040
GEO Care/S. FL Evaluation & Treatment Center	$36,000
GEO Care Treasure Coast Forensic Treatment Ctr	$31.000
Graceville Correctional Facility	$30,056
Lake City Correctional Facility	$29,474
Moore Haven Correctional Facility	$30,160
South Bay Correctional Facility	$30,056
South Bay Correctional Facility	$30,056

Source: Compiled from Florida Department of Law Enforcement (2014a). *Criminal Justice Agency Profile Report 2013.* Retrieved on October 29, 2014 from http://www.fdle.state.fl.us/Content/getdoc/ c67375a2-67bd-489a-9f4f-119e23bcc34c/2013-CJAP-Correctional-Agencies-Index-Page.aspx.

While most jail staffs are relatively small in size, two-thirds of all local correctional officers work in a county sheriff office. At the same time, the Florida jail population is quite substantial. Table 7.8 ranks the fifty largest jails throughout the nation in terms of

Table 7.5 Number of County Correctional Facilities and Full-Time Sworn Correctional Officers, 2013

	Sheriff Offices				Private & County			
	Agencies		Sworn Personnel		Agencies		Sworn Personnel	
Sworn Size	*n*	%	*n*	%	*n*	%	*n*	%
1–9	8	13	42	1	—	—	—	—
10–24	11	18	187	2	2	11	22	—
25–49	11	18	395	5	2	11	86	
50–99	8	13	580	7	3	16	213	4
100–249	15	25	2,341	30	9	47	1,598	31
250–499	4	7	1,300	17	1	5	261	5
500–999	4	7	2,935	38	1	5	992	19
1,000+	—	—	—	—	1	5	2,021	39
Total	61	101	7,780	100	19	100	5,193	100

Source: Compiled from Florida Department of Law Enforcement (2014a). *Criminal Justice Agency Profile Report 2013.* Retrieved on October 29, 2014 from http://www.fdle.state.fl.us/Content/getdoc/ c67375a2-67bd-489a-9f4f-119e23bcc34c/2013-CJAP-Correctional-Agencies-Index-Page.aspx.

**Table 7.6 Sworn Size, Race, and Gender of Full-Time Correctional
Officers, Florida Sheriff Offices, 2012**

Sworn Size	% White	% Nonwhite	% Female
1–9	81	19	39
10–24	70	30	38
25–49	79	21	32
50–99	73	27	29
100–249	62	38	30
250–499	54	46	36
500+	50	50	30
Total %	58	42	31
Total *n*	4,512	3.230	2,434

Source: Compiled from Florida Department of Law Enforcement (2014b). *Criminal Justice Agency Profile Report 2013*. Retrieved on October 30, 2014 from http://www.fdle.state.fl.us/Content/getdoc/ fe4a385f-32c8-445f-af50-b23e0216df70/2013-Sheriff-s-Office-Index-Page.aspx.

the average daily inmate population. The *average daily inmate population* reflects the total number of inmates held in jail each day of the year divided by 365 days (Minton, 2011, p. 3). Looking at the table, one can see that Florida places eight jails in this category. There were 55,282 persons under lock and key in Florida jails in June of 2014 (FDOC, 2014e). Another way to think about this number is to imagine that the all the undergraduate students at Florida Agricultural and Mechanical University, University of West Florida, University of North Florida, Florida Gulf Coast University, and Florida International University are placed in confinement.

**Table 7.7 Sworn Size and Average Entry-Level Salary of Correctional Officers,
Florida Sheriff Offices, 2013**

Sworn Size	Number of Agencies	Entry-Level Salary Average	Minimum	Maximum
1–9	5	$26,900	$22,500	$30,000
10–24	10	$25,539	$20,000	$33,009
25–49	11	$31,821	$28,840	$36,000
50–99	8	$35,479	$30,560	$39,401
100–249	15	$37,451	$28,521	$43,050
250–499	4	$38,100	$33,882	$47,220
Total	57	$33,271	$27,967	$39,002

Source: Compiled from Florida Department of Law Enforcement (2014b). *Criminal Justice Agency Profile Report 2010*. Retrieved on October 31, 2014 from http://www.fdle.state.fl.us/Content/getdoc/ fe4a385f-32c8-445f-af50-b23e0216df70/2013-Sheriff-s-Office-Index-Page.aspx .

**Table 7.8 50 Largest Local Jails in the United States by Average Daily
Inmate Population, 2010**

Rank	Facility	Rank	Facility
1	Los Angeles County, CA	26	Tarrant County, TX
2	New York, NY	27	Allegheny County, PA
3	Harris County, TX	28	**Pinellas County, FL**
4	Cook County,, IL	29	Gwinnet County, GA
5	Philadelphia City, PA	30	Clark County, NV
6	Maricopa County, AZ	31	District of Columbia
7	Dallas County, TX	32	**Palm Beach County, FL**
8	**Miami-Dade County, FL**	33	Milwaukee County, WI
9	Shelby County, TN	34	Travis County, TX
10	San Bernardino County, CA	35	Bernalillo County, NM
11	Orange County, CA	36	Kern County, CA
12	San Diego County, CA	37	Cobb County, GA
13	**Broward County, FL**	38	King County, WA
14	Alameda County, CA	39	York County, PA
15	Sacramento County, CA	40	Suffolk County, MA
16	Bexar County, TX	41	Mecklenburg County, NC
17	**Jacksonville City, FL**	42	Fulton County, GA
18	Baltimore City, MD	43	**Polk County, FL**
19	**Orange County, FL**	44	Salt Lake County, UT
20	Santa Clara County, CA	45	Essex County, NJ
21	DeKalb County, GA	46	Denver County, CO
22	Davidson County, TN	47	Oklahoma County, OK
23	Orleans Parish, LA	48	Marion County,, IN
24	Riverside County, CA	49	Clayton Co, GA
25	**Hillsborough County, FL**	50	Franklin County, OH

Source: Compiled by author from Todd D. Minton (2011). *Jail Inmates at Midyear 2010—Statistical
Tables*, pp. 10–11. Washington, DC: Bureau of Justice Statistics. Retrieved on October 30, 2014 from
http://bjs.ojp.usdoj.gov/content/pub/pdf/jim10st.pdf.

Community Supervision

There were 1,638 probation and parole officers monitoring over 147,000 additional
offenders in Florida during June of 2014 (FDOC, 2014f). Like correctional officers,
probation officers must meet the same set of minimum standards and then complete a
449-hour pre-service academy training module (FCJSTC, 2014b). In addition, they must
have earned a bachelor's degree prior to employment (FDOC, 2014g). A new correctional
probation officer earns a starting salary of $33,478 a year (FDOC, 2011h).

As Herberman and Bonczar (2014, p, 2) explain, probation refers to "a court-ordered
period of correctional supervision in the community, generally as an alternative to incarceration." Parole, on the other hand, "is a period of conditional supervised release in
the community following a prison term." The average length of time a person spends

Figure 7.5 Examples of Probation and Parole Officer Duties and Responsibilities

- Evaluates offender progress and recommends intensity of supervision based on observations from time of conviction through the period of adjustment after release from an institution.
- Assists offenders in securing jobs, maintains contacts with business organizations and employment agencies, and arrange for employment interviews.
- Counsels and refers offenders to specialized treatment services at guidance clinics, mental health clinics, and related organizations.
- Records offender restitution payments, cost of supervision, court costs, as well as other related payments.
- Maintains an awareness of offenders' daily activities and evaluates desirability to remain at liberty.
- Represents the Department of Corrections in all parole hearings for inmates assigned to caseload.
- Appears as a witness at parole or probation revocation hearings.
- Responsible for the case management of all assigned inmates.
- Serves as a team leader or member in all case reviews to determine the direction for each case.
- Serves as team chairman or member of all disciplinary due process hearings for inmates assigned to caseload.
- Evaluates information from reports, interviews and correspondence and prepares case histories for recommendations for inmate classification and job assignment.

Source: Florida Department of Corrections (2014j). *Correctional Probation Officer Careers: Examples of Duties and Responsibilities.* Tallahassee: Florida Department of Corrections. Retrieved on October 30, 2014 from http://www.fldocjobs.com/paths/cpo/duties.html.

under supervision is 4.1 years for probation and 17.1 years for parole (FDOC, 2014i). Figure 7.5 displays some of the typical duties that probation and parole officers perform.

The total number of full-time undergraduate students who attend the University of South Florida and Florida Atlantic University amounts to approximately 38,000 persons (Florida Board of Governors, 2014). Factoring in the 155,000 college students who go to school at the 31 private, not-for-profit, colleges and universities throughout the state (Independent Colleges & Universities of Florida, 2014) leads to a sobering realization. That is, the number of people in prisons, jails, or under community supervision in the Sunshine State almost equals the total number of Florida college students who are working on their four-year baccalaureate degrees in public and private institutions.

Accreditation

The topic of accreditation received some attention in the earlier chapter on Florida law enforcement agencies. There it was explained that accreditation focuses upon a set of minimum standards for law enforcement organizations. Essentially, *accreditation* means that an agency has undergone both internal and external review to make sure that its goals, objectives, and policies comply with the "best practices" in the field. Like law enforcement, the field of corrections is also involved in accreditation at both the national and the state level.

Figure 7.6 Benefits of Accreditation

- Improved management.
- Strengthens the facility's defense against lawsuits and complaints.
- Increased accountability.
- Enhanced public credibility for administrative and line staff.
- A safer and more humane environment for administrative and line staff.
- Potential reduction in liability through adoption of sound operating pratices.
- Demonstration of a "good faith" effort to improve conditions of confinement.
- Establishment of measurable criteria for upgrading programs, personnel, and physical plant.

Source: Taylor County Sheriff's Office (2014). *Corrections Accreditation.* Perry, FL: Taylor County Sheriff's Office. Retrieved on October 31, 2014 from http://taylorcountysherifffl.org/Corrections Accreditation.aspx.

The National Effort

The American Correctional Association (ACA) initiated a national campaign during the 1970s to upgrade correctional organizations. The ACA assembled a panel of representatives from a wide range of groups that dealt with adult corrections, juvenile rehabilitation, and other portions of the criminal justice system. These experts drafted a series of standards that promoted sound, state-of-the-art practices in such target areas as prison and jail operations, probation and parole services, detention facilities, training academies, boot camps, correctional industries, electronic monitoring, and so forth. Eventually, the ACA delegated responsibility for carrying out its accreditation program to the Commission on Accreditation for Corrections (CAC).

The CAC administers the daily operations of the ACA accreditation program. Whenever an agency decides to pursue accreditation, it contacts the CAC to determine what standards are applicable and how to proceed. The agency usually begins by selecting an accreditation manager from its staff members. The accreditation manager coordinates all the accreditation activities with the CAC. The next step is to assemble the appropriate documents that show how an agency complies with the relevant standards. Should the organization not be in compliance with a standard, the accreditation manager will implement a corrective plan. This self-evaluation process usually takes between twelve and eighteen months to complete. At that point, the agency is ready for an audit team to conduct an on-site inspection. If the audit uncovers any deficiencies, the assessors will suggest remedies that the accreditation manager can implement. Once all the standards have been addressed, the ACA will confer its seal of approval. The accreditation status is good for three years. After that, the agency must initiate another self-study, address any new or revised standards that have emerged during the interim, and then undergo another external inspection.

The ACA (2014) reports that almost 1,500 correctional agencies have become accredited since the program's inception in 1978. Florida was the first state to embrace the accreditation process and continues to be a leader in that endeavor (FDOC, 2014k). Today, 47 of the major correctional institutions, along with the probation and parole field services offices and 20 work release centers, have achieved ACA accreditation. As Figure 7.6 shows, proponents claim there are a number of benefits that accredited agencies enjoy.

The Florida Effort

Despite widespread participation, going through the accreditation process can be an expensive venture for many agencies. There are fees associated with the audit process, along with a consultant charge and travel expense reimbursement for each member who participates in the on-site review. An agency may incur additional costs for training, consultation, pre-accreditation site visits, and monitoring visits should the need arise. As the reader can see, these expenses place national accreditation beyond the reach of many smaller organizations.

In a move that paralleled developments in the law enforcement sector, the Florida Corrections Accreditation Commission (FCAC) is designed to oversee the accreditation process for correctional facilities operating in the Sunshine State. The attraction of this program is that it is geared towards problems, regulations, and laws that pertain to the state of Florida. In addition, accreditation fees are reduced and are graduated according to agency size, resulting in considerable savings for some locations. For example, smaller facilities that hold less than 50 prisoners are charged a $450 accreditation fee. Institutions that handle 50 or more inmates but less than 250, are assessed a $900 accreditation fee. The fee is $3,000 for agencies in the 250–1,000 range and $3,900 for larger facilities (Commission for Florida Law Enforcement Accreditation, 2014). Thus far, 34 county jails have earned the FCAC stamp of approval.

Questions concerning the impact of accreditation surface at this point. Unfortunately, a definitive body of literature that evaluates this effort to achieve greater professionalism simply does not exist at this time. In its place, though, one can locate an ample supply of supportive testimonials on the internet. However, these statements are largely anecdotal and do not emanate from independent third-party sources.

Private Prisons

One alternative to having the state operate correctional facilities has been the move towards allowing private enterprises to manage correctional facilities on behalf of the state. *Privatization* means that an independent business entity will contract with state officials to house prisoners after the corporation builds and staffs a facility. Once the prison is fully operational, the state then transfers convicts to that location. Although the private business houses the inmates, the state still retains authority over parole decisions, release, and other matters.

The attractive feature here is that relying upon the public sector helps the state avoid the costly construction process. It also allows the state to gain more bed space at a reduced price, especially at a time when some states have come under judicial scrutiny for overcrowded prison conditions. As a report from one investment firm stated, "private prison builders can more efficiently bring new facilities on line, with time savings of 50% and typical cost savings between 15% and 25%" (Coffey & Fox, 2002, p. 17). Despite these apparent pluses, there are some concerns about cost effectiveness and the direction that privatization is taking.

Growth

The private prison industry has enjoyed a lucrative growth spurt in recent years. In 1995, there were just 29 private prisons scattered throughout the United States. That figure jumped to 101 by 2000 and then inched up to 107 by 2005 (Stephan, 2008, p. 2; Stephan & Karberg, 2003, p. iv). In addition, for-profit corporations had assumed responsibility for running 308 community-based facilities (halfway houses, residential treatment centers, restitution centers, and pre-release centers) around the country (Stephan, 2008).

Private prisons held 12,736 state inmates in 1995 (Stephan & Karberg, 2003, p. v). That number rose to almost 86,000 inmates by 2005 (Stephan, 2008) and climbed to 92,000 state prisoners held in private prison confinement by the end of 2013 (Carson, 2014, p. 14). Factor in another 23,000 persons being processed in community-based facilities and one can see that privatization has managed to make substantial inroads. That expansion has made the industry very attractive to investors and the stock market (Coffey & Fox, 2002).

The Federal Bureau of Prisons reserved more than 41,000 beds in private prisons during 2013 (Carson, 2014). A number of states have also become involved in similar arrangements. By 2005, Texas had outsourced 15,131 inmates to private locations. In that same year, Florida housed 5,739 persons in 15 private facilities (Stephan, 2008, p. 3). Today, there are eleven private prisons doing business in the Sunshine State and together they account for almost 12,000 state prisoners (Carson, 2014).

Savings

Governmental officials envision privatization as a source of considerable savings for taxpayers. According to state law, private contractors must guarantee that their facilities will generate a cost savings of at least 7% when juxtaposed against comparable FDOC operations (*Florida Statutes 2014*, §957.07). Just as a gross point of comparison, the FDOC (2013, p. 9) reports that the average inmate per diem cost is $52.63 for all persons under state supervision. That figure compares with an average daily cost of $45.75 in a typical private institution. However, several differences make it difficult to conduct a direct comparison. For example, Hall and his co-authors (2010, p. 3) caution that "those who are more costly to handle are usually incarcerated in public prisons, such as those who are the highest security risks and those with extensive medical issues." At the same time, staff training and personnel qualifications must meet or exceed the minimum standards that FDOC employees must satisfy.

In spite of these directives, Florida officials have encountered obstacles that make it very difficult to pinpoint the actual dollar amount of savings (Brown & Vaughn, 1995; Harkness, Vaughn, Williams, & Holley, 209). One review flatly states "There is no compelling evidence that the privatization of prisons has actually resulted in savings" (Hall, Walsh, & Walsh, 2010, p. 4). The contracts with private management companies typically lack any specifications or standards that would enable a routine evaluation of such typical indicators as recidivism (Harkness, Vaughn, Williams, & Holley, 2008). Despite this shortcoming, one independent group of researchers was able to track over 81,000 Florida inmates who were released from both private and public prisons during the 1995–2001 interval (Bales, Bedard, Quinn, Ensley, & Holley, 2005). Those authors concluded there was "no convincing evidence that exposure to private prisons reduces recidivism" (p. 80).

Thwarted Expansion

The budget bill that took effect at the end of the Florida 2011 legislative session ignited a firestorm of activity on all sides. Tucked away in the fine print of the final budget was an allocation and language that allowed the FDOC to convert 29 public correctional facilities in the southern portion of the state immediately into private prisons. When FDOC Secretary Buss failed to pursue this matter quickly enough, Governor Scott relieved him of his official duties. Buss, whom the Governor had lured from a similar correctional leadership position in Indiana, had been on the job for only eight months.

While the movement towards privatization appeared to have gathered momentum, three developments obstructed the path. The first blockage occurred when officials realized that FDOC would incur an unanticipated $25 million tab to pay departing employees for their accumulated vacation days, sick time, and overtime. The transfer of prisons from a public employer to the private sector meant that the State of Florida would terminate the employment of more than 4,000 staff members. Those departures would trigger a payout that one official said "may just cripple the agency for the next year" (Bousquet, 2011). While proponents originally claimed that privatization would save the state $22 million during the first year of operation alone, they had overlooked this $25 million payout that would come due immediately. Thus, the highly touted savings that had energized the march towards privatization quickly evaporated.

A second sticking point arose when the Florida Police Benevolent Association (PBA), the collective bargaining agent for the soon-to-be displaced correctional officers, filed a lawsuit aimed at preventing the switch from governmental oversight to the private sector. The PBA, which had campaigned against Scott when he was a candidate for the governor's office, contended that the transfer was illegal under the state constitution. The PBA took the position that such a policy change needed to be promulgated through the normal legislative process instead of being slipped surreptitiously into the budget. After hearing both sides present their arguments, the judge ruled that not only had the FDOC violated procedures, so had the legislature (*Baiardi et al. v. Tucker*, 2011). Judge Fulford conceded that the Florida Legislature did possess the authority to privatize existing correctional facilities. However, she ultimately concluded that such a transfer could only be accomplished through the passage of substantive legislation and that path had to follow normal legislative procedures. As a result, the effort to privatize those 29 Florida prisons stalled.

A third development also unfolded. Mindful that privatization would reappear in the next legislative session, correctional officers throughout the state participated in an election to determine who their collective bargaining agent would be. The final ballot count resulted in the selection of the Teamsters Union to represent the 19,000 FDOC workers (Florida Public Employees Relations Commission, 2011). The Teamsters, of course, oppose privatization efforts, thus paving the way for confrontation in the near future.

Civil Rights Restoration

In addition to serving any sentence imposed by a judge, persons convicted of a felony in Florida also forfeit their civil rights. According to Article VI of the Florida Constitution, convicted felons automatically lose the right to vote, commonly referred to as d*isenfranchisement*, and the right to hold office. In addition, convicted felons forfeit the right to possess or use a firearm, to serve on a jury, and to hold certain state occupational licenses. These losses are permanent unless one applies for clemency and is granted restoration.

Convicted felons must complete the application form that appears in Figure 7.7 to initiate the process to have their civil rights restored. Clemency rules divide felonies into two groups. The less serious offenses require a waiting period of five years before applying for restoration, while the more serious crimes have a seven-year interval. Applicants must

Figure 7.7 The Florida Clemency Application

APPLICATION FOR CLEMENCY
Check box for type of clemency desired. All applications must have the proper court documents attached.

☐ **Restoration of Civil Rights for Florida/Federal/ Military, or Out-of-State conviction** (Eligible 5 or 7 years after completion of sentence)

☐ **Restoration of Alien Status Under Florida Law** (Eligible 5 or 7 years after completion of sentence)

☐ **Remission of Fine or Forfeiture**

☐ **Specific Authority to Own, Possess or Use Firearms** (Eligible 8 years after completion of sentence)

☐ **Full Pardon** (Eligible 10 years after completion of sentence)

☐ **Pardon Without Firearm Authority** (Eligible 10 years after completion of sentence)

Commutation of Sentence (Use Form "Request for Review")

If you have applied for a Full Pardon, Pardon Without Firearm Authority or Specific Authority to Own, Possess or Use Firearms and are determined ineligible due to not meeting the time requirement, you will be processed for Restoration of Civil Rights. If you have already received Restoration of Civil Rights, a Certificate for Restoration of Civil Rights will be mailed to you.

Your signature acknowledges you understand this action. _____
                                                                    SIGNATURE

PLEASE PRINT

Name When Convicted: _____

Current Name: _____ Other Names Used: _____

Date of Birth: _____ Race: _____ Sex: ☐ Male ☐ Female   Driver License #: _____

U.S. Citizen? ☐ Yes ☐ No - Alien Registration _____ Social Security #: _____

Home Address: _____
                        Street   City   County   State   Zip

Mailing Address: _____
                        Street   City   County   State   Zip

Home Telephone #: _____ Cellular Telephone #: _____

E-mail Address: _____

PRISON/PROBATION #: _____

CONVICTIONS: (Please list each conviction and provide court documents for each conviction. If you have more than two convictions, please attach a separate sheet of paper listing all the required information.) **YOU DO NOT NEED TO FILL OUT A SEPARATE APPLICATION FOR EACH CONVICTION.**

_____

_____

Court_____ County/State_____ Date Convicted _____ Date Sentenced_____

What was your sentence? _____

Date you completed/expired your sentence: _____ (Please Circle one of the following: Prison   Jail   Release   Parole   Probation)

_____   _____
             Signature   Date

YOU DO NOT HAVE TO HAVE AN ATTORNEY FOR THIS PROCESS. Do not list the attorney who represented you during the criminal proceedings. If you have chosen to be represented by an attorney for the clemency process, please provide the Attorney Name, Address & Telephone Number.

_____   _____   _____
     Attorney Name   Address   Telephone Number

Attach a certified copy of the following for EACH felony conviction: charging indictment/information; judgment; and sentence/community control/probation order.

APPLICATIONS SUBMITTED WITHOUT THE PROPER COURT DOCUMENTS WILL **NOT** BE ACCEPTED.

Mailing Address: Office of Executive Clemency   Form ADM 1501
                   4070 Esplanade Way   Updated 06/30/2014-JMc
                   Tallahassee, FL 32399-2450

UNDER THE FLORIDA CONSTITUTION, A CONVICTED FELON CANNOT VOTE, SERVE ON A JURY, OR HOLD PUBLIC OFFICE UNTIL CIVIL RIGHTS HAVE BEEN RESTORED.

Source: Florida Commission on Offender Review (2014). *Application for Clemency.* Tallahassee: Florida Parole Commission. Retrieved on October 30, 2014 from https://www.fcor.state.fl.us/docs/clemency/ClemencyApplication.pdf.

have completed all their sentencing conditions and be crime-free since their release before receiving any consideration (Florida Commission on Offender Review, 2011). Only the Governor, along with the support of two of the other three members who sit on the Clemency Board, can exercise the power to restore civil rights.

During his administration, Governor Crist had instituted an automatic restoration of all civil rights, except for firearms ownership, upon release from prison without having to petition for a formal hearing. However, Governor Scott changed the rules after he assumed office. As Governor Scott (2011) explained, "Felons seeking restoration of rights will also be required to demonstrate that they desire and deserve clemency by applying only after they have shown they are willing to abide by the law."

The ramifications of these changes are far-reaching. The Florida Advisory Commission to the U.S. Commission on Civil Rights (Flom, 2008) estimated that as many as 200,000 persons lost their right to cast a ballot during 1995–2005 period because of Florida's standing policy not to reinstate the right to vote to convicted felons. The number of affected minority voters probably reached the one-million mark. Since blacks are incarcerated more often than whites, many observers are of the opinion that this prohibition is designed intentionally to exert a disproportionate impact on minority voters and the political platforms they are most likely to support (Holloway, 2014; Nelson, 2013).

A Graying Inmate Population

Whenever policy changes are enacted, they are likely to generate two distinct types of outcomes: manifest and latent effects. *Manifest effects* refer to the intended consequences. For example, minimum mandatory sentencing laws are designed to keep people incarcerated for a specific term. *Latent effects*, on the other hand, refer to any unintended effects. Several writers blame Florida's minimum mandatory sentencing laws for igniting an explosive expansion in the number of persons kept under lock and key (Harris, 2013; McCarthy, 2014; Nauman, 2013). Unexpected costs that stem from minimum mandatory sentencing, such as rising health expenses due to an older inmate population, would fit here.

The Expanding Group of Senior Inmates

The Florida prison population has become increasingly older over the past nineteen years. The typical inmate was 33 years old in 1996. By 2014, the average age had increased to 38 years (FDOC, 1996; FDOC, 2013). In terms of sheer numbers, almost 20,000 prisoners in Florida have surpassed the 50-years-old mark (FDOC, 2013). Today, Florida prison cells are home for 1,091 persons in their seventies, 130 in their eighties, and 10 in their nineties (McCarthy, 2014, p. 4). Most of these advanced seniors, despite miniscule odds of recidivating, will not survive until their release dates.

Figure 7.8 displays further evidence of Florida's aging inmate population. While all the other age groups show a decline, the percent inmates over the age of 50 has increased from 6% in 1996 to 19% in 2013 (FDOC, 1996; FDOC, 2013). The 50+ age group is the fastest growing segment of the correctional population. And, there are no signs that this expansion is abating in the near future.

While age 50 is not necessarily a definitive marker for senior citizen status, it is a common cut-off point that many prison experts utilize (Kerbs & Jolley, 2009; Kerbs & Jolley, 2014). Quite often, inmates arrive at the prison gates already infected with a variety of communicable diseases, stemming from prior risky lifestyles and lack of regular medical treatment, and mental health issues. In addition, older inmates who have endured the rigors of prison life often face multiple health complications that the general public does

Figure 7.8 Florida Prison Population Composition by Age Groups, 1996–2013

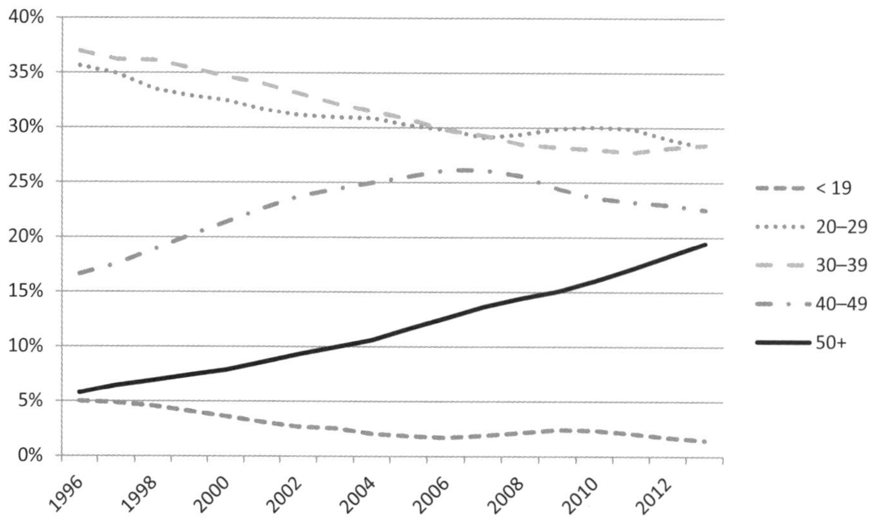

Source: Compiled by author from Florida Department of Corrections annual reports.

not experience. Florida prisons, for example, contain some of the highest counts of inmates who are HIV positive and are confirmed AIDS cases in the country (Maruschak, 2010; Maruschak, 2012). Clearly, Florida is facing an immense problem with its emerging elderly prisoner population.

How did the inmate population manage to reach this point? There are a number of contributing factors. For example, the 1995 Florida Legislature passed a law that requires offenders to serve at least 85% of their sentences prior to release (*Florida Statutes 2014*, § 944.275). That statutory requirement has increased the amount of time inmates must serve in Florida's correctional facilities (FDOC, 2014l; Sabol et al., 2002). In addition, minimum mandatory sentences now require offenders to serve specific periods before becoming eligible for release. Several writers blame Florida's minimum mandatory sentencing laws for igniting an explosive expansion in the number of persons kept under lock and key (Harris, 2013; McCarthy, 2014; Nauman, 2013).

These developments, along with other sentencing modifications, are keeping prisoners in confinement for longer periods of time (Kerbs & Jolley, 2009; Kerbs & Jolley, 2014). Florida has the dubious honor of leading the nation in terms of the lengthy sentences that prisoners serve (Gelb, Dhungana, Adams, McCann, & Zafft, 2014). The net result of these "get tough" policies is that the elderly segment of the Florida prison population is becoming increasingly larger, older, and, in turn, much more expensive to maintain. Medical expenditures for Florida prisoners have skyrocketed by 77% from 2001 to 2008 (Kyckelhahn, 2014). These costs siphon considerable amounts of money from other areas of the state budget. As Harris (2013, p. 435) notes, "Florida is among a list of states that spend more money on corrections than on education."

Health Needs of Senior Inmates

The Florida Correctional Medical Authority (CMA) is charged with monitoring the health needs of state prisoners and tracking medical service delivery (*Florida Statutes 2014*, §945.601). This body was created in response to a class action lawsuit by Florida inmates seeking better medical care (*Celestineo v. Singletary*, 1993). The CMA (2013) audits health care in the state's correctional facilities and makes recommendations for improvements in an effort to ward off further lawsuits.

The CMA (2013, p. 20) projects that at least a quarter of Florida's elderly inmates will eventually die of natural causes in custody while serving their prison terms. In addition, half of Florida's elderly prisoners suffer from some type of visual, hearing, physical, or developmental impairment (CMA, 2013, p. 22). While some of these difficulties can be handled by providing wheelchairs, lower bunks, hearing aids, and other accommodations, the medical needs of this group will become more chronic, pervasive, and costly as the prisoners age. These older inmates have twice as many sick calls compared to younger prisoners, require more medical prescriptions, undergo more surgeries, and need more medical attention (CMA, 2013, pp. 22–25). One estimate is that it takes $70,000 a year to maintain an older inmate, more than two to three times what it costs to incarcerate younger and healthier inmates (CMA, 2013, p. 27). Considerations such as these have prompted Gov. Scott to privatize prison health care in an effort to hold down expenditures (Galik, Gilroy, & Volokh, 2014).

These costs and their allied concerns have prompted some legislators to propose a medical parole program for elderly prisoners. Senator Smith introduced a bill in the 2012 session that would have created the "Elderly Rehabilitated Inmate Program." Among other things, inmates could petition the Parole Commission for early compassionate release if they:

- were at least 60 years old;
- had already served 25 consecutive years of incarceration;
- had not been sentenced for a capital felony;
- were not serving a minimum mandatory sentence; and
- had not received a disciplinary report during the previous six months.

Estimates were that 98 current inmates would be eligible for release in this program over the next few years. It was anticipated that this program would not have a significant impact on the Parole Commission (now renamed the Florida Commission on Offender Review) and would generate considerable savings for the FDOC. A conservative estimate is that a program like this, after one subtracts administrative and community supervision costs, would produce substantial savings associated with the provision of medical treatment and end-of-life care (Chettiar, Bunting, & Schotter, 2012). Continuation on this path is not a sustainable option. As one independent report explains,

> The addition of 4,100 elderly prisoners to the current population of 20,750 will take Florida to 24,850 elderly prisoners by the end of 2015. Assuming no interim policy changes to manage the elderly prison population, the number will further climb to 30,000 by 2018. Comparing this to national average predictions from the *Wall Street Journal*, which reports that "at current rates a third of all prisoners will be 50 or older by 2030," Florida will achieve this dubious distinction 10 years ahead of the rest of the nation (McCarthy, 2014, p. 12).

Summary

In addition to providing a description of the Florida correctional system, this chapter visited some of the complications and issues that have arisen with this facet of the criminal justice system. It has detailed some of the problems that are peculiar to Florida, while also looking at concerns that other states also face. At the same time, some of these developments are ongoing and still evolving. Hopefully, the background provided in this chapter will allow readers to monitor further developments that will take place in the near future. It is obvious that Florida has taken the lead on many fronts and the back seat on others.

Key Terms

accreditation
average daily inmate population
certification
community supervision
disenfranchisement
imprisonment rate
jails
latent effects
manifest effects
minimum standards
parole
prisons
privatization
probation

Selected Internet Sites

American Corrections Association
    http://www.aca.org

American Jail Association
    http://www.aja.org

Association of Private Correctional & Treatment Organizations
    http://apcto.org

Correctional Accreditation Managers' Association
    http://mycama.org

Corrections Corporation of America
    http://www.cca.com

Florida Accreditation
    http://www.flaccreditation.org

Florida Department of Corrections Teamsters Local 2011
    http://fdocteamsters.unionactive.com

Florida Rights Restoration Coalition
   http://www.restorerights.org

The GEO Group, Inc.
   http://www.geogroup.com

The Management and Training Corp.
   http://www.mtctrains.com

Review Questions

1.   What are "minimum standards"?

2.   Assemble a list of minimum standards for Florida correctional officers.

3.   What does "certification" mean?

4.   What are some of the topics that are covered in the correctional officer training academy curriculum?

5.   What are some of the duties and responsibilities that correctional officers perform?

6.   What is the "State Officer Certification Examination"?

7.   Give aspects that are covered in the "Florida Correctional Officer Code of Conduct"?

8.   What three units form the Florida correctional system?

9.   What types of inmates are housed in Florida prisons?

10. What types of inmates are housed in Florida jails?

11. Distinguish probation from parole.

12. How large is the Florida prison population compared to other states?

13. How large is the Florida imprisonment rate compared to other states?

14. Develop a demographic and salary profile of state correctional officers.

15. Develop a demographic and salary profile of county correctional officers.

16. How do Florida jails fare in comparison to the 50 largest jails in the United States?

17. What are some of the duties and responsibilities that probation and parole officers perform?

18. Compare the number of persons in Florida who are under correctional supervision with the number of students enrolled in colleges and universities.

19. What is accreditation?

20. Why does Florida have its own state accreditation body?

21. What benefits is accreditation purported to yield?

22. What does the term "privatization" mean for corrections?

23. What are some reasons why proponents favor privatization?

24. How has privatization grown over the past few years?

25. How has the effort to privatize Florida prisons become controversial?

26. What is disenfranchisement?

27. What civil rights do convicted felons forfeit in Florida?

28. How is civil rights restoration handled in Florida?

29. Why has Florida's prison population become older?

30. What impact does an aging inmate population have for health care?

31. Talk about the "Elderly Rehabilitated Inmate Program" proposal that has been introduced in recent state legislative sessions.

References

American Correctional Association (2014). *The Commission on Accreditation for Corrections*. Alexandria, VA: Standards and Accreditation Department. Retrieved on October 31, 2014 from http://www.aca.org/ACA_Prod_IMIS/ACA_Member/Standards___Accreditation/About_Us/CAC/ACA_Member/Standards_and_Accreditation/SAC_Commission.aspx?hkey=90da0502-afd8-4685-97c2-b8c7e1c803d3.

Baiardi et al. v. Tucker (September 30, 2011). Case No. 2011 CA 1838. Tallahassee: Second Judicial Circuit. Retrieved on November 1, 2014 from http://www.sunshinestatenews.com/sites/default/files/Injunction_PBA_v_DOC-4.pdf.

Bales, William D., Laura E. Bedard, Susan T. Quinn, David T. Ensley, and Glen P. Holley (2005). Recidivism of public and private state prison inmates in Florida. *Criminology & Public Policy, 4*, 57–82.

Bosquet, Steve (2011). Privatization of prison comes with an unexpected $25 million expense. *Miami Herald*, August 16.

Brown, D. Byron and Linda S. Vaughn (1995). *Review of Correctional Privatization: Report No. 95–12*. Tallahassee: Office of Program Policy Analysis and Government Accountability. Retrieved on November 1, 2014 from http://www.oppaga.state.fl.us/MonitorDocs/Reports/pdf/9512rpt.pdf.

Bureau of Justice Statistics (2011). *Local Jail Inmates and Jail Facilities*. Washington, DC: U.S. Department of Justice. Retrieved on October 28, 2014 from http://www.bjs.gov/index.cfm?ty=tp&tid=12.

Carson, E. Ann (2014). *Prisoners in 2013*. Washington, DC: Bureau fo Justice Statistics. Retrieved on October 29, 2014 from http://www.bjs.gov/content/pub/pdf/p13.pdf.

Celestineo v. Singletary, 147 F.R.D. 258 (1993).

Chettiar, Inimai, Will Bunting, and Geoff Schotter (2012). *At America's Expense: The Mass Incarceration of the Elderly*. New York: American Civil Liberties Union. Retrieved in November 5, 2014 from https://www.aclu.org/criminal-law-reform/report-americas-expense-mass-incarceration-elderly.

Coffey, Henry J., Jr., and Carrington Fox (2002). *Private Corrections Industry: Beds and Cons? Changing Dynamics, Areas of Potential Growth*. New York: Morgan Lewis Githens & Ahn, Inc. Retrieved on November 1, 2014 from http://www.apcto.org/logos/stockanalysis.pdf.

Commission for Florida Law Enforcement Accreditation (2014). *Program Requirements*. Tallahassee: Commission for Florida Law Enforcement Accreditation. Retrieved on October 31, 2014 from http://flaccreditation.org/prcr.htm.

Flom, Elena M. (2008). *Ex-Felon Voting Rights in Florida: Revised Rules of Executive Clemency That Automatically Restore Civil Rights to Level-1 Offenders Is the Right Policy.* Washington, DC: Florida Advisory Committee to the U.S. Commission on Civil Rights. Retrieved on November 1, 2014 from http://www.usccr.gov/pubs/EX-FelonVRFL.pdf.

Florida Board of Governors (2014). *State University System of Florida Facts and Figures.* Tallahassee: State University System of Florida. Retrieved on October 29, 2014 from http://www.flbog.edu/resources/factbooks/factbooks.php.

Florida Commission on Offender Review (2011). *Rules of Executive Clemency.* Tallahassee: Florida Parole Commission. Retrieved on November 1, 2014 from https://www.fcor.state.fl.us/docs/clemency/clemency_rules.pdf.

Florida Commission on Offender Review (2014). *Application for Clemency.* Tallahassee: Florida Parole Commission. Retrieved on October 30, 2014 from https://www.fcor.state.fl.us/docs/clemency/ClemencyApplication.pdf.

Florida Correctional Medical Authority (2013). *2012–2013 Annual Report and Report on Aging Inmates.* Tallahassee: Florida Department of Health. Retrieved on December 30, 2014 from http://www.flgov.com/wp-content/uploads/pdfs/correctional_medical _authority_2012-2013_annual_report.pdf.

Florida Criminal Justice Professionalism Program (2014a). State officer certification examination statistics second quarter, fy 2013–2014. *Quarterly Update, Spring 2014.* Tallahassee: Florida Department of Law Enforcement. Retrieved on October 10, 2014 from http://www.fdle.state.fl.us/Content/getdoc/bc16efd2-4c09-407a-8fad-a93832272357/Summer-2014-Quarterly-Update.aspx.

Florida Criminal Justice Professionalism Program (2014b). State officer certification examination statistics third quarter, fy 2013–2014. *Quarterly Update, Fall 2014.* Tallahassee: Florida Department of Law Enforcement. Retrieved on October 10, 2014 from http://www.fdle.state.fl.us/Content/getdoc/a9a4918f-f629-48be-a3bd-e477e2a 56528/Fall-2014-Quarterly-Update.aspx.

Florida Criminal Justice Standards and Training Commission (2014a), *Florida CMS Correctional Basic Recruit Training Program, ATMS #1190, Instructor Guide.* Tallahassee: Florida Department of Law Enforcement. Retrieved on October 28, 2014 from http://www.fdle.state.fl.us/Content/getdoc/e0f681e3-e361-4c21-a095-7c7ae787dd4e/2014_CO_IG.aspx.

Florida Criminal Justice Standards and Training Commission (2014b), *Florida Correctional Probation Basic Recruit Training Program, ATMS #1176, Course Guide.* Tallahassee: Florida Department of Law Enforcement. Retrieved on October 31, 2014 from http://www.fdle.state.fl.us/Content/getdoc/bbffbc1b-3283-4ab7-a4de-480a088e4ce8/2014-CPO-BRTP.aspx.

Florida Department of Corrections (1996). *Fiscal Year 1995–1996 Annual Report.* Tallahassee: Florida Department of Corrections. Retrieved on October 29, 2014 from http://www.dc.state.fl.us/pub/annual/9596/stats/stat_in.html.

Florida Department of Corrections (2013). *Fiscal Year 2011–2012 Annual Report.* Tallahassee: Florida Department of Corrections. Retrieved on October 29, 2014 from http://www.dc.state.fl.us/pub/annual/1112/AnnualReport-1112.pdf.

Florida Department of Corrections (2014a). *Correctional Officer Careers: Minimum Qualifications.* Florida Department of Corrections: Tallahassee. Retrieved on October 28, 2014 from http://www.fldocjobs.com/paths/co/qualifications.html.

Florida Department of Corrections (2014b). *Correctional Officer Careers: Salary Information.* Tallahassee: Florida Department of Corrections. Retrieved on October 28, 2014 from http://www.fldocjobs.com/paths/co/salary.html.

Florida Department of Corrections (2014c). *Correctional Officers Careers: Examples of Duties and Responsibilities.* Tallahassee: Florida Department of Corrections. Retrieved on October 28, 2014 from http://www.fldocjobs.com/paths/co/duties.html.

Florida Department of Corrections (2014d). *Code of Conduct.* Florida Department of Corrections: Tallahassee. Retrieved on October 28, 2014 from http://www.dc.state.fl.us/code.html.

Florida Department of Corrections (2014e). *Florida County Detention Facilities Average Inmate Population, June 2014.* Tallahassee: Florida Department of Corrections. Retrieved on October 31, 2014 from http://www.dc.state.fl.us/pub/jails/2014/06/FCDF.PDF.

Florida Department of Corrections (2014f). *Florida's Community Supervision Population. June 2014.* Tallahassee: Florida Department of Corrections. Retrieved on October 31, 2014 from http://www.dc.state.fl.us/pub/spop/2014/06/0614.pdf.

Florida Department of Corrections (2014g). *Correctional Probation Officer Careers: Minimum Qualifications.* Tallahassee: Florida Department of Corrections. Retrieved on October 31, 2014 from http://www.fldocjobs.com/paths/cpo/qualifications.html.

Florida Department of Corrections (2014h). *Correctional Probation Officer Careers: Salary Information.* Tallahassee: Florida Department of Corrections. Retrieved on October 31, 2014 http://www.fldocjobs.com/paths/cpo/salary.html.

Florida Department of Corrections (2014i). *Community Supervision Population: Average Sentence Length for those on Community Supervision on June 30, 2013 is 4.1 Years.* Tallahassee: Florida Department of Corrections. Retrieved on October 31, 2014 from http://www.dc.state.fl.us/pub/annual/1213/stats/csp_length.html.

Florida Department of Corrections (2014j). *Correctional Probation Officer Careers: Examples of Duties and Responsibilities.* Tallahassee: Florida Department of Corrections. Retrieved on October 31, 2014 from http://www.fldocjobs.com/paths/cpo/duties.html.

Florida Department of Corrections (2014k). *Accreditation in Florida: Leading the Nation.* Tallahassee: Florida Department of Corrections. Retrieved on October 31, 2014 from http://www.dc.state.fl.us/pub/ACA/index.html.

Florida Department of Corrections (2014l). *Doing Time: Most Florida Inmates Serving More than 85% of Their Sentences.* Tallahassee: Florida Department of Corrections. Retrieved on November 1, 2014 from http://www.dc.state.fl.us/pub/timeserv/doing/DoingTime2014.pdf.

Florida Department of Law Enforcement (2013). *Criminal Justice Agency Profile Report 2012.* Retrieved on October 29, 2014 from http://www.fdle.state.fl.us/Content/getdoc/8670ee78-1114-445c-ba74-cd0d03a14abe/2012-CJAP-Correctional-Agencies-Index-Page.aspx.

Florida Department of Law Enforcement (2014a). *Criminal Justice Agency Profile Report 2013.* Retrieved on October 29, 2014 from http://www.fdle.state.fl.us/Content/getdoc/c67375a2-67bd-489a-9f4f-119e23bcc34c/2013-CJAP-Correctional-Agencies-Index-Page.aspx.

Florida Department of Law Enforcement (2014b). *Criminal Justice Agency Profile Report 2013*. Retrieved on October 30, 2014 from http://www.fdle.state.fl.us/Content/getdoc/fe4a385f-32c8-445f-af50-b23e0216df70/2013-Sheriff-s-Office-Index-Page.aspx.

Florida Public Employees Relations Commission (2011). *Teamsters Local Union No. 2011 v. State of Florida, Department of Management Services, v. Florida Police Benevolent Association, Inc., and International Union of Police Associations, AFL-CIO, Case No. EL-2011-025*. Tallahassee: Florida Public Employees Relations Commission. Retrieved on November 1, 2014 from http://perc.myflorida.com/download.aspx/Prefix=Certs/File=1779-120511143757.pdf.

Florida Statutes 2014.

Gadsden County (2014). *About Gadsden County*. Quincy, FL: Gadsden County Commission. Retrieved on October 29, 2014 from http://www.gadsdengov.net/category/?categoryid=7.

Galik, Lauren, Leonard Gilroy, and Alexander Volokh (2014). *Annual Privatization Report 2014: Criminal Justice and Corrections*. Los Angeles, CA: Reason Foundation. Retrieved on October 31, 2014 from http://reason.org/files/apr-2014-criminal-justice.pdf.

Gelb, Adam, Karla Dhungana, Benjamin Adams, Ellen McCann, and Kathryn Zafft (2014). *Max Out: The Rise in Prison Inmates Released Without Supervision*. Washington, DC: The Pew Charitable Trusts. Retrieved on November 4, 2014 from http://www.pewtrusts.org/~/media/Assets/2014/06/04/MaxOut_Report.pdf.

Hall, John, Kelly Walsh, and Mike Walsh (2010). *Are Florida's Private Prisons Keeping Their Promise? Lack of Evidence to Show They Cost Less and Have Better Outcomes than Public Prisons*. Tallahassee: Florida Center for Fiscal and Economic Policy. Retrieved on November 1, 2014 from http://fcfep.org/attachments/20100409—Private%20Prisons.

Harkness, Marti, Linda Vaughn, Victor Williams and Glen Holley (2009). *While DMS Has Improved Monitoring, It Needs to Strengthen Private Prison Oversight and Contracts, Report No. 08-71*. Tallahassee: Office of Program Policy Analysis and Government Accountability. Retrieved on November 1, 2014 from http://www.oppaga.state.fl.us/MonitorDocs/Reports/pdf/0871rpt.pdf.

Harris, Maggie E. (2013). The cost of mandatory minimum sentences. *Florida Coastal Law Review*, 14, 419–450.

Herberman, Erinn J. and Thomas P. Bonczar (2014). *Probation and Parole in the United States, 2013*. Washington, DC: Bureau of Justice Statistics. Retrieved on October 29, 2014 from http://www.bjs.gov/content/pub/pdf/ppus13.pdf.

Holloway, Pippa. (2014). *Living in Infamy: Felon Disfranchisement and the History of American Citizenship*. New York: Oxford University Press.

Independent Colleges & Universities of Florida (2014). *About Us*. Tallahassee: The Independent Colleges & Universities of Florida. Retrieved on October 31, 2014 from http://www.icuf.org/newdevelopment/about-icuf/.

Kerbs, John J. and Jennifer M. Jolley (2009). A commentary on age segregation for older prisoners: Philosophical and pragmatic considerations for correctional systems. *Criminal Justice Review*, 34, 119–139.

Kerbs, John J. and Jennifer M. Jolley, Eds. (2014). *Senior Citizens Behind Bars: Challenges for the Criminal Justice System*. Boulder, CO: Lynne Rienner Publishers.

Kyckelhahn, Tracey (2014). *State Corrections Expenditures, FY 1982–2010*. Washington, DC: Bureau of Justice Statistics. Retrieved on November 4, 2014 from http://www.bjs.gov/content/pub/pdf/scefy8210.pdf.

Maruschak, Laura M. (2010). *HIV in Prisons, 2007–08*. Washington, DC: Bureau of Justice Statistics. Retrieved on November 1, 2014 from http://www.bjs.gov/content/pub/pdf/hivp08.pdf.

Maruschak, Laura M. (2012). *HIV in Prisons, 2001–2010*. Washington, DC: Bureau of Justice Statistics. Retrieved on November 1, 2014 from http://www.bjs.gov/content/pub/pdf/hivp10.pdf.

McCarthy, Dan (2014). *Over-Criminalization in Florida: An Analysis of Nonviolent Third-degree Felonies*. Tallahassee: The Florida Taxwatch Center for Smart Justice. Retrieved on November 4, 2014 from http://www.floridatrend.com/public/userfiles/news/pdfs/ThirdDegreeFINAL.pdf.

Minton, Todd D. (2011). *Jail Inmates at Midyear 2010—Statistical Tables*, pp. 10–11. Washington, DC: Bureau of Justice Statistics. Retrieved on October 30, 2014 from http://bjs.ojp.usdoj.gov/content/pub/pdf/jim10st.pdf.

Nelson, Janai S. (2013). The First Amendment, equal protection, and felon disenfranchisement: A new viewpoint. *Florida Law Review*, *65*, 111–172.

Sabol, William J., Katherine Rosich, Kamala Mallik-Kane, David P. Kirk, and Glenn Dubin (2002). *The Influences of Truth-in-Sentencing Reforms on Changes in States' Sentencing Practices and Prison Populations*. Washington, DC: Urban Institute. Retrieved on November 1, 2014 from http://www.urban.org/uploadedPDF/410470_FINAL TISrpt.pdf.

Scott, Rick Governor (2011). *Press Release: Governor Scott and Florida Cabinet Discuss Amended Rules of Executive Clemency*, March 9. Tallahassee: Office of the Governor.

Retrieved on November 1, 2014 from http://felonvoting.procon.org/sourcefiles/florida_clemency_press_release.pdf.

Stephan, James J. (2008). *Census of State and Federal Correctional Facilities, 2005*. Washington, DC: Bureau of Justice Statistics. Retrieved on October 31, 2014 from http://www.bjs.gov/content/pub/pdf/csfcf05.pdf.

Stephan, James J. and Jennifer C. Karberg (2003). *Census of State and Federal Correctional Facilities, 2000*. Washington, DC: Bureau of Justice Statistics. Retrieved on October 31, 2014 from http://www.bjs.gov/content/pub/pdf/csfcf00.pdf.

Taylor County Sheriff's Office (2014). *Corrections Accreditation*. Perry, FL: Taylor County Sheriff's Office. Retrieved on October 31, 2014 from http://taylorcountysherifffl.org/CorrectionsAccreditation.aspx.

U.S. Census Bureau (2014). *Florida QuickFacts from the U.S. Census Bureau*. Washington, DC: U.S. Census Bureau. Retrieved on October 10, 2014 from http://quickfacts.census.gov/qfd/states/12000.html.

CHAPTER 8

THE FLORIDA DEATH PENALTY

Learning Objectives

After reading this chapter, you should be able to:

- Provide a picture as to how frequently the death penalty is used.
- Explain the issue in *Furman v. Georgia* (1972).
- Tell how *Furman* involved the Eight Amendment of the U.S. Constitution.
- Present the four essential ingredients Justice Brennan utilized in *Furman* to determine if a punishment was civilized and humane.
- Outline the two strategies that Florida leaders had constructed in response to *Furman*.
- Differentiate aggravated from mitigating circumstances.
- Outline the role of the judge and the jury when it comes to the sentencing portion of a capital penalty case in Florida.
- Summarize the issue in *Gregg v. Georgia* (1976).
- Present the two principles used to determine whether a punishment is excessive.
- Explain what the "standards of decency" argument is.
- Tell why lethal injection is portrayed as a more humane method of execution.
- Link "botched executions" to the Eighth Amendment.
- Describe the current situation regarding the issues surrounding lethal injection.
- Discuss the issues addressed in *Baze v. Rees* (2008).
- Outline the post-conviction process for Florida death penalty cases.
- Explain how and why the post-conviction process consumes so much time.
- Compare incarceration costs for typical inmates and death row inmates.
- Talk about how Florida has handled the issue of public legal representation for death row inmates during the post-conviction appeals process.
- Present some issues associated with public legal representation for death row inmates.
- Explore the goals associated with the "Timely Justice Act."
- Detail the bases for Judge Martinez finding the Florida death penalty to be problematic in terms of the way Florida juries handle aggravating and mitigating circumstances in their sentence recommendation.
- Evaluate whether the call for a moratorium on the Florida death penalty is warranted.

Introduction

The death penalty has had a long and contentious history in the United States as well as in Florida. Up until 1923, county sheriffs were responsible for executing prisoners in Florida. Most executions were conducted by hanging. In 1923, the Florida Legislature adopted electrocution as the proper mode of execution. From that point forward, executions were carried out by the Florida Department of Corrections (FDOC). The first FDOC execution took place in 1924. Florida electrocuted 196 inmates between 1924 and 1964 (FDOC, no date). No executions took place from May 1964 through May 1979 due to pending litigation and court decisions.

Figure 8.1 contains a graph of the annual number of executions that have taken place from 1930 through 2014 in the United States. The number of executions peaked at a high of 199 in 1935 and dropped to just 2 deaths in 1967. The *Furman* case banned the use of capital punishment in 1972. In 1976, though, the United States Supreme Court overturned that ruling and reinstated the death penalty. As Figure 8.1 shows, there were no executions in this country from 1968 until 1977 when a firing squad shot Gary Gilmore to death in Utah. Florida became the second state to execute a prisoner in 1979 when it electrocuted John Spenkelink, who was convicted of committing a homicide in Tallahassee. The graph also shows how often death sentences have been carried out in the post-*Gregg* period.

Table 8.1 explains that there have been 1,359 executions in this country since the Supreme Court ruled the death penalty was constitutional in its 1976 *Gregg* decision. While Texas has led the country in executions during the post-*Gregg* era, Florida is in

Figure 8.1 Annual Executions in the United States, 1930–November 30, 2014

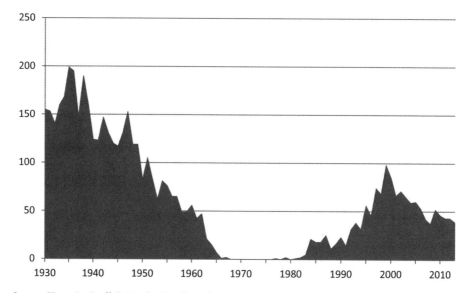

Source: Tracy L. Snell (2014a). *Number of Persons Executed in the United States.* Washington, DC: Bureau of Justice Statistics. Retrieved on December 17, 2014 from https://www.quandl.com/BJS/ CAP_PUN-Number-of-Persons-Executed-in-the-United-States; Tracy L. Snell (2014). *Capital Punishment, 2013 — Statistical Tables.* Washington, DC: Bureau of Justice Statistics. Retrieved on December 17, 2014 from http://www.bjs.gov/content/pub/pdf/cp13st.pdf.

Table 8.1 Death Row Population and Post-*Gregg* Executions by State as of December 31, 2013

State	Number of Inmates	Number of Executions	Average Years Under Sentence of Death	State	Number of Inmates	Number of Executions	Average Years Under Sentence of Death
AL	190	56	12.4	NV	81	12	17.7
AZ	122	36	12.4	NH	1	0	n/a
AR	37	27	14.7	NM	2	1	n/a
CA	735	13	16.1	NC	151	43	15.1
CO	3	1	n/a	OH	136	52	15.2
CT	10	1	11.9	OK	48	108	11.1
DE	17	16	8.2	OR	34	2	12.0
FL	398	81	15.0	PA	190	3	15.4
GA	82	53	15.5	SC	45	43	12.0
ID	12	3	16.2	SD	3	3	n/a
IN	14	20	9.7	TN	75	6	18.4
KS	9	0	n/a	TX	273	508	13.0
KY	33	3	18.3	UT	8	4	n/a
LA	84	28	14.0	VA	7	110	n/a
MD	5	5	n/a	WA	9	5	n/a
MS	50	21	13.0	WY	1	1	n/a
MO	45	70	12.4	Fed.	56	3	9.1
MT	2	3	n/a				
NE	11	3	11.3	Total	2,979	1,359	14.6

Source: Tracy L. Snell (2014b). *Capital Punishment, 2013—Statistical Tables.* Washington, DC: U.S. Department of Justice. Retrieved on December 17, 2014 from http://www.bjs.gov/content/pub/pdf/cp13st.pdf.

fourth-place behind Virginia and Oklahoma. Florida trails only California in the number of inmates currently housed on Death Row.

Further inspection of Table 8.1 reveals some other interesting aspects. A lot of time elapses between when the court imposes the death penalty at sentencing and when the inmate is executed. While the average Death Row inmate lives on that prison tier for 14.6 years, the typical execution in Florida takes 15 years to accomplish. We will focus on this aspect later in the chapter when the discussion centers upon the appeals process.

This brief sketch provides a convenient platform for studying Florida's death penalty. The chapter begins by explaining why the death penalty was banned in 1972, Florida's efforts to defeat this ban, and then the reinstatement of capital punishment in 1976. But, a number of unanticipated issues surfaced when Florida resumed executing prisoners. Those concerns prompted a move away from electrocution to lethal injection. However, this method of execution was prone to its own difficulties. Florida soon became entangled in a number of other challenges during the post-*Gregg* period. As a result, this chapter will identify some of those issues and see how Florida has resolved them.

Making the Death Penalty Constitutional Again

The following materials start by outlining the *Furman* decision that prohibited the imposition of the death penalty. The information then examines how Florida reacted to the death penalty ban. Finally, this section ends with an analysis of *Gregg*, the case that reinstated the death penalty.

The Case of *Furman v. Georgia* (1972)

On June 29, 1972, the United State Supreme Court declared the death penalty, as the states were currently administering it, to be unconstitutional. The Justices found that the practice of imposing capital punishment violated the Eighth Amendment in that it amounted to "cruel and unusual punishment" (see Figure 8.2). As Figure 8.3 demonstrates, the Florida Constitution contains very similar provisions.

The *Furman* decision actually consolidated three related cases into one proceeding. The first case involved a Georgia homicide conviction where the suspect was black and the victim was white. The second was another Georgia case where the defendant was black and the rape victim was white. The third case dealt with a rape conviction in Texas involving a black suspect and a white victim. Juries had found all the defendants in those cases guilty of the charges and all three defendants had received a death sentence.

The majority opinion explained that the Supreme Court would consider the death penalty as "'unusual,' if it discriminates against him [a defendant] by reason of his race,

Figure 8.2 The Eighth Amendment to the United States Constitution

> Excessive bail shall not be required, nor excessive fines imposed, nor cruel and unusual punishments inflicted.

Figure 8.3 The Prohibition against Excessive Punishments in the Florida Constitution

> Excessive fines, cruel and unusual punishment, attainder, forfeiture of estate, indefinite imprisonment, and unreasonable detention of witnesses are forbidden. The death penalty is an authorized punishment for capital crimes designated by the legislature. The prohibition against cruel or unusual punishment, and the prohibition against cruel and unusual punishment, shall be construed in conformity with decisions of the United States Supreme Court which interpret the prohibition against cruel and unusual punishment provided in the Eighth Amendment to the United States Constitution. Any method of execution shall be allowed, unless prohibited by the United States Constitution. Methods of execution may be designated by the legislature, and a change in any method of execution may be applied retroactively. A sentence of death shall not be reduced on the basis that a method of execution is invalid. In any case in which an execution method is declared invalid, the death sentence shall remain in force until the sentence can be lawfully executed by any valid method. This section shall apply retroactively.

Source: Florida Constitution, Article I, Section 17.

religion, wealth, social position, or class, or if it is imposed under a procedure that gives room for the play of such prejudices" (p. 242). Given this orientation, the Court took particular note of research which amply demonstrated that the death penalty was imposed more often on poor, young, undereducated, and black persons. As Justice Douglas wrote:

> we know that the discretion of judges and juries in imposing the death penalty enables the penalty to be selectively applied, feeding prejudices against the accused if he is poor and despite, and lacking political clout, or if he is a member of a suspect or unpopular minority.... (p. 255).

Going a step further, Justice Douglas admonished state authorities that the Eighth Amendment mandates:

> legislatures to write penal laws that are evenhanded, nonselective, and nonarbitrary, and to require judges to see to it that general laws are not applied sparsely, selectively and spottily to unpopular groups (p. 256).

In overturning the three death sentences, each Justice put forth the reasons behind his vote. While some statements conflicted with what others wrote, each individual opinion offered further insights as to the logic the Justice utilized and the positions each might hold in future cases. For example, Justice Brennan put forth four essential ingredients that a punishment had to satisfy if it was to be considered civilized and humane. They are:

1. The punishment should not extract undue physical or mental pain.

2. The punishment cannot be imposed arbitrarily.

3. The punishment must be endorsed as appropriate by society.

4. The punishment must be commensurate or proportionate to the crime. In other words, if a less severe penalty is equally effective, then that less severe penalty must be applied.

These are just a few of the remarks expressed by each of the Justices. As you might imagine, the volume and variety of comments left plenty of room for conjecture, debate, and interpretation. However, state officials did not feel they had the luxury of time to sit back and engage in pensive deliberations. The immediate effects of *Furman* were colossal. The death penalty was wiped off the books in 38 states and the District of Columbia. Over 600 inmates throughout the country were removed from death row and had their sentences reduced to a term of life imprisonment (Ehrhardt, Hubbart, Levinson, Smiley, & Wills, 1973, p. 7). For Florida, *Furman* resulted in 96 inmates being transferred from death row and having their sentences commuted to life imprisonment (Florida Department of Corrections, 2014a). In the meanwhile, legislators fretted that criminals were still committing crimes and preying upon innocent people. Obviously, there was a dire need for an immediate legislative solution to this crisis. The following section visits how Florida addressed this situation.

The Florida Reaction

The *Furman* decision left Florida leaders divided as to what steps they should take next. Each Supreme Court Justice had issued a separate opinion. In some instances, the arguments of one Justice conflicted with the positions taken by other Justices, either in whole or in part. In addition, it appeared that at least two Justices were absolutely opposed to the imposition of capital punishment. Whether the Supreme Court was issuing a decree that banned the death penalty forever or was trying merely to stimulate state legislatures to forge more responsible courses of action was left to the imagination. The immediate task at hand became three-fold (Ehrhardt & Levinson, 1973; Ehrhardt et al., 1973). First, Florida leaders had to divine what the Court had said and meant in its ruling and individual opinions. Second, state officials had to project the position each Justice would take in the future and determine how the Court members eventually would vote. Finally, the task for the Florida Legislature became one of constructing a statute that would silence these objections.

These considerations eventually resulted in two different camps, with both advocating the pursuit of a distinctly different legislative avenue. The first group took the position of pushing for the mandatory imposition of the death penalty for specific crimes. That list included such acts as the premeditated murder of a law enforcement or correctional officer, a felony murder, a contract murder, the assassination of a governmental official, and any death occurring during a hijacking (Stewart, 1992, p. 1308). Other legislative efforts amended the list to include additional crimes, such as sexual battery of a child. The thinking behind these efforts was that removing all discretion and simply imposing the death penalty on everybody convicted of these charges would sidestep the Supreme Court's objection that capital punishment was targeting select individuals in an arbitrary and capricious manner.

A second position emerged in which mercy became the focal point. This strategy called for two different checkpoints. The first safety valve was the installation of a *bifurcated hearing*. In other words, once there was an adjudication of guilty, then the trial would proceed to the second checkpoint, the penalty phase. There, a three-judge tribunal would consider whether the death penalty was warranted.

The Governor at the time, Reubin Askew, called the Florida Legislature into special session for the sole purpose of passing a revised death penalty statute. After much debate and parliamentary maneuvering, the Legislature moved away from the mandatory crime sentencing posture and endorsed the bifurcated hearing system that used a jury rather than the three-judge tribunal. In addition, the final version also included an analysis of aggravating and mitigating circumstances during the sentencing phase.

The new plan called for the sentencing jury to balance aggravating circumstances against mitigating circumstances. *Aggravated circumstances* refer to conditions that make the crime more heinous or despicable than usual (see Figure 8.4). *Mitigating circumstances*, on the other hand, are factors that make the crime less heinous or more understandable (see Figure 8.5). The jury's task would be to locate an appropriate balance between these two sets of circumstances. If the aggravating circumstances outweighed the mitigating circumstances, then the jury should recommend a death sentence. If, however, the mitigating circumstances were more prominent than the aggravating circumstances, then the recommendation should be life imprisonment. A simple majority vote by the jury to recommend the death penalty, as opposed to a unanimous decision, suffices.

Rather than allow the jury unfettered control over the case outcome, the jury's finding became advisory to the judge. If the judge and the jury concurred and reached the same conclusion (either death or life imprisonment), then that penalty stood as the final case outcome. If the judge and the jury disagreed, however, the judge could select what he or she thought was the appropriate punishment. If the jury recommended death, the judge had the authority to override that verdict and declare a life sentence as the penalty. However, if there was disagreement and the judge imposed the death penalty when the jury had recommended life imprisonment, the judge was required to provide a written

Figure 8.4 Examples of Aggravating Circumstances

- The defendant had a previous conviction of a capital felony.
- The defendant created a great risk of death to multiple persons.
- The defendant committed the capital felony in an effort to avoid arrest.
- The defendant committed the capital felony for monetary gain.
- The defendant committed the homicide in a cold, calculated, and premeditated manner.
- The victim was a law enforcement officer acting in an official capacity.
- The defendant was a gang member or a sexual predator.
- The victim was an elected or appointed official.
- The victim was a child under the age of twelve.

Source: Florida Statutes 2011, § 921.141(5).

Figure 8.5 Examples of Mitigating Circumstances

- The defendant had no significant criminal history.
- The defendant was under extreme mental or emotional duress.
- The defendant was an accomplice and had a minor role in the capital felony.
- The defendant had a substantially impaired mental capacity.
- The age of the defendant.
- The victim was a willing participant in the crime.

Source: Florida Statutes 2011, § 921.141(6).

explanation for his or her reasoning. As Chapter 6 explained, a death sentence would trigger an automatic appeal to the state supreme court.

After much debate, the Legislature adopted these provisions. This legislative action made Florida the first state in the Union to pass a revised death penalty statute in the wake of the *Furman* decision. Now, all eyes turned and focused on Washington, D.C. where the Supreme Court would have the final word on whether the revised death penalty was constitutional or not. The 1976 *Gregg v. Georgia* decision would provide just that forum.

The Case of *Gregg v. Georgia* (1976)

The case of *Gregg v. Georgia* afforded the United States Supreme Court the opportunity to review a death penalty statute that was revised in light of the earlier *Furman* decision. Gregg had shot two men to death and then robbed them of their belongings and vehicle. A jury found him guilty of homicide and armed robbery. Based upon the presence of aggravated circumstances, that same jury later sentenced Gregg to death for his misdeeds. The Georgia Supreme Court reviewed the case and agreed that the death penalty was appropriate in this instance. Eventually, the case found its way to the federal Supreme Court.

The issue at the heart of this case was whether the death penalty always amounts to a "cruel and unusual" punishment. The Court reiterated two principles to use when determining whether a punishment is excessive. "First, the punishment must not involve the unnecessary and wanton infliction of pain. Second, the punishment must not be grossly out of proportion to the severity of the crime" (p. 173).

Another consideration is continued public support for the death penalty. Proponents of *Furman* argued that "standards of decency had evolved to the point where capital punishment no longer could be tolerated" (p. 179). However, the Court reached the opposite conclusion. It noted that at least 35 states had revised their capital punishment statutes in the wake of *Furman*. In addition, there was strong undercurrent for keeping the death penalty, particularly for its deterrent value. In other words, the Court felt that "capital punishment is an expression of society's moral outrage at particularly offensive conduct" (p. 183).

In light of these observations, the Court was satisfied that Georgia had instituted sufficient procedural safeguards to ensure that the death penalty would not be imposed arbitrarily or capriciously. Thus, the *Gregg* decision upheld the validity of the Georgia death penalty statute and, by extension, the revisions crafted by the Florida Legislature.

The Resumption of Executions

A number of unanticipated difficulties arose once executions were allowed to resume. Malfunctions during some electrocutions caused observers to wonder whether this was a humane and dignified method. The persistence of these problems prompted many states to switch to lethal injection. However, this technique was not completely error-free either. As a result, this portion of the chapter traces the path that Florida took.

Problems with Electrocutions

The long hiatus between executions in Florida meant that the death apparatus had grown dusty and rusty. Nobody could remember how to operate the electric chair. State officials contacted Westinghouse and the company dispatched a consultant to test the machine and explain how to use it (Clendinen, 1999). Obviously, the machinery was not error-free. While these incidents may not happen regularly or often, "botched executions" sometimes do occur. A *botched execution* refers to an execution that encounters abnormal circumstances and does not unfold according to plan. Such was the case as the execution of Jesse Tafero unfolded on May 4, 1990.

After Tafero was readied and strapped into the electric chair, the executioner threw the first switch which unleashed the initial surge of electricity. Smoke and foot-long flames appeared almost immediately from Tafero's head area. A second jolt of electricity produced even more smoke and flames. After the third electric shock was delivered, Tafero was declared dead.

A subsequent investigation revealed that the electrical apparatus was in perfect working order. The culprit was a worn-out sponge inside the headpiece that had been replaced prior to Tafero's execution. However, the replacement was a synthetic, as opposed to a natural, sponge. It was this substituted synthetic sponge that caught fire during the procedure. Medical personnel were of the opinion that the initial electrical jolt rendered

Tafero unconscious and, as a result, he experienced no undue pain. The autopsy report documented extensive burn marks and charring on Tafero's head

Buenoano, a death row inmate under an active death warrant at this time, filed an appeal. She contended that a malfunctioning electrode was the real cause of the problem in the Tafero execution. The worker who had constructed that device testified that "he created the present Army-boot electrode by riveting different types of metal and roofing material into the boot, together with a stainless steel bolt obtained from a hardware store" (*Buenoano v. Florida*, 1990, p. 315). In light of this device being a homemade contraption, Buenoano maintained that executing her in the same electric chair would expose her needlessly to "cruel and unusual punishment." The courts disagreed and Buenoano was eventually executed. Ironically, a small puff of white smoke appeared from her right ankle area when she was electrocuted.

The execution of Pedro Medina on March 25, 1997 also produced flames and smoke when the electric switch was thrown. According to one newspaper report, "as thousands of volts of electricity coursed through the murderer's body, flames burst from his face mask, startling the assembled witnesses" (Kuntz, 1997). An autopsy confirmed there were distinct third-degree burn marks on Medina's head.

Another botched execution occurred with the death of Allen Lee Davis on July 8, 1999. Guards secured a leather mouth-strap across the bottom of Davis' chin as part of the preparation. However, the strap was so tight that it pushed the inmate's nostrils up and obstructed his airway. Right before the execution began, a nosebleed became evident. Davis also appeared to struggle and yelled twice, but the execution continued. An autopsy revealed that Davis partially suffocated prior to the execution and blood from the nose dripped down to form a pool on his shirt. There were also burn marks about the head area.

These experiences led another inmate to appeal his impending execution scheduled for the very next day (*Provenzano v. Florida*, 1999). Provenzano argued that Florida's electric chair was mechanically defective and that FDOC had failed to follow proper protocol. While the Florida Supreme Court ruled that electrocution was a constitutional method of execution, the case spurred a variety of concurring and dissenting opinions. Among other things, Justice Harding urged the Florida Legislature to end this line of challenges by considering the propriety of lethal injection. Five other Justices (Anstead, Pariente, Quince, Shaw, and Wells) lent their support this course of action. Perhaps Justice Quince summarized the situation best in her concurring opinion when she wrote:

> Execution by electrocution—with its attendant smoke and flames and blood and screams—is a spectacle whose time has passed. The fiery deaths of Jesse Tafero and Pedro Medina and the recent bloody execution of Allen Lee Davis are acts more befitting a violent murderer than a civilized state.... each of these deaths was a barbaric spectacle played by the State of Florida on the world stage. Each botched execution cast the entire criminal justice system of this state—including the courts—in ignominy (*Provenzano v. Florida*, 1999, p. 65).

In light of all these concerns, including botched executions in other jurisdictions, and mindful of what the United States Supreme Court might do in a pending case, Governor Bush convened a special session of the Florida Legislature. That body quickly passed a statute that replaced electrocution with lethal injection as the method of execution.

One commentator aptly noted that this legislative maneuvering was as predictable as it was problematic. As Denno (2007, p. 116) explained:

Historically, challenges to execution methods have followed a fairly predictable Eighth Amendment path. When one method of execution became problematic … states would sense constitutional vulnerability and switch to another method …. When those … methods established a record of serious botches, states switched to lethal injection.

As we shall see in the following section, that path soon proved to have its own set of thorny briars for the State of Florida.

Embracing Lethal Injections

Florida, like other states that rely upon lethal injection to execute condemned persons, had established a three-drug sequence for use in its execution procedure. Under the original protocol, the first drug administered to an inmate during an execution was sodium pentothal. Its purpose is to render the subject unconscious so that he or she does not suffer any pain. The second injection, pancuronium bromide, is given after the first drug has taken effect and the subject is unconscious. It paralyzes muscles so the inmate cannot move and stops respiration. The third drug, potassium chloride, causes the heart to cease beating and completes the death process (Denno, 2002; Denno, 2007).

Confronting New Problems with Lethal Injection

A number of questions quickly became apparent with lethal injection. The major concern is whether the procedure violates the Eighth Amendment protections against "cruel and unusual punishment." Some objections center around whether an execution in this manner produces excruciating pain, whether the dosage or amount of drugs administered is sufficient, and whether this execution technique is inherently flawed because it unwittingly creates lots of room for error.

This section utilizes a timeline of selected cases that have played pivotal roles in shaping Florida's lethal injection procedures. It starts with a review of how Florida responded to mishaps surrounding the Angel Diaz execution. The section then chronicles state and federal supreme court rulings that have shaped FDOC procedures.

The Jennings Commission

The circumstances surrounding the execution of Angel Diaz left many people wondering about whether the FDOC procedures were complete and appropriate. A number of death row inmates filed emergency writs with the Florida Supreme Court the day after the execution asking for an examination of the state's lethal injection procedures. In order to quell rumors and speculation, Governor Bush ordered an immediate moratorium on all executions in Florida (Liptak & Aguayo, 2006). He also appointed a special commission called "The Governor's Commission on Administration of Lethal Injection." William Jennings, an attorney with the Commission on Capital Cases, chaired that fact-finding body. Governor Bush tasked the Jennings Commission with reviewing current lethal injection procedures and recommending revisions wherever necessary. The Commission released its final report on March 1, 2007 (Jennings, 2007).

By some accounts, the Angel Diaz execution was a "botched execution." A *botched execution* refers to an execution that encounters abnormal circumstances and does not unfold according to plan. Observers reported that the Diaz execution took 34 minutes, almost three times longer than normal, to complete and required a second round of injections (Tisch & Krueger, 2006). Some witnesses reported that Diaz appeared to grimace and experience pain during the extended procedure. A post-mortem investigation involving interviews with the warden and members of the execution team revealed they had encountered some technical difficulties. Apparently, both IV needles had penetrated the veins, allowing the administered drugs to pool beneath the skin rather than enter the bloodstream directly. Other procedural irregularities involving the injections were also mentioned in the report (Changus, Bustle, Sorensen, & Sapp, 2006). But, Florida was not alone. Sketchy protocols and overlooked aspects typically characterized lethal injection protocols in many states (Denno, 2002; Denno, 2007).

The Jennings Commission compiled a lengthy list of 37 recommendations. Some of the improvements included the following items:

- Developing written procedures that specify the chain-of-command and the exact responsibilities of each person involved in the execution;
- Establishing a formal training program for all persons involved in the execution;
- Monitering and documenting all stages of the execution;
- Maintaining two independent logs of all the activities as an execution takes place;
- Instituting standard procedures to locate a suitable intravenous site;
- Planning for unexpected events that may arise and issuing guidelines for their resolution;
- Identifying appropriate procedures for administering the drug mix; and
- Conducting a formal post-execution debriefing process.

The Commission also noted a possible complication that had the potential to impede the development of a sound protocol. Members of the medical community, ranging from doctors and nurses to paramedics and emergency medical technicians, have serious reservations about participating in capital punishment procedures. The overarching principle that guides the medical community is the preservation of life. For example, the Code of Ethics adopted by the American Medical Association (2002) forbids physicians from participating in executions. Those prohibited activities include:

> selecting injection sites; starting intravenous lines as a port for a lethal injection device; prescribing, preparing, administering, or supervising injection drugs or their doses or types; inspecting, testing, or maintaining lethal injection devices; and consulting with or supervising lethal injection personnel.

The FDOC (2007) embraced the Jennings Commission Report and began taking action to comply with all the recommendations. More specifically, Secretary McDonough (2007, p. 2) emphasized the absolute need to provide "a humane and dignified death" in as timely a manner as possible. By August 1, 2007, the FDOC had a new set of procedures for how to conduct executions. That action set the stage for yet a new wave of litigation.

Lightbourne v. McCollum (2007)

Lightbourne, a death row inmate, challenged Florida's revised lethal injection procedures almost as soon as they were released. Essentially, Lightbourne contended that death by lethal injection amounted to cruel and unusual punishment, contrary to both the Florida Constitution and the United States Constitution. The Florida Supreme Court summarized the issue very succinctly:

> The claim is not about whether the death penalty is *per se* unconstitutional or whether lethal injection is *per se* unconstitutional under the Eighth Amendment. The claim is specifically about whether the method of execution through lethal injection, as currently implemented in Florida, is unconstitutional because it constitutes cruel and unusual punishment (pp. 14–15).

The ruling explained that a punishment must involve pain so extreme that it amounts to torture or a lingering death before it would be deemed unconstitutional. While acknowledging there had been mishaps in past executions, the court took note of all the changes and details the FDOC had instituted to avoid a repeat of the problems that arose during the Diaz execution. As a result, the Florida Supreme Court rejected Lightbourne's contentions and ruled that he had not "shown a substantial, foreseeable or unnecessary risk of pain in the DOC's procedures for carrying out the death penalty through lethal injection that would violate the Eighth Amendment protections" (p. 56).

Baze v. Rees (2008)

Arguments surrounding exactly how to execute a condemned prisoner made their way to the United States Supreme Court. Baze was convicted of committing two homicides in Kentucky and the lower court sentenced him to death. Baze accepted Kentucky's reliance upon the three-drug mix as a humane way of execution. However, he objected to the manner in which lethal injection was carried out. More specifically, Baze maintained there were a number of flaws with the Kentucky protocol that, if not followed precisely, could produce significant pain. The risk that the execution team might not adhere to the protocol led Baze to suggest that Kentucky should utilize an alternative protocol instead.

The United States Supreme Court rejected this entire line of reasoning. It noted:

> Simply because an execution method may result in pain, either by accident or as an inescapable consequence of death, does not establish the sort of "objectively intolerable risk of harm" that qualifies as cruel and unusual (p. 11).

Baze contended that the possibility of improperly administered drugs, combined with inadequate medical training, inconsistent ways to assess whether the procedure was working as intended, and other sources of human error warranted an entirely different execution methodology. The Justices noted that the mere possibility of a mishap was not sufficient grounds to overturn the way in which executions were conducted. Instead, there must be a "substantial risk of serious harm" to the inmate. The opinion also went on the say that a "State with a lethal injection protocol substantially similar to the protocol we uphold today would not create a risk that meets this standard" (p. 22).

Since the Florida procedure mirrored how Kentucky carried out lethal injections, state officials here were satisfied they had a constitutionally viable method of execution.

Further Challenges in Florida

Florida death row inmates resurrected some of these same issues before the Florida Supreme Court (*Schwab v. Florida*, 2008; *Ventura v. Florida*, 2009). Ventura argued that the Florida Supreme court, up to this point, had not applied the *Baze* standard to determine whether the state's lethal injection protocol was constitutional. After reviewing its past decisions, the court ruled that the state's lethal injection protocol was "substantially similar" to Kentucky's procedure. Furthermore, when evaluating the Florida method of execution, the court explained that it had utilized a more stringent standard. Hence, the court dismissed Ventura's appeal as baseless.

A second inmate, Manuel Valle, carried an appeal to the Florida Supreme Court after Governor Scott signed his death warrant (*Valle v. Florida*, 2011). The FDOC just changed its lethal injection protocol in June after learning that the pharmaceutical manufacturer had ceased production of sodium pentothal. As a result, the FDOC planned to substitute pentobarbital. Valle contended that this switch invalidated the Florida lethal injection procedures because he feared that the new drug might not be as effective as the old substance and, as a result, he could be subject to considerable pain.

Once again, *Baze* came into play. The Florida Supreme Court invoked the *Baze* standard that there must be a "substantial risk of serious harm" to the inmate. However, all the information gathered prior to the FDOC adoption of the substitute drug indicated that pentobarbital was just as effective as the original drug. In addition, the other issues Valle had raised (inadequate supervision and training for members of the execution team, issues with intravenous lines, the assessment of consciousness after administering the first drug, and so forth) had all been resolved in the earlier *Lightbourne* decision. As a result, the Florida Supreme Court ruled that the FDOC procedures, including use of the new drug, were constitutionally proper.

Drug shortages, drug substitutions for unavailable substances, manufacturers ceasing production of drugs used in lethal injection protocols, dependency upon unregulated compounding pharmacies, procedural changes implemented during botched executions, and other difficulties have left the states scrambling to find suitable ways to carry out executions appropriately. All these problems, according to one leading authority on the matter, have plunged execution strategies into sheer chaos. As Denno (2013, p. 1335) explains,

> States can — and do — modify virtually any aspect of their lethal injection procedures with a frequency that is unprecedented among execution methods in this country's history. There have been more changes in lethal injection protocols during the past five years [2008–2013] than there have been in the last three decades. The resulting protocols differ from state to state and even from one execution to the next within the same state. As a result, many states' lethal injection issues and procedures scarcely resemble those evaluated by the *Baze* Court.

In an effort to confront this developing swirl of objections, one Florida lawmaker filed a bill in the House during the 2012 session that would have eliminated lethal injection and substituted death by a firing squad in its place. That bill languished in committee and never received full consideration from the Florida Legislature. However, the topic of execution by lethal injection is certain to attract more attention in the near future.

The Post-Conviction Process

Rather than being the final destination after much legal wrangling, a death sentence only marks the start of a lengthy review process. Putting a person to death is not something that government officials wish to take lightly. As mentioned earlier, the imposition of the death penalty triggers an automatic appeal to the Florida Supreme Court. Estimates are that this direct appeal consumes, on average, over 2½ years from start to finish (Maas, 2011).

The diagram in Figure 8.6 shows that the post-conviction review process involves a number of steps. Once the automatic direct appeal to the Florida Supreme Court is completed, then the post-conviction review process can commence in earnest. Rule 3.850 and Rule 3.851 of the *Florida Rules of Criminal Procedure* (Florida Bar, 2014) impose time limits within which to apply for post-conviction relief. Under Rule 3.850, an inmate must initiate any challenges that deal with jurisdiction, improper sentencing, or other constitutional protections within two years. A petition on any other grounds proceeds under Rule 3.851 and requires the court appoint a new attorney to represent the convicted person. The purpose behind dismissing the original counsel and bringing in a second lawyer is to allow for a fresh set of eyes to examine the case. That way, if the original representation was defective or ineffectual, that claim can surface without any prejudice. Of course, that means the new attorney must gain physical custody of all case records, pour over the details, and identify any strategies that be worthwhile to pursue. Now that more files are being maintained electronically, it is much easier for the new attorney to access the materials. In any event, any motions filed under Rule 3.851 are supposed to be raised within the first year. The Florida Supreme Court can grant time extensions whenever necessary. In actuality, the typical case takes about two years to complete in Circuit Court and almost another two years to get resolved by the Florida Supreme Court (Maas, 2011).

In addition to a series of appeals within the Florida court system, inmates are afforded other opportunities to venture into the federal court system. The amount of time to resolve a filing in the federal system took on average 3 months for the U.S. Supreme Court, a little more than a year for the U.S. Court of Appeals, and over 2½ years in the U.S. District Court (Maas, 2011). Once these appeals are exhausted and the governor signs a death warrant (see Figure 8.7), another round of appeals automatically begins. The actual execution will take place only after these concerns have been aired and exhausted. According to Table 8.1 presented earlier, the average Florida Death Row inmate spends 15 years on that cell block. Now that we have visited the appeals process, perhaps this figure makes more sense.

Hidden Costs with the Post-Conviction Process

As one might imagine from this presentation, death penalty cases consume a lot of time, energy, and other resources. The former Speaker of the Florida House of Representatives, Rep. Cannon (2011), noted even although death penalty appeals make up only 12% of the state Supreme Court's docket, they gobble up over half the court's time. Another point to consider is that the FDOC must keep the inmate in its custody throughout this entire period. The FDOC (2013) estimates that it costs $47.50 a day to incarcerate the average inmate. By way of comparison, the average daily cost is $68.64 to maintain a Florida death row inmate. In other words, the typical adult male costs Florida taxpayers $16,403 to imprison annually. That figure rises to $25,071 for the average death row inmate (Florida Legislature Commission on Capital Cases, 2008). Also consider the amount of time inmates spend on death row. Figures compiled by the Florida House of Representatives show that as of March 3, 2013, "of the 404 inmates on death row, 155 have been in custody for more than 20 years and ten have been on death row for more than 35 years" (Florida House of Representatives, 2013, p. 2).

If one were to factor in the cost of litigation and the other sundry costs, Floridians pay an extra premium of $51 million every year to maintain the death row population (Date,

Figure 8.6 The Post-Conviction Process in Florida Death Penalty Cases

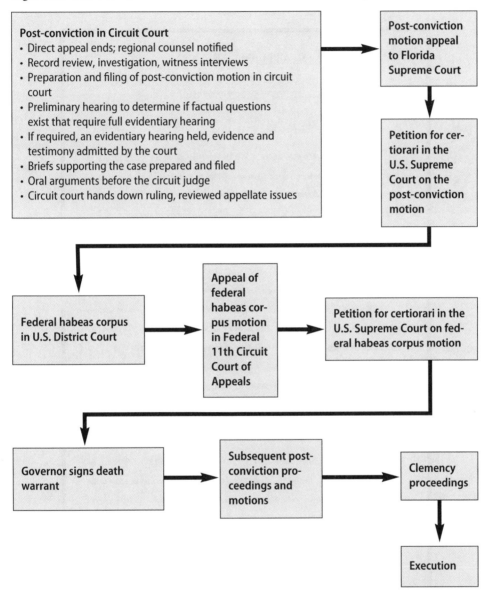

Source: Office of Program Policy Analysis & Government Accountability (2001). *Justification Review: Performance of Collateral Counsels Improved; Registry Accountability Needs to Be Revisited*, p. 2. Tallahassee, FL: Office of Program Policy Analysis & Government Accountability. Retrieved on October 11, 2011 from http://www.oppaga.state.fl.us/Summary.aspx?reportNum=01-52.

2000). The bottom line is that it is much more economical to imprison inmates for life than it is to execute them, especially in light of the fact that 25 Florida death row inmates have been exonerated from 1979 until December of 2014 (Death Penalty Information Center, 2014). When taken as a whole, these observations would lead some people to favor life imprisonment without the possibility of parole over capital punishment. Another

Figure 8.7 The Death Warrant Gov. Rick Scott Signed on October 10, 2011, for Death Row Inmate Chadwick Banks

DEATH WARRANT
STATE OF FLORIDA

WHEREAS, CHADWICK DEWELLYN BANKS, on or about the 24th day of September, 1992, murdered Cassandra Banks and Melody Cooper; and

WHEREAS, CHADWICK DEWELLYN BANKS, on the 29th day of April, 1994, after a plea of nolo contendere to the charges, was adjudicated guilty of two counts of first-degree murder and one count of sexual battery of a child, and was sentenced to death; and

WHEREAS, on the 28th day of August, 1997, the Supreme Court of Florida affirmed the convictions and death sentence of CHADWICK DEWELLYN BANKS; and

WHEREAS, on the 20th day of March, 2003, the Supreme Court of Florida affirmed the trial court's order denying CHADWICK DEWELLYN BANKS's Motion for Postconviction Relief, and denied his State Petition for Writ of Habeas Corpus; and

WHEREAS, on the 29th day of July, 2005, the United States District Court dismissed CHADWICK DEWELLYN BANKS's federal Petition for Writ of Habeas Corpus; and

WHEREAS, further postconviction motions and petitions have been denied, and affirmed on appeal; and

WHEREAS, executive clemency for CHADWICK DEWELLYN BANKS, as authorized by Article IV, Section 8(a), Florida Constitution, was considered pursuant to the Rules of Executive Clemency and it has been determined that executive clemency is not appropriate; and

WHEREAS, attached hereto is a certified copy of the record of the conviction and sentence pursuant to section 922.052, Florida Statutes.

Figure 8.7   The Death Warrant Gov. Rick Scott Signed on October 10, 2011 for Death Row Inmate Chadwick Banks, *continued*

NOW, THEREFORE, I, RICK SCOTT, as Governor of the State of Florida and pursuant to the authority and responsibility vested in me by the Constitution and Laws of Florida, do hereby issue this warrant, directing the Warden of the Florida State Prison to cause the sentence of death to be executed upon CHADWICK DEWELLYN BANKS, in accord with the provisions of the Laws of the State of Florida.

IN TESTIMONY WHEREOF, I have hereunto set my hand and caused the Great Seal of the State of Florida to be affixed at Tallahassee, the Capital, this 22nd day of September, 2014.

GOVERNOR

ATTEST:

SECRETARY OF STATE

2014 SEP 22 PM 1:38
DEPARTMENT OF STATE
TALLAHASSEE, FLORIDA
FILED

2

Source: No Author (2014, September 24). Gov. Rick Scott signs double murder's death warrant. *Space Coast Daily*. Melbourne, FL: Maverick Multimedia, Inc. Retrieved on December 18, 2014 from http://spacecoastdaily.com/2014/09/gov-rick-scott-signs-double-murders-death-warrant/.

alternative to abolishing the death penalty is to find ways to expedite case processing. The following section looks at Florida efforts to do just that.

Problems with Legal Representation

In 1985, Governor Graham signed execution warrants for two inmates. Inmates in those days were not entitled to post-conviction representation unless they themselves had secured the services of a private attorney. What this meant was that whenever the Governor signed an inmate's death warrant, a hectic scramble would ensue to locate a volunteer lawyer to handle the case, usually on a *pro bono* basis. One of the first things the newly acquired attorney would do routinely was to ask for a time extension so that he or she could become familiar with the case. That delay thwarted schedules and meant that post-collateral proceedings took even longer than normal to litigate.

Neither of the two inmates under Governor Graham's death warrants was able to find a lawyer. Rather than allow the executions to continue without the benefit of legal representation, the Florida Supreme Court intervened and cancelled the scheduled executions. Attorney General Smith knew full well that this dilemma had the potential to halt other executions in the future. As a result, he turned to the Legislature for funds that would enable capital defendants to have post-conviction legal representation at public expense. Legislative leaders responded by creating the Office of Capital Collateral Representative (CCR) to represent death row inmates in post-conviction appeals (Olive, 2007).

This approach soon proved to be just a temporary patch. A rapidly expanding caseload, coupled with administrative difficulties, quickly strained existing resources. The CCR needed more staffing and a larger budget. Citing an unmanageable workload, the CCR defiantly declined to take on any more death row inmates. As a result, Governor Chiles convened a commission, headed by retired Florida Supreme Court Justice McDonald, to evaluate the agency's performance.

The McDonald Report (1997) documented a number of ongoing problems. The perception in legal circles was that the CCR staff members had become antagonistic, abusive, and had overreached the agency's mandate. The CCR was more concerned with advocating against the death penalty and working for its repeal than with discharging its duty to represent clients. The McDonald Commission (1997, p. 3) concluded that "based on CCR's lack of institutional integrity, Florida should consider other models of post-conviction representation."

The Florida Legislature responded by disbanding the CCR and creating the Office of Capital Collateral Regional Counsel (CCRC). The original CCRC was divided into three regional offices covering the north, middle, and southern portions of the state. Later, the three locations were collapsed into two and put under the direction of the Commission on Capital Cases (CCC). The plan was to have CCC lawyers handle death penalty appeals in their respective regions and rely upon registry attorneys elsewhere. A *registry attorney* is a regular lawyer who is a member in good standing with the Florida Bar. He or she has spent at least three years practicing criminal law and has handled a combination of at least five felony trials, appeals, or post-conviction cases (Maas, 2004a). Whether registry attorneys could provide quality counsel in post-conviction capital proceedings was a major concern.

The American Bar Association (2003) had devised a series of guidelines aimed at providing the best legal representation possible for capital punishment defendants. The ABA felt that death penalty cases, both during the trial stage and post-conviction phase, had become so specialized and detailed that many regular attorneys simply could not provide adequate service to their clients. As a result, it recommended that each state develop an independent agency that would be responsible for assembling knowledgeable defense teams to represent capital punishment clients zealously and effectively.

Despite implementing some changes, lingering difficulties and differences of opinion continued to trail the CCRC (McGuire, Cline, & Turcotte, 2001; Maas, 2004b; Turcotte, 2002). Florida Supreme Court Justice Cantero was quoted as saying that the work done by private attorneys in post-conviction appeals amounted to "some of the worst lawyering I have seen" and "some of the worst briefs I have read" (Pudlow, 2005). Justice Cantero went on to say:

> I'm talking about minimum standards. I'm not talking about requiring Clarence Darrow-quality high standards. I'm talking about whether this person should be doing these cases at all.

While all these exchanges were occurring, the American Bar Association (2003) had called for a moratorium on all executions in this country until the states could demonstrate they had sound procedures in place to protect against executing innocent persons. After that announcement, the ABA embarked on an analysis of capital punishment procedures in several states. The ABA released a report in 2006 that was critical of the Florida death penalty system. That investigation noted a number of ongoing deficiencies, including the area of legal representation, and made several recommendations for improvement.

Three Contemporary Developments

A series of three recent developments have prompted ongoing concerns for Florida's death penalty statute. The following pages explain what each of these events entailed. As of this writing, other related issues are also surfacing that may impact how Florida approaches the administration of the death penalty.

The Demise and Resurrection of Formal Legal Representation

For a variety of reasons, the Florida Legislature voted to abolish the Commission on Capital Cases as of July 1, 2011. This agency apparently had not managed to escape the haunts of its predecessor, the CCR. This action left a void in that Florida now lacked a formal agency that would provide legal representation to handle post-conviction death penalty appeals. Instead, the Justice Administrative Commission was tasked with maintaining the capital collateral registry of attorneys.

Exasperation over the ever-growing gap between the imposition of a capital sentence and the actual date on which the execution is carried out prompted Florida lawmakers to pass the "Timely Justice Act," which Governor Scott signed in June of 2013. Among many other things, this new law establishes the goal of resolving all post-conviction proceedings as quickly as possible after sentencing. The hope, of course, is that imposing stricter time limits on Rule 3.850 and Rule 3.851 proceedings would produce speedier resolutions.

The new law incorporated several elements to meet this streamlined time limit. For example, the legislation requires the Secretary of State to maintain all the records of a death penalty case in a central location. That move was designed to reduce problematic delays associated with new lawyers acquiring case documents.

Another portion of the new law re-authorized capital collateral regional counsel, basically a public defender's office that handles only capital punishment cases during the appeal process. Also, the background requirements of death-qualified attorneys listed on the registry were tightened in an effort to achieve greater quality control over legal representation and to reduce this avenue as possible grounds for yet another appeal.

Finally, a new provision now requires the clerk of the Florida Supreme Court notify the Governor whenever a death row inmate's case has exhausted all apparent avenues of state and federal appeals. In other words, that inmate is now death-ready. The Governor then has 30 days in which to issue a death warrant authorizing the warden to conduct an execution in the immediate future. Until this provision was enacted, the Governor was not required to take any action once all appeals were exhausted. Now it appeared that the Governor would be required to sign 132 death warrants within the next month (Hernandez, 2014).

As one might expect, a lawsuit challenging this new legislation materialized almost immediately (*Muhammad v. State of Florida*, 2013). Death row inmate Muhammad was already the subject of a death sentence when he stabbed and killed a correctional officer. While his suit raised a number of issues, three concerns are pertinent to our immediate discussion. First, the defendant objected to the substitution of midazolam hydrochloride as the first drug in the three-drug series used in the lethal injection protocol. The Florida Supreme Court, however, found no legitimate basis for Muhammad's contention that reliance upon this substitute drug rose to the level of cruel and unusual punishment as forbidden under the 8th Amendment to the U.S. Constitution.

A second consideration dealt with the separation of powers between the various branches of government. Muhammad maintained that the provisions of the "Timely Justice Act" requiring the clerk of the Florida Supreme Court to notify the Governor's Office of the expiration of appeals and the legislative requirement that the Governor then issue a death warrant violated the independence of these branches. Furthermore, Muhammad argued that various agencies had not complied with his records requests under the new time limits established by this legislation. The court determined that Muhammad's requests for volumes of records amounted to nothing more than a fishing expedition and had no plausible basis for creating a viable argument in his defense.

A third objection Muhammad raised was that "adding execution to the lengthy period of time he has served on death row constitutes cruel and unusual punishment" (*Muhammad v. State of Florida*, 2013, p. 52). The court was not persuaded by the argument that having resided on death row since 1975 was an extenuating circumstance, particularly when Muhammad availed himself of several series of appeals that delayed execution. The State of Florida finally executed the defendant on January 7, 2014 (FDOC, 2014b).

The Florida Supreme Court revisited the claim regarding the constitutionality of the "Timely Justice Act" in *Abdool v. Bondi* (2014). There, Abdool questioned whether the legislative branch of government had impinged upon the judicial and executive branches when it mandated the automatic issuance of a death warrant by the Governor upon completion of the clemency process. In response, the Florida Supreme Court drew a firm distinction between substantive laws and procedural laws.

Basically, substantive laws are the domain of the legislature, while procedural laws fall within the scope of the judiciary. Establishing deadlines is completely within the Legislature's purview and does not infringe upon the Florida Supreme Court's ability to issue a stay of execution whenever appropriate. After an extended analysis, the Florida Supreme Court ruled the "Timely Justice Act" did not interfere with the separation of powers and, therefore, appeared to be constitutional.

As one might guess, reaction to this ruling has been mixed. Supporters contend that this statute will put Florida executions back on track and justice will prevail. Opponents, however, worry that Florida has done nothing to improve the quality of justice and "will exacerbate existing problems in a system already plagued by errors and a lack of funding and resources" (Bagdasarova, 2013). Whether this arrangement will work or succumb to concerns over the quality of legal representation remains an open question.

Florida's Death Penalty Statute Ruled Unconstitutional

U.S. District Court Judge Martinez declared the Florida death penalty unconstitutional on June 20, 2011. The trial court found the defendant Evans guilty of first-degree murder and issued a sentence of death, which the Florida Supreme Court upheld. During a federal appeal hearing, Evans maintained that the Florida death penalty procedures violate the U.S. Supreme Court holding in *Ring v. Arizona* (2002). According to *Ring*, once the jury in a capital punishment cases makes a finding of guilt, the defendant automatically faces a sentence of life imprisonment. When the jury goes on to consider the presence of mitigating and aggravating circumstances, the stakes immediately increase. Now the defendant is exposed to the possibility of death. Under these conditions, it should be the jury, not just the judge, who must determine whether an aggravating circumstance is present using the proof-beyond-a-reasonable-doubt standard.

Judge Martinez pointed to a number of defects in how Florida conducts the sentencing phase. For one thing, "there are no specific findings of fact made by the jury. Indeed, the reviewing courts never know what aggravating or mitigating factors the jury found" (p. 90). In other words, the jury does not have report which factors were found relevant. All the jury has to do is report that a factor was found relevant. Second, there is a distinct possibility that although the jurors collectively recommended for the death penalty, each juror may have focused on a completely different aggravating factor. Third, it takes a majority vote of the twelve-person jury, as opposed to a unanimous vote, to recommend death in Florida. Other states require a unanimous vote. Finally, if the judge does sentence the defendant to death, there is no way to determine whether the judge and jury relied upon the same or different aggravating circumstances. In light of these troublesome areas, Judge Martinez declared the Florida death penalty provisions unconstitutional. As best as can be determined, this ruling had the potential to affect about 40 death row cases.

A flurry of litigation ensued. Ultimately, a death row inmate filed a writ of *certiorari* asking the U.S. Supreme Court to hear the case and evaluate its constitutional merit (*Evans v. McNeil*, 2011). As one might expect, Florida Attorney General Bondi opposed the writ. Eventually, the federal Supreme Court declined to entertain the case. That inaction meant that the Florida death penalty had escaped intense scrutiny.

In all fairness, Judge Martinez's ruling was not unanticipated. These same trouble spots had received notice in several venues (ABA, 2006; Eaton, 2004). One observer offered the assessment that "Florida's death penalty statute is at a crossroads" (Ryan, 2013, p. 973) and goes on to suggest that statutory revisions could sidestep future controversy. However, despite repeated calls for reform (Cantero & Schlakman, 2013; Kogan, White & Wilkinson, 2014; Pudlow, 2014), Florida has not seen fit to address these issues. Bills introduced in both the House and the Senate during 2013 and 2014 never found their way out of committee and, thus, died. That stagnation led to an editorial penned by a former Florida Supreme Court Justice in conjunction with a member of the 2006 ABA report. There, they chastised the Florida Legislature:

> Ironically, controversy involving the Timely Justice Act diverted attention from these issues and other serious concerns about Florida's death-penalty process documented in a 2006 American Bar Association report, including that Florida is the only state that allows juries to find the requisite "aggravating circumstances" to support capital punishment and recommend death during penalty-phase proceedings by simple majority, e.g. 7–5 (Cantero & Schlakman, 2013).

Other commentators have also urged legislators to fix this gap. The Constitution Project, a national organization, recently produced a report chaired by former Florida Supreme Court Chief Justice Kogan. In a scathing critique, the report notes:

> In the most egregious departure from unanimous decision-making, Florida requires only that a simple majority of jurors find an aggravating factor for the death penalty to be imposed. Florida jurors do not even have to agree on which aggravating factor exists. The death penalty may be imposed in Florida if seven of twelve jurors — just over 50 percent — each find a different aggravating factor and recommend a sentence of death (Kogan et al., 2014, pp. 98–99).

A Call to Abolish Florida's Death Penalty

This stubborn recalcitrance to modify the Florida death penalty statute prompted Representative Rehinkle Vasilinda to file a bill in the 2012 legislative session that would abolish the Sunshine State's death penalty. The accompanying news release (Rehinkle Vasilinda, 2011) explained:

> [The death penalty] costs at least $51 million a year and [the process took] over 30 years to arrive at the day of execution for Manuel Valle.... With that $51 million we could put 850 law enforcement officers on Florida's streets, as well as adding more FDLE investigators and equipment to our arsenal against crime.

On the same day, Rep. Rehinkle Vasilinda delivered a letter to Governor Scott urging him to impose a moratorium on the Florida death penalty (see Figure 8.8). A *moratorium* means that the Governor would suspend all death warrants and no executions would take place during this period. What eventually will happen with Florida's death penalty provisions remains to be seen.

Summary

As this chapter demonstrates, capital punishment has had a tumultuous history, both in the United States and in Florida. Aside from the larger ethical question of whether the death penalty is an appropriate punishment, the various practices associated with the administration of the death penalty have raised a number of equally important questions. The resolution of these questions, in turn, has generated even more concerns. As this chapter shows, Florida is now on the brink of several new challenges. No matter what the future portends, it is safe to assume that Florida will be in the midst of those issues.

Figure 8.8 Letter from Representative Vasilinda to Governor Scott Requesting a Moratorium on the Death Penalty

September 27, 2011

The Honorable Rick Scott
Governor
The Capitol
Tallahassee, Florida 32399

Dear Governor Scott:

As public servants, we are not in the business of dispensing vengeance. Ours is the business of making decisions to help keep Floridians safe from crime while spending the public's tax dollars prudently. Towards that end, I have filed HB 4051 which would repeal the death penalty in Florida.

I urge you not to sign any death warrants that may be on your desk awaiting consideration. Instead, I respectfully request that you enact a moratorium on the death penalty in the State of Florida. I believe that life without parole, as an alternative to the death penalty, is the better path.

Executions are carried out at staggering cost to taxpayers. In its 2000 report, "The High Price of Killing Killers," the Palm Beach Post found that Florida spent approximately $51 million each year to enforce the death penalty. With that $51 million, we could put 850 law enforcement officers on Florida's streets, as well as adding more FDLE investigators and equipment to our arsenal against crime.

Life without parole is a sensible alternative to the death penalty. Unlike decades ago, a sentence of life without parole means exactly what it says—convicts locked away in prison until they die. In reality, it is much less expensive to keep criminals in prison for life than it is for the state to execute them. A sentence of life in prison without parole allows mistakes to be corrected or new evidence to come to light, serving to increase faith and fairness in our justice system.

One of the underlying questions in the debate about state-sponsored executions is the proper role and place of government. The appropriate question for state government is: how do we keep people safe from crime in the most cost effective way? When you analyze the numbers, state-sponsored execution is not the correct answer. On the basis of what is best for the citizens of our great state, I urge you to impose a moratorium on executions in Florida.

Thank you for your consideration.

Sincerely,

Rep. Michelle Rehwinkel Vasilinda
District 09

Source: No Author (2011). Rep. Rehwinkle Vasilinda wants moratorium on death penalty. *WCTV.* Tallahassee: WCTV News. Retrieved on December 19, 2014 from http://www.wctv.tv/news/headlines/Rep_Rehwinkel_Vasilinda_Wants_Moratorium_on_Death_Penalty_130709433.html.

Key Terms

aggravating circumstances
bifurcated hearing

botched execution
mitigating circumstances
moratorium
registry attorney

Selected Internet Sites

American Civil Liberties Union of Florida
    https://aclufl.org/

Florida Commission on Capital Cases
    http://www.floridacapitalcases.state.fl.us/#index

Florida Justice Administrative Commission
    http://www.justiceadmin.org/

Death Penalty Information Center
    http://www.deathpenaltyinfo.org

Florida Capital Resource Center
    http://floridacapitalresourcecenter.org/

Floridians for Alternatives to the Death Penalty
    http://www.fadp.org

National Coalition to Abolish the Death Penalty
    http://www.ncadp.org

Review Questions

1. What kind of a pattern emerges when one graphs the number of executions that have taken place in the United States from 1930 until now?

2. How does Florida's death row inmate population compare with the other states in terms of overall size, number of executions, and the time it takes to carry out the sentence of death?

3. What does the Eighth Amendment phrase "cruel and unusual punishment" mean?

4. Explain the *Furman* case.

5. What were the four principles Justice Brennan used to determine whether a punishment was civilized and humane?

6. What impact did *Furman* have on the death row population in Florida and in the United States?

7. Why did some Florida officials endorse the post-*Furman* plan that automatically imposed the death penalty for specific crimes?

8. What is a bifurcated hearing?

9. What are aggravating circumstances?

10. What are mitigating circumstances?

11. How are aggravating and mitigating circumstances intended to work at sentencing?

12. Explain the *Gregg* case.

13. What two principles did the U.S. Supreme Court use when determining whether a punishment is excessive?

14. What is a "botched execution"?

15. How are botched executions relevant for Eighth Amendment challenges?

16. Why did Florida switch its method of execution from electrocution to lethal injection?

17. What types of objections did inmates raise concerning executions in the post-*Gregg* period?

18. What are the three steps in the typical lethal injection procedure?

19. What was the Jennings Commission and what did it recommend?

20. How does the medical community react to member involvement in executions?

21. How did death penalty opponents invoke "standards of decency"?

22. What standard did the *Baze v. Rees* (2008) ruling create and how did that influence Florida?

23. What is the current state of affairs with respect to execution by lethal injection?

24. What are the stages in the post-conviction process for Florida death penalty cases?

25. How much time does a death penalty appeal case take after sentencing?

26. How much money do death penalty cases cost Florida taxpayers?

27. Why does Florida provide legal representation for post-conviction appeals in death penalty cases?

28. What does the term "life sentence without the possibility of parole" mean?

29. Why does Florida not rely solely on *pro bono* lawyers during post-conviction appeals?

30. What is a "registry lawyer"?

31. How effective are registry lawyers?

32. What is the "Timely Justice Act" and what is it intended to accomplish?

33. What are some of the objection to the "Timely Justice Act"?

34. What four defects did federal Judge Martinez find objectionable in the sentencing phase of the Florida death penalty process where the jury considers aggravating and mitigating circumstances?

35. What is a moratorium?

References

Abdool v. Bondi, No. SC 13-1123 (Fla. 2014).

American Bar Association (2003). *Guidelines for the Appointment and Performance of Defense Counsel in Death Penalty Cases* (Revised Edition). Chicago: American Bar Association. Retrieved on December 18, 2014 from http://www.americanbar.org/

content/dam/aba/uncategorized/Death_Penalty_Representation/Standards/National/
2003Guidelines.authcheckdam.pdf.

American Bar Association (2006). *Evaluating Fairness and Accuracy in State Death Penalty
Systems: The Florida Death Penalty Assessment Report: An Analysis of Florida's Death
Penalty Laws, Procedures, and Practices.* Chicago: American Bar Association. Retrieved
on December 18, 2014 from http://www.americanbar.org/content/dam/aba/migrated/
moratorium/assessmentproject/florida/executivesummary.authcheckdam.pdf.

American Medical Association (2000). *Code of Medical Ethics: Opinion 2.06 — Capital
Punishment.* Chicago: American Medical Association. Retrieved on December 8,
2014 from http://www.ama-assn.org/ama/pub/physician-resources/medical-ethics/
code-medical-ethics/opinion206.page?.

Bagdasarova, Susanna (2013). Florida accelerates death penalty process with "Timely
Justice Act." *Death Penalty Representation Project, Summer Newsletter.* Washington,
DC: American Bar Association. Retrieved on December 19, 2014 from http://
www.americanbar.org/publications/project_press/2013/summer/<d>florida-accelerates-
death-penalty-process-with-timely-justice-ac.html.

Baze v. Rees, 553 U.S. 35 (2008).

Buenoano v. Florida, 565 So. 2d 309 (Fla. 1990).

Cannon, Dean (2011). Opposing view: Make the judiciary responsive. *USA Today*, April
14. Retrieved on December 18, 2014 from http://usatoday30.usatoday.com/news/
opinion/editorials/2011-04-14-reform-floridas-courts.htm.

Cantero, Raoul and Mark Schlakman (2013). State's death-penalty overhaul: Require
juries to be unanimous. *Orlando Sentinel*, August 27. Retrieved on December 19,
2014 from http://articles.orlandosentinel.com/2013-08-27/news/os-ed-death-sentence-
appeals-082713-20130826_1_florida-bar-require-juries-death-penalty-process.

Changus, Miximillian J., Electra Bustle, Bohita J. Sorensen, and George B. Sapp (2006).
*Summary of the Findings of the Department of Corrections' Task Force Regarding the
December 13, 2006 Execution of Angel Diaz.* Tallahassee, FL: Florida Department of
Corrections. Retrieved on December 18, 2014 from http://lethal-injection-
florida.blogspot.com/2007/02/florida-december-13-2006-execution-of_11.html.

Clendinen, Dudley (1999). Editorial observer: The long search for a civilized way to kill.
New York Times, November 7. Retrieved on December 18, 2014 from http://
www.nytimes.com/1999/11/07/opinion/editorial-observer-the-long-search-for-a-
civilized-way-to-kill.html?scp=6&sq=jesse+tafero&st=nyt.

Date, S. V. (2000). What price for vengeance on society's worst killers? *Palm Beach Post*,
January 4. Retrieved on December 18, 2014 from http://www.deathpenaltyinfo.org/
node/2289.

Death Penalty Information Center (2014). *Exonerations by State.* Washington, DC: Death
Penalty Information Center. Retrieved on December 18, 2014 from http://www.
deathpenaltyinfo.org/innocence-and-death-penalty#inn-st.

Denno, Deborah W. (2002). When legislatures delegate death: The troubling paradox
behind state uses of electrocution and lethal injection and what is says about us. *Ohio
State Law Journal*, *63*, 63–104.

Denno, Deborah W. (2007). The lethal injection quandary: How medicine has dismantled
the death penalty. *Fordham Law Review*, *76*, 49–128.

Denno, Deborah W. (2013). Lethal inject chaos post-*Baze*. *Georgetown Law Journal, 102*, 1331–1382.

Eaton, O. H., Jr. (2004). Capital punishment: An examination of current issues and trends and how these developments may impact the death penalty in Florida. *Stetson Law Review, 34*, 9–54.

Ehrhardt, Charles W., Phillip A. Hubbart, L. Harold Levinson, William McKinley Smiley, Jr., and Thomas A Wills (1973). The future of capital punishment in Florida: Analysis and recommendations. *Journal of Criminal Law and Criminology, 64*, 2–10.

Ehrhardt, Charles W. and L. Harold Levinson (1973). Florida's legislative response to *Furman*: An exercise in futility? *Journal of Criminal Law and Criminology, 64*, 10–21.

Evans v. NcNeil, (2011), Case 2:08-cv-14402-JEM, U.S. District Court for the Southern District of Florida, Miami Division, June 20.

Florida Bar (2014). *Florida Rules of Criminal Procedure*. Tallahassee: Florida Supreme Court. Retrieved on December 17, 2014 from http://www.floridabar.org/TFB/ TFBResources.nsf/0/BDFE1551AD291A3F85256B29004BF892/$FILE/Criminal.pdf? OpenElement.

Florida Department of Corrections (2007). *Department of Corrections' Response to The Governor's Commission on Administration of Lethal Injections' Final Report with Findings and Recommendations*. Tallahassee: Florida Department of Corrections. Retrieved on December 18, 2014 from http://www.floridacapitalcases.state.fl.us/DeathWarrant Files/Schwab/Exhibit%202%20and%203.pdf.

Florida Department of Corrections (2013). *Budget Summary (FY 20129–2013)*. Tallahassee: Florida Department of Corrections. Retrieved on December 18, 2014 from http:// www.dc.state.fl.us/pub/annual/1213/budget.html.

Florida Department of Corrections (2014a). *Death Row*. Tallahassee: Florida Department of Corrections. Retrieved on December 17, 2014 from http://www.dc.state.fl.us/oth/ deathrow.

Florida Department of Corrections (2014b). *Execution List: 1976 – Present*. Tallahassee: Florida Department of Corrections. Retrieved on December 18, 2014 from http:// www.dc.state.fl.us/oth/deathrow/execlist.html.

Florida Department of Corrections (no date). *Execution List 1924–1964*. Tallahassee: Florida Department of Corrections. Retrieved on December 18, 2014 from http:// www.dc.state.fl.us/oth/deathrow/execlist2.html.

Florida House of Representatives (2013). *HB 7083 Final Analysis*. Tallahassee: State of Florida. Retrieved on December 18, 2014 from http://www.myfloridahouse.gov/ Sections/Documents/loaddoc.aspx?FileName=h7083z1.CRJS.DOCX&Document Type=Analysis&BillNumber=7083&Session=2013.

Florida Legislature Commission on Capital Cases (2008). *Daily and Annual Costs of Housing Florida Death Row Inmates*. Tallahassee: Commission on Capital Cases. Retrieved on December 18, 2014 from http://www.floridacapitalcases.state.fl.us/ Publications/Costs%20Analysis%20FINAL%2006.11.08.pdf.

Florida Statutes 2014.

Furman v. Georgia, 408 U.S. 238 (1972).

Gregg v. Georgia, 428 U.S. 153 (1976).

Hernandez, Antonio M. (2014). Florida—America's first death warrant fulfilment center?: Timely Justice Act of 2013's death warrant issuance provision and a proposed holding for *Abdool v. Bondi. University of Miami Law Review*, forthcoming. Retrieved on December 19, 2014 from http://papers.ssrn.com/sol3/papers.cfm?abstract_id=2411233.

Jennings, John W. "Bill" (2007). *Final Report with Findings and Recommendations.* Tallahassee, FL: The Governor's Commission on Administration of Lethal Injection. Retrieved on December 18, 2014 from http://sentencing.nj.gov/downloads/pdf/articles/2007/Apr2007/document08.pdf.

Kogan, Gerald, Mark White, and Beth A. Wilkinson (2014). *Irreversible Error: Recommended Reforms for Preventing and Correcting Errors in the Administration of Capital Punishment.* Washington, DC: The Constitution Project. Retrieved on December 19, 2014 from http://www.constitutionproject.org/wp-content/uploads/2014/06/Irreversible-Error_FINAL.pdf.

Kuntz, Tom (1997). Tightening the nuts and bolts of death by electric chair. *New York Times*, August 3. Retrieved on December 18, 2014 from http://www.nytimes.com/1997/08/03/weekinreview/tightening-the-nuts-and-bolts-of-death-by-electric-chair.html?pagewanted=all&src=pm.

Lightbourne v. McCollum, 969 So. 2d 326 (Fla. 2007).

Liptak, Adam and Terry Aguayo (2006). Bush's brother suspends Florida death penalty after botched execution. *New York Times*, December 16. Retrieved on December 18, 2014 from http://www.nytimes.com/2006/12/16/world/americas/16iht-web.1216death.3921915.html?_r=0.

Maas, Roger (2004a). *Transfer of Responsibilities from Capital Collateral Regional Counsel–North to the Statewide Attorney Registry.* Tallahassee: Commission on Capital Cases. Retrieved on December 18, 2014 from http://www.floridacapitalcases.state.fl.us/Publications/mid-fiscal-year-report.pdf.

Maas, Roger (2004b). *Fiscal Year 2003–2004 Report Pilot Project.* Tallahassee: Commission on Capital Cases. Retrieved on December 18, 2014 from http://www.floridacapitalcases.state.fl.us/Publications/fiscal%20report%202004.pdf.

Maas, Roger R. (2011). *Appellate Time Frames: A Comprehensive Statistical Examination.* Tallahassee, FL: Commission on Capital Cases. Retrieved on December 17, 2014 from http://www.floridacapitalcases.state.fl.us/Publications/Appellate%20Time%20Frame%20Statistics%20&%20Appendix2.pdf.

McDonald, Parker Lee (1997). *Study of Postconviction Representation of Death Row Inmates.* Tallahassee: Commission for the Review of Post-Conviction Representation. Retrieved on December 18, 2014 from http://www.floridacapitalcases.state.fl.us/Publications/McDonaldReport.pdf.

McDonough, James R. (2007). *Execution by Lethal Injection Procedures: Effective for Executions after August 1, 2007.* Tallahassee: Florida Department of Corrections. Retrieved on December 18, 2014 from http://www.floridacapitalcases.state.fl.us/DeathWarrantFiles/Schwab/Exhibit%202%20and%203.pdf.

McGuire, Kathy, Cynthis Cline, and John W. Turcotte (2001). *Performance of Collateral Counsels Improved; Registry Accountability Needs to Be Revisited.* Tallahassee: Office of Program Policy Analysis and Government Accountability. Retrieved on December 18, 2014 from http://www.oppaga.state.fl.us/MonitorDocs/Reports/pdf/0152rpt.pdf.

Muhammad v. State of Florida, No. SC13-2105 (Fla. 2014).

No Author (2011). Rep. Rehwinkle Vasilinda wants moratorium on death penalty. *WCTV*. Tallahassee: WCTV News. Retrieved on September 28, 2011 from http://www.wctv.tv/news/headlines/Rep_Rehwinkel_Vasilinda_Wants_Moratorium_on_Death_Penalty_130709433.html.

No Author (2014). Gov. Rick Scott signs double murder's death warrant. *Space Coast Daily*, September 24. Melbourne, FL: Maverick Multimedia, Inc. Retrieved on December 18, 2014 from http://spacecoastdaily.com/2014/09/gov-rick-scott-signs-double-murders-death-warrant/.

Office of Program Policy Analysis & Government Accountability (2001). *Justification Review: Performance of Collateral Counsels Improved; Registry Accountability Needs to Be Revisited*. Tallahassee, FL: Office of Program Policy Analysis & Government Accountability. Retrieved on December 17, 2014 from http://www.oppaga.state.fl.us/Summary.aspx?reportNum=01-52.

Olive, Mark E. (2007). Capital post-conviction representation models: Lessons from Florida. *American Journal of Criminal Law*, 34, 277–291.

Provenzano v. Moore, 744 So. 2d. 413 (Fla. 1999).

Pudlow, Jan (2005). Justice rips shoddy work of private capital case lawyers. *The Florida Bar News*, March 1. Retrieved on December 18, 2014 from http://www.floridabar.org/DIVCOM/JN/jnnews01.nsf/Articles/6D34A7C218AE74C385256FB0004F3311.

Pudlow, Jan (2014). Take a hard look at the real cost of the death penalty. *The Florida Bar News*. Tallahassee: The Florida Bar. Retrieved on December 18, 2014 from http://www.floridabar.org/divcom/jn/jnnews01.nsf/8c9f13012b96736985256aa900624829/bce3cb33c0857da4852576ce0066f7b4!OpenDocument.

Rehwinkel Vasilinda, Michelle (2011). Representative Rehwinkel Vasilinda files death penalty repeal bill. *Flhousedems*. Retrieved on December 18, 2014 from https://www.facebook.com/notes/flhousedems/representative-rehwinkel-vasilinda-files-death-penalty-repealer-bill/10150452601290130?ref=nf.

Ring v. Arizona, 536 U.S. 584 (2002).

Ryan, Brendan (2013). The *Evans* case: A Sixth Amendment challenge to Florida's capital sentencing statute. *University of Miami Law Review*, 67, 933–974.

Schwab v. Florida, 995 So. 2d 922 (Fla. 2008).

Snell, Tracy L. (2014a). *Number of Persons Executed in the United States*. Washington, DC: Bureau of Justice Statistics. Retrieved on December 17, 2014 from https://www.quandl.com/BJS/CAP_PUN-Number-of-Persons-Executed-in-the-United-States.

Snell, Tracy L. (2014b). *Capital Punishment, 2013 — Statistical Tables*. Washington, DC: U.S. Department of Justice. Retrieved on December 17, 2014 from http://www.bjs.gov/content/pub/pdf/cp13st.pdf.

Stewart, Malcolm (1992). Enactment of the Florida death penalty statute, 1972: History and analysis. *Nova Law Review*, 16, 1299–1355.

Tisch, Chris and Curtis Krueger (2006). Executed man takes 34 minutes to die. *St. Petersburg Times*, December 13. Retrieved on December 18, 2014 from http://www.sptimes.com/2006/12/13/State/Executed_man_takes_34.shtml.

Turcotte, John W. (2002). *Council Report on OPPAGA Justification Review of the Capital Collateral Regional Counsels "Performance of Collateral Counsels Improved; Registry Accountability Needs to be Revised" (OPPAGA Report No. 01-52)*. Tallahassee: Council for Healthy Communities, Florida House of Representatives. Retrieved on December 18, 2014 from http://www.leg.state.fl.us/data/publications/2002/house/reports/ 1145Hcc_021902.pdf.

Valle v. Florida, No. SC11-1387 (Fla. 2011).

Ventura v. Florida, No. SC08-60 (Fla. 2009).

CHAPTER 9

FLORIDA JUVENILE JUSTICE

Learning Objectives

After reading this chapter, you should be able to:

- Reiterate some of the problems associated with the accuracy of crime rate statistics.
- Explain what an arrest rate is.
- Compare and contrast national and Florida juvenile arrest rates.
- Compare and contrast adult and juvenile arrest rates within Florida.
- Evaluate the mix of offenses in Florida juvenile arrest rates.
- Outline the activities that take place at the referral stage.
- Elaborate on the civil citation program.
- Summarize the criteria a juvenile must meet to participate in the civil citation program.
- Talk about the benefits of the civil citation program.
- Describe what takes place at the intake stage.
- Outline the activities involved at the detention hearing.
- Separate non-judicial handling from judicial handling in terms of the petition stage.
- Comment on what happens at the arraignment.
- Offer an explanation of what waiver is and what it is intended to accomplish.
- Discuss what happens at the adjudicatory hearing.
- Expound upon the alternatives available to judges at the disposition hearing.
- Convey the role that the Department of Juvenile Justice plays.
- Give some reasons why some people think that a curfew reduces juvenile delinquency.
- Relay why the courts have struck down some curfew laws as being unconstitutional.
- Tell what is to be gained by diversion.
- Illustrate how teen court is intended to be a diversion program.
- Explain what waiver is.
- Enunciate how popular waiver is in Florida.
- Describe the type of juveniles for whom waiver is intended.
- Evaluate whether waiver handles "the worst of the worst."
- Present the practice of "leapfrogging."

- Evaluate Florida's gang problem.
- Present some of the statewide grand jury findings pertaining to gang activity.
- Address the efforts Florida has taken to eradicate gangs.
- Explain how United State Supreme Court rulings have affected the imposition of the death penalty on juveniles.

Introduction

Earlier in Chapter 3 we raised the question of whether Florida has a crime problem. Statistics from the *Uniform Crime Reports* helped craft a response to that query. At this point, we have arrived at a similar juncture, except now our attention has turned to juvenile delinquency. Does Florida have a problem with juvenile delinquency? If so, how does the Sunshine State deal with that problem? Once we determine how to respond to that question, the chapter can look at how Florida handles juvenile delinquency. The text then moves to an explanation of how a case winds its way through the juvenile justice system by exploring what takes place at each stage of the process. Finally, the discussion focuses on a series of topics that have corralled much attention in Florida. These aspects include whether a juvenile curfew helps curb delinquency, the use of teen court as a way to divert children out of the formal system, how waiver can remove chronic and calloused offenders from the juvenile court process and transfer them into the adult justice system, the concern with the growing gang problem in the state, and how federal Supreme Court decisions have affected juveniles being sentenced to death for their crimes. By the time you finish reading this chapter, you will have a much broader understanding of issues surrounding juvenile justice in the Sunshine State.

Is Delinquency a Concern in Florida?

One way to assess the level of a problem is to rely upon official crime statistics. Chapter 3 took advantage of official crime data to determine how big or extensive illegal behavior is within Florida. You will recall that a crime rate divides the number of offenses known to the police by the number of residents and then multiplies that outcome by a constant, usually 100,000 people. That strategy allows observers to make numerous comparisons. Chapter 3 utilized several comparisons, including a state-by-state look, a city-by-city comparison, and a temporal analysis. While that approach yielded a number of interesting findings, it was limited by the dark figure of crime, episodes that the authorities either did not know about or did not record. There was also a worry about accurate population figures. An accurate head count of people, especially for Florida, can be elusive or difficult to obtain. A steady influx of tourists, something the state actively promotes, causes the daily population to fluctuate. Commuters arriving at work are another blip on the population count screen. Seasonal residents also come and go at different times of the year, affecting the population size of an area. In short, while crime rates can offer some interesting insights, they are surrounded by a number of shortcomings.

A similar situation shrouds delinquency. One might be able to rely upon victim reports to come up with an accurate estimate of how much crime actually occurs. However, delinquency is another matter. Only juveniles can commit delinquent acts and, in many instances, information about the suspect is lacking. In the absence of any information about the age of the offender, it is extremely difficult to construct an accurate measure of delinquency rates.

Arrest rates might provide some helpful data when trying to piece together a picture of Florida delinquency. An *arrest rate* divides the number of persons taken into custody who possess a trait by the number of people in the population who possess that trait, multiplied by a constant. This calculation enables researchers to compute arrest rates by race, gender, age, and other characteristics.

One obstacle to computing relevant crime rates that Chapter 3 mentioned involved the notion of "population at risk." Basically, the idea was that a more appropriate denominator would reflect the number of vulnerable units. Most juvenile courts handle children as young as ten years old, some maybe around age eight. Consequently, constructing arrest rates that utilize a base of everybody under the age of 18 invites some inaccuracy. The lack of available age-specific data for the nation and states means these numbers are very difficult to find. However, it is possible to locate information that tallies the number of children who are four years old and younger. Taking advantage of these databases allows the denominators in juvenile arrest rates to be adjusted so that they reflect the age categories of five through seventeen years old. While this approach may not be a perfect solution, it does whittle away some imprecision.

Another problem with interpreting an arrest rate is that it is hard to determine whether these figures stem from police activity or from that group's proclivity to be involved in deviant behavior. Even so, examining arrest rates might be productive if we can keep these caveats in mind.

Violent Arrest Rates

The UCR, among other things, contains tallies of how many people the police arrest, the charge underlying the arrest, and characteristics of the arrested person. This information enables one to compare arrest rates in a variety of ways. For instance, Figure 9.1 examines annual violent juvenile arrest rates (murder, forcible rape, robbery, and aggravated assault) for the entire United States and for Florida. A closer look at the graphs will help determine whether the juvenile arrest rates in the Sunshine State are problematic.

A glance at Figure 9.1 shows that, in all four instances, the Florida juvenile arrest rates surpass the national norm. In terms of murder, the Florida rate tracks the U.S. trend in the first part of the decade, but then soars dramatically upward. The gap between the national average and the state's forcible rape arrest rates indicates that Florida is much more violent. Similarly, Florida robbery arrest rates and aggravated assault arrest rates are much higher than the rest of the nation. Even though murder, forcible rape, robbery, and aggravated assault display downward trends over the decade, the Florida rates remain elevated in comparison to the rest of the country.

Figure 9.2 offers a comparison of adult and juvenile arrest rates within the state. While juvenile arrest rates for murder are lower than the corresponding adult rates in the first half of the decade, the juvenile graph spikes in 2005 and then shows a dramatic surge in 2007 before settling down in 2010. Juvenile arrest rates for forcible rape parallel the adult rates, while the juvenile robbery figures are much higher than the adult rates. While the aggravated assault rates converge at the start of the decade, the adult figures are more dominant for most of that ten-year period.

Figure 9.1 United States (Broken Line) and Florida (Solid Line) Juvenile Serious Violent Crime Arrest Rates, 2000–2013

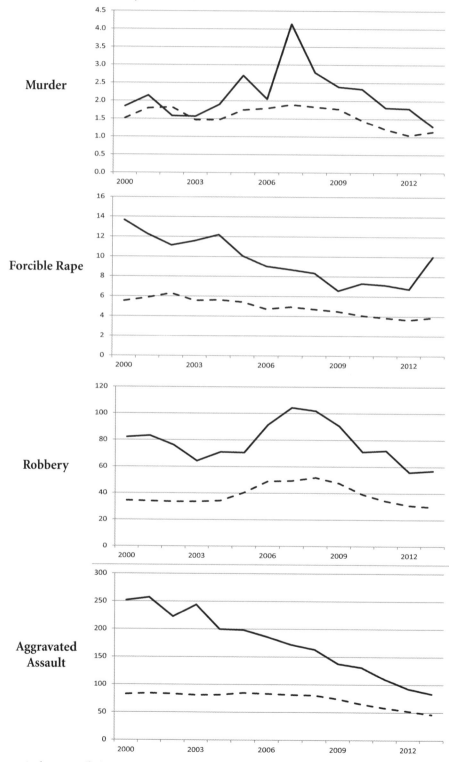

Source: Author compilation.

Figure 9.2 Florida Serious Violent Arrest Rates for Juveniles (Solid Line) and Adults (Broken Line), 2000–2013

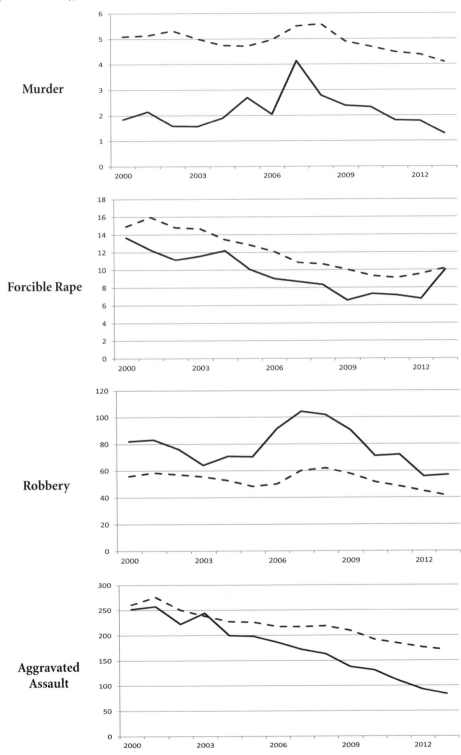

Source: Author compilation.

Property Arrest Rates

A comparison of annual juvenile property arrest rates (burglary, larceny-theft, and motor vehicle theft) for the nation and for Florida appears in Figure 9.3. All in all, the Florida juvenile arrest rates are higher than the norm. Florida juvenile burglary and larceny-theft rates dwarf the national rates. While the gap for motor vehicle theft rates closes considerably by 2010, the graphs indicate that the Florida rates are two-and-a-half times higher than the national average.

Attention switches in Figure 9.4 to a comparison of juvenile and adult arrest rate patterns within the Sunshine State. Florida juveniles display considerably higher arrest rates for burglary, larceny-theft, and motor vehicle theft over the series. Even though the juvenile arrest rate for larceny-theft dips below the adult standard by 2012, it is too early to tell whether this trend will continue. While motor vehicle theft arrest rates draw closer by the end of the decade, the juvenile arrest rates are much more pronounced for most of that period.

The Offense Mix

Another consideration to take into account is the mixture of the arrest charges. Even though two jurisdictions might register the exact same total arrest rate, there could be some distinctive qualitative differences hidden within the summary numbers. One jurisdiction might record all violent felony arrests and officials in the other area could be making arrests for just misdemeanor property offenses. As you can see, reliance upon a summary statistic could risk overlooking the underlying seriousness of juvenile activity.

The national and state data contained in Figure 9.5 present the nature of juvenile arrest charges. Of the Florida juvenile arrests, 44% are for serious property crimes (burglary, larceny-theft, motor vehicle theft) compared with 37% for the nation. Arrests for serious violent crimes (murder, forcible rape, robbery, and aggravated assault) are relatively higher in Florida than in the rest of the country. Altogether, serious crimes constitute 54% of all juvenile arrests in Florida, compared with 45% for all the other states. Thus, these data demonstrate that a much higher proportion of the Florida juvenile arrests are made for more serious offenses.

Summary

It is difficult to determine whether arrest rates reflect police activity or greater juvenile involvement in illicit activities. However, three points are abundantly clear from the analyses presented in this section. First, Florida juvenile arrest rates are much higher than the national norm. Second, comparatively speaking, Florida juveniles have much more elevated arrest rates than do adults. Third, juveniles are arrested for more serious crimes in Florida than elsewhere. The picture that does evolve is that juvenile delinquency is a problem the Sunshine State needs to be addressed.

Figure 9.3 United States (Broken Line) and Florida (Solid Line) Juvenile Serious Property Crime Arrest Rates, 2000–2013

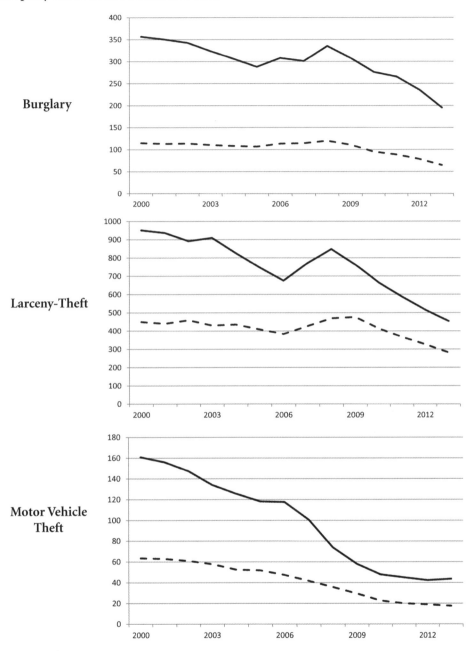

Source: Author compilation.

Figure 9.4 Florida Serious Property Arrest Rates for Juveniles (Solid Line) and Adults (Broken Line), 2000–2013

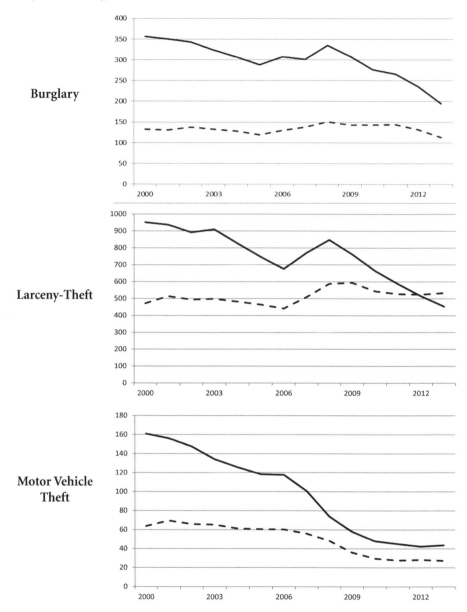

Source: Author compilation.

The Florida Juvenile Justice System

The Florida juvenile justice system is housed within the circuit courts of Florida. As Figure 9.6 demonstrates, there are a number of steps or stages within the juvenile justice

Figure 9.5 Relative Composition of Selected Juvenile Arrests in Florida (Black) and the United States (Gray), 2013

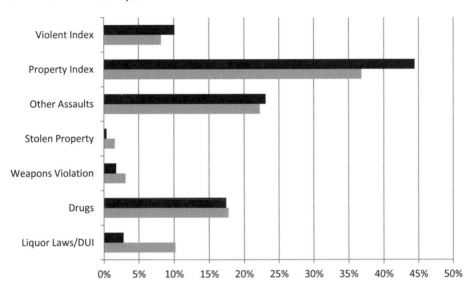

Source: Author compilation.

system. This section of the chapter will ferry you through what happens in those various stages.

Referral

Just like the adult system, the most common way for a juvenile to come to the attention of the juvenile court is through *referral* or contact with a law enforcement officer. The usual procedure is that the investigating officer takes the child into custody, prepares an offense report, and swears out an affidavit. The affidavit explains when and where the violation took place and then outlines how the juvenile's behavior matches the elements of the criminal charge. The officer then transports the youth to a Juvenile Assessment Center (JAC) and turns custody over to the Florida Department of Juvenile Justice (FDJJ) where a counselor then screens the case.

An alternative path to the above procedure, outlined in Figure 9.7, is the juvenile *civil citation program* (CCP). Under this procedure, the investigating officer can bypass JAC and handle the case informally in an alternative fashion, provided certain conditions are met (*Florida Statutes 2014*, §985.12). These conditions include:

- The incident is a misdemeanor or a local ordinance violation;
- The juvenile admits being responsible for the offense;
- The juvenile does not have a prior arrest history;
- The juvenile does not have a prior civil citation;
- The juvenile agrees to participate in the civil citation process; and
- The juvenile is a local resident.

Figure 9.6 Florida Juvenile Delinquency Case Flowchart

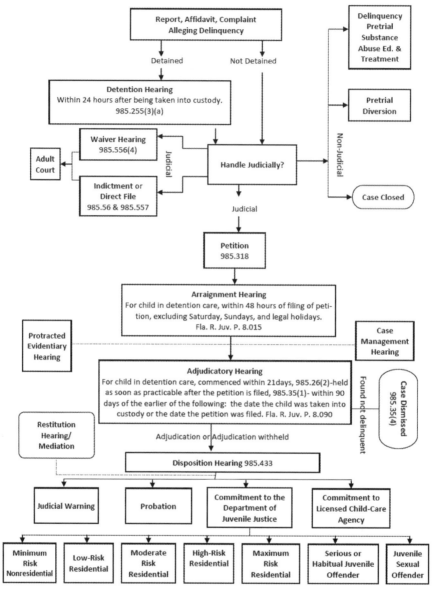

Source: Office of the State Courts Administrator (2010). *Florida's Juvenile Delinquency Benchbook*, p. xi. Tallahassee: U.S. Supreme Court. Retrieved on December 27, 2014 from http://www.flcourts.org/core/fileparse.php/260/urlt/DelinquencyBenchbook091410.pdf.

If all these criteria are fulfilled, then the investigating officer has some latitude in how to proceed with the case. Instead of transporting the juvenile to JAC, the officer can return the child home and discuss the matter with the parent or guardian. If there is agreement, the officer can enroll the youngster in a diversion program. The diversion program requires the participant to perform up to 50 hours of community service. Counseling or any other

Figure 9.7 The Florida Civil Citation Process

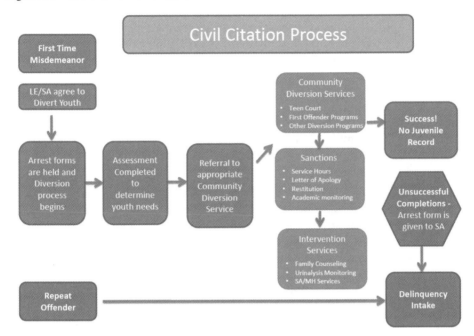

Source: Florida Department of Juvenile Justice (2012b). *Civil Citation Flow Chart.* Tallahassee: Florida Department of Juvenile Justice. Retrieved on December 27, 2014 from http://www.djj.state.fl.us/docs/partners-providers-staff/flowchart-dec-2012.pdf?sfvrsn=0.

appropriate form of intervention can also be a requirement of enrollment. The juvenile, in turn, must report to a coordinator within seven working days and start program participation. The expectation is that the child will complete a minimum of five hours per week in the program. Upon completion of the program, the case is closed and the child avoids a criminal history. Should the juvenile fail to finish the program or become involved in a new offense while enrolled in the program, the civil citation is suspended, the original charges are reinstated, and the case returns to the juvenile justice system for handling.

Supporters of this approach endorse the CCP for at least four reasons. First, successful completion spares juveniles the stigma of a delinquent history. Second, the CCP keeps first-time offenders from entering the system and becoming exposed to unintended consequences (FDJJ, 2014a). Third, the CCP delivers social services to youth who benefit more from counseling than from formal handling. Fourth, the CCP represents a more fiscally responsible alternative to formal processing. One report pegs the cost of a civil citation case at $386, compared with $5,000 for a case processed through the juvenile justice system (Bishop, Walters, & Olk, 2010). As of October of 2014, CCP programs were active in 59 of Florida's 67 counties (FDJJ, 2014b). If the CCP were uniformly available throughout the entire state, then Florida would save an estimated $158 million annually (FDJJ, 2014c).

Intake

The intake process begins after the investigating law enforcement officer completes the referral tasks and turns custody of the juvenile over to FDJJ personnel at JAC. The purpose of *intake* is to determine whether the juvenile should remain in custody prior to the actual detention hearing which must take place within 24 hours (*Florida Statutes 2014*, §985.255(3)(a)). There are three possible placements. The juvenile may return home, enter a non-secure residential facility, or remain in secure detention. Children will remain in custody if they are a flight risk, have committed a violent crime or a weapons violation, have a history of committing new offenses while out on release, been found in contempt of court in the past, or request to stay in a facility (*Florida Statutes 2014*, §985.24).

The intake officer also prepares a *Detention Risk Assessment Inventory* (DRAI) to determine whether the child is a high-risk candidate. DRAI is a screening tool that rates the minor's propensity to commit another offense in the immediate future and/or not show up at scheduled court hearings. Three basic considerations propel DRAI. They are objectivity, uniformity, and verified behavior (Steinhart, 2006, p. 7). As one FDJJ (2009, p. 1) document explains, "the purpose of these instruments is to apply criteria for detention uniformly for all juveniles, to use criteria that measure specific detention-related risks for the juveniles, and to objectively determine which juveniles should be detained."

The DRAI is a form that the intake officer uses to assess the juvenile's risk status. Information is gathered regarding the seriousness of the current offense, prior record (especially incidents involving a firearm), a confirmed history of abuse or neglect, and any other special circumstances (Strange, 2013). A juvenile who scores high on this inventory is considered to be a danger to public safety and will be recommended to remain in secure detention until the case is resolved. A juvenile who grades out as a moderate or low risk will be released prior to the final case disposition. While the DRAI instrument is useful, periodic monitoring and recalibration is necessary.

Detention Hearing

The detention hearing in the juvenile justice system is similar to first appearance in the adult court. Three activities occur here. First, the juvenile court judge examines the investigating officer's materials and evaluates whether there is sufficient probable cause to believe that the youth committed a delinquent act. If probable cause is absent, the judge will release the minor and the case ends. Second, the judge will advise the minor about the nature of the charges, the privilege against self-incrimination, and the right to consult with an attorney. Third, the judge must also decide whether to release the child or to detain him or her (Florida Bar, 2014, Rule 8.010). Under normal conditions, the maximum detention stay is 21 days. Longer stays automatically trigger a judicial review (*Florida Statutes 2014*, §985.26).

Delinquency Petition

At this point, the state attorney's office (SAO) has to decide whether to handle the case informally or formally. If the decision is for an informal or non-judicial handling, then

Figure 9.8 Common Juvenile Diversion Programs in Florida

QUESTION: What were some of the most common diversion programs found in the statewide circuit profiles?

ANSWER: **Teen Court** is a diversion program in which volunteer teens act as attorneys, clerks, bailiffs, and jurors. They conduct a "teen trial" to handle the diverted juveniles.

Arbitration is a diversion program in which juveniles discuss their delinquency charges with victims. Juveniles and victims assist in crafting an individualized plan of consequences, education and treatment.

Intensive Diversion (IDDS) involves providing individualized treatment to the juvenile through counseling and various other services.

Civil citation focuses on the juvenile providing service to the community in which the criminal act was committed.

Source: Office of the State Courts Administrator (2003). *Florida's Juvenile Delinquency Court Assessment*, p. 35. Tallahassee: Florida Supreme Court. Retrieved on December 27, 2014 from http://jud18.flcourts. org/gen_public/family/bin/delinquencyassessment.pdf.

the case is diverted out of the system. The juvenile might be directed to appear before a teen court, enter a community service program, become involved in family counseling, receive mental health treatment, participate in a substantive intervention program, or pursue any other option deemed appropriate (see Figure 9.8). Completion of these alternatives can result in an expunction or expungement (see Figure 9.9). An *expungement* means that the juvenile's record is closed after satisfactory completion of the program and avoids a formal arrest record (*Florida Statutes 2014*, § 943.0582).

If the SAO elects to handle the case formally, then it must submit a delinquency petition to the court. The petition lists the charges that are being filed and the probable cause for each charge. Once a petition is filed, the next step is to go to an arraignment hearing within 48 hours (Florida Bar, 2014, Rule 8.015).

Arraignment

Like the adult court proceedings, a juvenile court arraignment is the point at which the court reviews the charges, advises the child of his or her rights, checks on the status of counsel for the juvenile, and asks the minor to enter a plea. The juvenile can plead not guilty, guilty, or *nolo contendere*. If the plea is not guilty, then an adjudicatory hearing is scheduled. Meanwhile decisions will be made about pre-trial detention, speedy trial, and other matters.

Figure 9.9 A Florida Affidavit Form Regarding a Petition to Expunge a Juvenile Arrest Record

IN THE CIRCUIT COURT OF THE
SECOND JUDICIAL CIRCUIT, IN AND
FOR LEON COUNTY, FLORIDA

IN THE INTEREST OF,   CASE #: _____
                                                        Juvenile Division

_____
Name of Child.

_____
Current Mailing Address

_____
City/State/Zip

_____
Home Phone   /   Work Phone

AFFIDAVIT

STATE OF FLORIDA
COUNTY OF LEON

      I, _____, am the child in the above-styled case, and I do hereby
swear or affirm that:

   1. I fully understand the meaning of all of the terms of this affidavit.
   2. I have never been adjudicated guilty of a criminal offense or a comparable ordinance violation.
   3. I was arrested on the _____ day of _____, _____, by the
       _____ (arresting agency), and I have not been adjudicated guilty of
       the charges stemming from that arrest or the alleged criminal activity surrounding my arrest.
   4. I am eligible for the relief requested, to the best of my knowledge and belief, and do not have any
       other petition to expunge or seal pending before any court.
   5. I have never secured a prior records expunction or sealing under any law.

                              _____
                              Child

      Sworn to and subscribed before me this _____ day of _____, _____.

_____   _____
Notary Public/Deputy Clerk   Print/Type Notary/Deputy Clerk Name
My Commission Expires:

      _____Personally known or _____Produced ID   Type of ID Produced_____

Source: Leon County Clerk of the Court (n.d.). *Juvenile Expunction Packet.* Tallahassee: Leon County Clerk of the Court. Retrieved on December 27, 2014 from http://cvweb.clerk.leon.fl.us/clerk_services/online_forms/juvenile_delinquency/juvenile_expunge.pdf.

Waiver

Waiver, also known as transfer, means that the juvenile court relinquishes jurisdiction over the youthful offender and sends the case over to the adult court for processing. The judge can invoke waiver if he or she determines the minor is not amenable to treatment or considers the youth to be a danger or menace to society. From that point forward, whenever the juvenile commits a subsequent offense, the charges are handled in the adult court (*Florida Statutes 2014*, § 985.556). "Once an adult, always an adult" is the standard here.

There are three types of waiver in Florida. A *voluntary waiver* occurs when the child, the child's parent, or the child's guardian asks the juvenile court judge to transfer the case to the adult system. The second type, an *involuntary discretionary waiver*, describes the situation where the SAO asks the juvenile court to remand the youth to the adult court.

There are two conditions that underlie the third type, an *involuntary mandatory waiver* to the adult court system. First, the juvenile must have been at least 14 years old at the time of the alleged crime. The second condition can be satisfied in one of two ways. The first route is when the minor has a prior felony adjudication for a violent crime and is charged with a second violent felony. The other possibility is if the youth is facing the fourth felony charge of his or her career and one of the past convictions was for a violent felony crime involving a firearm.

A motion to this effect triggers an automatic waiver hearing within seven business days. The juvenile court judge must consider a number of aspects. They include:

- The seriousness of the current offense;
- Whether the offense was done in an aggressive, violent, premeditated or willful manner;
- Whether the offense was a crime against a person;
- The probable cause statement in the investigating officer's affidavit;
- The sophistication and maturity of the child;
- The child's criminal history and prior institutional commitments; and
- The prospects for rehabilitation balanced against the need for public safety.

If the judge determines that waiver is not an appropriate avenue and the SAO disagrees, the SAO can consider a direct file. A *direct file* means that the state bypasses the juvenile court and has the case tried in the adult court. There are two types of direct filing: a discretionary direct file and a mandatory direct file.

A *discretionary direct file* involves a juvenile who is 14 or 15 years of age and is charged with a serious felony offense. A *mandatory direct file* is reserved for situations where a 16- or 17-year-old, with a prior serious felony conviction. uses a firearm in the commission of a forcible felony. Both a discretionary and a mandatory direct filing move the case to the adult court where the youthful offender faces charges as an adult (Office of the State Courts Administrator, 2010, pp. 189–190).

Adjudicatory Hearing

For those cases that remain in the juvenile justice system, the next step is the adjudicatory hearing. The adjudicatory hearing must take place within 90 days of the arrest or within 90 days of the SAO filing a petition, whichever is earlier (Florida Bar, 2014, Rule 8.090). Of course, the judge can grant an extension if the need for extra time is appropriate.

After hearing both sides present their cases, the judge must decide whether the child is delinquent or not delinquent. If the finding is a lack of delinquency, the judge will dismiss the case and release the child. If the judge finds the juvenile to be delinquent, then the case moves to the dispositional phase. At this point, the judge will also determine whether the juvenile should be released or stay in secure detention during the interim.

Disposition Hearing

The period between adjudication and the disposition hearing is when the Department of Juvenile Justice prepares a *predisposition report* (PDR) or rehabilitative assessment. A juvenile probation officer will review the child's social history, family background, medical records, psychological interviews, school reports, and delinquency history to arrive at an appropriate treatment plan and commitment recommendation. There are five levels of restriction for the judge to consider. They are:

- Minimum-risk nonresidential;
- Low-risk residential;
- Moderate-risk residential;
- High-risk residential; and
- Maximum-risk residential.

Typical *minimum-risk nonresidential programs* involve the child remaining in the home, a probation order, and participation in community-based services. The judge can impose such conditions as school attendance, participation in counseling, maintaining a part-time job, restitution, community service, loss of a driver's license, periodic drug testing, a curfew, and anything else that might benefit the youngster (*Florida Statutes 2014*, § 985.435). However, the length of the probation period cannot exceed the normal term associated with the offense. In other words, if the maximum penalty associated with a first-degree misdemeanor is one year of confinement, then the length of probation cannot exceed one year. Failure to honor these provisions could result in a probation revocation and re-sentencing.

The second level, *low-risk residential program*, removes the child from the home and places him or her in a nonsecure residential facility. This facility could be a halfway-house, foster care, or other suitable residential arrangement. The conditions discussed in the minimum-risk nonresidential program typically apply here.

A *moderate-risk residential commitment* is reserved for juveniles who pose some risk to the community if left unsupervised. Like a road camp, these facilities are staffed on a 24-hour basis and are somewhat secure. Residents may attend school in the larger community during the day, but then they return to the supervised location for after-hours care.

High-risk residential facilities are much more secure and residents are not allowed to leave the compound. These locations typically have perimeter fencing, locked doors, 24-hour staffing, and very structured activities. Youths are sent to these facilities because they are considered to be genuine threats to public safety. All programs (educational, vocational, and counseling) are held on the campus.

The final tier is reserved for youth who require a *maximum-risk residential program* in a secure setting. These facilities are basically juvenile correctional facilities or juvenile prisons. Commitments are usually for longer periods and supervision is much more intense.

Figure 9.10 Department of Juvenile Justice Operating Budget, FY 2014–2015

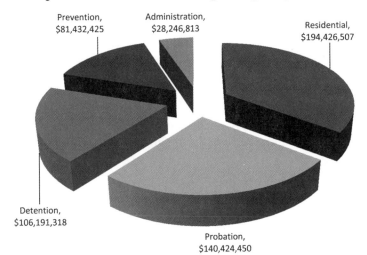

Prevention,
$81,432,425

Administration,
$28,246,813

Residential,
$194,426,507

Detention,
$106,191,318

Probation,
$140,424,450

Source: Florida Department of Juvenile Justice (2014d). *2014 Legislative Report.* Tallahassee: Florida Department of Juvenile Justice. Retrieved on December 27, 2014 from http://www.djj.state.fl.us/docs/par-data/2014-legislative-wrap-up-report.pdf?sfvrsn=0.

The Florida Department of Juvenile Justice

The Florida Department of Juvenile Justice is charged with administering services to children throughout the state. The FDJJ mission statement calls for the agency "to increase public safety by reducing juvenile delinquency through effective prevention, intervention and treatment services that strengthen families and turn around the lives of troubled youth" (FDJJ, 2012a). FDJJ operates 21 secure juvenile detention centers throughout the state with a total capacity of 1,342 beds. These centers provided court-ordered detention, educational, health, and residential services to 17,475 juveniles during fiscal year 2012–13 (FDJJ, 2013a).

As Figure 9.10 shows, the FDJJ 2014–15 operating budget totaled $551 million. The largest portion of the budget was spent on confinement or juvenile commitments. Probation costs amounted to $140 million, while detention facilities accounted for 19% of the budget. The

Table 9.1 FDJJ Service Categories and Number of Clients, Fiscal Year 2012–13

Category	Number of Clients
Prevention and Victim Services	26,268
Detention	32,655
Probation and Community Services	62,275
Residential Services	5,665
Total	**128,863**

Source: Florida Department of Juvenile Justice (2013b). *2013 Comprehensive Accountability Reports (CAR).* Tallahassee: Florida Department of Juvenile Justice. Retrieved on December 27, 2014 from http://www.djj.state.fl.us/research/reports/car.

prevention category represents money spent on children who have exhibited pre-delinquent behaviors such as ungovernability, truancy, running away from home, and the like. A true cost estimate for juvenile services would also factor in the partnering costs that local governments must shoulder. In addition, municipal and county law enforcement costs involving juvenile delinquents are not included in these numbers. Keeping all these things in mind, the juvenile justice system translates into quite an expensive venture for Florida taxpayers.

Table 9.1 presents the number of clients FDJJ handled in each service category during fiscal year 2012–13. Almost 129,000 children had some kind of formal contact with FDJJ. To put that number into context, it is estimated that the Sunshine State was home to approximately 1.8 million children between the ages of ten and seventeen during 2013.

Special Topics

There are a number of issues facing the Florida juvenile justice system that will be explored in this portion of the chapter. These items include whether curfews curtail delinquency, the reliance upon teen court as a diversion program, the practice of waiver or transferring chronic juveniles to the adult court for handling, the problem of gang activity throughout the state, and whether juveniles should be subjected to the death penalty. As you will see each of these topics addresses a different facet of the juvenile delinquency problem. Unfortunately, the question of how effective these approaches are is still under investigation.

Curfews

One appealing way to counter juvenile delinquency and violent crime has been for local governments to enact ordinances that establish a curfew for youths. A *curfew* sets the hours during which young people cannot be present in public places. For example, a locality may prohibit juveniles from being out and about on the streets from 10 o'clock at night until 6:00 AM unless accompanied by an adult, running an errand for an adult, being involved in an emergency situation, or other conditions.

There is ample public support for proposals that restrict juveniles from late night wandering and the accompanying expectation that curfews act as a crime reduction tool (Adams, 2003; Hemmens & Bennett, 1999; Kline, 2012; Ruefle & Reynolds, 1996). Given this base, juvenile curfews swept the country, including Florida, during the 1990s (Bannister, Carter, & Schafer, 2001; Lersch & Sellers, 2000; Levy, 1997; Lubensky, 2006; Ruefle & Reynolds, 1996). By 1997, 80% of cities with a minimum population of 30,000 had a nighttime curfew on the books (U.S. Conference of Mayors, 1997). However, there are some questions about whether curfews produce the desired outcomes and whether they are constitutionally sound.

Analyses of juvenile curfew laws generally report very unimpressive results (Adams, 2003; Cole, 2003; McDowall, Loftin, & Wiersema, 2000). These ordinances have little, if any, effect on crime. Researchers offer a variety of explanations for this lack of impact (Reynolds, Seydlitz, & Jenkins, 2000). For one thing, juveniles as an overall age group do not constitute the largest category of victims or offenders. Second, most offenses generated by juveniles take place after school and not during the hours that curfews target. Third, the police enforce curfew provisions sporadically and on a selective basis.

Juvenile curfew laws have displayed some vulnerability to legal challenges. Tampa officials sought a legal opinion from Attorney General Butterworth (1994) when they were drafting a juvenile curfew ordinance. The Attorney General cautioned them about the reasons why the courts had overturned curfews in Pensacola, Palmetto, and Jacksonville as being unconstitutional. After reviewing the Tampa proposal and making some other suggestions, General Butterworth concluded that:

> Tampa may enact a valid city ordinance imposing a juvenile curfew, if the ordinance is crafted to further the compelling state interest of protecting the safety of minors and reducing juvenile crime, while providing exemptions and defenses that adequately inform people of conduct that is allowed and limiting minors' rights without infringing on basic constitutional rights.

Despite this apparent green light and reliance upon Florida laws, Tampa eventually became embroiled in a lawsuit about its curfew ordinance when police officers arrested J.P., a juvenile, who was out riding his bicycle around 2 o'clock in the morning. A second case involved a Pinellas Park provision. There, authorities arrested T.M and two companions on criminal charges for curfew violations.

Both parties challenged the legality of the county ordinances and the trial judge agreed. The state appealed to the District Court which upheld the curfew laws. Those conflicting rulings paved the way to a hearing in Tallahassee before the Florida Supreme Court (*State of Florida v. J.P. and T.M.*, 2004). At issue was whether the lower courts had applied the appropriate standard when evaluating the curfew laws and whether these two ordinances were constitutional.

The critical point when analyzing a curfew statute is to determine the appropriate balance between protecting juveniles and fighting crime while, at the same time, honoring everybody's constitutional rights (Lubensky, 2006, p. 1384). The Florida Supreme Court faced the question of whether it should apply a "strict scrutiny standard" or the lesser "lenient rational basis." A *strict scrutiny standard* is invoked whenever there might be a civil rights violation or if a fundamental right is violated. Basically, the issue boils down to two concerns. First, do juveniles possess the same array of rights under the Florida constitution as adults do? Second, does the restriction under review serve a compelling governmental interest and, if so, does the law do so in a minimally intrusive way? As Judge Levy of Florida's Third District Court of Appeal explained:

> This is the most rigorous form of judicial review. Under strict scrutiny, the Ordinance will be upheld only if it serves a compelling state interest and, even then, only if the Ordinance is sufficiently narrowly tailored such that it furthers the compelling interest by the least intrusive means (1997, p. 526).

The Florida Supreme Court chose to follow the strict scrutiny standard and, in a 4–3 decision, ruled that the Tampa and Pinellas Park juvenile curfew laws were unconstitutional. The ordinances violated the Florida constitutional right to freedom of movement, as well as freedom of privacy. In addition, the ordinances punished juveniles who were out in public after hours even if these juveniles had parental permission to do so. In the opinion of one analyst, had the curfew codes imposed only civil sanctions, made allowances for youth to parental permission to be out in public after hours, and had the need for a curfew been demonstrated empirically, then these local laws might have been in a better position to survive judicial scrutiny (Lubensky, 2006, p. 1399).

As Figure 9.11 shows, state law grants local governments the option of establish a juvenile curfew. Both Jacksonville and Miami-Dade County are two Florida locations that have revised juvenile curfews in force today (Jacksonville, 2014; Miami-Dade County, 2014). The Miami experience offers a prime demonstration of the gripping power of anecdotal evidence. After a spate of drive-by shootings in Liberty City left 11 people dead in just three months, City Commissioner Dunn requested police beef up enforcement of the curfew ordinance (Rabin, 2010). Now after police intervention, the problem seems to have been curtailed and supporters point to the curfew as a major tool in reducing youthful violence. Whether or not that is actually the case requires further monitoring and analysis.

Figure 9.11 Legislative Intent Section of the Statute Permitting Local Juvenile Curfew Ordinances

It is the intent of the Legislature to protect minors in this state from harm and victimization, to promote the safety and well-being of minors in this state, to reduce the crime and violence committed by minors in this state, and to provide counties and municipalities with the option of adopting a local juvenile curfew ordinance ....

Source: Florida Statutes 2014, § 877.20.

Teen Court

Teen courts have grown very popular throughout the United States and in Florida. At least 54 Florida counties have established such a program in their area (Florida Association of Teen Courts, 2014). The Florida Legislature allows each county the option of deciding whether to authorize a teen court program. If a county does proceed with a teen court program, the local courts can assess a $3 surcharge on all criminal fines and use this money to fund the local teen court program (*Florida Statutes 2014*, § 938.19).

Teen court is a diversion program. *Diversion* means that a case is channeled out of the normal juvenile justice system and is handled informally. One task the intake officer has to consider during the screening process is whether to insert the juvenile's case into the formal justice system or to divert the child to a teen court program or other alternative (*Florida Statutes 2014*, § 985.145). Usually, cases involving first-time offenders who are typically charged with vandalism, stealing, or any other minor misdemeanors are placed into the teen court program. Once the child completes the sanction imposed by the teen court, the case is dismissed and adjudication is withheld. *Adjudication withheld* means there is no finding of guilt and the juvenile is spared an arrest history.

While there are some different variations, a *teen court* mimics the real court, except for being staffed by juveniles. Youths assume the various court personnel roles (clerk, bailiff, prosecuting attorney, defense attorney, and jurors) and the case is processed in front of a jury or panel of peers. Both sides (prosecutor and defense) follow a script whereby they present opening arguments, call witnesses to the stand for questioning, cross-examine witnesses, present closing arguments, and then ask the jurors to determine culpability. The presiding judge is usually a local practicing attorney who volunteers his or her time. Once the jury makes its finding, the judge decides on an appropriate sentence. Sanctions may include such alternatives as community service, writing an apology letter to the victim, constructing an essay about the consequences of one's actions, attending special classes to help make better choices in the future, or other similar penalties. In many instances, juveniles who complete these terms are expected to serve as jurors in future teen court deliberations. If a juvenile fails to finish the teen court program, then he or she returns to the juvenile justice system for further processing.

Several evaluations have examined whether being immersed in teen court restructures participant attitudes and impacts future delinquent behavior. The results vary with some analyses appearing to be promising and others showing no desired effects. There are research findings which suggest that teen court involvement can diminish delinquency in the short-term and do promote positive attitudinal adjustments (Butts, Buck-Willison, & Coggeshall, 2002; Forgays, 2008). On the other hand, some studies show less-than-stellar results (Norris, Twill, & Kim, 2011; Rasmussen, 2004; Rasmussen & Diener, 2005; Stickle, Connell, Wilson, & Gottfredson, 2008). One Florida study (Smith & Blackburn, 2011) demonstrates that peer influence may be an important ingredient in avoiding future delinquent behavior. Obviously, more incisive research is needed.

Perhaps the best assessment comes from the comments offered by Butts and Buck (2000, p. 15) who wrote:

> State and local jurisdictions across the country are embracing teen court as an alternative to the traditional juvenile justice system for their youngest and least serious offenders.... Researchers are beginning to accumulate a body of findings on the effectiveness of teen courts, but more detailed information is needed for future practice and policy development.

Waiver

As mentioned earlier, the purpose behind *waiver* is to transfer youths who are not amenable to treatment or who are especially dangerous to others out of the juvenile justice system and into the adult court system. Rising juvenile crime, coupled with a preoccupation with juvenile gangs, fueled public perception that harsher crime control measures would provide more effective remedies (Jan, Ball, & Walsh, 2008; Lane & Meeker, 2000). In fact, public opinion surveys reveal that while Floridians support a separate system for juveniles that focuses upon treatment and rehabilitation, they also think it is appropriate to send "the worst of the worst" to the adult court system (Applegate, Davis, & Cullen, 2009; Mears, Hay, Gertz, & Mancini, 2007). "Get-tough" reforms, such as waiver, are seen as one way to sidestep a system that merely coddled juvenile offenders. As Figure 9.12 demon-

Figure 9.12 The Florida Constitution Provision Allowing Juvenile Waiver to the Adult Court

When authorized by law, a child as therein defined may be charged with a violation of law as an act of delinquency instead of crime and tried without a jury or other requirements applicable to criminal cases. Any child so charged shall, upon demand made as provided by law before a trial in a juvenile proceeding, be tried in an appropriate court as an adult. A child found delinquent shall be disciplined as provided by law.

Source: Florida Constitution, Article I, Section 16.

strates, the Florida Constitution contains explicit provisions for removing youth out of the juvenile justice system and into the adult arena.

Florida became a leader in this crusade. The legislature enacted laws that loosened waiver restrictions and modified how juveniles were handled. A telling statistic is that 7,000 of the 9,700 judicial waivers that occurred during 1997 throughout the entire United States took place here in Florida (Mears, 2003, p. 159). Further evidence that the pendulum had swung away from a rehabilitative focus to a more punitive approach is echoed in the following remarks:

> Since 1978, Florida has transferred more juveniles to criminal court than most other states together .... Florida has more juveniles in adult prison, including those under 16 years of age, than any other state (Frazier, Bishop, & Lanza-Kaduce, 1999, p. 168).

Given this background, one would expect that youths who are waived would display some very distinct characteristics. In addition, one might also anticipate that youths who are waived because they are dangerous should receive some differential handling by the adult system. Fortunately, there are several studies that examine these issues in Florida.

An analysis of transfer cases right after the Florida Legislature made extensive reforms in the juvenile justice system in 1995 showed very little change from past practices. While three-quarters of the waived cases involved felony offenses, 25% were for misdemeanors (Frazier et al., 1999, p. 174). Less than 10% of the cases were slated for reverse waiver. *Reverse waiver* means that the adult court adjudicates the juvenile as guilty, but then imposes a sentence to a juvenile, rather than an adult, facility (Burrow, 2008). Instead of sending convicted transferees to prison or jail, the sentencing judge makes use of a youthful commitment facility. While reverse waiver might appear to be a more lenient alternative, starting in 1995, youths in both locations began serving longer sentences. Thus, it would appear that both the adult and the juvenile court systems had begun to crack down on chronic juvenile offenders.

Curiosity led Frazier et al. (1999) to interview a number of Florida judges and state attorneys. They discovered a large rift between the two groups. While most judges felt that direct filing and waiver practices were adequate, prosecutors were not so happy with the provisions and favored more powerful and sweeping reforms. Specifically, the state attorneys wanted more latitude to direct file against younger juvenile offenders. Similar professional differences have surfaced in jurisdictions outside of Florida (Mears, Shollenberger, Willison, Owens, & Butts, 2010; Myers, Lee, Giever, & Gilliam, 2011).

Digging further, Lanza-Kaduce and his colleagues (1999) probed local court records to determine whether transferred juveniles represented "the worst of the worst." About one-third of the cases involved violent crimes while 44% were for serious property crimes. If you recall, the leading criteria for invoking waiver is that the current offense is a violent crime or involved a firearm. Furthermore, even though some youth were incarcerated in either adult or juvenile facilities, the most common sentence administered to convicted transferees was supervised release back into the community. Given these observations, it does not appear that waiver always involves "the worst of the worst." After combing the data for more information, the researchers (1999, p. 299) concluded that they could not locate "any pattern of additional problems among transfers that could be used to characterize the transfers as being unusually 'bad.'" Thus, changes in Florida waiver practices were not very dramatic in the initial days of implementation.

Another way researchers have evaluated waiver is to investigate recidivism. Bishop and her research team (1996) compared waived juveniles with a matched sample of youths who remained in the juvenile system. They found that transferred youth had higher short-term re-offending rates. Despite being incarcerated and, thus, out of circulation for that time, waived juveniles had more prolific re-arrest rates. This failure to deter is not novel and is a finding that has been repeated elsewhere (Myers, 2003).

Intrigued by this outcome, one group of researchers wondered whether leapfrogging was at the heart of this recidivism problem (Johnson, Lanza-Kaduce, & Woolard, 2011). *Leapfrogging* means that case handling skips over the usual increments or the next step in the rehabilitative process and subjects the transferred youth to harsher or more punitive sanctions than usual. Seen in this light, waiver represents a logical next-step only in those situations where the juvenile has exhausted all previous remedies. Tracking a group of waived and non-waived cases into early adulthood revealed that accelerating cases past the usual treatment modes by pushing them into adult court jurisdiction impeded rehabilitation and fostered greater criminality.

Interviews with youth who were waived into the adult system and youth who stayed in the juvenile system shed some additional light (Lane, Lanza-Kaduce, Frazier, & Bishop, 2002). Participants in low-end programs (community supervision) had mostly negative things to say about their experiences. They viewed the low-key interventions as unhelpful and virtually meaningless. Sporadic contact with probation officers and a lack of consequences when probationers failed to honor those conditions led them to rate these delinquency-prevention efforts as meaningless. Juveniles subjected to deep-end sanctions (residential facilities) were confined for relatively longer periods. Those extended stays made the treatment programs more intensive and more likely to take root. Compared to their current experiences, incarcerated youth felt that the low-end programs were far too soft. The third group, juveniles who were waived and punished in the adult system, portrayed their sanctions in a negative light. The experience of prison life with all its deprivations made them realize that imprisonment was harsh and a future to be avoided if at all possible. Consolidating all these findings prompted Lane and her colleagues (2002) to question the wisdom of leapfrogging.

To summarize, the purpose of waiver is to remove chronic violent offenders, especially those who have not benefited from previous rehabilitative efforts, away from the protection of the juvenile court and to punish these dangerous offenders as if they were adults. The Florida experience suggests that waived juveniles are not always the "worst of the worst." In addition, there are suggestions that waived youth continue on their already established criminal paths. If that is the case, then maybe waiver does target the correct audience after all.

Gangs

In June of 2007, then-Governor Crist petitioned the Florida Supreme Court to seat a statewide grand jury for the purpose of investigating gang-related activity throughout the state. The grand jury report, released later in December of that same year, painted a grim picture (Eighteenth Statewide Grand Jury, 2007). Gang activity was flourishing and eclipsing existing law enforcement capacities to deal with the problem. The grand jury took special note of a report that ranked Florida second in the nation in terms of drive-by shootings. Those incidents left 18 people dead and another 47 injured (Sugarman & Newth, 2007, p. 5). A *drive-by shooting* takes place when a "shooter fires a firearm from a motor vehicle at another person, vehicle, building, or other stationary object" (Sugarman

Figure 9.13 How Florida Determines Whether Someone Is a Gang Member

(3) "Criminal gang member" is a person who meets two or more of the following criteria:

  (a) Admits to criminal gang membership.

  (b) Is identified as a criminal gang member by a parent or guardian.

  (c) Is identified as a criminal gang member by a documented reliable informant.

  (d) Adopts the style of dress of a criminal gang.

  (e) Adopts the use of a hand sign identified as used by a criminal gang.

  (f) Has a tattoo identified as used by a criminal gang.

  (g) Associates with one or more known criminal gang members.

  (h) Is identified as a criminal gang member by an informant of previously untested reliability and such identification is corroborated by independent information.

  (i) Is identified as a criminal gang member by physical evidence.

  (j) Has been observed in the company of one or more known criminal gang members four or more times.

  (k) Has authored any communication indicating responsibility for the commission of any crime by the criminal gang.

Source: Florida Statutes 2014, § 874.03(3).

& Newth, 2007, p. 1). While not all drive-by shootings are gang-related, this type of an assault is one hallmark or signature of gang violence.

Florida defines a *gang* as any "formal or informal ongoing organization, association, or group that has as one of its primary activities the commission of criminal or delinquent acts, and that consists of three or more persons who have a common name or common identifying signs, colors, or symbols, including, but not limited to, terrorist organizations and hate groups" (*Florida Statutes 2014*, § 874.03(1)). How Florida determines whether somebody is a gang member appears in Figure 9.13 for your consideration. Interviews with prosecutors from the Alachua County State Attorney's Office show how their perceptions of gangs and "emerging gangs" are influenced by these statutes (Fox & Lane, 2010).

The statewide grand jury was alarmed by how quickly gang membership and its associated violent activities were spreading throughout the state. Current estimates are that Florida is now home to over 1,223 gangs which have almost 47,000 documented members and associates and in excess of 8,700 other affiliates (Office of the Florida Attorney General, 2013, p. 7). Virtually all these groups are involved in such criminal enterprises as drug distribution, robberies, burglaries, thefts, and deadly forms of criminal violence.

The statewide grand jury noted a number of major shortcomings in the efforts to protect Floridians from gang violence. First, Florida's laws were seriously outdated. These aging statutes, last updated in the 1990s, hamstrung law enforcement officials in their efforts to abate gang activity. Second, criminal justice officials needed more training and greater resources. More precisely, police departments and state attorney offices should have specialized personnel who concentrated solely on gang-related activity. Third, penalties for gang-initiated crimes, especially offenses utilizing firearms and other weapons, needed to become stiffer. Fourth, witness protection needed to become enhanced so that state attorney offices could gain the assistance of the general public. Finally, the grand jury noted there was a need for members of the criminal justice system to share information with each other. For instance, the Department of Corrections should notify law enforcement authorities whenever a known gang member is being released back into the community. Also, a computerized gang member registry would be a valuable resource to officers in the field. Eventually, the Florida Legislature acted on many of these recommendations.

One tool that lawmakers provided state attorneys was sentencing enhancements. A *sentencing enhancement* means that the punishment associated with the crime is bumped up a notch if the state attorney can demonstrate that the offense was intended to benefit, promote, or further gang interests. Under this scheme, a first-degree misdemeanor moves up to a third-degree felony, a third-degree felony is punished as a second-degree felony, and so forth. Thus, a sentencing enhancement is a tool to incarcerate gang members for longer periods of time (*Florida Statutes 2014*, § 874.04).

The Florida Attorney General has spearheaded an effort aimed at devising ways to eradicate gangs. As Figure 9.14 illustrates, the strategy revolves around three pillars. The first leg, prevention/intervention, calls for efforts to target at-risk and gang-involved youth. The second activity involves law enforcement efforts in gang suppression. The last

Figure 9.14 The Florida Gang Reduction Pyramid Strategy

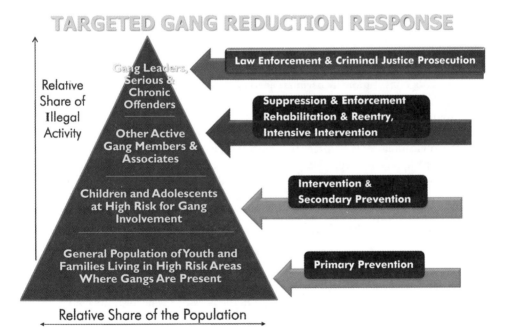

Source: Office of the Florida Attorney General (2014). *Targeted Gang Reduction Response.* Tallahassee: Office of the Florida Attorney General. Retrieved on December 28, 2014 from http://www.floridagangreduction.com/webfiles.nsf/WF/KGRG-7UESXF/$file/GangReductionStrategy-pyramid.pdf.

pillar focuses on rehabilitation and re-entry of incarcerated gang members back into the community. Each of the three efforts is accompanied by a series of objectives to fulfill those goals (Office of the Florida Attorney General, 2012). The Attorney General has organized the state into seven regional gang reduction task forces to implement these recommendations. Given its infancy and brief period of existence, it is too early to tell whether the interventions are effective.

The Death Penalty

As mentioned in the earlier chapter on capital punishment, Florida has been a proponent of the death penalty. However, three U.S. Supreme decisions altered the landscape. This portion of the chapter looks at each of those decisions and the impact on Florida.

Thompson v. Oklahoma *(1988)*

Thompson was 15 years old when he, along with three other adults, shot his former brother-in-law to death and then gutted him with a knife. The group chained the deceased's body to a concrete block and dumped the remains in a nearby river. The authorities eventually recovered the body. All four participants were found guilty and sentenced to death.

Because Thompson was a juvenile at the time of the incident, the prosecutor asked the juvenile court to waive the defendant to the adult court. Given Thompson's previous history of criminal violence and the failure of previous rehabilitative efforts to change him, the judge certified Thompson as an adult. There, Thompson was adjudicated guilty. During the sentencing phase, the jury found the homicide was committed in a particularly heinous manner and recommended the death penalty. The judge concurred and sentenced Thompson to death.

The case made its way to the United State Supreme Court where the Justices decided that it was not constitutionally permissible to execute somebody under the age of sixteen. The reasoning was that juveniles under the age of sixteen did not have the capacity to appreciate the full impact of their actions. As the majority opinion explained, "Given the lesser culpability of the juvenile offender, the teenager's capacity for growth, and society's fiduciary obligations to its children, this conclusion is simply inapplicable to the execution of a 15-year-old offender" (pp. 836–837). While Thompson's life was spared, the decision did not resolve the issue of whether 16- and 17-year-old defendants could be subject to the death penalty.

Stanford v. Kentucky *(1989)*

This decision involved two juveniles in two separate homicide cases in two different states. The first defendant, Stanford, was 17 years and 4 months old when he robbed, sodomized, and then murdered the victim. Stanford confessed that he shot the victim at point-blank range once in the face and once in the back of the head so she would not be able to identify him. The second case involved Wilkins who was 16 years and 6 months old when he committed a homicide. He, too, robbed his victim and then stabbed her to death so she would not be able to identify him. Both defendants were waived to the adult court where they were convicted and sentenced to death. The issue in both cases was whether the death penalty amounted to a cruel and unusual punishment because the defendants were juveniles when they committed their crimes.

The argument that Stanford and Wilkins presented was that executing juveniles was contrary to the "evolving standards of decency." Their attorneys noted that a number of states had abolished the death penalty and others had banned the death penalty for 16- and 17-year-olds. This trend was an indication that society was developing a consensus against imposing the death penalty on non-adults. Essentially, the defendants were arguing that all juveniles lacked the maturity and moral responsibility of adults. As Justice Brennan explained in the dissenting opinion (pp. 401–402), "Juveniles very generally lack that degree of blameworthiness that is, in my view, a constitutional prerequisite for the imposition of capital punishment."

Despite these and other objections, the U.S. Supreme Court upheld the death penalty in these two cases. The Court drew a bright line with this decision. Although it was not constitutionally permissible to execute a defendant who was younger than 16 at the time of the crime, 16- and 17-year-olds did not enjoy a similar blanket protection. They could be sentenced to death.

Roper v. Simmons *(2005)*

Simmons was 17 years old when he and an accomplice whom he had recruited burglarized an occupied residence. Fearful that the victim could identify him, Simmons bound her hands and feet together. He then pushed the victim off a bridge into the river below where she drowned. The case was moved to the adult court and, after he turned 18, Simmons was found guilty and sentenced to death.

Simmons maintained that an earlier decision provided ample justification to vacate his death sentence. The Court had ruled recently that evolving standards of decency forced it to overrule its earlier decision and institute a categorical ban on the execution of mentally retarded persons (*Atkins v. Virginia*, 2002). Simmons seized upon the same logic the Court employed in *Atkins*. There the Court had found that the diminished intellectual capacity of retarded persons exempted that class of individuals from capital punishment. Simmons argued that juveniles, by virtue of their lack of maturity and development, suffered a similar limitation. Hence, executing juveniles was no longer proper.

The Court concurred. It decreed that juvenile executions had become unconstitutional under the "cruel and unusual punishments" clause of the Eight Amendment. As the majority opinion explained:

> Drawing the line at 18 years of age is subject, of course, to the objections always raised against categorical rules. The qualities that distinguish juveniles from adults do not disappear when an individual turns 18 .... however, a line must be drawn (p. 20).

The Impact on Florida

Florida was not one of the states that had banned the juvenile death penalty prior to the *Roper v. Simmons* (2005) decision. That federal ruling means that Florida can no longer impose the death penalty on juveniles convicted of murder. While arrest numbers may differ substantially from conviction numbers, Figure 9.15 displays the number of juvenile suspects arrested for murder since that U.S. Supreme Court decision. Although the data do not take the age of the juvenile suspect into account, *Roper v. Simmons* has potentially influenced a maximum of 617 cases in the Sunshine State. Depending upon one's perspective and the considerations being contemplated, the ramifications of *Roper v. Simmons* may be beneficial or detrimental.

Figure 9.15 Annual Number of Juvenile Murder Arrests in Florida, 2005–2013

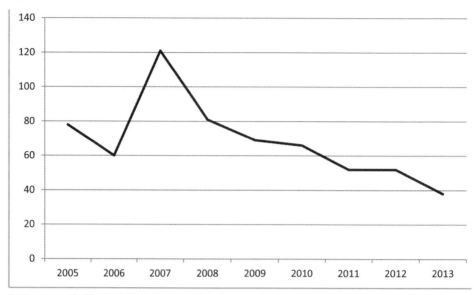

Source: Compiled by author from annual FDLE reports.

Summary

This brief exploration into the Florida juvenile justice system has alerted us to a number of current issues. First, official statistics reveal that Florida does have a long-standing problem with juvenile delinquency. Some observers would contend that this problem is quite serious and worrisome. Second, the chapter spends some time detailing how the juvenile justice system works. The materials present what typically transpires at each stage and point to some operational concerns that have arisen. Third, establishing this foundation provides an opportunity to delve into some current topics Florida is facing and some of the solutions the Sunshine State has employed. What is obvious from that discussion is that there is no "one-size-fits-all" remedy. Rather, dealing with the problems posed by juvenile delinquency requires continuous coordination between the usual crime-fighting apparatus and community service providers.

Key Terms

adjudication withheld
arrest rate
civil citation program
curfew
Detention Risk Assessment Inventory
direct file
discretionary direct file
diversion

drive-by shooting
expungement
gang
gang member
high-risk residential facilities
intake
involuntary discretionary waiver
involuntary mandatory waiver
leapfrogging
low-risk residential program
mandatory direct file
maximum-risk residential program
minimum-risk nonresidential program
moderate-risk residential commitment
predisposition report
referral
reverse waiver
sentencing enhancement
strict scrutiny standard
teen court
voluntary waiver
waiver

Selected Internet Sites

Eckerd Support Center
    http://www.eckerd.org

Florida Association of Teen Courts, Inc.
    http://www.flteencourt.net

Florida Department of Juvenile Justice
    http://www.djj.state.fl.us

Florida Gang Investigators Association
    http://www.fgia.com

Florida Gang Reduction
    http://floridagangreduction.com/flgangs.nsf/pages/Home

Florida Juvenile Justice Foundation
    http://www.djj.state.fl.us/fjjf

Florida Sheriffs Youth Ranches
    http://www.youthranches.org

National Association of Youth Courts
    http://www.youthcourt.net

National Gang Center
    http://www.nationalgangcenter.gov

Review Questions

1. Explain how one constructs an arrest rate.
2. How do Florida juvenile arrest rates for violent crimes compare with national figures?
3. How do Florida juvenile arrest rates for violent crimes compare with adult figures?
4. How do Florida juvenile property rates for violent crimes compare with national figures?
5. How do Florida juvenile arrest rates for property crimes compare with adult figures?
6. How does the mix of juvenile arrest charges in Florida compare with national figures?
7. Explain what a juvenile civil citation program is.
8. What conditions must a juvenile meet to participate in the civil citation program?
9. List some reasons why people support a juvenile civil citation program.
10. What is the purpose of intake?
11. What is a Detention Risk Assessment Inventory and what is it used for?
12. What takes place at the detention hearing?
13. What outcomes accompany the delinquency petition?
14. What is expunction or expungement?
15. What happens at arraignment?
16. What is the goal behind waiver?
17. What does "once an adult, always an adult" mean?
18. What are the three types of waiver?
19. What variables must a judge take into account during a waiver consideration?
20. What is a direct file?
21. What is the point of the adjudicatory hearing?
22. What happens at the disposition hearing?
23. What are the five levels of restrictions available to juvenile court judges at sentencing?
24. What does the Florida Department of Juvenile Justice do?
25. What is a curfew?
26. What is the logic behind installing a curfew?
27. Why are curfews generally ineffective?
28. On what grounds have curfews been challenged in the Florida courts?
29. Describe teen court.
30. What is diversion?
31. Who typically gets diverted to teen court?
32. What does "adjudication withheld" mean?
33. What is the purpose of waiver?
34. Who is eligible for waiver?

35. What is the purpose of reverse waiver?

36. Is waiver reserved for "the worst of the worst"?

37. What is leapfrogging?

38. Is leapfrogging an effective tool in efforts to reduce recidivism?

39. What is a drive-by shooting?

40. How does Florida define a gang?

41. How does Florida define a gang member?

42. How extensive is Florida's gang problem?

43. What recommendations emerged from the statewide grand jury that focused on Florida gangs?

44. What is a sentencing enhancement and how is it used to fight gangs?

45. Discuss the gang eradication strategy endorsed by the Florida Attorney General.

46. What is the significance of *Thompson v. Oklahoma* (1988) with respect to the death penalty for juveniles?

47. What happened in the *Stanford v. Kentucky* (1989) court ruling?

48. How did *Roper v. Simmons* (2005) usher in a new perspective on the juvenile death penalty?

49. How does *Roper v. Simmons* (2005) affect the death penalty in Florida?

References

Adams, Kenneth (2003). The effectiveness of juvenile curfews at crime prevention. *Annals of the American Academy of Political and Social Science, 587,* 136–159.

Applegate, Brandon K., Robin King Davis, and Francis T. Cullen (2009). Reconsidering child saving: The extent and correlates of public support for excluding youths from the juvenile court. *Crime & Delinquency, 55,* 51–77.

Atkins v. Virginia, 536 U.S. 302 (2002).

Bannister, Andra J., David L. Carter, and Joseph Schafer (2001). A national police survey on the use of juvenile curfews. *Journal of Criminal Justice, 29,* 233–240.

Bishop, Barney T. III, Wansley Walters, and Tom Olk (2010). *Getting Smart on Juvenile Crime in Florida: Taking It to the Next Level—Reducing Juvenile Arrests by 40%.* Tallahassee: Associated Industries of Florida. Retrieved on December 28, 2014 from http://www.americanbar.org/content/dam/aba/administrative/criminal_justice/AIFgettingsmart.authcheckdam.pdf.

Bishop, Donna M., Charles E. Frazier, Lonn Lanza-Kaduce, and Lawrence Winner (1996). The transfer of juveniles to criminal court: Does it make a difference? *Crime & Delinquency, 42,* 171–191.

Burrow, John (2008). Reverse waiver and the effects of legal, statutory, and secondary legal factors on sentencing outcomes for juvenile offenders. *Crime & Delinquency, 54,* 34–64.

Butterworth, Robert A. (1994). *Advisory Legal Opinion AGO 94–02: Juvenile Curfew Ordinance*. Tallahassee: Office of the Florida Attorney General. Retrieved on December 28. 2014 from http://www.myfloridalegal.com/ago.nsf/Opinions/1F9BF8FDEAA40B04 8525621F006633E0.

Butts, Jeffrey A. and Janeen Buck (2000). *Teen Courts: A Focus on Research. Juvenile Justice Bulletin*. Washington, DC: Office of Juvenile Justice and Delinquency Prevention. Retrieved on December 28, 2014 from http://www.urban.org/UploadedPDF/ 1000233_teencourtsfocus.pdf.

Butts, Jeffrey A., Janeen Buck-Willison, and Mark B. Coggeshall (2002). *The Impact of Teen Court on Young Offenders*. Washington, DC: The Urban Institute. Retrieved on December 28, 2014 from http://www.urban.org/publications/410457.html.

Cole, Danny (2003). The effect of a curfew law on juvenile crime in Washington, D.C. *American Journal of Criminal Justice, 27*, 217–232.

Eighteenth Statewide Grand Jury, Case No. SC 97-1128 (2007). *First Interim Report of the Statewide Grand Jury: Criminal Gangs and Gang-Related Violence*. Tallahassee: Florida Supreme Court. Retrieved on December 28, 2014 from http://www.florida supremecourt.org/pub_info/summaries/briefs/07/07-1128/Filed_01-15-2008_First_ Interim_Report.pdf.

Florida Association of Teen Courts (2014). *Teen Court Info*. Sarasota: Florida Association of Teen Courts. Retrieved on December 28, 2014 from http://www.flteencourt.net/ TC_info.html.

Florida Bar (2014). *Florida Rules of Juvenile Procedure*. Tallahassee: Florida Bar. Retrieved on December 27, 2014 from http://www.floridabar.org/TFB/TFBResources.nsf/ Attachments/E2AD7DEF01F6F90685256B29004BFA7E/$FILE/Juvenile.pdf.

Florida Constitution.

Florida Department of Juvenile Justice (2009). *Detention Risk Assessment Instrument (DRAI) Validation Contract #A2012*. Madison, WI: APS Healthcare.

Florida Department of Juvenile Justice (2012a). *Mission*. Tallahassee: Florida Department of Juvenile Justice. Retrieved on December 27, 2014 from http://www.djj.state.fl.us/ about-us/mission.

Florida Department of Juvenile Justice (2012b). *Civil Citation Flow Chart*. Tallahassee: Florida Department of Juvenile Justice. Retrieved on December 27, 2014 from http:// www.djj.state.fl.us/docs/partners-providers-staff/flowchart-dec-2012.pdf?sfvrsn=0.

Florida Department of Juvenile Justice (2013a). *Comprehensive Accountability Report: Detention Services*. Tallahassee: Florida Department of Juvenile Justice. Retrieved on December 27, 2014 from http://www.djj.state.fl.us/docs/research2/%282012-13- car%29-detention-services-%28final%29-%287-1-14%29.pdf?sfvrsn=0.

Florida Department of Juvenile Justice (2013b). *2013 Comprehensive Accountability Reports (CAR)*. Tallahassee: Florida Department of Juvenile Justice. Retrieved on December 27, 2014 from http://www.djj.state.fl.us/research/reports/car.

Florida Department of Juvenile Justice (2014a). *Civil Citation Model Plan*. Tallahassee: Florida Department of Juvenile Justice. Retrieved on December 27, 2014 from http:// www.djj.state.fl.us/docs/partners-providers-staff/model-plan.pdf?sfvrsn=8.

Florida Department of Juvenile Justice (2014b). *Civil Citation Implementation by County as of October 7, 2014*. Tallahassee: Florida Department of Juvenile Justice. Retrieved on December 27, 2014 from http://www.djj.state.fl.us/docs/probation-policy-memos/counties-with-cc-as-of-april-21-2014.pdf?Status=Master&sfvrsn=2.

Florida Department of Juvenile Justice (2014c). *Civil Citation Powerpoint*. Tallahassee: Florida Department of Juvenile Justice. Retrieved on December 27, 2014 from http://www.djj.state.fl.us/docs/probation-policy-memos/2014-civil-citation-powerpoint.pdf?Status=Master&sfvrsn=8.

Florida Department of Juvenile Justice (2014d). *2014 Legislative Report*. Tallahassee: Florida Department of Juvenile Justice. Retrieved on December 27, 2014 from http://www.djj.state.fl.us/docs/par-data/2014-legislative-wrap-up-report.pdf?sfvrsn=0.

Florida Statutes 2014.

Forgays, Deborah Kirby (2008). Three years of teen court offender outcomes. *Adolescence*, *43*, 473–484.

Fox, Kathleen A. and Jodi Lane (2010). Perceptions of gangs among prosecutors in an emerging gang city. *Journal of Criminal Justice*, *38*, 595–603.

Frazier, Charles E., Donna M. Bishop, and Lonn Lanza-Kaduce (1999). Get-tough juvenile justice reforms: The Florida experience. *The Annals of the American Academy of Political and Social Science*, *564*, 167–184.

Hemmens, Craig and Katherine Bennett (1999). Juvenile curfews and the courts: Judicial response to a not-so-new crime control strategy. *Crime & Delinquency*, *45*, 99–121.

Jacksonville, Florida (2014). *Code of Ordinances, Title XVI — Judicial Code, Chapter 603 — Children's Curfew*. Tallahassee: Municipal Code Corporation. Retrieved on December 28, 2014 from https://library.municode.com/index.aspx?clientID=12174&stateID=9&statename=Florida.

Jan, I-Fang, Jeremy D. Ball, and Anthony Walsh (2008). Predicting public opinion about juvenile waivers. *Criminal Justice Policy Review*, *19*, 285–300.

Johnson, Kristin, Lonn Lanza-Kaduce, and Jennifer Woolard (2011). Disregarding graduated treatment: Why transfer aggravates recidivism. *Crime & Delinquency*, *57*, 756–777.

Kline, Patrick (2012). The impact of juvenile curfew laws on arrests of youth and adults. *American Law and Economics Review*, *14*, 44–67.

Lane, Jodi and James W. Meeker (2000). Subcultural diversity and the fear of crime and gangs. *Crime & Delinquency*, *46*, 497–521.

Lane, Jodi, Lonn Lanza-Kaduce, Charles E. Frazier, and Donna M. Bishop (2002). Adult versus juvenile sanctions: Voices of incarcerated youths. *Crime & Delinquency*, *48*, 431–455.

Lanza-Kaduce, Lonn, Charles E. Frazier, and Donna M. Bishop (1999). Juvenile transfers in Florida: The worst of the worst? *University of Florida Journal of Law and Public Policy*, *10*, 277–312.

Leon County Clerk of the Court (n.d.). *Juvenile Expunction Packet*. Tallahassee: Leon County Clerk of the Court. Retrieved on December 27, 2014 from http://cvweb.clerk.leon.fl.us/clerk_services/online_forms/juvenile_delinquency/juvenile_expunge.pdf.

Lersch, Kim Michelle and Christine S. Sellers (2000). A comparison of curfew and noncurfew violators using a self-report delinquency survey. *American Journal of Criminal Justice*, *24*, 259–269.

Levy, David L. (1997). The Dade County juvenile curfew ordinance: A retrospective examination of the ordinance and the law that supports its constitutionality. *St. Thomas Law Review, 9,* 517–545.

Lubensky, Ellen (2006). Constitutional law—individual rights—Florida juvenile curfew ordinances held unconstitutional because the curfews were not narrowly tailored to further an admittedly compelling governmental interest. *State v. J.P.,* 907 So. 2d 1101 (Fla. 2004). *Rutgers Law Journal, 37,* 1371–1401.

McDowall, David, Colin Loftin, and Brian Wiersema (2000). The impact of youth curfew laws on juvenile crime rates. *Crime & Delinquency, 46,* 76–91.

Mears, Daniel P. (2003). A critique of waiver research: Critical next steps in assessing the impacts of laws for transferring juveniles to the criminal justice system. *Youth Violence and Juvenile Justice, 1,* 156–172.

Mears, Daniel P., Carter Hay, Marc Gertz, and Christina Mancini (2007). Public opinion and the foundation of the juvenile court. *Criminology, 45,* 223–258.

Mears, Daniel P., Tracey L. Shollenberger, Janeen B. Willison, Colleen E. Owens, and Jeffrey A. Butts (2010). Practitioner views of priorities, policies, and practices in juvenile justice. *Crime & Delinquency, 56,* 535–563.

Miami-Dade County, Florida (2014). *Code of Ordinances, Part III, Chapter 21—Offenses and Miscellaneous Provisions. Article XIII—Juvenile Curfew Program.* Tallahassee: Municipal Code Corporation. Retrieved on December 28, 2014 from https://library.municode.com/index.aspx?clientID=10620&stateID=9&statename=Florida.

Myers, David L. (2003). The recidivism of violent youths in juvenile and adult court: A consideration of selection bias. *Youth Violence and Juvenile Justice, 1,* 79–101.

Myers, David L., Daniel Lee, Dennis Giever, and Jay Gilliam (2011). Practitioner perceptions of juvenile transfer in Pennsylvania. *Youth Violence and Juvenile Justice, 9,* 222–240.

Norris, Michael, Sarah Twill, and Chigon Kim (2011). Smells like teen spirit: Evaluating a midwestern teen court. *Crime & Delinquency, 57,* 199–221.

Office of the Florida Attorney General (2012). *Florida Gang Reduction Strategy 2008–2012.* Tallahassee: Office of the Florida Attorney General. Retrieved on December 28, 2014 from http://www.floridagangreduction.com/webfiles.nsf/WF/KGRG-7FVPNR/$file/GangReductionReportWEB.pdf.

Office of the Florida Attorney General (2013). *Florida Gang Reduction 2013 Annual Report.* Tallahassee: Office of the Florida Attorney General. Retrieved on December 28, 2014 from http://www.floridagangreduction.com/flgangs.nsf/pages/APAE9LSMFM/$file/FGRS+2013+for+web.pdf.

Office of the Florida Attorney General (2014). *Targeted Gang Reduction Response.* Tallahassee: Office of the Florida Attorney General. Retrieved on December 28, 2014 from http://www.floridagangreduction.com/webfiles.nsf/WF/KGRG-7UESXF/$file/GangReductionStrategy-pyramid.pdf.

Office of the State Courts Administrator (2003). *Florida's Juvenile Delinquency Court Assessment.* Tallahassee: Florida Supreme Court. Retrieved on December 28, 2014 from http://www.5dca.flcourts.org/gen_public/family/bin/delinquencyassessment.pdf.

Office of the State Courts Administrator (2010). *Florida's Juvenile Delinquency Benchbook.* Tallahassee: Florida Supreme Court. Retrieved on December 27, 2014 from http://www.flcourts.org/core/fileparse.php/260/urlt/DelinquencyBenchbook091410.pdf.

Rabin, Charles (2010). Miami's teen curfew law sparks debate. *The Miami Herald, May 17.* Retrieved on December 28, 2014 from http://articles.sun-sentinel.com/2010-05-17/news/fl-miami-teen-curfew-20100517_1_teen-curfew-miami-police-cmdr-juvenile.

Rasmussen, Andrew (2004). Teen court referral, sentencing, and subsequent recidivism: Two proportional hazards models and a little speculation. *Crime & Delinquency, 59,* 615–635.

Rasmussen, Andrew and Carol I. Diener (2005). A prospective longitudinal study of teen court's impact on offending youths' behavior. *Juvenile and Family Court Journal, 56,* 17–32.

Reynolds, K. Michael, Ruth Seydlitz, and Pamela Jenkins (2000). Do juvenile curfew laws work? A time-series analysis of the New Orleans law. *Justice Quarterly, 17,* 205–230.

Roper v. Simmons, 543 U.S. 551 (2005).

Ruefle, W., and K. Michael Reynolds (1996). Keep them at home: Juvenile curfew ordinances in 200 American cities. *American Journal of Police, 15* (1), 63–84.

Smith, Kenneth S. and Ashley G. Blackburn (2011). Is teen court the best fit? Assessing the predictive validity of the teen court peer influence scale. *Journal of Criminal Justice, 39,* 198–204.

Stanford v. Kentucky, 492 U.S. 361 (1989).

State of Florida v. J.P and T.M., 907 So.2d 11-1 (Fla. 2004).

Steinhart, David (2006). *Juvenile Detention Risk Assessment: A Practice Guide to Juvenile Detention Reform #1.* Baltimore: The Annie E. Casey Foundation. Retrieved on December 28, 2014 from http://www.aecf.org/resources/a-practice-guide-to-juvenile-detention-reform-1/.

Stickle, Wendy Povitsky, Nadine M. Connell, Denise M. Wilson, and Denise Gottfredson (2008). An experimental evaluation of teen courts. *Journal of Experimental Criminology, 4,* 137–163.

Strange, Julia (2013). *Interoffice Memorandum PCI-13-002: Detention Risk Assessment Instrument (DRAI)—Amendment 1.* Tallahassee: Florida Department of Juvenile Justice. Retrieved on December 27, 2014 from http://www.djj.state.fl.us/docs/probation-policy-memos/drai.pdf?Status=Master&sfvrsn=2.

Sugarman, Josh and Aimee Newth (2007). *Drive-By America.* Washington, DC: Violence Policy Center. Retrieved on December 28, 2014 from http://www.vpc.org/studies/driveby.pdf.

Thompson v. Oklahoma, 487 U.S. 815 (1988).

U.S. Conference of Mayors (1997). *A Status Report on Youth Curfews in America's Cities: A 347–City Survey.* Washington, DC: U.S. Conference of Mayors. Retrieved on December 28, 2014 from http://usmayors.org/publications/curfew.htm.

CHAPTER 10

FLORIDA VICTIMS

Learning Objectives

After reading this chapter, you should be able to:

- Explain the Victim Rights Amendment contained in the Florida Constitution.
- Understand the constitutional reform promoted by the President's Task Force.
- Introduce the efforts behind the proposed 26th Amendment to the federal Constitution.
- Discuss the procedure for amending the U.S. Constitution.
- Give three reasons why supporters switched their efforts to amending state constitutions. ·
- Explore the similarity in language that appears in the proposed 6th Amendment change, the new version of the 26th Amendment, and the Florida VRA.
- Assess Florida's role in the state VRA movement.
- Compare and contrast victim compensation with offender restitution.
- Sketch out six shortcomings associated with offender restitution.
- Talk about what a civil restitution lien is.
- Pit the social contract perspective against the social welfare argument.
- Use Figure 10.4 to exemplify the philosophical orientation of Florida's approach to victim compensation.
- Show how adherence to the social contract perspective might be affected by the amount of crime in Florida.
- List some cost-containment measures present in the Florida victim compensation law.
- Link these cost-containment measures back to the two philosophical orientations to victim compensation.
- Demonstrate how Florida decided to deal with "unjust enrichment."
- Provide a list of the types of expenses the Florida crime compensation program covers.
- Explain how victim compensation is a "source of last resort."
- Offer a reason why victim compensation is a "source of last resort."
- Present other requirements that appear in the Florida crime compensation program.
- Demonstrate how the application form in Figure 10.5 reflects the two philosophical orientations.

- Tell where Florida gets the money to operate its crime compensation program.

- Address the three broad areas covered in the Florida victim rights legislation.

- Relay how judges accomplish the task of informing victims of their rights.

- Itemize what information goes into a victim impact statement.

- Offer a major concern that some people have regarding victim impact statements.

- Summarize the Florida VIS statute.

- Visit the Florida Supreme Court's warning in the *Booker* case about balancing defendant and victim issues.

- Outline the Florida Supreme Court's position in the *Deparvine* decision.

- Explain the stance the Florida Supreme Court took in the *Wheeler* decision.

Introduction

All too often, the interests of victims and witnesses are neglected and they become the forgotten parties in the pursuit of justice. The fixation on the accused supersedes and supplants the goals of true justice. In fact, the scant attention paid to victims has prompted some observers to conclude that the system marginalizes these citizens to the point that the system has lost its credibility. The only way to counter this erosion and get back on track is to transform the *criminal's* justice system into the *victim's* justice system (Doerner & Lab, 2014).

Florida, like many other states, has become cognizant of the urgent need to pay more attention to the forgotten member in the criminal-victim dyad if the system wishes to retain its legitimacy. What this chapter does, then, is alert the reader to the mounting wave of enthusiasm behind the institutionalization of victim rights. A quick visit to constitutional reform efforts at the national level provides the reader with a context to understand developments in the Sunshine State. We will also look at how victim compensation and victim rights legislation have nurtured a growing recognition of victim concerns. Florida, as you will come to learn, has played a very active role in the challenge to make justice more meaningful.

Victim Rights Amendment

Floridians went to the polls on Election Day in 1988. One item on the ballot was the so-called *Victim Rights Amendment* (VRA) (see Figure 10.1). Once the votes were counted, the tabulation revealed that 90% of the voters in the Sunshine State favored the VRA. Hence, the initiative passed and became an integral part of the Florida Constitution.

We need to look more closely at the context and what was happening at that time in order to understand the Florida VRA more fully. The following materials examine efforts to enact a federal amendment, how that federal movement fizzled, and why proponents switched their focus to amending state constitutions. Florida, as you will see shortly, played a very visible role in this endeavor.

Figure 10.1 The Florida Victim Rights Amendment

Section 16. Rights of accused and of victims.

(a) In all criminal prosecutions the accused shall, upon demand, be informed of the nature
and cause of the accusation, and shall be furnished a copy of the charges, and shall have
the right to have compulsory process for witnesses, to confront at trial adverse witnesses,
to be heard in person, by counsel or both, and to have a speedy and public trial by
impartial jury in the county where the crime was committed. If the county is not known,
the indictment or information may charge venue in two or more counties conjunctively
and proof that the crime was committed in that area shall be sufficient; but before
pleading the accused may elect in which of those counties the trial will take place. Venue
for prosecution of crimes committed beyond the boundaries of the state shall be fixed
by law.

(b) Victims of crime or their lawful representatives, including the next of kin of homicide
victims, are entitled to the right to be informed, to be present, and to be heard when
relevant, at all crucial stages of criminal proceedings, to the extent that these rights do
not interfere with the constitutional rights of the accused.

Source: Florida Constitution, Article 1, Section 16.

Reforming the Federal Constitution

President Reagan empaneled a blue-ribbon commission and charged the members
with reviewing the plight of crime victims. The goal was to have the panel identify ways
"to improve our efforts to assist and protect victims of crime" (Reagan, 1982). When the
Task Force issued its final report, one recommendation towered over the others. That
proposal called for altering the 6th Amendment of the United States Constitution. Figure
10.2 presents the exact wording of that Amendment, along with the highlighted change.

This effort to catapult victim rights into the federal Constitution attracted a wave of
proponents and a corresponding body of resistors. While advocates viewed the proposed
change as fairly innocuous, dissenters responded with loud protests. One fear the opposition

**Figure 10.2 The Proposed Change to the U.S. Constitution Recommended by the
President's Task Force on Victims of Crime (1982)***

In all criminal prosecutions the accused shall enjoy the right to a speedy and public trial, by
an impartial jury of the State and district wherein the crime shall have been committed,
which district shall have been previously ascertained by law, and to be informed of the nature
and cause of the accusation; to be confronted with the witnesses against him; to have
compulsory process for obtaining witnesses in his favor and to have the Assistance of Counsel
for his defense. *Likewise, the victim, in every criminal prosecution shall have the right to be
present and to be heard at all critical stages of judicial proceedings.*

---

* Proposed changes appear in italics.

Source: The President's Task Force on Victims of Crime (1982). *Final Report*. Washington, DC: U.S.
Government Printing Office.

**Figure 10.3 The Proposed 26th Amendment to the U.S. Constitution Protecting
            Victim Rights**

> Victims of crime are entitled to certain basic rights including, but not limited to, the right
> to be informed, to be present, and to be heard at all critical stages of the federal and state
> criminal justice process to the extent that these rights do not interfere with existing
> Constitutional rights.

Source: Young, Marlene A. (1987). A constitutional amendment for victims of crime: The victim's
perspective. *Wayne Law Review, 34*, pp. 51–52.

voiced was that piggy-backing victim rights onto offender rights would unleash a storm
of lawsuits that would challenge many of the hard-fought Supreme Court decisions. After
much heated debate, the momentum ground to a halt. Sensing that they were at an
impasse, the supporters of constitutional reform selected a new strategy. They proposed
an entirely new, free-standing amendment for consideration (see Figure 10.3). Eventually,
this effort would also falter and fail.

Changing the federal Constitution is not a very easy task to accomplish. The procedure
outlined in Article 5 of the U.S. Constitution involves two stages. The first step calls for
passage of a resolution by a two-thirds vote in the House of Representatives and a two-
thirds vote in the Senate. The second phase is to route the resolution to the states. Three-
quarters or 38 of the states must vote in favor of the resolution if the Constitution is to
be amended. This entire process must be completed within seven years. Given the uphill
battle and insurmountable odds of being successful, a new strategy would emerge. That
plan was to shift the emphasis away from the U.S. Constitution and, instead, to concentrate
efforts on reforming the state constitutions. That development is what gave rise to the
Florida VRA.

Reforming the State Constitutions

This tactical maneuver to lobby for changes at the state level made sense for several
reasons. First, there already was a lot of grass-roots support in a number of communities.
Second, many states had enacted legislation formalizing the recognition of victim rights.
Third, modifying state constitutions would help gauge the level of support for reform
and provide the momentum needed for another federal initiative.

It is important not to gloss over this last point. Go back and re-read the Florida VRA
(see Figure 10.1), the proposed addition to the 6th Amendment (see Figure 10.2), and
the new version of the 26th Amendment (see Figure 10.3). Take special notice of the
congruity or agreement between the three statements. Was this happenstance? Not really.
The hope here was that employing similar language and concepts when modifying the
state constitutions should make a subsequent parallel effort at the federal level much easier
to achieve.

Florida was the 29th state to pass a VRA. As of this writing, 33 states have ratified similar
changes to their constitutions (National Center for Victims of Crime, 2014). While that
number is still shy of the 38 states needed to alter the federal Constitution, it does allow
observers to take the pulse of the movement. In fact, supporters have begun to renew their
efforts and are now trying to get Congress to take up the cause again (Doerner & Lab, 2014).

Victim Compensation

The launching of the Florida victim compensation program in 1978 was the culmination of more than 13 years of legislative debate and wrangling. Two questions trail the formation of this program. First, why did it take so long to pass such a law? Second, what did the contents of the final version of this statute look like? As we shall see in a moment, two major orientations framed the deliberations over why Florida had the responsibility of compensating innocent crime victims. Depending upon which perspective one endorses, there are ramifications for how such a program will operate. First, though, we need to look at the shortcomings of offender restitution in order to justify branching out into victim compensation.

The Shortcomings of Offender Restitution

Before going further, let us distinguish victim compensation from offender restitution. *Victim compensation* refers to the state reimbursing innocent crime victims for their crime-related losses, while *offender restitution* refers to the suspect assuming this responsibility. This distinction between who pays crime victims leads some people to ask why offenders are not repaying their victims. A number of reasons come into play and, when taken together, provide ample justification for incorporating victim compensation into the picture.

First, the authorities have to locate and arrest the suspect to start the process. A look at the Florida *Uniform Crime Reports* for 2013 reveals an overall *clearance rate* of 26% for murder, rape, robbery, aggravated assault, burglary, larceny, and motor vehicle theft (Florida Department of Law Enforcement, 2014). That figure means three out of every four suspects are never identified or captured. So three-quarters of the victim group is excluded immediately from any restitution consideration whatsoever.

Second, once the authorities make an arrest, the state attorney has to secure either a guilty plea or a conviction. This funneling process further shrinks the pool of suspects who are subjected to a restitution order.

Third, even though the state may have won a conviction in a case, the court has to impose a restitution order as part of the sentence. Estimates are that only 20% of criminal sentences cases involve a restitution order (Reaves, 2013, p. 32), thereby further depleting the pool of restitution-eligible victims. Florida legislators sidestepped this thorny issue when they enacted a statute that requires judges to consider a *civil restitution lien* as part of the sentence (*Florida Statutes 2014*, § 960.292). In other words, Florida judges can order that any property or assets the convicted person owns or comes to own in the next twenty years can be seized by the state and used to provide restitution to the victim.

Fourth, most offenders come from economically disadvantaged backgrounds. They typically have had a less-than-adequate education and are either unemployed or under-employed. In other words, many offenders simply lack the earning power necessary to repay their crime victims.

Fifth, trying to determine the fair market value of some damaged or stolen items can be very difficult at times. For example, a family heirloom that has a special meaning or sentimental value to one party may not carry that same price tag in the open market. Furthermore, some items depreciate over time due to built-in obsolescence or wear-and-tear from normal use. Restoring a victim completely back to his or her pre-crime status might not be possible.

Finally, the entire process of collecting, administering, and disbursing funds means that a method to handle restitution must be put into place. Sometimes, these operations become bureaucratized and lose sight of the fact that they have been instituted to help victims, not merely to ensure organizational survival. In these instances, victims play second fiddle and receive a dwindling return on their restitution orders.

When all these aspects are taken into consideration, it becomes apparent that offender restitution is not the perfect solution that it may have appeared to be at the onset. A different mechanism is needed to ensure that innocent victims do not suffer needlessly. Depending upon one's perspective, victim compensation may or may not be that remedy.

The Promise of Victim Compensation

Why should the state compensate or reimburse innocent crime victims for their losses? Two competing schools of thought offer justifications. Let us look at each viewpoint.

The first orientation is the *social contract* argument. Everybody pays taxes and government uses this revenue to provide services for the common good. One function that citizens expect government to perform is law enforcement. The thinking here is that when a person becomes victimized, government has failed to live up to its promise. As a result, it is incumbent upon government to take the steps necessary to restore the victimized party back to his or her original status (Doerner & Lab, 2014, p. 110).

The second position is called the *social welfare* argument. One function of government is to provide a decent standard of living for unfortunate persons. That is why there are programs to help special needs persons, the sick, the elderly, the poor, orphans, the disabled, and other persons in need. Advocates of this approach would maintain that when a person incurs unanticipated hardships because of a victimization episode, then government has the obligation to step in and lend a helping hand in this moment of need (Doerner & Lab, 2014, pp. 110–111).

Sometimes, these competing philosophies clash and lead to opposite conclusions. If one embraces the social contract argument, then the compensation program will have certain features. However, if one adheres to the social welfare notion, then the program will take some different twists.

Figure 10.4 Legislative Intent Section of the Florida Crimes Compensation Act: An Example of the Social Contract or Social Welfare Philosophy?

The Legislature recognizes that many innocent persons suffer personal injury or death as a direct result of adult and juvenile criminal acts or in their efforts to prevent crime or apprehend persons committing or attempting to commit adult and juvenile crimes. Such persons or their dependents may thereby suffer disabilities, incur financial hardships, or become dependent upon public assistance. The Legislature finds and determines that there is a need for government financial assistance for such victims of adult and juvenile crime. Accordingly, it is the intent of the Legislature that aid, care, and support be provided by the state, as a matter of moral responsibility, for such victims of adult and juvenile crime. It is the express intent of the Legislature that all state departments and agencies cooperate with the Department of Legal Affairs in carrying out the provisions of this chapter.

Source: Florida Statutes 2014, § 960.02.

As mentioned earlier, it took a long time and many compromises to get the Florida crimes compensation program up and running. One result of the bargaining process and the concessions that were made is that, at times, the program may appear to be more of a hybrid than a thoroughbred. Bear in mind during the remainder of the discussion that critics and supporters alike worried about the possibility of the costs associated with running a compensation program would escalate. They did not want this program to drain the state coffers and evaporate. Before we turn to some of the more prominent provisions in the Florida victim compensation program, the reader should take a look at Figure 10.4 and determine which philosophical orientation the Florida Legislature embraced. That brief exercise will make some of the provisions more understandable.

Provisions

The first consideration that Florida lawmakers had to resolve was what crimes should be compensable. If you flip back to Chapter 3, you will realize that Florida historically has had one of the highest, if not the highest, serious violent crime rates in the country. The same is true for serious property crime rates. In 2013 alone, there were 1.1 million serious violent offenses and another 8.6 million serious property offenses. The price tags associated with just these 9.7 million crimes would be astronomical. As a result, Florida leaders decided to limit victim compensation to crimes in which a person was injured or killed (*Florida Statutes 2014*, § 960.03(3)(a)). This move means that approximately 11% of all serious crime victims start out in the eligibility pool.

Florida also implemented other cost-containment measures in its compensation statute. For instance, eligibility is reserved for crime victims who experience a serious financial hardship as a result of their victimization (*Florida Statutes 2014*, § 960.13(8)). Here is another example of how the adoption of a philosophical orientation can affect the provisions in a statute.

Florida took some very explicit steps to avoid *unjust enrichment*. In other words, the state did not want offenders to profit from their misdeeds. For example, domestic violence victims who continue to reside with their violent partners would be excluded from compensation for their injuries. However, if a domestic violence victim is in the process of leaving or divorcing the assailant, then he or she could be eligible for benefits. Another eligibility restriction is that the claimant cannot have precipitated or caused the criminal event. *Victim precipitation* means that the victim instigated or was responsible for setting the incident into motion. Suppose that Albert pushes Zachary. Zachary retaliates by punching Albert in return and, in doing so, breaks Albert's nose. Since Albert initiated the fracas, Albert is ineligible for compensation.

Some expenses that are normally eligible for repayment include medical services, financial losses due to missing work, mental health treatment, and funeral expenses. The original Florida law prohibited reimbursement for property losses. However, that portion of the statute was later revised to include payments to senior citizens under special circumstances (*Florida Statutes 2014*, § 960.195). Once again, the philosophical orientation one takes determines some of the statutory contents.

Florida instituted caps or ceilings on how much money it would award victims in order to curtail some of these expenses. The maximum allowable payment is $25,000 per event. In addition, victim compensation is a *source of last resort*. In other words, Florida will underwrite expenses only after insurance and other sources of funds (i.e., worker compensation, social security benefits, restitution, civil awards, and the like) are exhausted.

There are a number of other stipulations aimed at supporting criminal justice operations. For one thing, the crime must have been reported to the authorities within 72 hours. A second requirement is that the victim must cooperate completely with the police investigation. Third, the victim must also cooperate completely with the prosecution. Finally, the victim or his/her representative must adhere to filing deadlines.

Operations

Figure 10.5 contains a copy of the actual claim form that victims must complete when seeking compensation from the State of Florida. The items on that form and the information being sought give the reader some further ideas about how the statute works. The materials also provide details that staff members need to access when they investigate and verify a claim.

Where does Florida get the money to run its victim compensation program? Interestingly enough, not a single penny comes out of taxpayer pockets. Financing comes from four general sources. They include:

- Mandatory court costs imposed on offenders;
- A surcharge on fines, bail, and bond forfeitures;
- Offender restitution; and
- Any available grants or donations.

Mandatory court costs account for 84% of the program funding (Office of Attorney General Pam Bondi, 2013, p. 16). The federal Victims of Crime Act (VOCA), administered by the Department of Justice, is a primary grant source for state compensation programs and other victim services throughout the country. Florida received almost $24 million from VOCA during fiscal year 2012–13 (Office of Attorney General Pam Bondi, 2013). A total of 19,675 claims were received during that same period, along with 5,595 requests to fund sexual battery evidentiary examinations, which the statute allows. The total amount of local money deposited in Florida's Crimes Compensation Trust Fund for fiscal year 2012–13 was $19 million. As you can see, the losses that Floridians experience are large.

Victim Rights Legislation

Now that Floridians had placed a VRA into the state constitution, many agencies were perplexed. Exactly what obligations and duties were they expected to honor? The Florida Legislature responded to this dilemma by passing a new law titled "Guidelines for Fair Treatment of Victims and Witnesses in the Criminal Justice and Juvenile Justice Systems" (*Florida Statutes 2014*, § 960.001 *et seq.*). For ease of presentation, we will group these rights into broad categories and give a general overview of what the statute means.

The first group of rights deals with providing relevant information to victims and witnesses. Most people are not aware of what social services exist in their locales, the availability of crime compensation, how the system works, or what other recourses they can pursue. This section of the statute directs law enforcement agencies and other members of the criminal justice community to furnish this information to victims. FDLE, for example, has produced information cards and brochures that local agencies can distribute to victims in general (FDLE, 2012) and to sexual battery victims in particular (FDLE,

Figure 10.5 Florida Victim Compensation Application Form

Office of the Attorney General

The Capitol, PL-01 • Tallahassee, FL 32399-1050 • Office: (800) 226-6667 Fax: (850) 414-6197
Bill Status Information for Providers (850) 414-3331 • TDD users may call through Florida Relay Service at 1-800-955-8771
Website: http://myfloridalegal.com • Email address: vcintake@myfloridalegal.com

BUREAU OF VICTIM COMPENSATION CLAIM FORM

Instructions

Please read the Eligibility Requirements to see if you qualify for this program. Fill out this form completely (please print), attach all required documentation, and submit to the above address. If you move or change your address, you are required to notify this office.

CHECK THE TYPE OF VICTIM COMPENSATION BENEFITS YOU ARE REQUESTING:

☐ **DISABILITY** - compensation for the victim who suffered a permanent disability. (Attach documentation as outlined in Section 3.)

☐ **WAGE LOSS** - compensation for the victim who lost wages because of the crime. (Attach documentation as outlined in Section 3.)

☐ **LOSS OF SUPPORT** - compensation for the dependent(s) of a deceased victim who was employed at the time of the crime. (Attach documentation as outlined in Section 4.)

☐ **EXPENSES** - payment or reimbursement on behalf of the victim for crime-related funeral/burial, medical/dental treatment, and mental health counseling expenses; as well as prescriptions, eyeglasses, dentures, or a prosthetic device lost, damaged, or required because of the crime. (Attach itemized bills and receipts from treatment/funeral providers.)
  ☐ FUNERAL/BURIAL   ☐ MEDICAL/DENTAL TREATMENT   ☐ MENTAL HEALTH COUNSELING

☐ **EMERGENCY ASSISTANCE** - reimbursement for documented wage loss and out-of-pocket expenses related to the crime. (Attach receipts.)

CHECK ALL OTHER TYPES OF BENEFITS YOU ARE REQUESTING: (Separate claim numbers will be assigned.)

☐ **PROPERTY LOSS** - for an adult over the age of 60 or disabled adult (attach proof of disability prior to the date of crime from a physician or the Social Security Administration) who suffered the loss of tangible personal property as the result of a criminal or delinquent act. Attach a receipt or written estimate from a vendor or merchant identifying the comparable replacement value. Compensable items must be identified by the law enforcement report and the crime reported to the proper authorities within 72 hours from the discovery of the loss.

☐ **SEXUAL BATTERY RELOCATION ASSISTANCE** - for the victim of sexual battery seeking assistance to relocate due to reasonable fear. A certified rape crisis center, state attorney, or statewide prosecutor certification form must be submitted with the application.

☐ **DOMESTIC VIOLENCE RELOCATION ASSISTANCE** - for the victim of domestic violence seeking assistance to relocate to a safe environment. A shelter certification form and application must be submitted within 30 days from the date of crime.

☐ **HUMAN TRAFFICKING RELOCATION ASSISTANCE** - for the victim of sexual trafficking seeking assistance to relocate due to reasonable fear. A certified rape crisis or domestic violence center, state attorney, or statewide prosecutor certification form must be submitted with the application. If certified by a certified rape crisis or domestic violence center, there must also be sufficient cooperation approval by a state attorney or statewide prosecutor.

Section 1. Victim and Applicant Information

VICTIM'S NAME (last, first, middle)			DATE OF BIRTH / /
SOCIAL SECURITY NO.	E-MAIL ADDRESS	WOULD YOU LIKE ALL CORRESPONDENCE SENT BY EMAIL? ☐ YES ☐ NO	
ADDRESS	CITY	STATE	ZIP CODE
TELEPHONE NUMBER ( )	ALTERNATE PHONE NUMBER ( )	OCCUPATION	

THIS INFORMATION IS COLLECTED FOR FEDERAL REPORTING PURPOSES AND IS OPTIONAL.
RACE: ☐ CAUCASIAN ☐ AFRICAN AMERICAN ☐ HISPANIC ☐ AMERICAN INDIAN or ALASKAN NATIVE ☐ ASIAN or PACIFIC ISLANDER ☐ OTHER, IDENTIFY: GENDER: MALE ☐ FEMALE ☐

NATIONAL ORIGIN   WAS VICTIM DISABLED BEFORE THE CRIME OCCURRED? ☐ YES ☐ NO

The applicant filing on behalf of a victim is required to provide claimant information below. When requesting compensation on behalf of an incompetent adult victim, proof of legal guardianship must be attached, and the applicant's signature on the claim form must be witnessed by a Notary Public.

IS THE VICTIM (check one) ☐ DECEASED ☐ INJURED MINOR ☐ MINOR WITNESS - NOT INJURED ☐ INCOMPETENT

APPLICANT NAME (last, first, middle)			DATE OF BIRTH / /
SOCIAL SECURITY NO.	E-MAIL ADDRESS	WOULD YOU LIKE ALL CORRESPONDENCE SENT BY EMAIL? ☐ YES ☐ NO	
ADDRESS	CITY	STATE	ZIP CODE
TELEPHONE NUMBER ( )	ALTERNATE PHONE NUMBER ( )	RELATIONSHIP TO VICTIM	OCCUPATION

BVC 100 (10/14)   *The Office of the Attorney General, Bureau of Victim Compensation is an equal opportunity provider and employer.*   Page 1 of 4

n.d.). FDLE also advertises brochures that other entities have constructed regarding civil injunctions (Florida Coalition Against Domestic Violence, n.d.).

The second area of victim rights addresses notification concerns. Some of these aspects include contacting involved parties about upcoming legal proceedings, prompt advisement

Figure 10.5 Florida Victim Compensation Application Form, *continued*

Section 2. Referral Source Information

Individuals who assisted with or filled out any sections of this application are required to provide referral information below. By signing this application, the victim/applicant affirms that all information provided is true and correct, and thus, all sections should be reviewed before the application is signed. (Treatment providers can request training on the Victim Compensation Program, which is recommended prior to becoming a referral source.)

NAME OF PERSON ASSISTING WITH APPLICATION (last, first, middle)	E-MAIL ADDRESS
NAME OF AGENCY/ORGANIZATION	
AGENCY/ORGANIZATION'S ADDRESS (address, city, state, zip code)	TELEPHONE NUMBER ( )

Section 3. Disability or Lost Wages Information

When requesting compensation for lost wages, attach a copy of your pay stub or earnings statement which identifies your employment status and wages at the time of the crime. If you are self-employed or work for a family member, attach a copy of your latest income tax return and applicable IRS schedule forms. If more than 5 work days were missed as a result of the crime, attach a doctor's letter which excused you for this absence. When requesting disability compensation, attach a doctor's letter which specifies each crime related permanent disability rating according to the American Medical Association Guidelines or Florida Impairment Rating Guidelines, and forward Social Security Administration award letters.

SUPERVISOR'S NAME	TELEPHONE NUMBER ( )
NAME OF COMPANY/BUSINESS (if more than one [1] employer, please attach additional sheet)	
COMPANY ADDRESS (address, city, state, zip code)	

IS WAGE LOSS COVERED BY INSURANCE? ☐ YES ☐ NO	IS VICTIM DISABLED AS A RESULT OF THE CRIME? ☐ YES ☐ NO
IS WAGE LOSS COVERED BY WORKER'S COMPENSATION? ☐ YES ☐ NO	

Section 4. Loss of Support Information or Grief Counseling Information

Indicate the name(s) and date(s) of birth of the deceased victim's surviving spouse, parent, sibling, or child. For loss of support, attach a copy of the deceased victim's latest income tax return and individual earnings statement, unemployment compensation benefit statement, court order for support, birth certificate which identifies dependent relationship, marriage certificate, or legal documentation proving principal support.

DEPENDANT/MINOR CLAIMANT NAME(S)	DATE OF BIRTH	RELATIONSHIP TO VICTIM

Section 5. Insurance Information

Claimants who are determined eligible for the Victim Compensation and Property Loss Programs may be exempt from the insurance deductible, co-payment, or coinsurance provisions of their insurance policy(ies).

IS INSURANCE OR MEDICAID AVAILABLE TO ASSIST WITH THESE EXPENSES?   ☐ YES   ☐ NO   MEDICAID NUMBER:

If yes, provide the following for all insurance policies, including Medicaid, Medicare, life, homeowner's, automobile, or major medical. Attach all related insurance Explanation of Benefits statement(s).

1. COMPANY NAME	POLICY NUMBER		TELEPHONE NUMBER ( )
ADDRESS	CITY	STATE	ZIP CODE
2. COMPANY NAME	POLICY NUMBER		TELEPHONE NUMBER ( )
ADDRESS	CITY	STATE	ZIP CODE

Section 6. Other Compensation, Settlement, and Attorney Information

If you have received, or if you anticipate receiving compensation or any benefits from any other source as a result of this incident, you must notify this office.

STATE THE SOURCE AND DATE RECEIVED (IF APPLICABLE)	ARE YOU REPRESENTED BY LEGAL COUNSEL? ☐ YES ☐ NO	ATTORNEY'S NAME
ADDRESS		E-MAIL ADDRESS
CITY	STATE	ZIP CODE	TELEPHONE NUMBER ( )

BVC 100 (10/14)   *The Office of the Attorney General, Bureau of Victim Compensation is an equal opportunity provider and employer.*   Page 2 of 4

Source: Office of the Florida Attorney General (2014). *Bureau of Victim Compensation Claim Form.* Tallahassee: Office of the Florida Attorney General. Retrieved on December 22, 2014 from http://myfloridalegal.com/webfiles.nsf/WF/RMAS-9P7GFD/$file/VictimCompClaimFormEng.pdf.

whenever there is a scheduling change in a case, letting victims know if and when the offender is released back into the community, allowing the state attorney's office to intercede with employers and creditors on behalf of victims, informing victims about the

Figure 10.6 Text of the Announcement Judges Must Read at Criminal Proceedings or Display in Their Courtroom

---

If you are the victim of a crime with a case pending before this court, you are advised that you have the right:

1. To be informed.

2. To be present.

3. To be heard, when relevant, at all crucial stages of criminal proceedings to the extent that these rights do not interfere with the constitutional rights of the accused.

4. To receive advance notification, when possible, of judicial proceedings and notification of scheduling changes.

5. To seek crimes compensation and restitution.

6. To consult with the state attorney's office in certain felony cases regarding the disposition of the case.

7. To make an oral or written victim impact statement at the time of sentencing of a defendant.

For further information regarding additional rights afforded to victims of crime, you may contact the state attorney's office or obtain a listing of your rights from the Clerk of Court.

Source: Florida Statutes 2014, § 960.0021(2)(a).

possibility of offender restitution, and providing victims an opportunity to make a victim impact statement to the court.

A third block deals with general assistance. Some of these items include help with directions to the courthouse, transportation to proceedings, where to park at the courthouse, having an appropriate waiting area away from the suspect, translator services, coordinating with victim advocates, and doing other things that make system participation go smoothly. There is also a victim's right to a *speedy trial* that limits the number of continuances to three requests and requires scheduling court hearings within a reasonable period of time.

Finally, in an effort to ensure that there are no victims who may have fallen through the cracks, judges are required to inform victims of their rights. This advisement can be a verbal announcement at the start of a proceeding or via posters displayed at the entrance to the courtroom. Figure 10.6 shows the wording of the exact statement that must be used.

Victim Impact Statements

The practice of allowing victim impact statements has had a tumultuous history. A *victim impact statement* (VIS) is an opportunity for the victim or the victim's representative to explain to the court during the sentencing phase exactly how the episode has affected his or her life. A VIS can be delivered in the form of either verbal testimony or a written statement. The VIS form that appears in Figure 10.7 is used in the Florida 10th Judicial Circuit (Hardee, Highlands, and Polk counties). A glance at the contents shows that victims can use this window to provide information about their reaction to the incident,

Figure 10.7 Victim Impact Statement Form Used in the Florida 10th Judicial Circuit

Office of the State Attorney
10th Judicial Circuit

Victim Impact Statement

Jerry Hill, State Attorney, 10ᵗʰ Judicial Circuit   ~ Drawer SA, P.O. Box 9000 ~ Bartow, Florida 33831-9000

Victim:_____ Case # _____
ASA_____ State v. _____

This form will allow the sentencing judge and the prosecutor to know your feelings about being the victim of a crime and how the crime has affected you. *If you need extra space, please attach additional pages.*

Victim's Personal Reaction:
Write your feelings on how being a victim of this crime has affected you personally and those around you.

_____
_____
_____
_____

Victim's Personal Injury:
Explain and injuries and the treatment you received (Please send to us copies of all related bills).

_____
_____
_____

Victim's Property Loss:
List any property that was damaged, destroyed or lost and the value of than property. (Please keep copies of any bills).

_____
_____
_____

Financial or Other Loss:
List the days and hours you missed work because of this crime and the amount of wages you have lost, if any.

_____
_____
_____

Any Additional Comments or Concerns you would like to express:

_____
_____
_____

THIS STATEMENT IS SUBSCRIBED AND AFFIRMED AS TRUE BY THE AFFIANT, UNDER PENALTY OF PERJURY.

_____ Date Signed_____
Signature of Victim or Aggrieved Party

SWORN TO AND SUBSCRIBED BEFORE ME THIS _____ DAY OF _____, 20_____, AT _____COUNTY,
_____.

PERSONALLY KNOWN___ OR PRODUCED IDENTIFICATION_____ TYPE OF IDENTIFICATION_____

_____
Notary Public

Notary Seal and Expiration Date:

Source: Office of the State Attorney, 10th Judicial Circuit (n.d.). *Victim Impact Statement Form*. Bartow: Office of the State Attorney. Retrieved on December 22, 2014 from http://www.sao 10.com/vis.pdf.

any injuries and subsequent treatment, property losses they incurred, and any other financial impact the crime created.

One general concern with a VIS is that it might unduly influence court decisions by injecting too much emotion into the judicial process. As we discussed earlier in the death penalty chapter, a major objective is to ensure the fairness of the sentencing decision. Inflammatory statements or any prejudicial materials that could compromise the defendant's right to a fair and unbiased trial are to be minimized whenever possible.

The legal wrangling that led up to the federal Supreme Court decision in *Payne v. Tennessee* (1991) is one example of the judicial struggle to remain impartial and keep court proceedings as sterile as possible. Payne was found guilty of murdering a mother and her infant. A three-year-old child who was also attacked during that escapade managed to survive his life-threatening wounds. During the sentencing phase, the child's grandmother testified about the emotional upheaval and the nightmares the child experienced stemming from the attack. The jury went on to impose the death penalty. On appeal, Payne maintained that the grandmother's recounting was so emotional that it devastated any chance he had of receiving an impartial consideration. The Supreme Court disagreed. They upheld the sentence and ruled that state statutes could allow the prosecutor to introduce VIS testimony.

The Florida Legislature responded to this situation by passing a law that allows the jury to hear VIS evidence as part of the sentencing deliberation. As that statute explains, the VIS:

> shall be designed to demonstrate the victim's uniqueness as an individual human being and the resultant loss to the community's members by the victim's death. Characterizations and opinions about the crime, the defendant, and the appropriate shall not be permitted as a part of victim impact evidence (*Florida Statutes 2014*, § 921.141(7)).

The Florida Supreme Court has weighed in on the matter of a VIS on several occasions. The foundation for monitoring the balance between defendant and victim interests was laid in *Booker v. State* (2000). In a statement reminiscent of the tensions in the early debate over federal constitutional reform, the court warned that "the rights provided to victims and victims' families under Article I, Section 16(b) [the Victim Rights Amendment in the Florida Constitution] are not absolute, as they are subordinate to the rights of an accused when the rights involved are in conflict" (p. 36).

In another matter, the Florida Supreme Court concluded that allowing multiple victims an opportunity to deliver their own individual VIS was not redundant nor excessive (*Deparvine v. State*, 2008). After Deparvine was convicted of first-degree homicide, the proceeding moved to the penalty phase. Five witnesses participated during that portion of the trial by presenting their own VIS testimony. Deparvine's attorney objected on the grounds that parading five witnesses into the court would be redundant and excessive. In other words, the sheer number of VIS deliveries might sway the jury. The Court ruled against Deparvine and noted that it "has never drawn a bright line holding that a certain number of victim impact witnesses are or are not permissible" (*Deparvine v. State*, 2008, pp. 49–51).

More recently, the Florida Supreme Court indicated that the inclusion of pictures of the victim in a VIS did not introduce overly emotionally-charged evidence (*Wheeler v. State*, 2009). During the penalty phase, the trial judge reviewed four written VIS testimonies prior to these statements being read in court. After Wheeler's lawyer objected to several passages in the VIS, the judge redacted those materials. In other words, those portions of the testimony were left out of the formal presentation. In addition, 54 photographs of the deceased victim and his family were presented. On appeal, Wheeler maintained that the introduction of so many pictures posed a due process violation. Although the Court disagreed and ruled against Wheeler's objection, the opinion contained the following warning:

> Prosecutors should make every effort to ensure that the rights of victims and families, who naturally want their loved one to be remembered through testimony and pictures, do not interfere with the right of the defendant to a fair trial. We also remind prosecutors of the admonition in *Payne* . . . [and] . . . we encourage trial judges to assist in ensuring that the proper balance is struck (p. 20).

Summary

While this chapter has focused on some of the progress that Florida has made in the area of victim rights, several other deserving developments have gone without mention. For example, we have not visited the reforms and gains associated with intimate partner violence, child maltreatment, elderly abuse and neglect, sexual battery, hate crimes, and a host of other forms of victimization. Those topics, of course, represent just a portion of the larger picture. By taking a broader view of the victimological landscape, the reader is now positioned to appreciate the paths that victim advocates have taken and the journey to justice that still awaits Floridians.

Key Terms

civil restitution lien
clearance rate
offender restitution
social contract
social welfare
source of last resort
unjust enrichment
victim compensation
victim impact statement
victim precipitation
victim rights amendment

Selected Internet Sites

Florida Coalition Against Domestic Violence
    http://www.fcadv.org

Florida Council Against Sexual Violence
    http://www.fcasv.org

Florida Crime Prevention Training Institute
   http://www.fcpti.com

Florida Network of Victim Witness Services
   http://www.fnvws.org

Florida State University Victim Advocate Program
   http://victimadvocate.fsu.edu

Mothers Against Drunk Driving Florida
   http://www.madd.org/local-offices/fl/

National Organization for Victim Assistance
   http://www.trynova.org

Office of the Attorney General of Florida, Crime Victims' Services
   http://myfloridalegal.com

Review Questions

1.   What are the contents of the "Victim Rights Amendment" in the Florida Constitution?

2.   What change did reformers wish to make to the 6th Amendment of the U.S. Constitution?

3.   Why did some people oppose amending the U.S. Constitution?

4.   Summarize efforts to introduce the 26th Amendment to the U.S. Constitution.

5.   What steps are involved in amending the U.S. Constitution?

6.   Why did the switch to reforming state constitutions make sense?

7.   Compare the language used in the Florida VRA, the 6th Amendment, and the 26th Amendment.

8.   Where do efforts to amend the U.S. Constitution lie today?

9.   Define victim compensation.

10. Explain what offender restitution is.

11. Give six objections to relying on offender restitution as the main way to remedy the plight of victims.

12. Explain what a civil restitution lien is.

13. What is the social contract philosophy with respect to victim compensation?

14. What is the social welfare philosophy with respect to victim compensation?

15. Using Figure 10.4 of your text, does Florida embrace the social contract or the social welfare philosophy in its legislative intent statement?

16. What implications do the social contract philosophy and the social welfare philosophy have in light of the Florida crime rate?

17. Does a serious financial hardship eligibility requirement reflect the social contract or the social welfare orientation?

18. What is unjust enrichment and how does it affect victim compensation provisions?

19. How does victim precipitation (one's responsibility for the criminal act) affect compensation?

20. What crime-related expenses does the Florida victim compensation program cover?

21. What crime-related expenses does the Florida victim compensation program not cover?

22. What does it mean when one says that compensation is a source of last resort?

23. What restrictions are there in terms of cooperating with the authorities?

24. Where does Florida get the money to fund its compensation program?

25. What informational concerns does the Florida victim rights legislation address?

26. What notification concerns does the Florida victim rights legislation address?

27. What general assistance aspects does the Florida victim rights legislation address?

28. What does the victim's right to a speedy trial mean?

29. What is contained in the statement that Florida judges must use when advising victims of their rights?

30. What is a victim impact statement (VIS)?

31. What are some of the contents of a VIS?

32. What argument did the defendant make in *Payne v. Tennessee*?

33. What is the intention behind the Florida VIS law?

34. What does the Florida VIS law say can be included in testimony?

35. What does the Florida VIS law say cannot be included in testimony?

36. What was the issue and what was the outcome in the Florida Supreme Court *Deparvine* decision?

37. What was the issue and what was the outcome in the Florida Supreme Court *Wheeler* decision?

References

Booker v. State, 773 So. 2d 1079 (Fla. 2000). Retrieved on December 22, 2014 from http://www.floridasupremecourt.org/decisions/pre2004/ops/sc93422.pdf.

Deparvine v. State, 995 So. 2d 351 (Fla. 2008). Retrieved on December 22, 2014 from http://www.floridasupremecourt.org/decisions/2008/sc06-155.pdf.

Doerner, William G. and Steven P. Lab (2014). *Victimology* (7th ed.) Waltham, MA: Elsevier/Anderson Publishing Company.

Florida Coalition Against Domestic Violence (n.d.). *Florida's Civil Injunction for Protection System for Victims of Domestic Violence, Dating Violence, Sexual Violence, Stalking, Repeat Violence.* Retrieved on December 22, 2014 from http://www.fdle.state.fl.us/Content/getdoc/f55c51ad-33d3-4b1a-9021-e95235fb136c/Legal-Brochure_2013.aspx.

Florida Constitution.

Florida Department of Law Enforcement (n.d.). *Sexual Battery: Victim Rights and Services.* Tallahassee: Florida Department of Law Enforcement. Retrieved on December 22,

2014 from http://www.fdle.state.fl.us/Content/getdoc/a8b678b2-3bd7-461c-a0bf-5c8f61b76917/SBVIctimsRightsBrochureSB1312.aspx.

Florida Department of Law Enforcement (2012). *Notice of Legal Rights and Remedies for Victims of Domestic Violence, Dating Violence, Repeat Violence, Sexual Violence, Stalking.* Tallahassee: Florida Department of Law Enforcement. Retrieved on December 22, 2014 from http://www.fdle.state.fl.us/Content/getdoc/df5333dd-d343-46c1-bf51-5d8939cf787f/2012DomesticViolenceVictimRights-RemediesEng.aspx.

Florida Department of Law Enforcement (2014). *County and Municipal Offense Data January – December 2013.* Tallahassee, FL: Florida Department of Law Enforcement. Retrieved on December 22, 2014 from http://www.fdle.state.fl.us/Content/getdoc/2c79e16b-8846-4383-be92-c7c16e227813/CoMuOff2013annual.aspx.

Florida Statutes 2014.

National Center for Victims of Crime (2014). *Issues: Constitutional Amendments.* Washington, DC: National Center for Victims of Crime. Retrieved on December 22, 2014 from http://www.victimsofcrime.org/our-programs/public-policy/amendments.

Office of Attorney General Pam Bondi (2013). *Division of Victim Services and Criminal Justice Programs Annual Report 2012–2013.* Tallahassee: Office of the Florida Attorney General. Retrieved on December 22, 2014 from http://myfloridalegal.com/webfiles.nsf/WF/RMAS-9ENQXB/$file/2012-2013AnnualReport.pdf.

Office of the Florida Attorney General (2014). *Bureau of Victim Compensation Claim Form.* Tallahassee: Office of the Florida Attorney General. Retrieved on December 22, 2014 from http://myfloridalegal.com/webfiles.nsf/WF/RMAS-9P7GFD/$file/VictimCompClaimFormEng.pdf.

Office of the State Attorney, 10th Judicial Circuit (n.d.). *Victim Impact Statement Form.* Bartow: Office of the State Attorney. Retrieved on December 22, 2014 from http://www.sao10.com/vis.pdf.

Payne v. Tennessee, 111 S. Ct. 2597 (1991).

The President's Task Force on Victims of Crime (1982). *Final Report.* Washington, DC: U.S. Government Printing Office.

Reagan, Ronald (1982). *Executive Order 12360—President's Task Force on Victims of Crime.* Washington, DC: The White House. Retrieved on December 22, 2014 from http://www.presidency.ucsb.edu/ws/index.php?pid=42438#axzz1SBopWwdg.

Reaves, Brian A. (2013). *Felony Defendants in Large Urban Counties, 2009—Statistical Tables.* Washington, DC: U.S. Department of Justice. Retrieved on December 22, 2014 from http://www.bjs.gov/content/pub/pdf/fdluc09.pdf.

Wheeler v. State, 4 So. 2d 599 (Fla. 2009). Retrieved on December 22, 2014 http://www.floridasupremecourt.org/decisions/2009/sc06-2323.pdf

Young, Marlene A. (1987). A constitutional amendment for victims of crime: The victim's perspective. *The Wayne Law Review*, 34, 51–68.

INDEX

Note: *f* denotes figure; *t*, table.

10-20-Life law, 47, 48*f*
2013 Criminal Justice Agency Profile
    (FDLE), 9–10

A
Abdool v. Bondi, 180
Academically Adrift (Arum; Roksa), 7–8
accreditation
    benefits of, 146*f*
    of college and university police de-
        partments, 76, 77
    in correctional system, 145–47
    defined, 76, 145
    in law enforcement agencies, 76–77
    of municipal police departments, 76,
        77
    of sheriff offices (SOs), 76, 77
    of special jurisdiction agencies, 77
acquittal, judgment of, 103, 112
adjudication, 114
adjudication withheld (juvenile justice
    system), 210
adjudicatory hearing (juvenile justice
    system), 205–6
affidavit, 106, 199
age
    and juvenile delinquency, 193
    percent of population by, 49, 50*f*
aggravated assault(s)
    about, 47–48, 47*f*

FBI definition, 26*f*
frequency of, 27, 28*f*
juvenile arrest rates, 193, 194*f*, 195*f*
rates, 29*f*, 30, 31*f*
aggravated battery, 48–49
aggravated circumstances (death
    penalty), 166, 167*f*
American Bar Association (ABA), on
    death penalty, 178–79
American Correctional Association
    (ACA), 146
American Medical Association Code of
    Ethics, 171
Americans with Disabilities Act, 63
Anthony, Casey, 102–3, 113
Arizona, Ring v., 181
armed robbery, 50
arraignment, 108
arraignment (juveniles), 203
arrest rates, 193–96
arson, 27–28
Arum, Richard, *Academically Adrift*,
    7–8
Askew, Reubin, 166
assaults
    aggravated (*see* aggravated assaults)
    simple, 46–47, 47*f*
    simple battery, 46–47
    weapons involved in, 47–48
assisting self-murder, 45
Atkins v. Virginia, 217
attorney general (AG), 104, 106

attorneys. (*see* lawyers)
average daily inmate population, 143, 144*t*

B

Baiardi et al. v. Tucker, 149
bail, 107, 108
Bales, William, 122, 148
Banks, Chadwick, 176–77*f*
battery
    aggravated, 48–49
    sexual (*see* sexual battery)
    simple, 46–47, 47*f*
Baze v. Rees, 172, 173
bench trials, 109
bifurcated hearing, 166
Bishop, Donna M., 212–13
Bob Graham Center for Public Service, 4
bona fide occupational qualification (BFOQ), 63
Bonczar, Thomas P., 138
bondable offenses, 107
Bondi, Abdool v., 180
Bondi, Pam, 106, 181
bonds, 107
Booker v. State, 239
booking, 106–7
botched executions, 168, 170, 171, 173
breaking and entering, 52
breaking and exiting, 53
Brennan, William J., 165, 217
Buck, Janeen, 211
Buenoano v. Florida, 169
burglary
    about, 52–53
    FBI definition, 27*f*
    frequency of, 27, 28*f*
    juvenile arrest rates, 196
    rates, 30, 32*f*
Bush, Jeb, 91, 169, 170
Buss, Edwin, 149
Butterworth, Bob, 106, 113, 209
Butts, Jeffrey A., 211

C

Cannon, Dean, 174
Cantero, Raoul G., 179, 182
Capitol Police (FDLE program), 68
carjacking, 51
caseloads, 96*f*, 97–99, 98*f*, 99*f*
cash bonds, 107
castle doctrine, 43, 44*f*
Celestineo v. Singletary, 153
certification, 134
certiorari, 100, 181
challenge by cause, 110
Chief Justice, 90
Chiles, Lawton, 178
circuit courts
    about, 92, 97
    criminal cases in, 97–98, 98*f*
    and death penalty post-conviction process, 174
    and juvenile justice system, 198
    map of, 93*f*
    SAO and, 100
city police departments. *See* police departments
civic responsibility, 4–5, 5*f*
civil citation program (CCP), 199–201, 201*f*
civil restitution lien, 231
civil rights restoration, 149–51
clearance rates, 77, 231
clemency, 17, 149–50, 150*f*, 180
clerk of the circuit court (CCC), 104
clerk of the court (COC), 101
closing arguments, 112
college degrees
    in criminal justice system, 4, 9–10
    and Department of Law Enforcement agents, 67, 68, 75
    and employment, 8
    police officers and, 9, 72–73, 76
    probation officers and, 144
    in security and protective services, 75
    sheriff offices and, 10
colleges and universities
    Florida Board of Governors, 75

law enforcement agencies in, 73–74,
   74t, 76, 77
quality of education, 6–9
Collie, Tim, 5
Commission for Florida Law Enforcement Accreditation (CFA), 77
Commission on Accreditation for Corrections (CAC), 146
Commission on Accreditation for Law
   Enforcement Agencies (CALEA), 76,
   77
Commission on Capital Cases (CCC),
   170, 178, 179
community supervision, 138, 144–45
Constitution (Florida)
   about, 15–20
   amending, 18–19, 19f
   and branches of government, 16–17,
      180
   and clerk of the circuit court (CCC),
      104
   on court system's availability to
      everybody, 95
   and death penalty, 164, 172
   Declaration of Rights, 17–18, 86
   and felons' forfeiture of civil rights,
      149
   and Governor's term of office, 91
   and hierarchy of law, 15
   history of, 16
   and juvenile waiver to adult court,
      211–12
   and right to counsel, 101
   on right to jury trial, 109–10
   on right to pretrial release from de-
      tention, 107, 107f
   on sheriffs, 69
   on state attorneys, 100
   on Supreme Court, 90, 91
   Victim Rights Amendment (VRA),
      228, 229f, 230
Constitution (U.S.)
   and cruel and unusual punishment,
      180
   and death penalty, 164, 172

Florida Declaration of Rights and
   federal Bill of Rights in, 17–18
and hierarchy of law, 15–16
and right to counsel, 101
and trial by jury, 110
victim rights in, 229–30, 229f, 230f
Constitution Project, 182
Constitution Revision Commission
   (CRC), 18
correctional officers
   academy training, 134–36, 136t
   certification of, 134, 137–38
   code of conduct, 138, 138f
   duties and responsibilities, 135, 137f
   gender representation among, 139–
      40, 141, 141t, 143t
   mandatory job requirements, 58–59
   minimum standards for, 134, 135f
   numbers in jails, 141, 142t
   private prisons and, 140, 141t, 149
   racial composition of, 139–40, 141,
      141t, 143t
   salaries, 140, 141, 142t
   in sheriff offices, 142, 144t
   and SOCE, 137–38
correctional system
   accreditation in, 145–47
   and prison overcrowding, 120–21
   size of facilities in, 141t
   structure of, 138–45
Costello v. Wainwright, 120
county courts
   about, 92–93, 97
   criminal cases in, 98–99, 99f
   SAO and, 100
court system
   appropriations for, 96f
   caseloads, 96f, 97–99, 98f, 99f
   Judicial Branch and, 17
   personnel, 99–106 (see also judges;
      lawyers)
courts
   administration, 93–95
   appellate-level, 87
   cases filed in, 96f

operations, 95–99
structure, 87–93, 88*f*
trial-level, 87
courts of general jurisdiction. *See* circuit
   courts
courts of limited jurisdiction. *See*
   county courts
crime(s). *See also* property crime(s); violent crime(s)
   as bondable vs. nonbondable of-
      fenses, 107
   crime clock, 27–28, 28*f*
   dark figure of, 30, 32, 192
   trends, 30–34
crime statistics
   crime rate, 28–30, 29*f*
   crime reporting vs. non-reporting
      and, 30, 33–34, 33*f*
   and delinquency, 192–93
   FBI on pitfalls of ranking, 36*f*
   in Florida cities, 34–35, 35*t*
   police crime recording and, 30,
      33–34
   tourism and, 34–35
Criminal Investigations and Forensic
   Science (FDLE program), 67
Criminal Justice Information (FDLE
   program), 68
Criminal Justice Professionalism (FDLE
   program), 68
Criminal Justice Standards and Training
   Commission (CJSTC), 58–62, 73,
   134, 137
criminal justice system
   arraignment in, 108
   booking in, 106–7
   Constitution and, 15, 19–20
   filing of formal charges, 108
   first appearance, 107–8
   investigation and deposition, 108–9
   post-arrest/pretrial activities, 106–9
   and right to attorney, 101
   trial activities, 109–13
Criminal Punishment Code (CPC), 121,
   122

criminology and criminal justice (CCJ)
   programs
   mission statements in, 10–11
   students in, 9–10
Crist, Charlie, 74, 113, 151, 213
Cromartie v. State of Florida, 115
cross-examination, 111–12
Crow, Matthew S., 122
curfews (juveniles), 208–10

D
Dantzker, Mark, 10
dark figure of crime, 30, 32, 192
Davis, Allen Lee, 169
death penalty. *See also* executions
   aggravating vs. mitigating circum-
      stances and, 166, 167*f,* 181, 182
   appeals process, 163, 167, 174
   ban/moratorium on, 162, 163, 165,
      182, 183*f*
   bifurcated hearing and, 166
   and commutation to life imprison-
      ment, 165
   constitutionality of, 162, 164–68,
      172, 181–82
   as cruel and unusual punishment,
      164, 164*f,* 168, 172, 216–17
   history of, 162–63
   jury and, 166–67, 181, 182
   in juvenile justice system, 216–18
   lawyers in post-conviction process,
      174, 178–81
   life imprisonment without possibility
      of parole vs., 175
   mandatory imposition of, 166
   post-conviction process, 173–79,
      175*f*
   race and, 164–65
   reinstatement of, 163
   sentencing phase of trial, 181
   separation of powers and, 180–81
Death Row
   costs of, 174–75
   post-*Gregg* population, 163*t*
   time spent on, 163, 174

defense
    and investigation and deposition, 108–9
    and jury selection, 110
    presentation, 112
    in trials, 110, 111
    and witnesses, 111–12
delinquency. *See also* juvenile justice system
    about, 192–98
    adjudicatory hearing and determination of, 205–6
    age and, 193
    crime statistics and, 192–93
    petition, 202–3
    teen courts and, 211
Denno, Deborah W., 169–70, 173
Denslow, David, 8
Deparvine v. State, 239
depositions, 108–9
detention hearing (juvenile justice system), 202
Detention Risk Assessment Inventory (DRAI), 202
Dewey, Jim, 8
Diaz, Angel, 170–71, 172
direct examination, 111
direct file (juvenile justice system), 205, 212
discretionary direct file (juvenile justice system), 205
disenfranchisement, 149
disposition hearing (juvenile justice system), 206
district courts of appeal (DCA)
    about, 90–92
    budget apportionment, 96f, 97
    caseloads, 96f, 97f
    judges, 90–91
    jurisdiction, 92
    map of, 92f
diversion programs (juveniles), 200–201, 203, 203f, 210–11
Doerner, William G., 77
Doerner, William M., 77

Douglas, William O., 165
drive-by shootings, 213–14

E
elderly
    and assisting self-murder, 45
    and criminal law, 49, 50f
    larceny-theft and, 52
    as prisoners, 151–53, 152f
Elderly Rehabilitated Inmate Program, 153
electrocution, 162, 163, 168–70
Evans v. McNeil, 181
excusable homicides, 43
executions. *See also* death penalty
    botched, 168, 170, 171, 173
    county sheriffs and, 162
    methods of, 164f
    moratorium on, 179
    numbers of, 162–63, 163t
    post-*Gregg,* 162–63, 163t
    resumption of, 168–70
    time lapse between sentencing and, 163, 179
Executive Branch, 17
expungement (juvenile justice system), 203, 204f

F
Farole, Donald J. Jr., 103
Federal Bureau of Investigation (FBI)
    and crime clock, 27–28, 28f
    definitions of serious property offenses, 26f
    definitions of serious violent offenses, 26f
    on pitfalls of crime rankings, 36f
felonies, 47–48, 47f, 48f, 52
felons, civil rights restoration for, 149–51
firearms. *See* weapons
firing squad, death by, 173
first appearance (criminal justice system), 107–8
first-degree murder, 43–45

Fish and Wildlife Conservation Com-
    mission (FWCC), 65, 75
flight risk, 108
Florida
    gender representation in, 65
    percent of population by age, 50*f*
    population, 87
    racial composition, 65
    size of, 65, 87
Florida Bar Association (FBA), 87, 93,
    94, 95
    Board Certification Plan, 95
    Florida Rules of Criminal Procedure
        (FRCP), 106
Florida Board of Bar Examiners (FBBE),
    93–94, 95
Florida Board of Governors, 75
Florida Commission on Offender Re-
    view, 153
Florida Correctional Medical Authority
    (CMA), 153
Florida Corrections Accreditation Com-
    mission (FCAC), 147
Florida Crimes Compensation Act,
    232*f*, 233*f*
Florida Department of Highway Safety
    & Motor Vehicles (DHSMV), 65, 68
Florida Department of Juvenile Justice
    (FDJJ), 199, 206, 207–8
Florida Department of Law Enforce-
    ment (FDLE)
    2013 Criminal Justice Agency Profile,
        9–10
    about, 66–68
    and clearance rates, 77
    entrance requirements for agents,
        64*f*, 67*f*, 75
    programs, 66–68
    Uniform Crime Reports (UCR) Pro-
        gram, 25–26
Florida Highway Patrol (FHP), 65, 68,
    69*f*, 75
Florida Parole Commission, 153
Florida Police Benevolent Association
    (PBA), 149

Florida Police Chiefs' Association, 77
Florida Rules of Criminal Procedure
    (FRCP), 106, 174
Florida Sheriffs' Association, 77
formal charges, filing, 108
Frazier, Charles E., 212
Fulford, Jackie, 149
Furman v. Georgia, 162, 164–67, 168

G
gain time, 121
gangs, 213–16
gender
    of judicial appointees, 91
    over- vs. underrepresentation in
        agencies, 65–66, 66*t*
    in police departments, 72, 72*t*
    in population composition, 65, 139
    representation among correctional
        officers, 139–40, 141, 141*t*, 143*t*
    representation in college/university
        law enforcement agencies, 74, 74*t*
    representation in law enforcement
        agencies, 65–66, 66*t*
    representation in sheriff offices, 70,
        70*t*
general jurisdiction courts. *See* circuit
    courts
Georgia, Furman v., 162, 164–67, 168
Georgia, Gregg v., 162–63, 167–68
Gideon v. Wainwright, 100–101
Gilmore, Gary, 162
Governor
    and civil rights restoration, 150–51
    and death warrant, 174, 176–77*f*, 180
    and justices of District Courts of Ap-
        peal, 91
    and justices of Supreme Court,
        87–88, 91
Graham, Bob, 178
grand jury, 113, 213–15
Gregg v. Georgia, 162–63, 167–68
Griset, Pamela L., 120–21
Gubernatorial Task Force for University
    Campus Security, 74

Guidelines for Fair Treatment of Victims and Witnesses in the Criminal Justice and Juvenile Justice Systems, 234–37

H

Hall, John, 148
Hanrahan, Kate, 9
Harding, Major, 169
Harris, Maggie E., 152
Herberman, Erinn J., 138
hierarchical reporting, 26
hierarchy of law, 15–16, 16*f*, 18
high school education, 5–6
high-risk residential programs (juveniles), 206
Hillsborough County Supervisor of Elections, 4–5
home-invasion robbery, 51
homicide(s). *See also* murder
  assisting self-murder and, 45
  castle doctrine and, 43, 44*f*
  defined, 42
  excusable, 43
  first-degree murder, 43–45
  justifiable, 43
  lawful, 43
  manslaughter, 45
  unlawful, 43–45
  vehicular, 45
  vessel, 45
hung jury, 113
Hunter, Ronald, 3, 11

I

imprisonment. *See also* jails; prisoners; prisons
  10-20-Life law, 47, 48*f*
  costs of, 174–75
  geography and, 122
  length of sentence and, 122
  life, 165, 175
  race and, 122
  rate, 139
  sentencing and, 115, 117, 122
indigent status, 101–4, 102*f*, 108

information (criminal justice system), 108
intake (juveniles), 202, 210
involuntary discretionary waiver (juvenile justice system), 205
involuntary mandatory waiver (juvenile justice system), 205

J

jails
  about, 141–44
  accredited, 147
  defined, 138
  educational levels of personnel in, 10
  functions/services, 139*f*
  numbers of, 141, 142*t*
  numbers of correctional officers in, 141, 142*t*
  population size, 142, 144*t*
  sheriff offices and, 141, 142*t*
Jennings Commission, 170–71
J.P. and T.M., State of Florida v., 209
judges
  application form, 89*f*
  and bench trials, 109
  circuit court, 92
  county court, 93
  and death penalty, 166–67
  of District Courts of Appeal, 90–91
  diversity of, 91
  gender representation among, 91
  and judicial activism, 91
  and jurors' identity, 113
  jury instructions, 112
  juvenile court, 202, 205–6
  and juvenile justice system, 212
  merit retention vote, 90
  Office of State Courts Administrator and, 93
  and pre-sentence investigation, 114
  racial representation among, 91
  and sentencing, 115–17, 121
  Supreme Court, 87–90
judgment of acquittal, 103, 112
judicial activism, 91

Judicial Branch
   about, 17
   budget, 95, 96f, 97, 98–99, 99f
Judicial Nominating Commission
   (JNC), 87, 90, 91
jurisdiction
   booking and, 106
   defined, 65
   and establishing of crime
     location/time, 106
jury
   castle doctrine case instructions, 44f
   challenges, 110–11
   and death penalty, 166, 181, 182
   deliberations, 112–13
   foreperson, 112
   grand, 113, 213–15
   hung, 113
   and identity of jurors, 113
   instructions, 112
   oath, 111f
   selection, 110–11
   sequestering, 112–13
   size of, 110, 111
   summons, 110
   trials, 109–10
   verdict, 112, 113
Justice Administrative Commission, 179
justifiable homicides, 43
Juvenile Assessment Center (JAC), 199,
   200, 202
juvenile courts
   and adult courts, 211–13
   and age of juveniles, 193
   and transfer to adult court, 204–5
   adjudicatory hearing, 205–6
   arraignment, 203
   circuit courts and, 198
   civil citation program (CCP), 199–
     201, 201f
   death penalty in, 216–18
   delinquency petition, 202–3
   detention hearing, 202
   Detention Risk Assessment Inventory
     (DRAI), 202
   disposition hearing, 206

   diversion program, 200–201, 203,
     203f
   expungement in, 203, 204f
   and gangs, 213–16
   intake process, 202, 210
   leapfrogging in, 213
   referral in, 199–201
   rehabilitative vs. punitive approaches,
     212
   residential programs, 206, 213
   steps/stages within, 198–99, 200f
   teen courts in, 210–11
   waiver in, 204–5, 211–13
juveniles
   arrest rates and, 193–96, 199f
   curfews for, 208–10
   and delinquency, 192–98
   murder arrests, 217, 218f
   property arrest rates, 196, 197f, 198f
   violent crime arrest rates, 193, 194f,
     195f, 196
   juvenile justice system

K

Kentucky, Stanford v., 216–17
killing of unborn child by injury to
   mother, 45
Knuckey, Jonathan, 5
Kogan, Gerald, 182

L

Lane, Jodi, 213
Langton, Lynn, 103
Lanza-Kaduce, Lonn, 212
larceny-theft
   about, 51–52
   elderly and, 52
   FBI definition, 27f
   juvenile arrest rates, 196
   and misdemeanor vs. felony theft, 52
   rates, 27, 28f, 29f, 30, 32f
   tourism and, 52
latent effects, 151
law enforcement agencies
   accreditation in, 76–77
   college and university, 73–74, 74t

gender representation in, 65–66, 66*t*

local, 68–73

professionalization of, 76

racial distribution in, 65, 66*t*

special jurisdiction, 73–74

state, 65–68

law enforcement officers. *See also* police
officers

arresting, 106–7

bona fide occupational qualification
(BFOQ), 63

certification, 59

jurisdiction, 65

minimum standards, 58–59

oath of office, 64

path to becoming, 58

screening in, 62

selection process, 62–64, 63*f*

sworn, 58

weeding out, 62

law enforcement system

length of careers in, 75

job prospects in, 75

structure of, 65–74

lawful homicides, 43

lawyers. *See also* attorney general (AG);
defense; public defender's office
(PDO); state attorneys

Bar Association and, 93, 94, 95

Board Certification Plan and, 95

Board of Bar Examiners and, 93–94

in death penalty post-conviction
process, 174, 178–81

Oath of Admission to Bar, 94, 94*f*

pro bono program and, 95, 178

registry, 178

right to, 101

and suitable moral character, 94

Supreme Court and discipline of, 95

leapfrogging, 213

Legislative Branch, 16–17

lethal injection, 163, 168, 169, 170–73,
180

Levy, David L., 209

Lightbourne v. McCollum, 171–72, 173

limited jurisdiction courts. *See* county
courts

Lou Frey Institute of Politics and Government, 4

low-risk residential programs (juveniles), 206

M

mandatory direct file (juvenile justice
system), 205

mandatory sentencing laws, 47

Mandel, Roberta G., 103–4

manifest effects, 151

manslaughter, 26*f*, 45

Martin, Jamie S., 9

Martin, Trayvon, 113

Martinez, Jose E., 181

maximum-risk residential programs
(juveniles), 206

McCarthy, Dan, 153

McCollum, Lightbourne v., 171–72, 173

McDonald Commission/Report, 178

McDonough, James R., 171

McNeil, Evans v., 181

Medina, Pedro, 169

merit retention vote, 90

minimum standards

for correctional officers, 134, 135*f*

defined, 58–59

for law enforcement officers, 58–59

for probation officers, 144

minimum-risk nonresidential programs
(juveniles), 206

misdemeanors, 47, 47*f*, 52

mitigating circumstances (death
penalty), 166, 167*f*

mitigation (of sentences), 121

moderate-risk residential programs (juveniles), 206

moratorium (death penalty), 179, 182,
183*f*

motor vehicle theft

FBI definition, 27*f*

frequency of, 27, 28*f*

juvenile arrest rates, 196

and population at risk, 29–30
rates, 29f, 30, 32f
Muhammad v. State of Florida, 180
municipal police officers. *See* police officers
murder. *See also* homicide(s)
  FBI definition, 26f
  felony-, 43
  first-degree, 43–45
  juvenile arrest rates, 193, 194f, 195f, 217, 218f
  rates, 29f, 30, 31f

N
National Assessment Governing Board, 5–6
National Center for State Courts, 97–98
National Conference on Citizenship (NCoC), 4
National Crime Victimization Survey (NCVS), 30
National Fire Incident Reporting System (NFIRS), 27–28
Nelson, Debra, 113
nonbondable offenses, 107

O
offender restitution, 231–32
Office of Capital Collateral Regional Counsel (CCRC), 178–79, 180
Office of Capital Collateral Representative (CCR), 178–179
Office of State Courts Administrator (SCA), 93, 95
Oklahoma, Thompson v., 216
opening arguments, 111
overrepresentation, 65–66, 66t

P
parole
  defined, 138, 144
  life imprisonment without possibility of, 175
  medical program, 153
  officers, 144, 145f

and prison population crisis, 121
Payne v. Tennessee, 239
peremptory challenge, 110–11
Perry, Belvin, 113
police departments
  about, 71–73
  accreditation of, 76, 77
  entrance requirements, 64, 64f, 73–74
  gender representation, 72, 72t
  numbers of, 71–72
  over- vs. underrepresentation of race/gender among, 72, 72t
  racial backgrounds, 72, 72t
  reporting by, 77
  salaries in, 72, 73t
  size of, 72t, 75
police officers. *See also* law enforcement officers
  academy training, 59–61, 60–61t
  and college degrees, 76
  crime reporting to, 30, 33, 33f
  educational levels, 9
  jurisdiction, 65
  mandatory job requirements, 58–59
  numbers of, 71–72
  recording practices, 30, 33–34, 33f
  reporting by, 33–34, 33f
  State Officer Certification Examination (SOCE), 62
Polston, Ricky, 99
population
  and court system, 87
  crime rates and, 29
  gender composition of, 65, 139
  racial composition of, 65, 139
  at risk, 29–30, 193
post-conviction process
  and court caseloads, 97
  in death penalty, 173–81, 175f
predisposition report (PDR), 206
pregnant women
  battery of, as aggravated battery, 49
  injury to, and killing of unborn child, 45

President's Commission (1967), 76
President's Task force on Victims of
    Crime (1982), 229f
pretrial motions, 109
prisoners
    by age groups, 152f
    civil rights of, 149–51
    deaths of, 153
    early-release mechanisms and, 121
    elderly as, 151–53, 152f
    length of time served, 121, 152
    medical expenditures for, 152–53
    numbers in private prisons, 148
    numbers of, 143, 144t, 145
prisons
    about, 139–40
    defined, 138
    early-release mechanisms, 121
    expansion of, 120–21
    overcrowding in, 120–21
    private, 140, 141t, 147–49
    time spent in, vs. sentence, 114
privatization, defined, 147
pro bono program, 95, 178
pro se, 100
probable cause, 106
probation
    defined, 138, 144
    first-time defendants and, 116
    in juvenile justice system, 206
    numbers placed on, 115
probation officers
    academy training, 144
    duties and responsibilities, 145f
    minimum standards for, 144
    numbers of, 144
    salaries, 144
procedural laws, 180–81
proof beyond a reasonable doubt, 111
property crime(s)
    clearance rates, 77
    FBI definitions for serious, 27f
    frequency of, 27, 28f
    juvenile arrest rates, 196, 197f, 198f
    rates, 24–25, 24t, 29t, 30, 32f

Provenzano v. Florida, 169
public defender's office (PDO),
    100–104, 180

Q
Quince, Peggy Ann, 99, 169

R
race
    and death penalty, 164–65
    and disenfranchisement, 151
    and incarceration, 122
    of judicial appointees, 91
    over- vs. underrepresentation in
        agencies, 65, 66t
    population composition, 65, 139
    and prison sentences, 122
    representation among correctional
        officers, 139–40, 141, 141t, 143t
    representation in college/university
        law enforcement agencies, 74, 74t
    representation in law enforcement
        agencies, 65, 66t
    representation in police departments,
        72, 72t
    representation in sheriff offices, 70,
        70t
rape. See sexual battery
Reagan, Ronald, 229
recidivism
    and imprisonment, 117
    in juvenile justice system, 212–13
Rees, Baze v., 172, 173
referral (juveniles), 199–201
registry attorneys, 178
release
    at booking, 107
    at first appearance, 108
    pretrial, 107, 108
    on recognizance (ROR), 108
reporting practices, 30, 33–34, 33f
residential programs (juveniles), 206,
    213
reverse waiver (juvenile justice system),
    212

Ring v. Arizona, 181
robbery
  about, 50–51
  armed, 50
  carjacking, 51
  defined, 50
  FBI definition, 26*f*
  frequency of, 27, 28*f*
  home-invasion, 51
  juvenile arrest rates, 193, 194*f*, 195*f*
  rates, 29*f*, 30, 31*f*
  strong-armed, 50
  by sudden snatching, 51
  violence and, 51
Roksa, Josipa, *Academically Adrift*, 7–8
Roper v. Simmons, 217
Rule, the, 111

S
salaries
  of assistant public defenders, 103
  of assistant state attorneys, 103
  of correctional officers, 140, 141,
    142*t*
  incentive program, 73
  in police departments, 72, 73, 73*t*,
    74*t*
  of probation officers, 144
  in sheriff offices (SOs), 71, 71*t*
sanctions, 115, 119*f*, 120*f*
Scott, Rick, 91, 106, 149, 151, 153, 173,
  176–77*f*, 179, 182
screening in, 62
self-murder, assisting, 45
Senack, Ethan, 8
sentencing
  10-20-Life law, 47, 48*f*
  enhancements, 215
  geography and, 122
  guidelines, 114–15, 115*f*, 120–22
  habitual-offender, 122
  hearing, 115–20
  mandatory sentencing laws, 47, 48*f*,
    151, 152
  mitigating circumstances and, 119*f*,
    121

offender's criminal history and, 115,
  120*f*
phase in death penalty trials, 181
pre-sentence investigation, 114–15,
  116–18*f*
race and, 122
scoresheet, 114–15, 116–18*f*
structured vs. unstructured, 114
truth in, 114, 121
sequestering, 112–13
sexual battery
  about, 49–50
  aggravating circumstances, 49–50
  FBI definition, 26*f*
  frequency of, 27, 28*f*
  juvenile arrest rates, 193, 194*f*, 195*f*
  rates, 29*f*, 30, 31*f*
  UCR history of, 25
sheriff offices (SOs)
  about, 68–71, 70*t*, 71*t*
  accreditation of, 76, 77
  annual salary in, 71, 71*t*
  deputies' salaries in, 71, 71*t*
  educational levels in, 10
  entrance requirements, 64, 64*f*, 73
  and executions, 162
  and jails, 141, 142*t*
  jurisdiction, 65
  numbers of correctional officers in,
    142, 143*t*, 144*t*
  over- vs. underrepresentation of
    race/gender in, 70, 70*t*
  racial representation in, 70, 70*t*
  size of, 70*t*, 75
  and unionization, 71
Simmons, Roper v., 217
simple assault, 46–47, 47*f*
simple battery, 46–47, 47*f*
Singletary, Celestineo v., 153
Smith, Christopher, 153
Smith, James C., 178
social contract argument, 232
social welfare argument, 232
source of last resort, 233
special investigators, 100
special jurisdiction agencies, 73–74, 77

speedy trial, 109, 110, 237
Spenkelink, John, 162
standard bail/bond schedule, 107
"Stand-Your-Ground" law, 113
Stanford v. Kentucky, 216–17
State Attorney Offices (SAO)
    and assistant state attorneys, 100
    and juvenile justice system, 202–3,
      205
state attorneys
    about, 100
    and jury selection, 110
    and juvenile justice system, 212
    and mitigation of sentences, 121
    presentation in trials, 111
    and witnesses, 111–12
State of Florida v. Casey Marie Anthony,
    113
State of Florida v. J.P. and T.M., 209
State Officer Certification Examination
    (SOCE), 62, 137–38
strict scrutiny standard (juvenile curfew
    laws), 209
strong-armed robbery, 50
structured sentencing, 114
subpoena, 104
subpoena duces tecum, 104, 105*f*
substantive laws, 180–81
suicide, assisted, 45
suitable moral character, 94
supremacy clause, 15
Supreme Court (Florida)
    about, 87–88, 90
    budget appropriations for, 96*f*, 97
    Chief Justice, 90
    and collective bargaining for sheriff
      deputies, 71
    Constitution on, 90, 91
    and constitutional amendment, 18
    on court system's availability to
      everybody, 95
    and death penalty, 167, 172, 174, 180
    division into two, 87–88
    and FBBE, 93
    Governor and justices of, 87–88, 91

    in hierarchy of law, 15
    judges of, 87–90
    and juvenile curfew laws, 209
    and lawyer discipline, 95
    mission statement, 86
    and Office of State Courts Adminis-
      trator (SCA), 95
    and victim impact statements,
      239–40
Supreme Court (U.S.)
    and death penalty, 162, 164, 165,
      172, 174
    on death penalty for juveniles, 216,
      217
    and *Gideon v. Wainwright*, 100–101
    in hierarchy of law, 15
    on jury size, 110*f*
    and victim impact statements, 239
sworn officers, 58

T
Tafero, Jesse, 168–69
Taxation and Budget Reform Commis-
    sion (TBRC), 19
Teamsters Union, 149
teen courts, 210–11
Tennessee, Payne v., 239
theft. *See* larceny-theft
Thompson v. Oklahoma, 216
Timely Justice Act, 179–81, 182
tourism
    and crime statistics, 34–35
    larceny-theft and, 52
trespass, 52, 53
trials
    activities, 109–13
    bench, 109
    closing arguments, 112
    courts, 87, 96*f*, 97
    defense's presentation, 112
    jury, 109–10
    jury deliberations, 112–13
    jury instructions, 112
    opening arguments, 111
    penalty phase, 166

post-trial activities, 113, 114–20
pretrial activities, 106–9
sentencing phase, 114–20
speedy, 109, 110
state's presentation, 111–12
"The Rule" in, 111
types of, 109–10
verdict, 112, 113
witnesses in, 111–12
Tucker, Baiardi et al. v., 149

U

unborn child, killing of, 45
underrepresentation, 65–66, 66*t*
Uniform Crime Reports (UCR) Program,
    25–26, 193, 231
unjust enrichment, 233
unnecessary killing to prevent unlawful
    act, 45
unstructured sentencing, 114

V

Valle, Manuel, 173, 182
Valle v. Florida, 173
Vasilinda, Rehinkle, 182
vehicular homicide, 45
venire, 110
Ventura v. Florida, 172–73
verdict, 112, 113
victim compensation
    about, 231–34
    application form, 235–36*f*
    and mandatory court costs, 234
    operations of, 234, 235–36*f*
    provisions, 233–34
    shortcomings of, 231–32
    social contract argument, 232
    social welfare argument, 232
    as source of last resort, 233
victim impact statements (VIS), 237–
    40, 238*f*
victim precipitation, 233
victim rights
    in constitutions, 228–30

courtroom announcement, 237*f*
general assistance, 237
legislation, 234–37
notification concerns, 235–36
provision of relevant information to
    victims/witnesses, 235–37
to speedy trial, 237
Victim Rights Amendment (VRA), 228,
    229*f,* 230
victims
    crime reporting/disclosure, 30, 33,
        33*f,* 34
    reporting practices, 192–93
Victims of Crime Act (VOCA), 234
violent crime(s)
    clearance rates, 77
    FBI definitions for, 26*f*
    juvenile arrest rates, 193, 194*f,* 195*f,*
        196
    rates, 24, 24*t,* 29*f,* 30, 31*f*
Virginia, Atkins v., 217
voir dire, 110
voluntary waiver (juvenile justice sys-
    tem), 205

W

Wainwright, Costello v., 120
Wainwright, Gideon v., 100–101
waiver (juvenile justice system), 204–5,
    211–13
weapons
    in aggravated battery, 48–49
    and aggravated vs. simple assault,
        47–48, 48*f*
    deadly vs. non-deadly, 48
weeding out, 62
Wheeler v. State, 239–40
Williams, Marian R., 103
witnesses
    investigation and deposition, 108–9
    in trials, 111–12

Z

Zimmerman, George, 113